MILLENNIUM

THE GIRL WHO DANCED WITH DEATH

TITAN®
COMICS

FROM TITAN COMICS AND
HARD CASE CRIME

GRAPHIC NOVELS

THE ASSIGNMENT

BABYLON BERLIN

MICKEY SPILLANE'S MIKE HAMMER: THE NIGHT I DIED

MILLENNIUM: THE GIRL WITH THE DRAGON TATTOO

MILLENNIUM: THE GIRL WHO PLAYED WITH FIRE

MILLENNIUM: THE GIRL WHO KICKED THE HORNET'S NEST

MILLENNIUM: THE GIRL WHO DANCED WITH DEATH

MINKY WOODCOCK: THE GIRL WHO HANDCUFFED HOUDINI

NORMANDY GOLD

PEEPLAND

THE PRAGUE COUP

QUARRY'S WAR

TRIGGERMAN

TYLER CROSS: BLACK ROCK

TYLER CROSS: ANGOLA

NOVELS

361

A BLOODY BUSINESS

A DIET OF TREACLE

A TOUCH OF DEATH

A WALK AMONG THE TOMBSTONES

BABY MOLL

BINARY

BLACKMAILER

BLOOD ON THE MINK

BORDERLINE

BRAINQUAKE

BRANDED WOMAN

BROTHERS KEEPERS

BUST

CASINO MOON

CHARLESGATE CONFIDENTIAL

CHOKE HOLD

THE COCKTAIL WAITRESS

THE COMEDY IS FINISHED

THE CONFESSION

THE CONSUMMATA

THE CORPSE WORE PASTIES

THE COUNT OF 9

CUT ME IN

THE CUTIE

THE DEAD MAN'S BROTHER

DEAD STREET

DEADLY BELOVED

DRUG OF CHOICE

DUTCH UNCLE

EASY DEATH

EASY GO

FADE TO BLONDE

FAKE I.D.

FALSE NEGATIVE

FIFTY-TO-ONE

FOREVER AND A DEATH

GETTING OFF: A NOVEL OF SEX AND VIOLENCE

THE GIRL WITH THE DEEP BLUE EYES

THE GIRL WITH THE LONG GREEN HEART

GRAVE DESCEND

GRIFTER'S GAME

GUN WORK

THE GUTTER AND THE GRAVE

HELP I AM BEING HELD PRISONER

HOME IS THE SAILOR

HONEY IN HIS MOUTH

HOUSE DICK

JOYLAND

KILL NOW PAY LATER

KILLING CASTRO

THE KNIFE SLIPPED

THE LAST MATCH

THE LAST STAND

LEMONS NEVER LIE

LITTLE GIRL LOST

LOSERS LIVE LONGER

LUCKY AT CARDS

THE MAX

MEMORY

MONEY SHOT

MURDER IS MY BUSINESS

THE NICE GUYS

NIGHT WALKER

NO HOUSE LIMIT

NOBODY'S ANGEL

ODDS ON

PASSPORT TO PERIL

PIMP

PLUNDER OF THE SUN

ROBBIE'S WIFE

SAY IT WITH BULLETS

SCRATCH ONE

THE SECRET LIVES OF MARRIED WOMEN

SEDUCTION OF THE INNOCENT

SINNER MAN

SLIDE

SNATCH

SO MANY DOORS

SO NUDE, SO DEAD

SOHO SINS

SOMEBODY OWES ME MONEY

SONGS OF INNOCENCE

STOP THIS MAN!

STRAIGHT CUT

THIEVES FALL OUT

TOP OF THE HEAP

THE TRIUMPH OF THE SPIDER MONKEY

TURN ON THE HEAT

THE TWENTY-YEAR DEATH

TWO FOR THE MONEY

THE VALLEY OF FEAR

THE VENGEFUL VIRGIN

THE VENOM BUSINESS

WEB OF THE CITY

WITNESS TO MYSELF

THE WOUNDED AND THE SLAIN

ZERO COOL

QUARRY

THE FIRST QUARRY

THE LAST QUARRY

QUARRY

QUARRY'S CHOICE

QUARRY'S CLIMAX

QUARRY'S CUT

QUARRY'S DEAL

QUARRY'S EX

QUARRY IN THE BLACK

QUARRY IN THE MIDDLE

QUARRY'S LIST

QUARRY'S VOTE

THE WRONG QUARRY

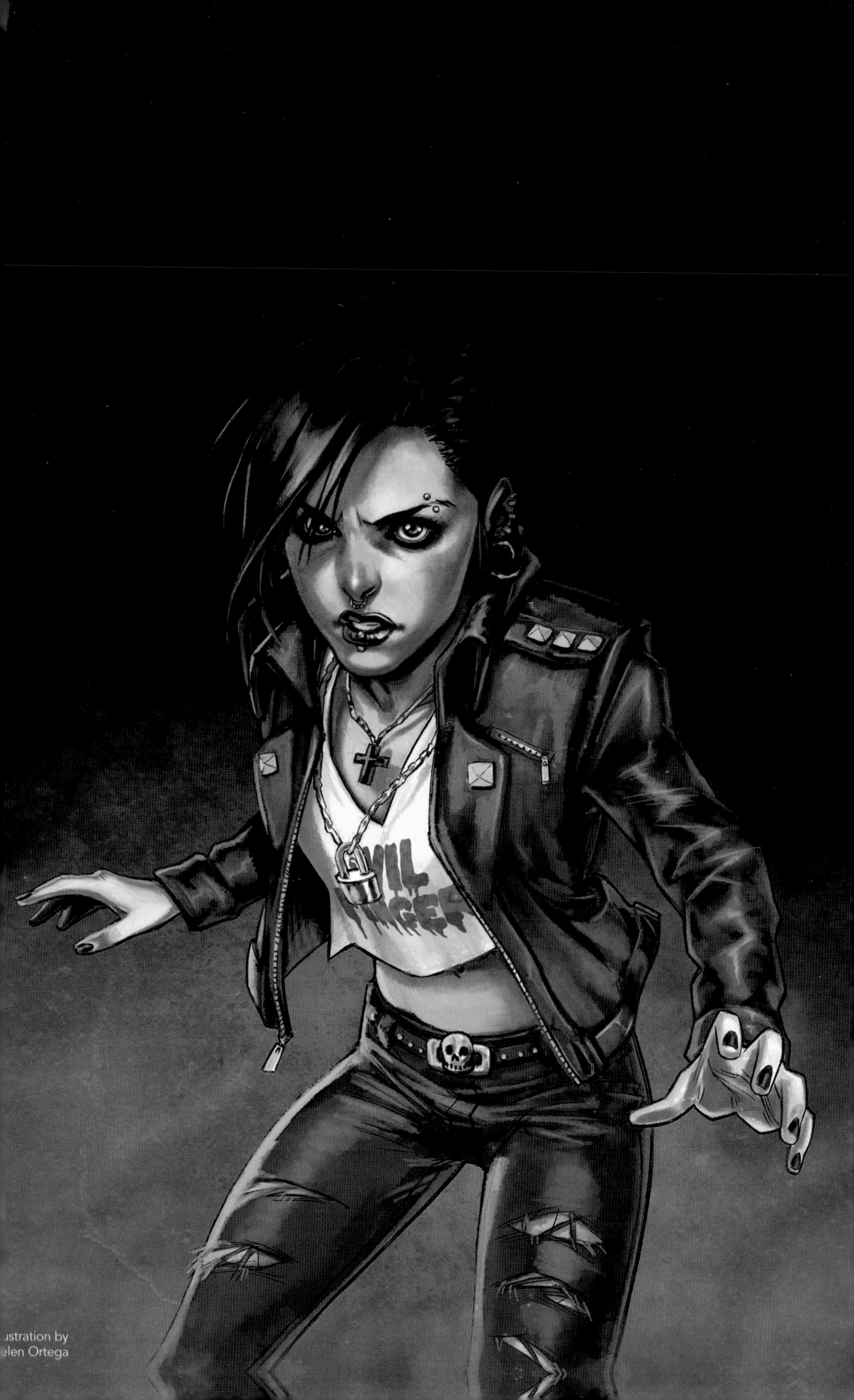

ustration by
elen Ortega

THE GIRL WHO DANCED WITH DEATH

TITAN COMICS
EDITOR: LAUREN BOWES
ART DIRECTOR: OZ BROWNE

Consulting Editor: Charles Ardai
Line Editor: Jonathan Stevenson
Titan Comics Editorial: Dan Boultwood
Managing & Launch Editor: Andrew James
Senior Production Controller: Jackie Flook
Production Controller: Peter James
Production Assistant: Rhiannon Roy
Circulation Executive: Frances Hallam
Sales & Circulation Manager: Steve Tothill
Marketing Assistant: Charlie Raspin
Brand Manager: Chris Thompson
Press Officer: Will O'Mullane
Publicist: Imogen Harris
Ads & Marketing Assistant: Bella Hoy
Direct Sales & Marketing Manager: Ricky Claydon
Commercial Manager: Michelle Fairlamb
Publishing Manager: Darryl Tothill
Publishing Director: Chris Teather
Operations Director: Leigh Baulch
Executive Director: Vivian Cheung
Publisher: Nick Landau

MILLENNIUM: THE GIRL WHO DANCED WITH DEATH
9781785866937
Published by Titan Comics
A division of Titan Publishing Group Ltd.
144 Southwark St., London, SE1 0UP
Titan Comics is a registered trademark of Titan Publishing Group Ltd. All right reserved.

Originally published as *Millennium Saga: Les Âmes froides* EDITIONS DUPUIS S.A © Dupuis 2016; *Millennium Saga: Les Nouveaux Spartiates* EDITIONS DUPUIS S.A © Dupuis 2017; and *Millennium Saga: La fille qui ne lâichait jamais prise.* EDITIONS DUPUIS S.A © Dupuis 2018 by Runberg, Ortega.

A CIP catalogue record for this title is available from the British Library

10 9 8 7 6 5 4 3 2 1
First Published January 2019
Printed in Spain.
Titan Comics.

MILLENNIUM
THE GIRL WHO
DANCED WITH DEATH

WRITTEN BY
SYLVAIN RUNBERG

ARTWORK BY
BÉLEN ORTEGA

TRANSLATED BY
RACHEL ZERNER

BASED ON THE NOVEL
TRILOGY BY
STIEG LARSSON

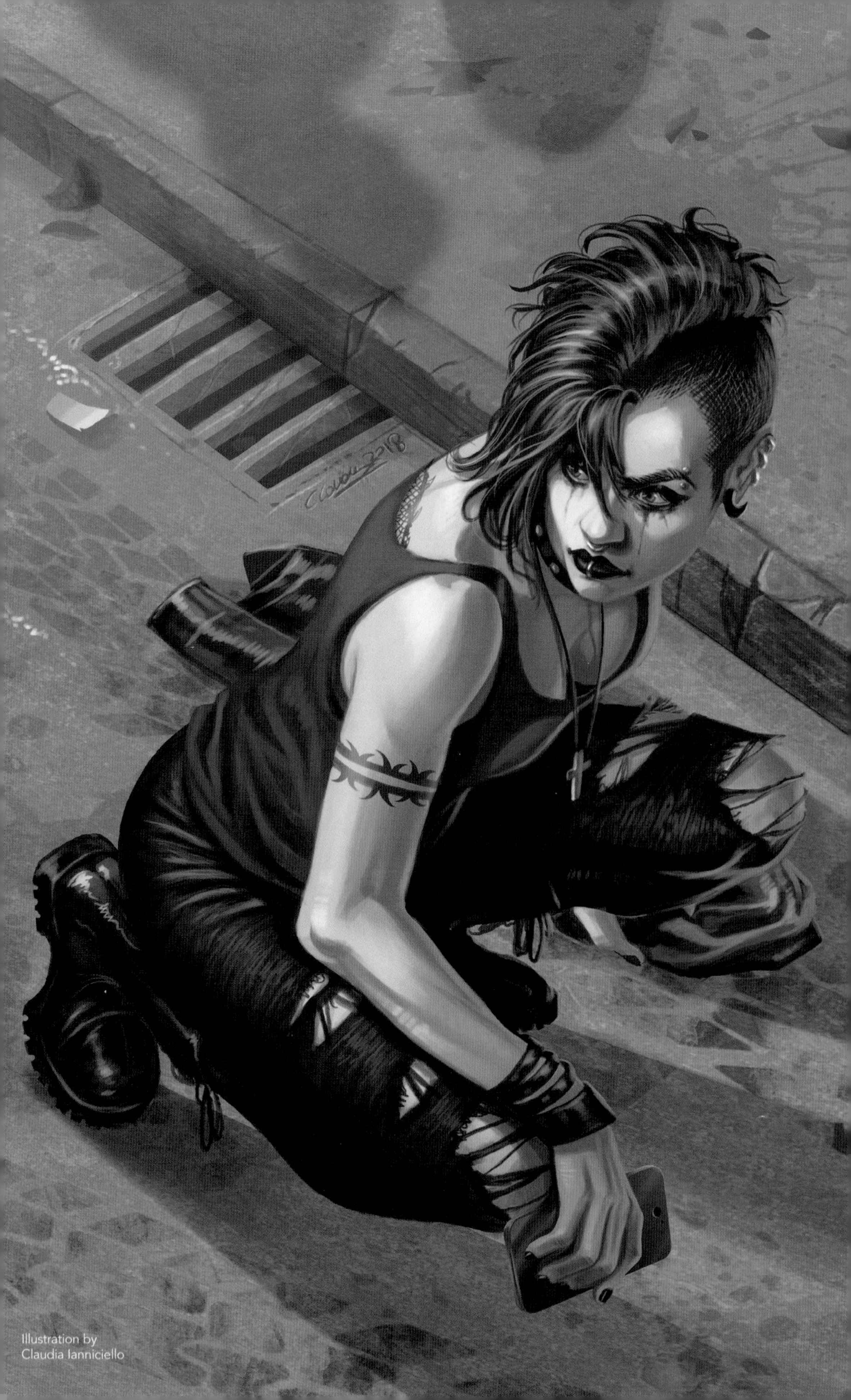

Illustration by
Claudia Ianniciello

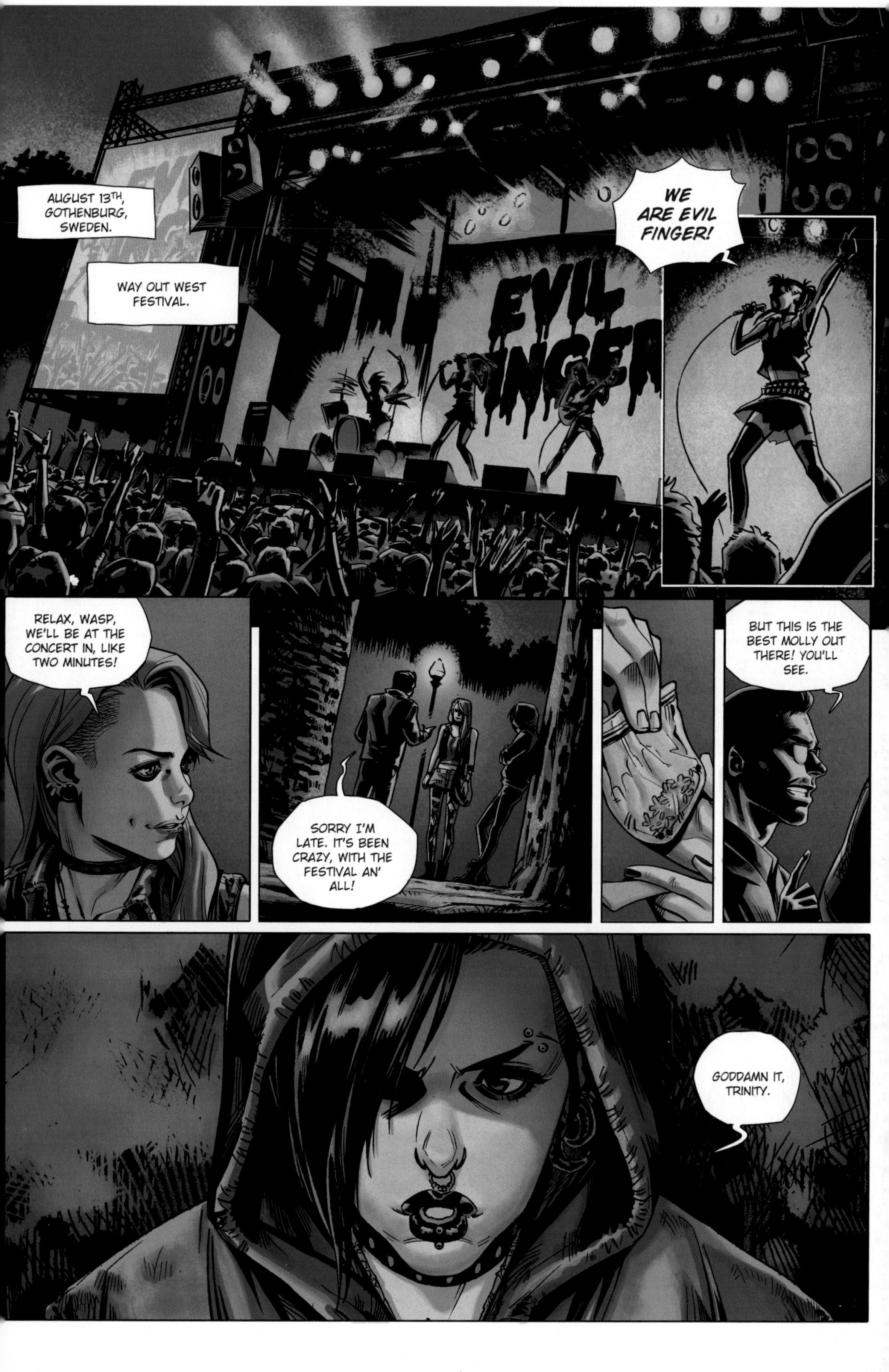
AUGUST 13TH, GOTHENBURG, SWEDEN.
WAY OUT WEST FESTIVAL.
EVIL FINGER
WE ARE EVIL FINGER!
RELAX, WASP, WE'LL BE AT THE CONCERT IN, LIKE TWO MINUTES!
SORRY I'M LATE. IT'S BEEN CRAZY, WITH THE FESTIVAL AN' ALL!
BUT THIS IS THE BEST MOLLY OUT THERE! YOU'LL SEE.
GODDAMN IT, TRINITY.

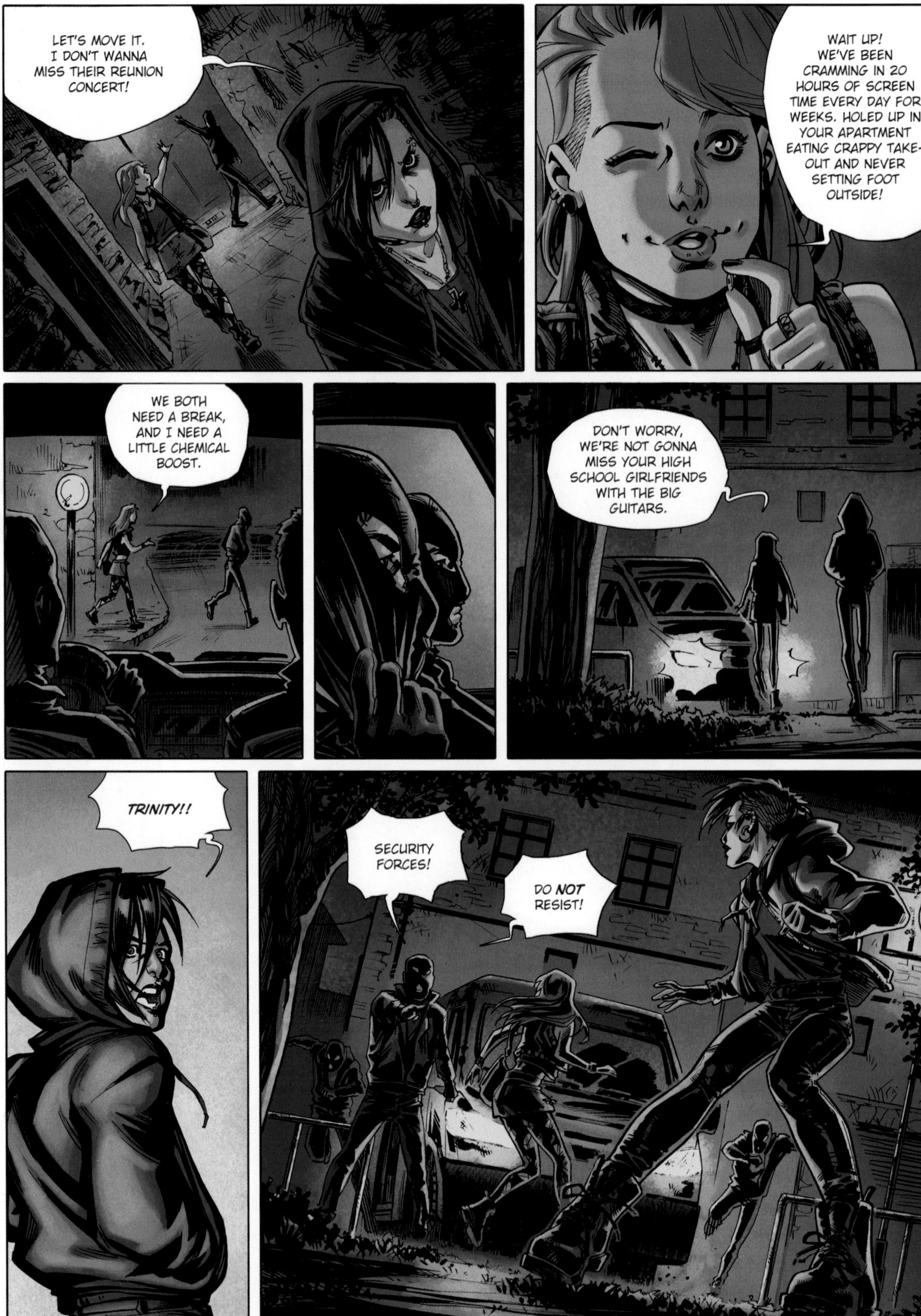
LET'S MOVE IT. I DON'T WANNA MISS THEIR REUNION CONCERT!
WAIT UP! WE'VE BEEN CRAMMING IN 20 HOURS OF SCREEN TIME EVERY DAY FOR WEEKS. HOLED UP IN YOUR APARTMENT EATING CRAPPY TAKE-OUT AND NEVER SETTING FOOT OUTSIDE!
WE BOTH NEED A BREAK, AND I NEED A LITTLE CHEMICAL BOOST.
DON'T WORRY, WE'RE NOT GONNA MISS YOUR HIGH SCHOOL GIRLFRIENDS WITH THE BIG GUITARS.
TRINITY!!
SECURITY FORCES!
DO NOT RESIST!

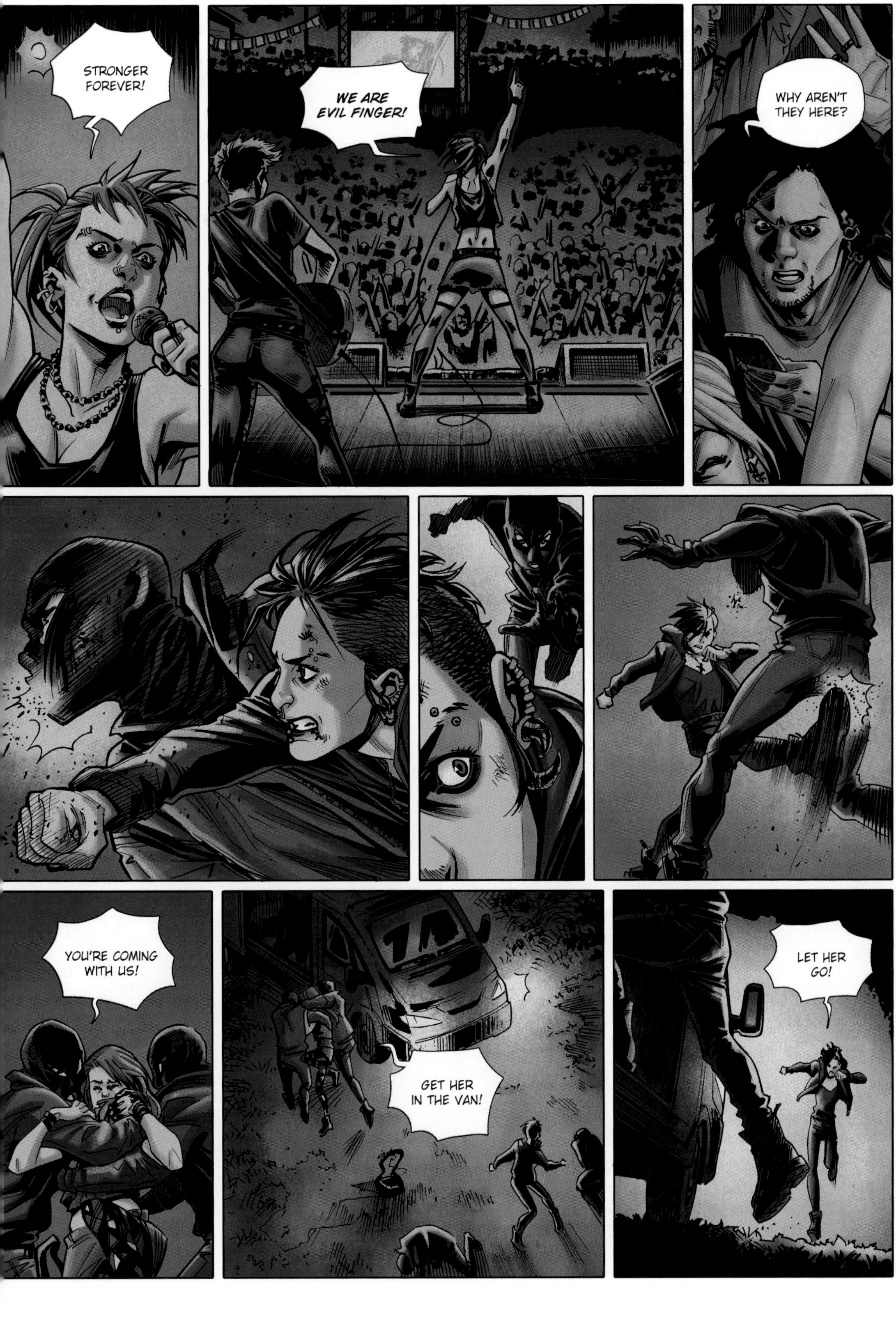
STRONGER FOREVER!
WE ARE EVIL FINGER!
WHY AREN'T THEY HERE?
YOU'RE COMING WITH US!
GET HER IN THE VAN!
LET HER GO!

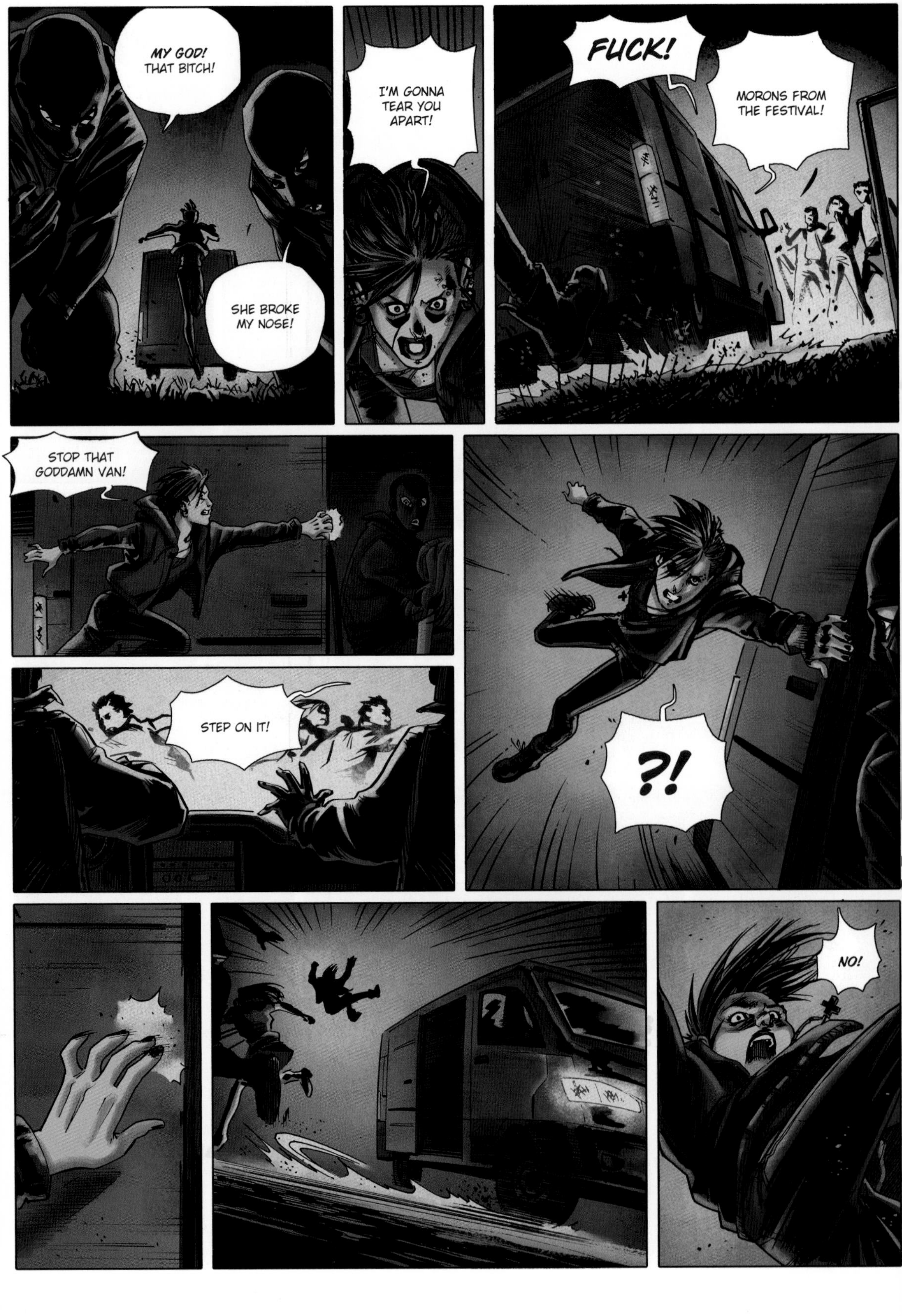
MY GOD! THAT BITCH!
SHE BROKE MY NOSE!
I'M GONNA TEAR YOU APART!
FUCK!
MORONS FROM THE FESTIVAL!
STOP THAT GODDAMN VAN!
STEP ON IT!
?!
NO!

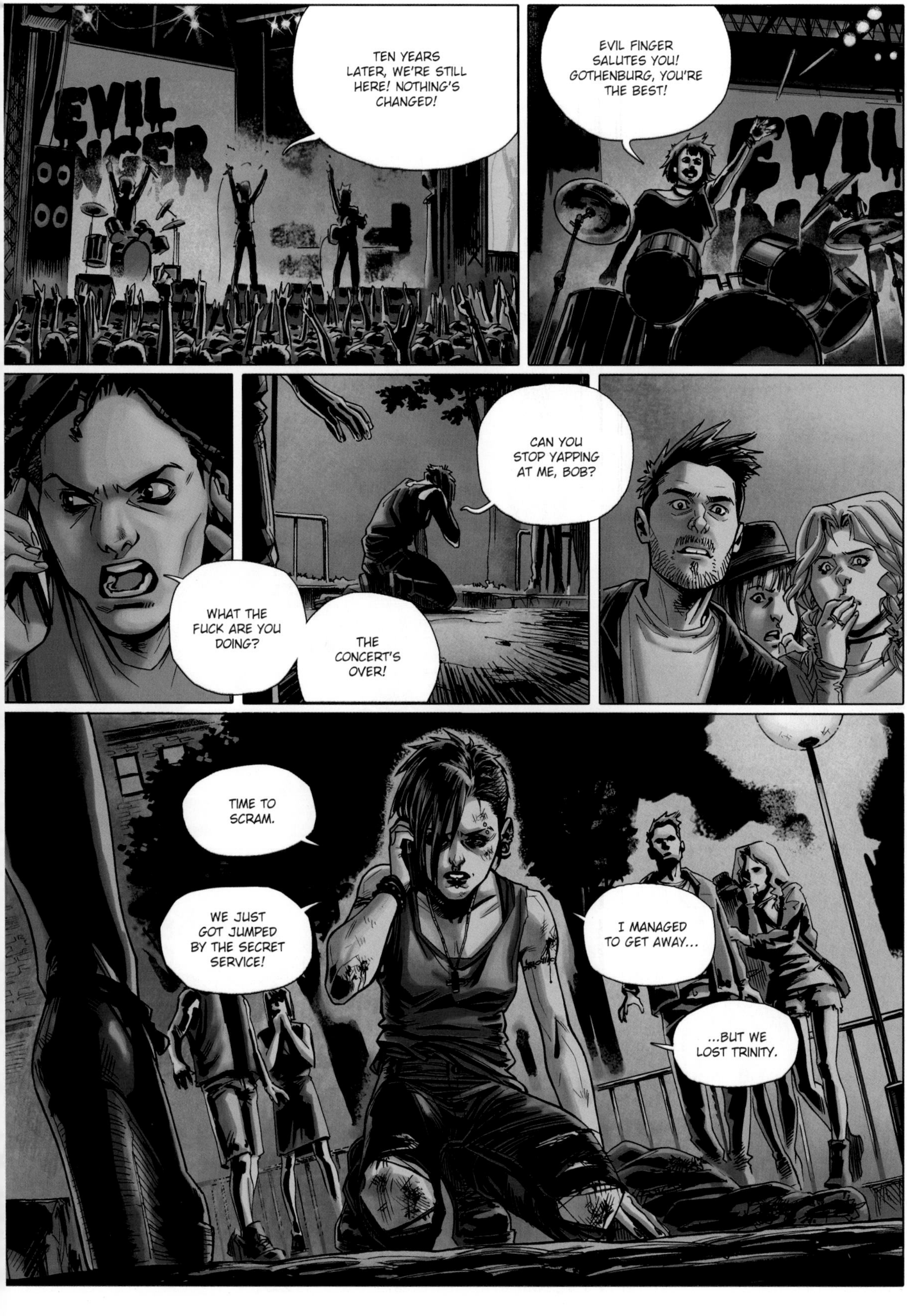
TEN YEARS LATER, WE'RE STILL HERE! NOTHING'S CHANGED!
EVIL FINGER
EVIL FINGER SALUTES YOU! GOTHENBURG, YOU'RE THE BEST!
WHAT THE FUCK ARE YOU DOING?
THE CONCERT'S OVER!
CAN YOU STOP YAPPING AT ME, BOB?
TIME TO SCRAM.
WE JUST GOT JUMPED BY THE SECRET SERVICE!
I MANAGED TO GET AWAY...
...BUT WE LOST TRINITY.

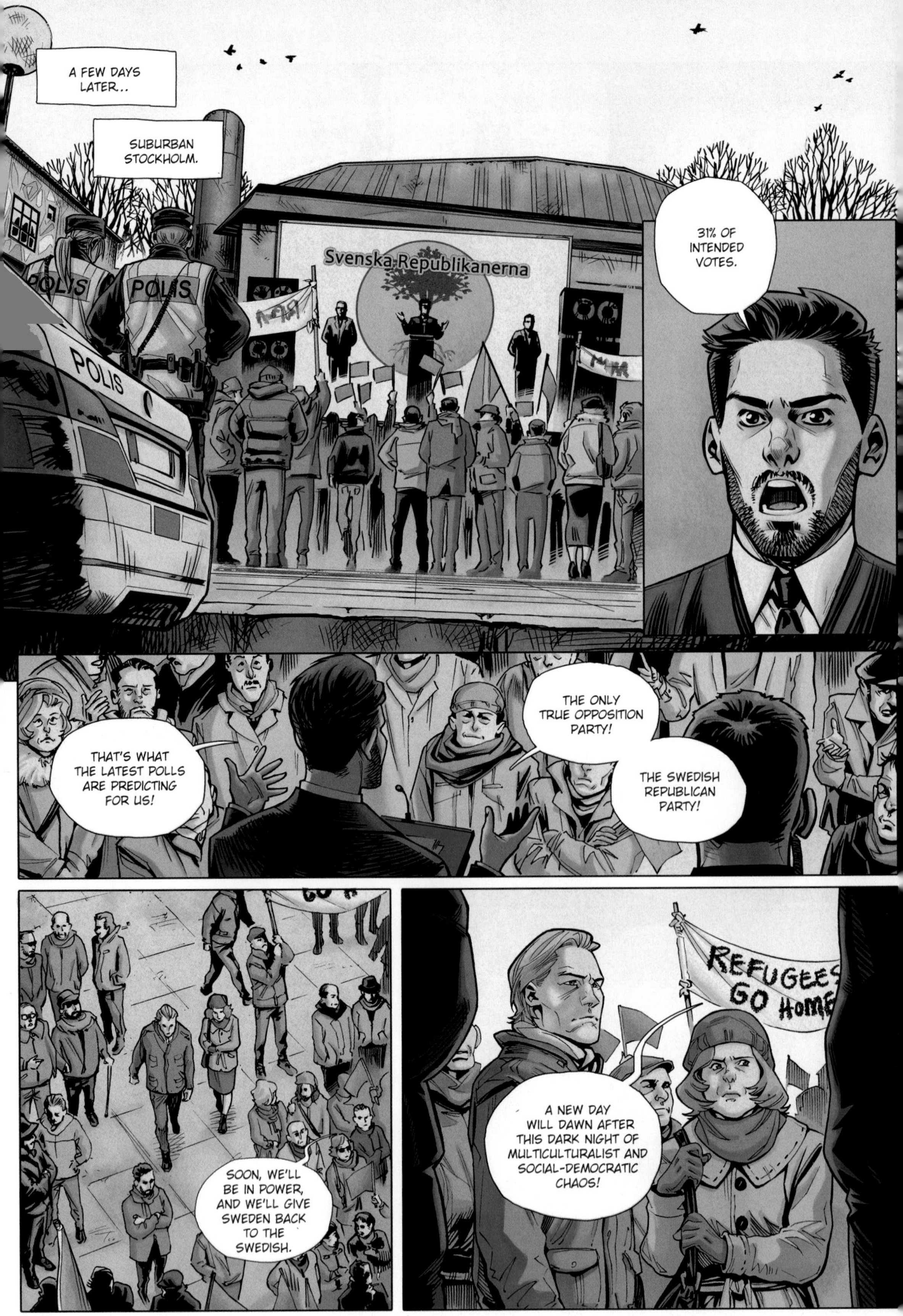
A FEW DAYS LATER...
SUBURBAN STOCKHOLM.
POLIS
POLIS
POLIS
Svenska Republikanerna
31% OF INTENDED VOTES.
THAT'S WHAT THE LATEST POLLS ARE PREDICTING FOR US!
THE ONLY TRUE OPPOSITION PARTY!
THE SWEDISH REPUBLICAN PARTY!
SOON, WE'LL BE IN POWER, AND WE'LL GIVE SWEDEN BACK TO THE SWEDISH.
REFUGEES GO HOME
A NEW DAY WILL DAWN AFTER THIS DARK NIGHT OF MULTICULTURALIST AND SOCIAL-DEMOCRATIC CHAOS!

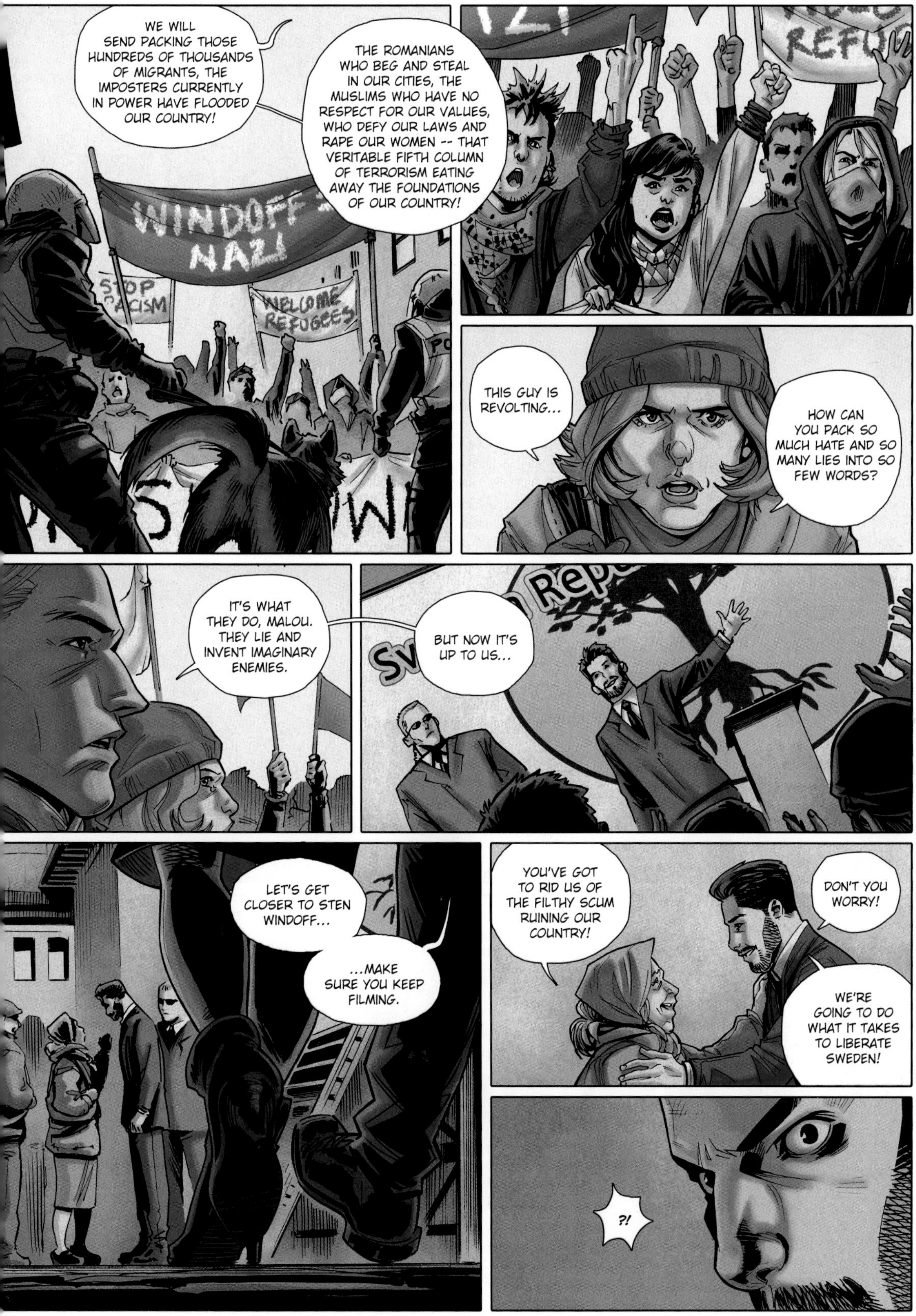
WE WILL SEND PACKING THOSE HUNDREDS OF THOUSANDS OF MIGRANTS, THE IMPOSTERS CURRENTLY IN POWER HAVE FLOODED OUR COUNTRY!
THE ROMANIANS WHO BEG AND STEAL IN OUR CITIES, THE MUSLIMS WHO HAVE NO RESPECT FOR OUR VALUES, WHO DEFY OUR LAWS AND RAPE OUR WOMEN -- THAT VERITABLE FIFTH COLUMN OF TERRORISM EATING AWAY THE FOUNDATIONS OF OUR COUNTRY!
WINDOFF
NAZI
WELCOME REFUGEES
THIS GUY IS REVOLTING...
HOW CAN YOU PACK SO MUCH HATE AND SO MANY LIES INTO SO FEW WORDS?
IT'S WHAT THEY DO, MALOU. THEY LIE AND INVENT IMAGINARY ENEMIES.
BUT NOW IT'S UP TO US...
LET'S GET CLOSER TO STEN WINDOFF...
...MAKE SURE YOU KEEP FILMING.
YOU'VE GOT TO RID US OF THE FILTHY SCUM RUINING OUR COUNTRY!
DON'T YOU WORRY!
WE'RE GOING TO DO WHAT IT TAKES TO LIBERATE SWEDEN!
?!

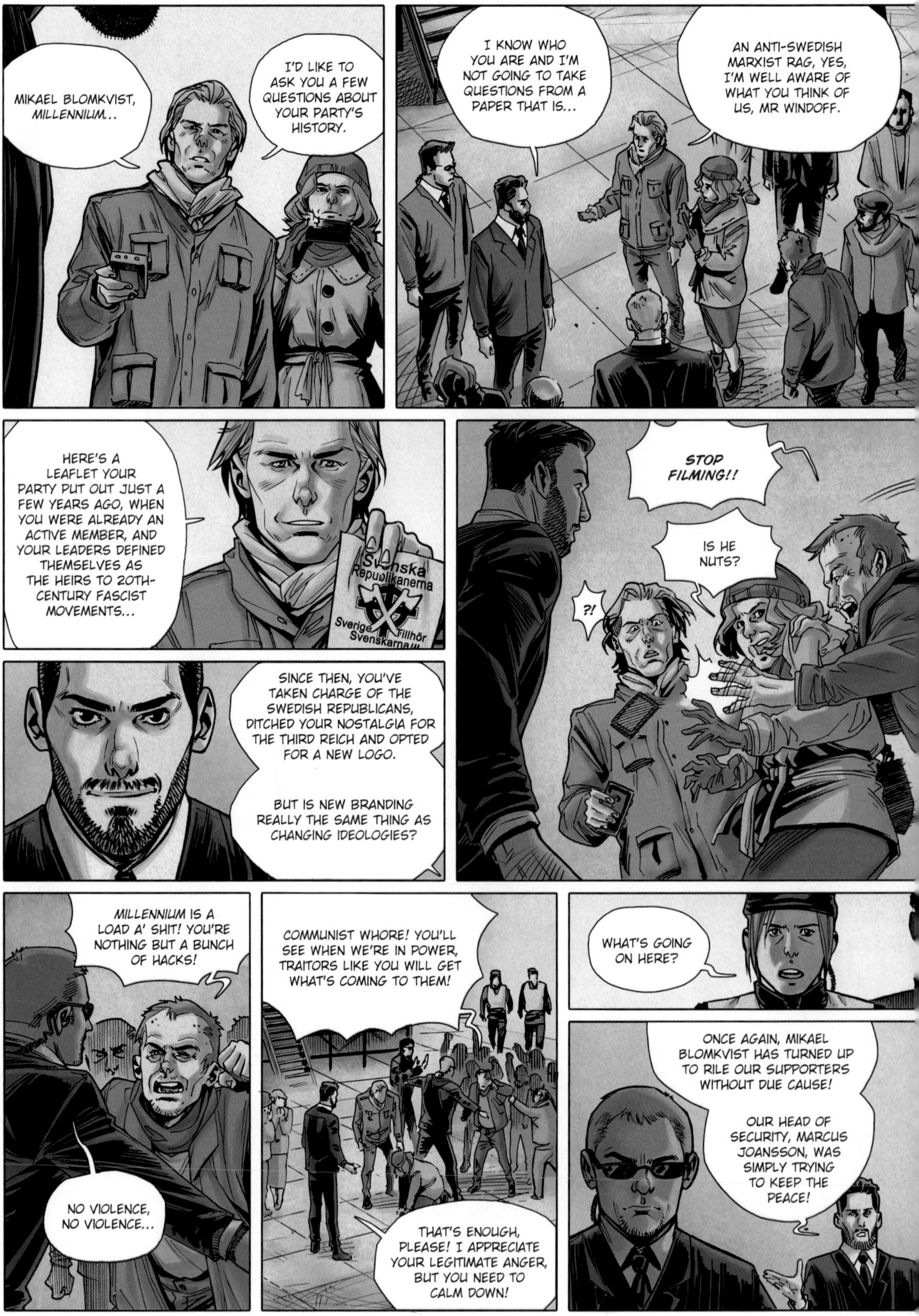
MIKAEL BLOMKVIST, MILLENNIUM...
I'D LIKE TO ASK YOU A FEW QUESTIONS ABOUT YOUR PARTY'S HISTORY.
I KNOW WHO YOU ARE AND I'M NOT GOING TO TAKE QUESTIONS FROM A PAPER THAT IS...
AN ANTI-SWEDISH MARXIST RAG, YES, I'M WELL AWARE OF WHAT YOU THINK OF US, MR WINDOFF.
HERE'S A LEAFLET YOUR PARTY PUT OUT JUST A FEW YEARS AGO, WHEN YOU WERE ALREADY AN ACTIVE MEMBER, AND YOUR LEADERS DEFINED THEMSELVES AS THE HEIRS TO 20TH-CENTURY FASCIST MOVEMENTS...
Svenska Republikanerna
Sverige Tillhör Svenskarna
SINCE THEN, YOU'VE TAKEN CHARGE OF THE SWEDISH REPUBLICANS, DITCHED YOUR NOSTALGIA FOR THE THIRD REICH AND OPTED FOR A NEW LOGO.
BUT IS NEW BRANDING REALLY THE SAME THING AS CHANGING IDEOLOGIES?
STOP FILMING!!
IS HE NUTS?
?!
MILLENNIUM IS A LOAD A' SHIT! YOU'RE NOTHING BUT A BUNCH OF HACKS!
NO VIOLENCE, NO VIOLENCE...
COMMUNIST WHORE! YOU'LL SEE WHEN WE'RE IN POWER, TRAITORS LIKE YOU WILL GET WHAT'S COMING TO THEM!
THAT'S ENOUGH, PLEASE! I APPRECIATE YOUR LEGITIMATE ANGER, BUT YOU NEED TO CALM DOWN!
WHAT'S GOING ON HERE?
ONCE AGAIN, MIKAEL BLOMKVIST HAS TURNED UP TO RILE OUR SUPPORTERS WITHOUT DUE CAUSE!
OUR HEAD OF SECURITY, MARCUS JOANSSON, WAS SIMPLY TRYING TO KEEP THE PEACE!

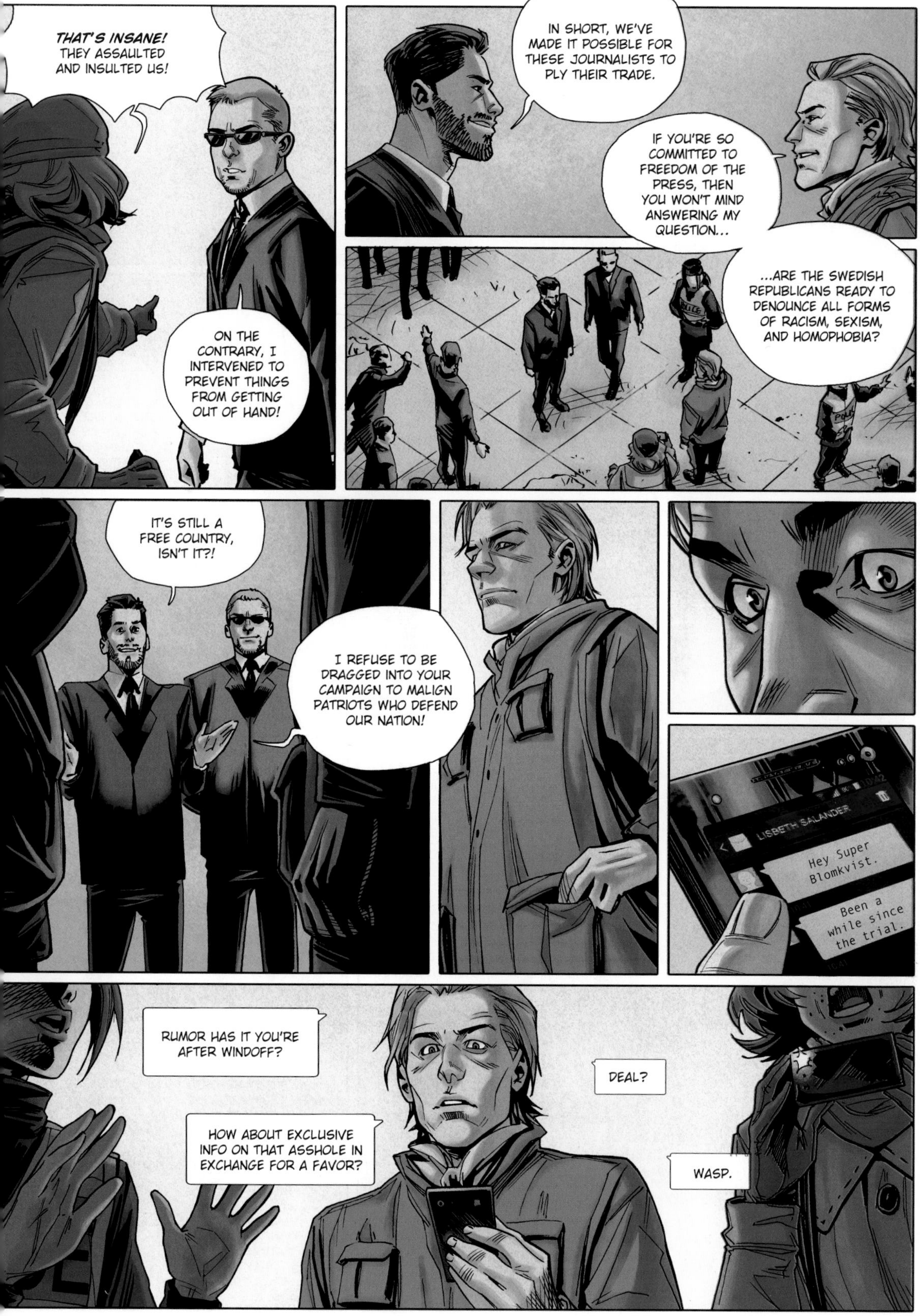
THAT'S INSANE! THEY ASSAULTED AND INSULTED US!
ON THE CONTRARY, I INTERVENED TO PREVENT THINGS FROM GETTING OUT OF HAND!
IN SHORT, WE'VE MADE IT POSSIBLE FOR THESE JOURNALISTS TO PLY THEIR TRADE.
IF YOU'RE SO COMMITTED TO FREEDOM OF THE PRESS, THEN YOU WON'T MIND ANSWERING MY QUESTION...
...ARE THE SWEDISH REPUBLICANS READY TO DENOUNCE ALL FORMS OF RACISM, SEXISM, AND HOMOPHOBIA?
POLICE
IT'S STILL A FREE COUNTRY, ISN'T IT?!
I REFUSE TO BE DRAGGED INTO YOUR CAMPAIGN TO MALIGN PATRIOTS WHO DEFEND OUR NATION!
LISBETH SALANDER
Hey Super Blomkvist.
Been a while since the trial.
RUMOR HAS IT YOU'RE AFTER WINDOFF?
HOW ABOUT EXCLUSIVE INFO ON THAT ASSHOLE IN EXCHANGE FOR A FAVOR?
DEAL?
WASP.

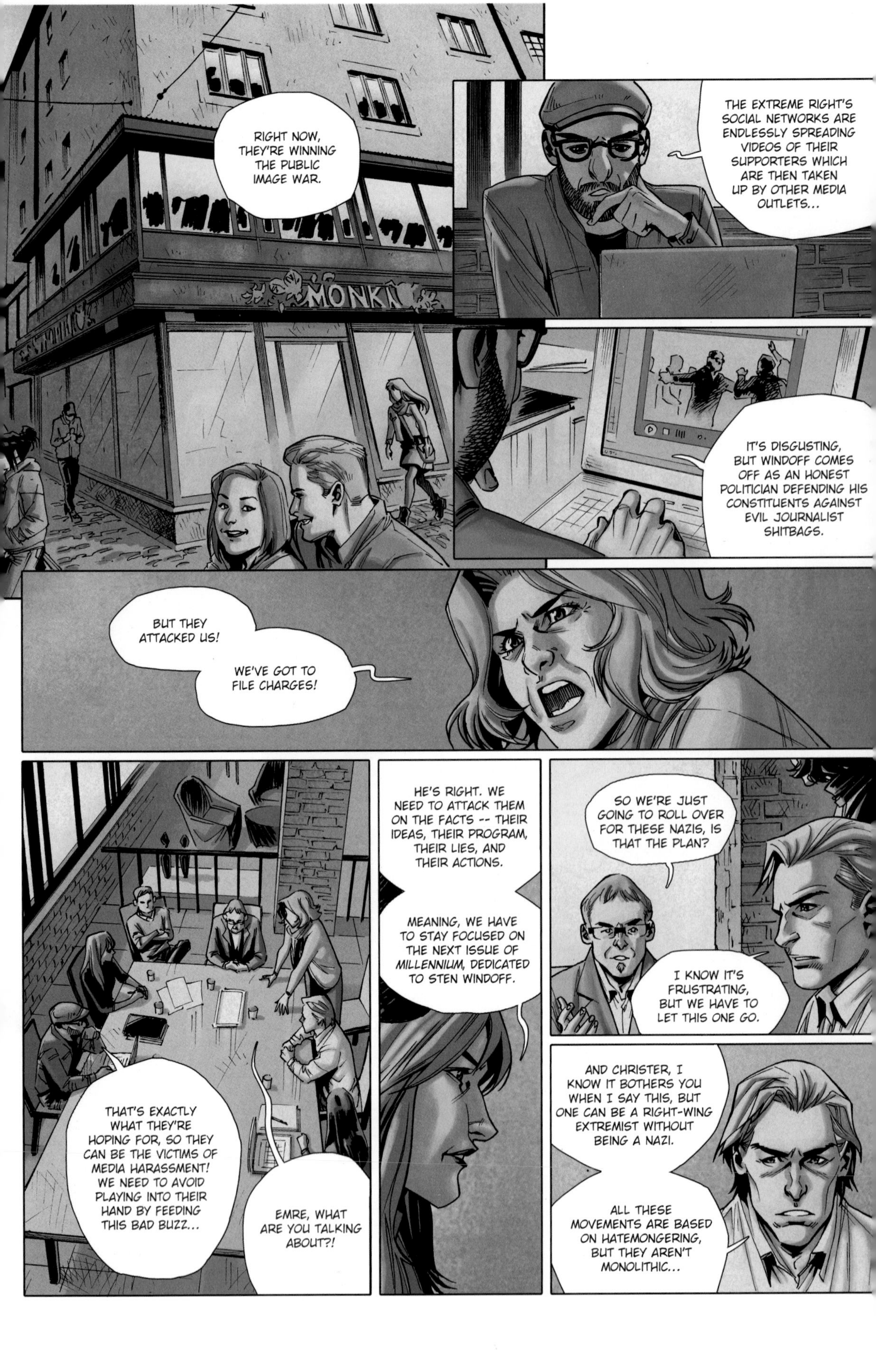
RIGHT NOW, THEY'RE WINNING THE PUBLIC IMAGE WAR.
MONKA
THE EXTREME RIGHT'S SOCIAL NETWORKS ARE ENDLESSLY SPREADING VIDEOS OF THEIR SUPPORTERS WHICH ARE THEN TAKEN UP BY OTHER MEDIA OUTLETS...
IT'S DISGUSTING, BUT WINDOFF COMES OFF AS AN HONEST POLITICIAN DEFENDING HIS CONSTITUENTS AGAINST EVIL JOURNALIST SHITBAGS.
BUT THEY ATTACKED US!
WE'VE GOT TO FILE CHARGES!
THAT'S EXACTLY WHAT THEY'RE HOPING FOR, SO THEY CAN BE THE VICTIMS OF MEDIA HARASSMENT! WE NEED TO AVOID PLAYING INTO THEIR HAND BY FEEDING THIS BAD BUZZ...
EMRE, WHAT ARE YOU TALKING ABOUT?!
HE'S RIGHT. WE NEED TO ATTACK THEM ON THE FACTS -- THEIR IDEAS, THEIR PROGRAM, THEIR LIES, AND THEIR ACTIONS.
MEANING, WE HAVE TO STAY FOCUSED ON THE NEXT ISSUE OF *MILLENNIUM*, DEDICATED TO STEN WINDOFF.
SO WE'RE JUST GOING TO ROLL OVER FOR THESE NAZIS, IS THAT THE PLAN?
I KNOW IT'S FRUSTRATING, BUT WE HAVE TO LET THIS ONE GO.
AND CHRISTER, I KNOW IT BOTHERS YOU WHEN I SAY THIS, BUT ONE CAN BE A RIGHT-WING EXTREMIST WITHOUT BEING A NAZI.
ALL THESE MOVEMENTS ARE BASED ON HATEMONGERING, BUT THEY AREN'T MONOLITHIC...

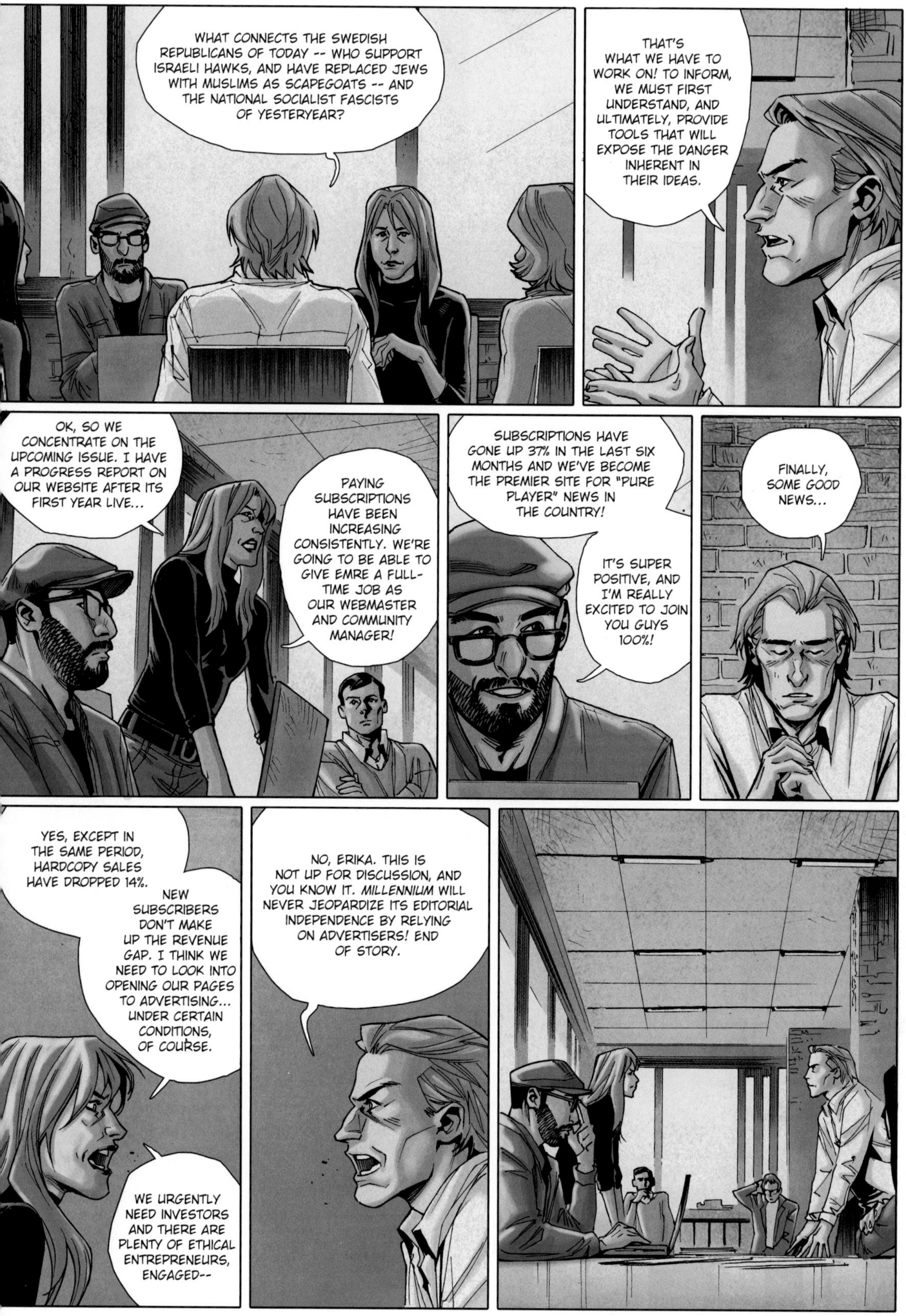
WHAT CONNECTS THE SWEDISH REPUBLICANS OF TODAY -- WHO SUPPORT ISRAELI HAWKS, AND HAVE REPLACED JEWS WITH MUSLIMS AS SCAPEGOATS -- AND THE NATIONAL SOCIALIST FASCISTS OF YESTERYEAR?
THAT'S WHAT WE HAVE TO WORK ON! TO INFORM, WE MUST FIRST UNDERSTAND, AND ULTIMATELY, PROVIDE TOOLS THAT WILL EXPOSE THE DANGER INHERENT IN THEIR IDEAS.
OK, SO WE CONCENTRATE ON THE UPCOMING ISSUE. I HAVE A PROGRESS REPORT ON OUR WEBSITE AFTER ITS FIRST YEAR LIVE...
PAYING SUBSCRIPTIONS HAVE BEEN INCREASING CONSISTENTLY. WE'RE GOING TO BE ABLE TO GIVE EMRE A FULL-TIME JOB AS OUR WEBMASTER AND COMMUNITY MANAGER!
SUBSCRIPTIONS HAVE GONE UP 37% IN THE LAST SIX MONTHS AND WE'VE BECOME THE PREMIER SITE FOR "PURE PLAYER" NEWS IN THE COUNTRY!
IT'S SUPER POSITIVE, AND I'M REALLY EXCITED TO JOIN YOU GUYS 100%!
FINALLY, SOME GOOD NEWS...
YES, EXCEPT IN THE SAME PERIOD, HARDCOPY SALES HAVE DROPPED 14%.
NEW SUBSCRIBERS DON'T MAKE UP THE REVENUE GAP. I THINK WE NEED TO LOOK INTO OPENING OUR PAGES TO ADVERTISING... UNDER CERTAIN CONDITIONS, OF COURSE.
WE URGENTLY NEED INVESTORS AND THERE ARE PLENTY OF ETHICAL ENTREPRENEURS, ENGAGED--
NO, ERIKA. THIS IS NOT UP FOR DISCUSSION, AND YOU KNOW IT. *MILLENNIUM* WILL NEVER JEOPARDIZE ITS EDITORIAL INDEPENDENCE BY RELYING ON ADVERTISERS! END OF STORY.

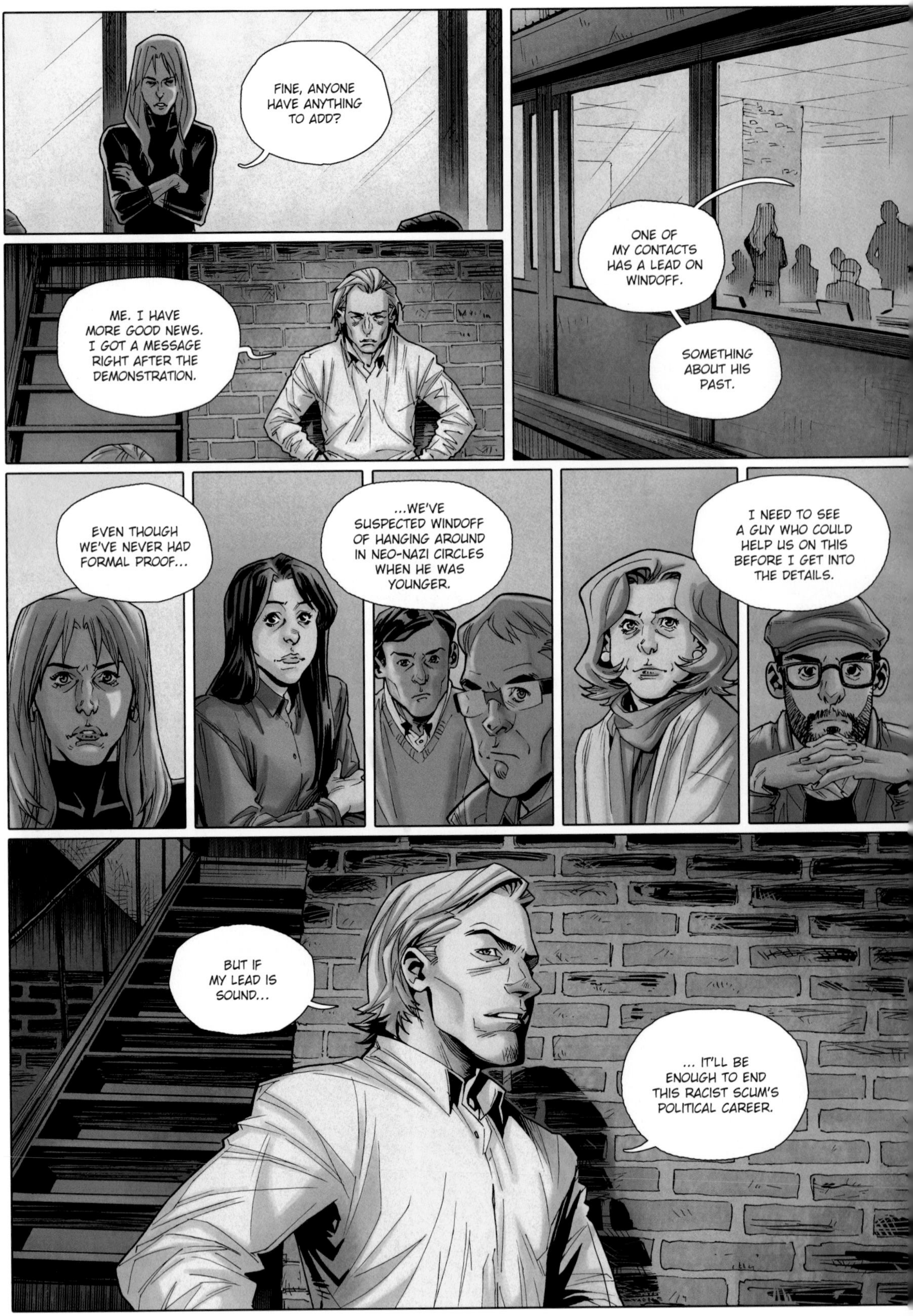
FINE, ANYONE HAVE ANYTHING TO ADD?
ME. I HAVE MORE GOOD NEWS. I GOT A MESSAGE RIGHT AFTER THE DEMONSTRATION.
ONE OF MY CONTACTS HAS A LEAD ON WINDOFF.
SOMETHING ABOUT HIS PAST.
EVEN THOUGH WE'VE NEVER HAD FORMAL PROOF...
...WE'VE SUSPECTED WINDOFF OF HANGING AROUND IN NEO-NAZI CIRCLES WHEN HE WAS YOUNGER.
I NEED TO SEE A GUY WHO COULD HELP US ON THIS BEFORE I GET INTO THE DETAILS.
BUT IF MY LEAD IS SOUND...
... IT'LL BE ENOUGH TO END THIS RACIST SCUM'S POLITICAL CAREER.

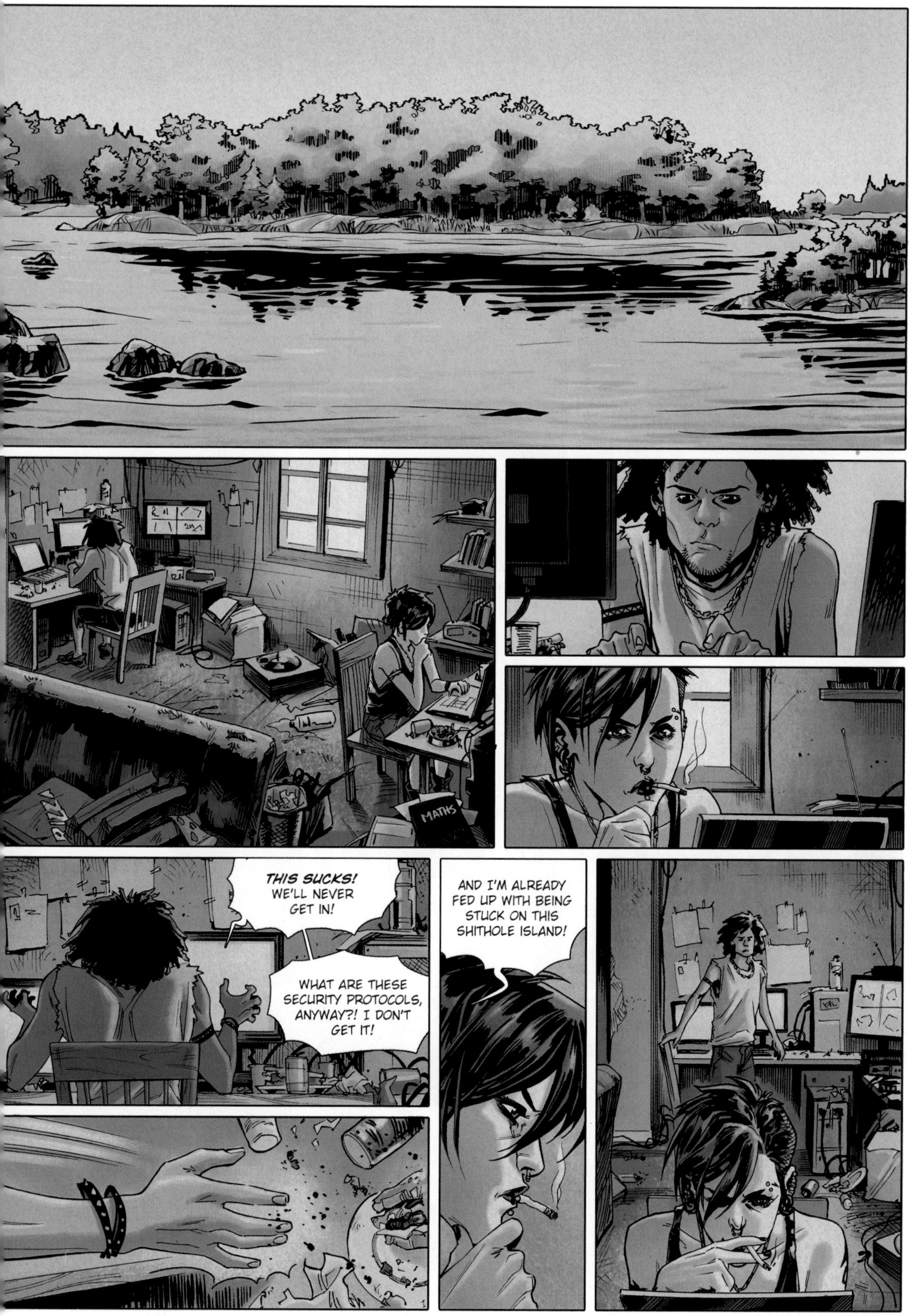

THIS SUCKS! WE'LL NEVER GET IN!
WHAT ARE THESE SECURITY PROTOCOLS, ANYWAY?! I DON'T GET IT!
AND I'M ALREADY FED UP WITH BEING STUCK ON THIS SHITHOLE ISLAND!
MATHS

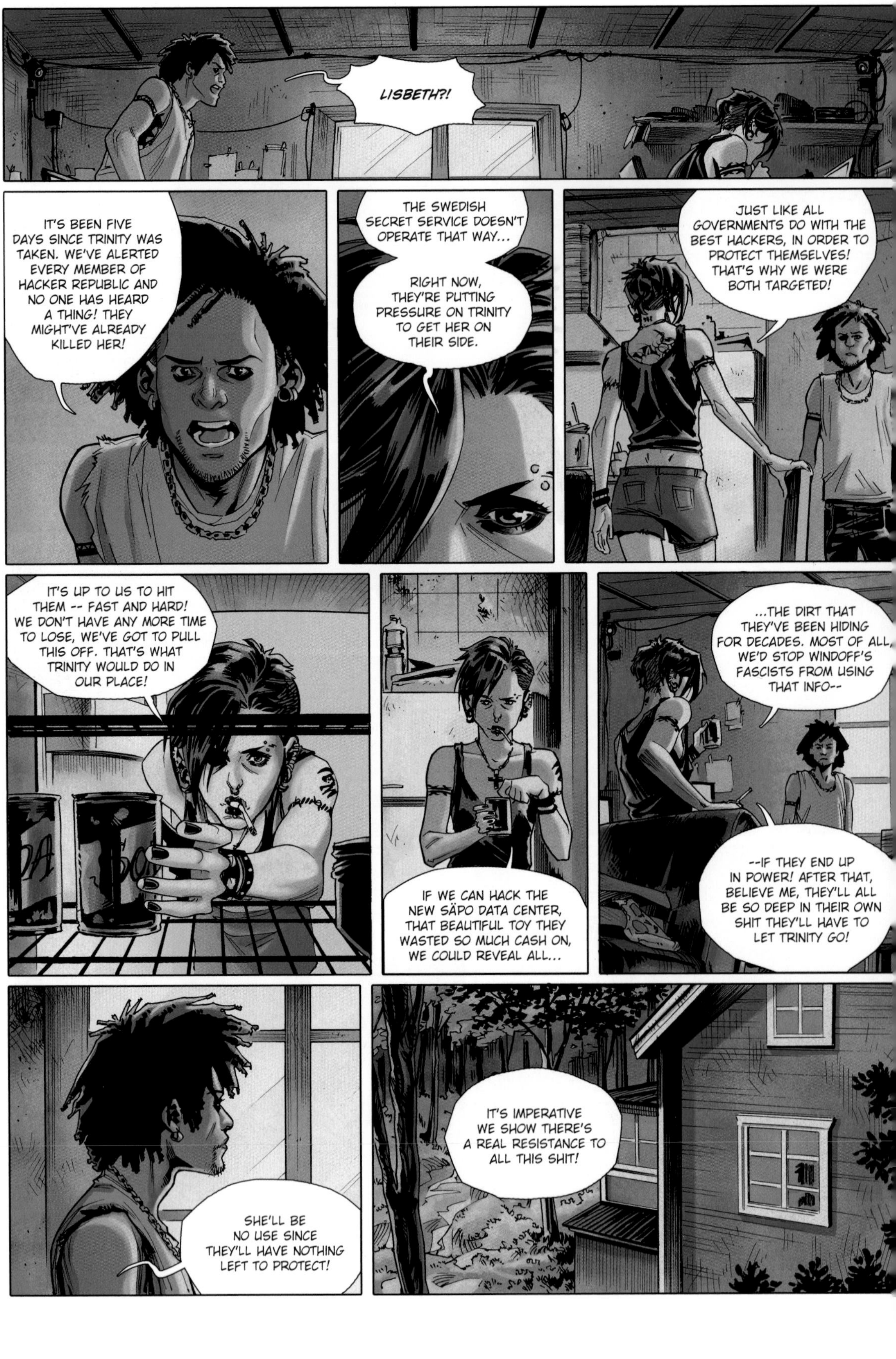
LISBETH?!
IT'S BEEN FIVE DAYS SINCE TRINITY WAS TAKEN. WE'VE ALERTED EVERY MEMBER OF HACKER REPUBLIC AND NO ONE HAS HEARD A THING! THEY MIGHT'VE ALREADY KILLED HER!
THE SWEDISH SECRET SERVICE DOESN'T OPERATE THAT WAY...
RIGHT NOW, THEY'RE PUTTING PRESSURE ON TRINITY TO GET HER ON THEIR SIDE.
JUST LIKE ALL GOVERNMENTS DO WITH THE BEST HACKERS, IN ORDER TO PROTECT THEMSELVES! THAT'S WHY WE WERE BOTH TARGETED!
IT'S UP TO US TO HIT THEM -- FAST AND HARD! WE DON'T HAVE ANY MORE TIME TO LOSE, WE'VE GOT TO PULL THIS OFF. THAT'S WHAT TRINITY WOULD DO IN OUR PLACE!
IF WE CAN HACK THE NEW SÄPO DATA CENTER, THAT BEAUTIFUL TOY THEY WASTED SO MUCH CASH ON, WE COULD REVEAL ALL...
...THE DIRT THAT THEY'VE BEEN HIDING FOR DECADES. MOST OF ALL, WE'D STOP WINDOFF'S FASCISTS FROM USING THAT INFO--
--IF THEY END UP IN POWER! AFTER THAT, BELIEVE ME, THEY'LL ALL BE SO DEEP IN THEIR OWN SHIT THEY'LL HAVE TO LET TRINITY GO!
SHE'LL BE NO USE SINCE THEY'LL HAVE NOTHING LEFT TO PROTECT!
IT'S IMPERATIVE WE SHOW THERE'S A REAL RESISTANCE TO ALL THIS SHIT!

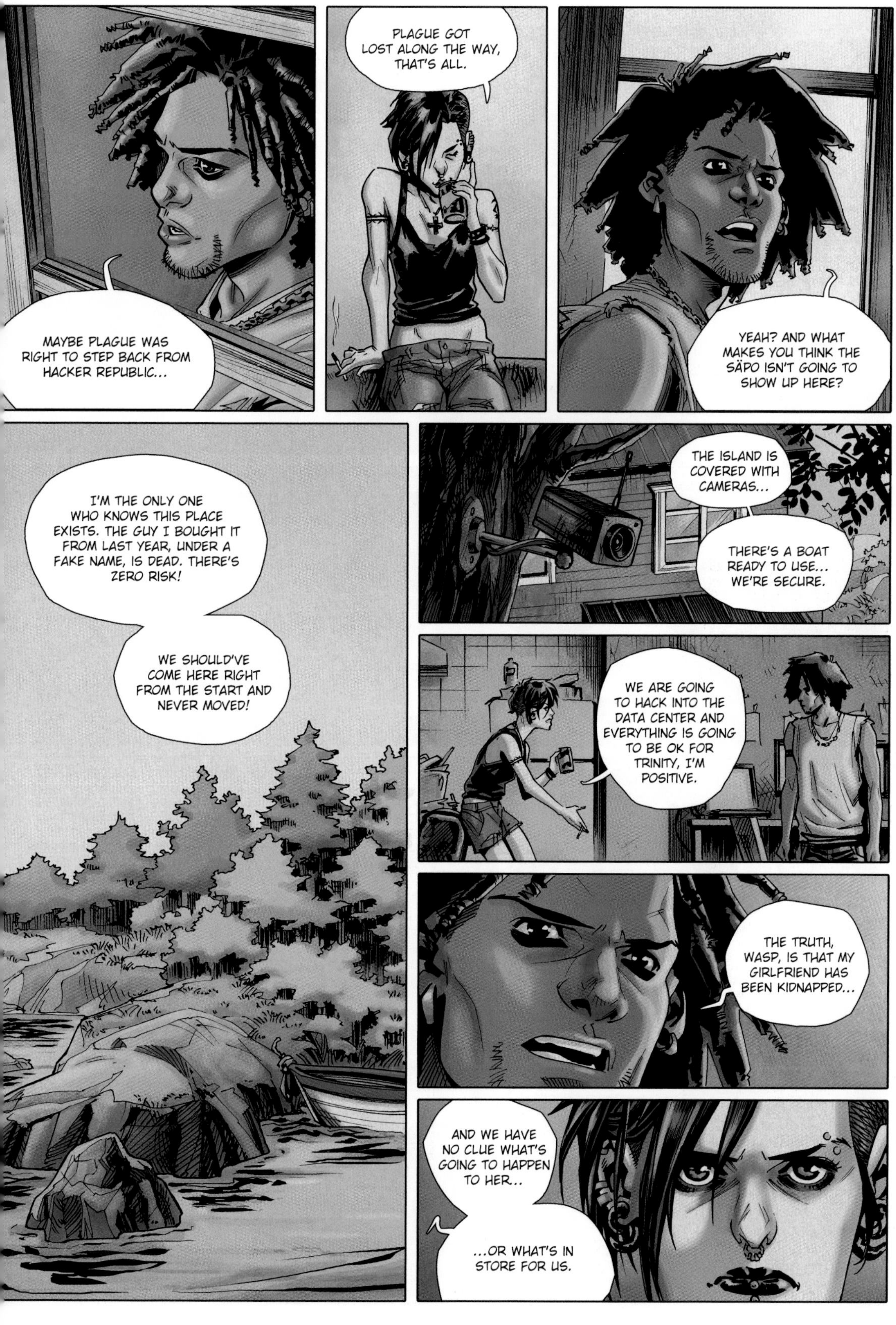
MAYBE PLAGUE WAS RIGHT TO STEP BACK FROM HACKER REPUBLIC...
PLAGUE GOT LOST ALONG THE WAY, THAT'S ALL.
YEAH? AND WHAT MAKES YOU THINK THE SÄPO ISN'T GOING TO SHOW UP HERE?
I'M THE ONLY ONE WHO KNOWS THIS PLACE EXISTS. THE GUY I BOUGHT IT FROM LAST YEAR, UNDER A FAKE NAME, IS DEAD. THERE'S ZERO RISK!
WE SHOULD'VE COME HERE RIGHT FROM THE START AND NEVER MOVED!
THE ISLAND IS COVERED WITH CAMERAS...
THERE'S A BOAT READY TO USE... WE'RE SECURE.
WE ARE GOING TO HACK INTO THE DATA CENTER AND EVERYTHING IS GOING TO BE OK FOR TRINITY, I'M POSITIVE.
THE TRUTH, WASP, IS THAT MY GIRLFRIEND HAS BEEN KIDNAPPED...
AND WE HAVE NO CLUE WHAT'S GOING TO HAPPEN TO HER..
...OR WHAT'S IN STORE FOR US.

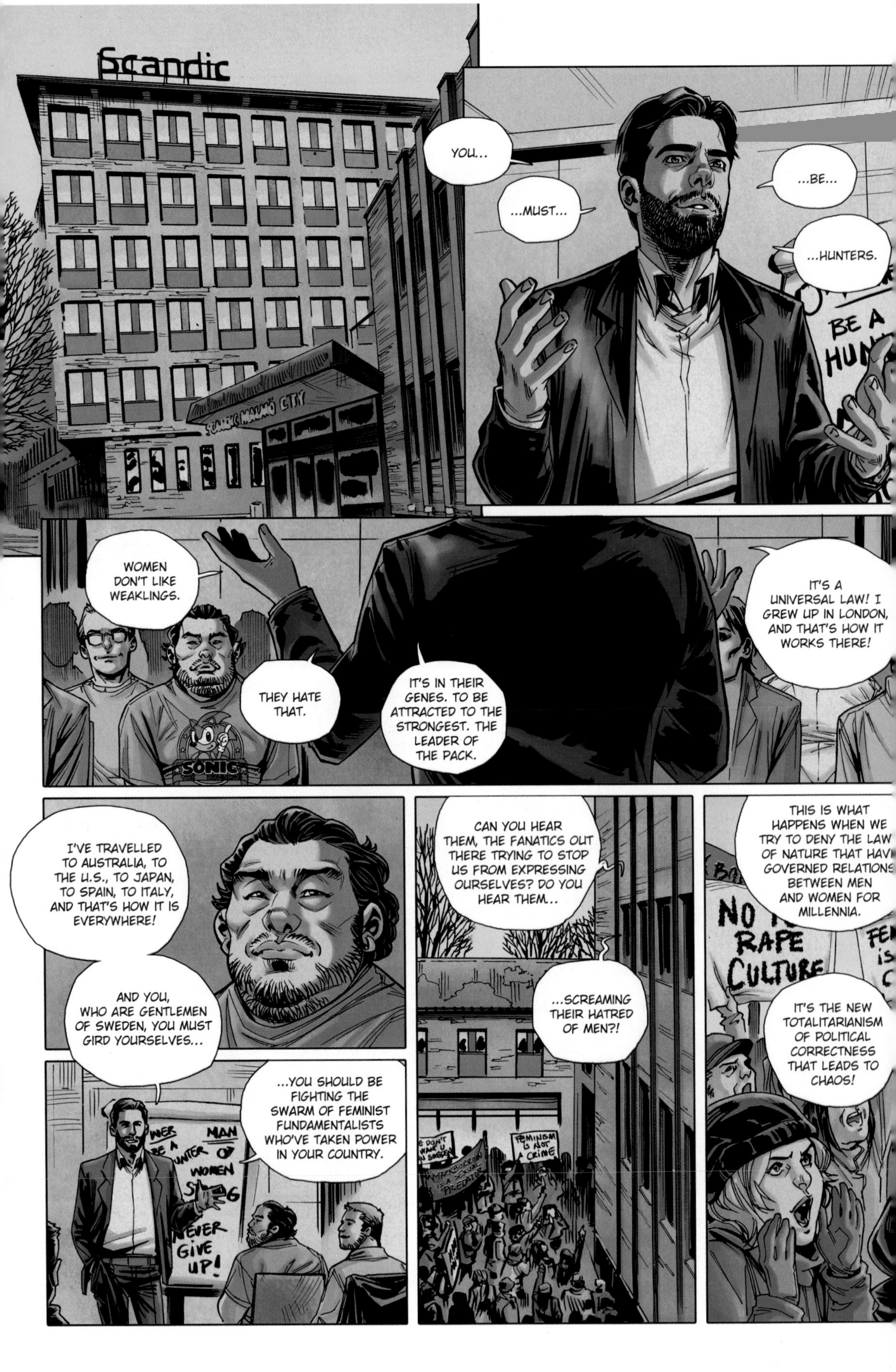
Scandic
YOU...
...MUST...
...BE...
...HUNTERS.
WOMEN DON'T LIKE WEAKLINGS.
THEY HATE THAT.
IT'S IN THEIR GENES. TO BE ATTRACTED TO THE STRONGEST. THE LEADER OF THE PACK.
IT'S A UNIVERSAL LAW! I GREW UP IN LONDON, AND THAT'S HOW IT WORKS THERE!
I'VE TRAVELLED TO AUSTRALIA, TO THE U.S., TO JAPAN, TO SPAIN, TO ITALY, AND THAT'S HOW IT IS EVERYWHERE!
AND YOU, WHO ARE GENTLEMEN OF SWEDEN, YOU MUST GIRD YOURSELVES...
...YOU SHOULD BE FIGHTING THE SWARM OF FEMINIST FUNDAMENTALISTS WHO'VE TAKEN POWER IN YOUR COUNTRY.
NEVER GIVE UP!
CAN YOU HEAR THEM, THE FANATICS OUT THERE TRYING TO STOP US FROM EXPRESSING OURSELVES? DO YOU HEAR THEM...
...SCREAMING THEIR HATRED OF MEN?!
FEMINISM IS NOT A CRIME
THIS IS WHAT HAPPENS WHEN WE TRY TO DENY THE LAW OF NATURE THAT HAVE GOVERNED RELATIONS BETWEEN MEN AND WOMEN FOR MILLENNIA.
IT'S THE NEW TOTALITARIANISM OF POLITICAL CORRECTNESS THAT LEADS TO CHAOS!

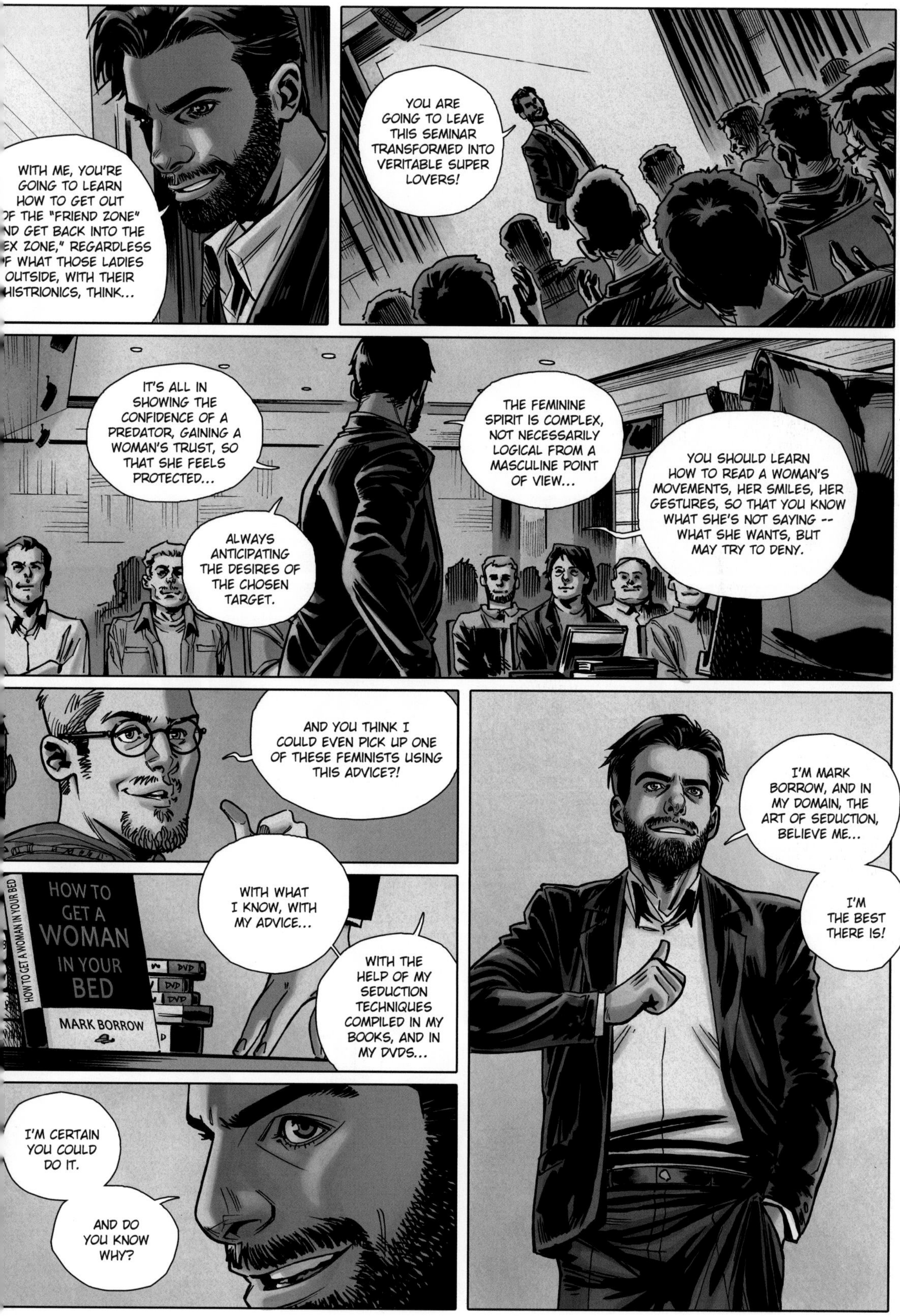
WITH ME, YOU'RE GOING TO LEARN HOW TO GET OUT F THE "FRIEND ZONE" ND GET BACK INTO THE EX ZONE," REGARDLESS F WHAT THOSE LADIES OUTSIDE, WITH THEIR HISTRIONICS, THINK...
YOU ARE GOING TO LEAVE THIS SEMINAR TRANSFORMED INTO VERITABLE SUPER LOVERS!
IT'S ALL IN SHOWING THE CONFIDENCE OF A PREDATOR, GAINING A WOMAN'S TRUST, SO THAT SHE FEELS PROTECTED...
ALWAYS ANTICIPATING THE DESIRES OF THE CHOSEN TARGET.
THE FEMININE SPIRIT IS COMPLEX, NOT NECESSARILY LOGICAL FROM A MASCULINE POINT OF VIEW...
YOU SHOULD LEARN HOW TO READ A WOMAN'S MOVEMENTS, HER SMILES, HER GESTURES, SO THAT YOU KNOW WHAT SHE'S NOT SAYING -- WHAT SHE WANTS, BUT MAY TRY TO DENY.
AND YOU THINK I COULD EVEN PICK UP ONE OF THESE FEMINISTS USING THIS ADVICE?!
WITH WHAT I KNOW, WITH MY ADVICE...
WITH THE HELP OF MY SEDUCTION TECHNIQUES COMPILED IN MY BOOKS, AND IN MY DVDS...
HOW TO GET A WOMAN IN YOUR BED
HOW TO GET A WOMAN IN YOUR BED
MARK BORROW
DVD
I'M CERTAIN YOU COULD DO IT.
AND DO YOU KNOW WHY?
I'M MARK BORROW, AND IN MY DOMAIN, THE ART OF SEDUCTION, BELIEVE ME...
I'M THE BEST THERE IS!

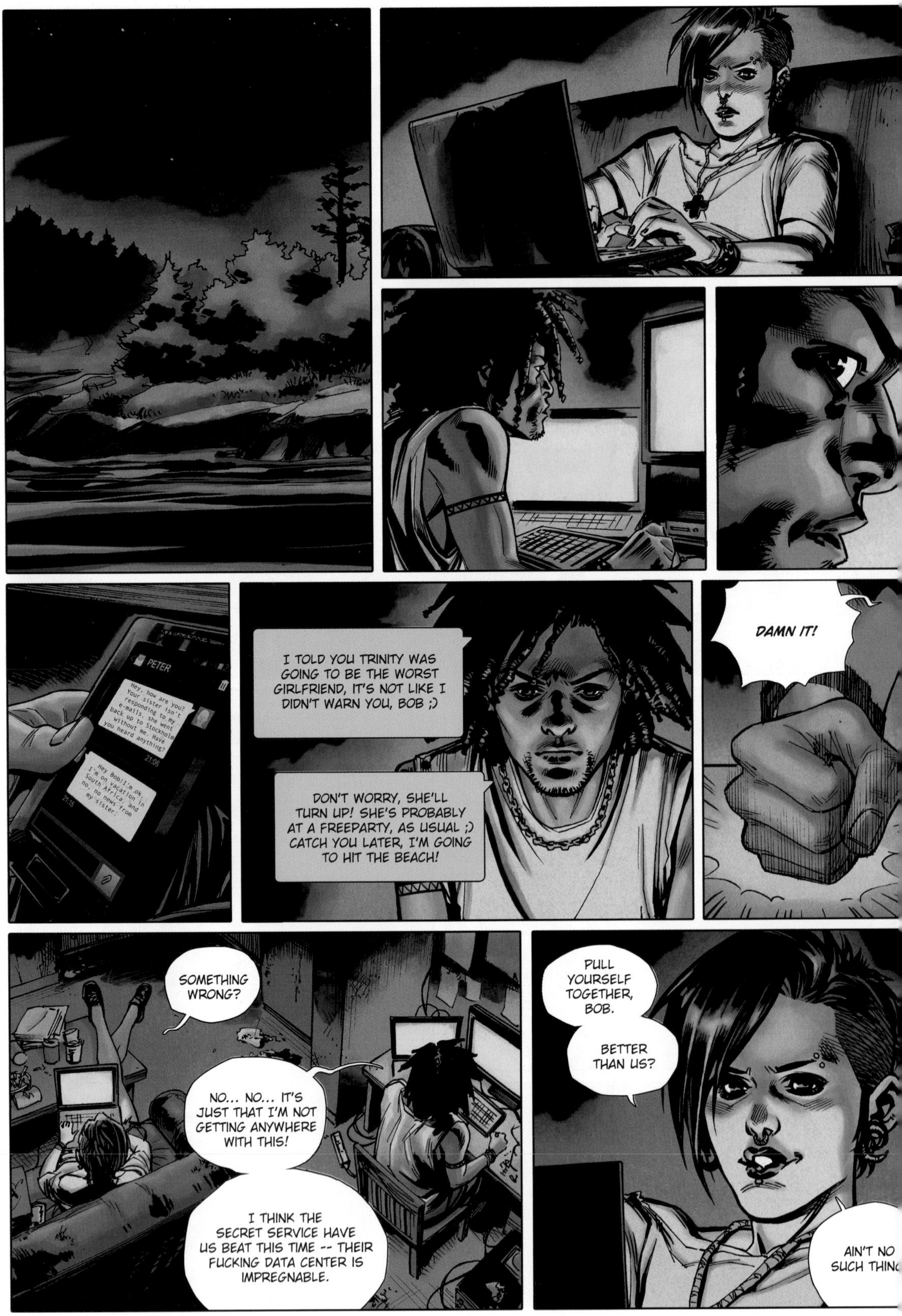
PETER
Hey, how are you? Your sister isn't responding to my e-mails, she went back up to Stockholm without me. Have you heard anything?
21:08
Hey Bob!I'm ok, I'm on vacation in South Africa, and no, no news from my sister.
21:15
I TOLD YOU TRINITY WAS GOING TO BE THE WORST GIRLFRIEND, IT'S NOT LIKE I DIDN'T WARN YOU, BOB ;)
DON'T WORRY, SHE'LL TURN UP! SHE'S PROBABLY AT A FREEPARTY, AS USUAL ;) CATCH YOU LATER, I'M GOING TO HIT THE BEACH!
DAMN IT!
SOMETHING WRONG?
NO... NO... IT'S JUST THAT I'M NOT GETTING ANYWHERE WITH THIS!
I THINK THE SECRET SERVICE HAVE US BEAT THIS TIME -- THEIR FUCKING DATA CENTER IS IMPREGNABLE.
PULL YOURSELF TOGETHER, BOB.
BETTER THAN US?
AIN'T NO SUCH THING

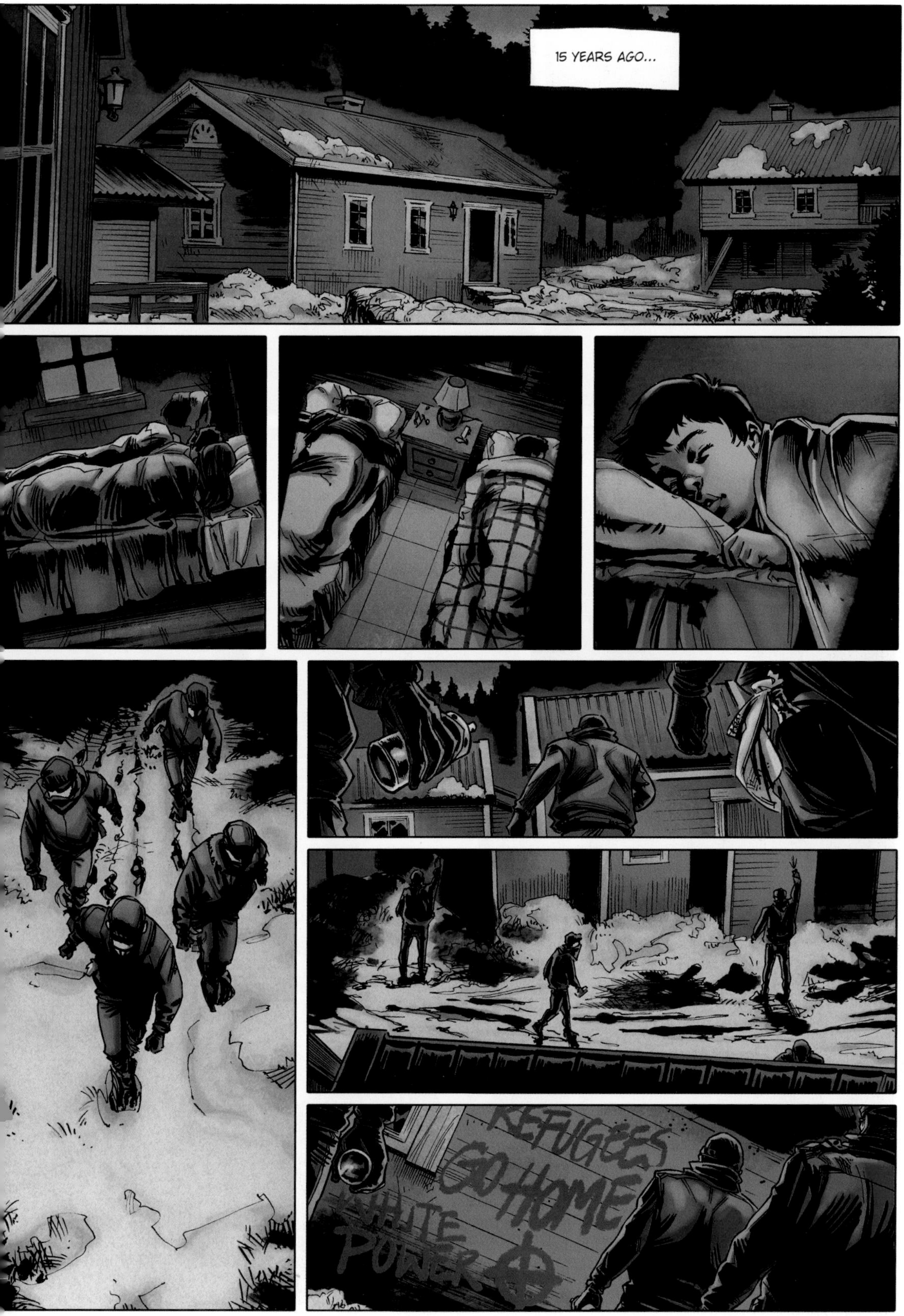
15 YEARS AGO...
REFUGEES GO HOME
WHITE POWER

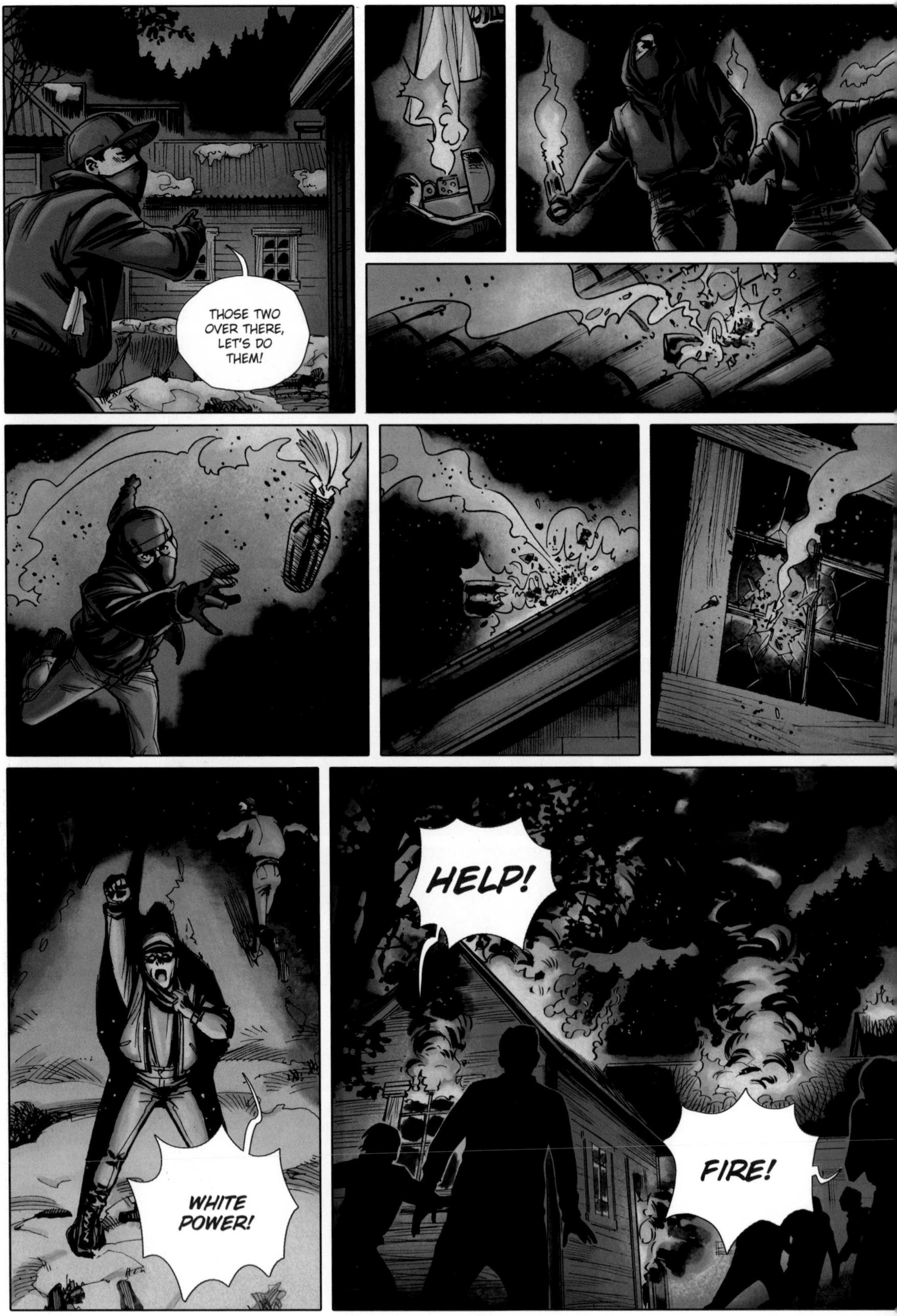
THOSE TWO OVER THERE, LET'S DO THEM!
WHITE POWER!
HELP!
FIRE!

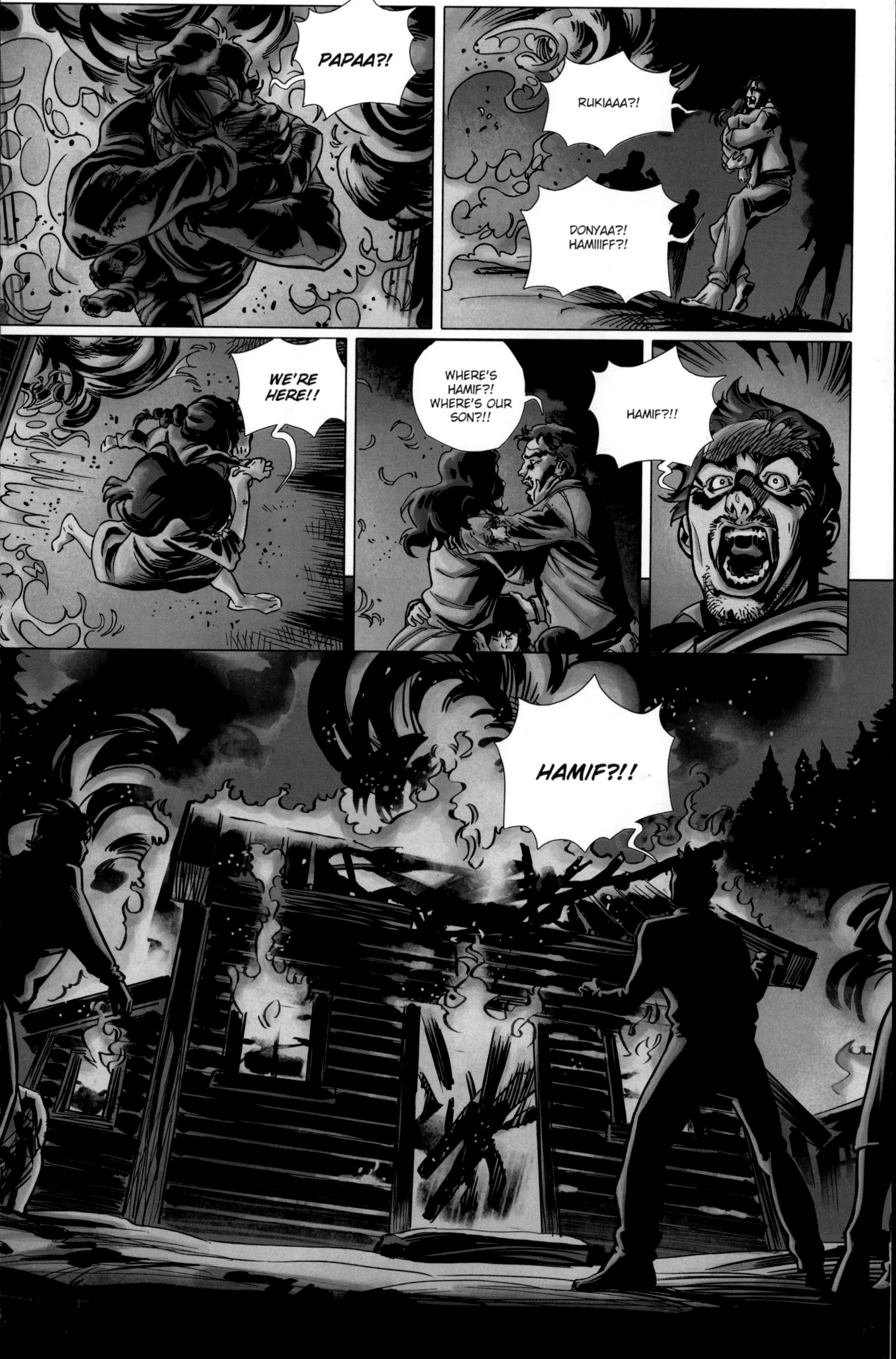
PAPAA?!
RUKIAAA?!
DONYAA?! HAMIIIFF?!
WE'RE HERE!!
WHERE'S HAMIF?! WHERE'S OUR SON?!!
HAMIF?!!
HAMIF?!!

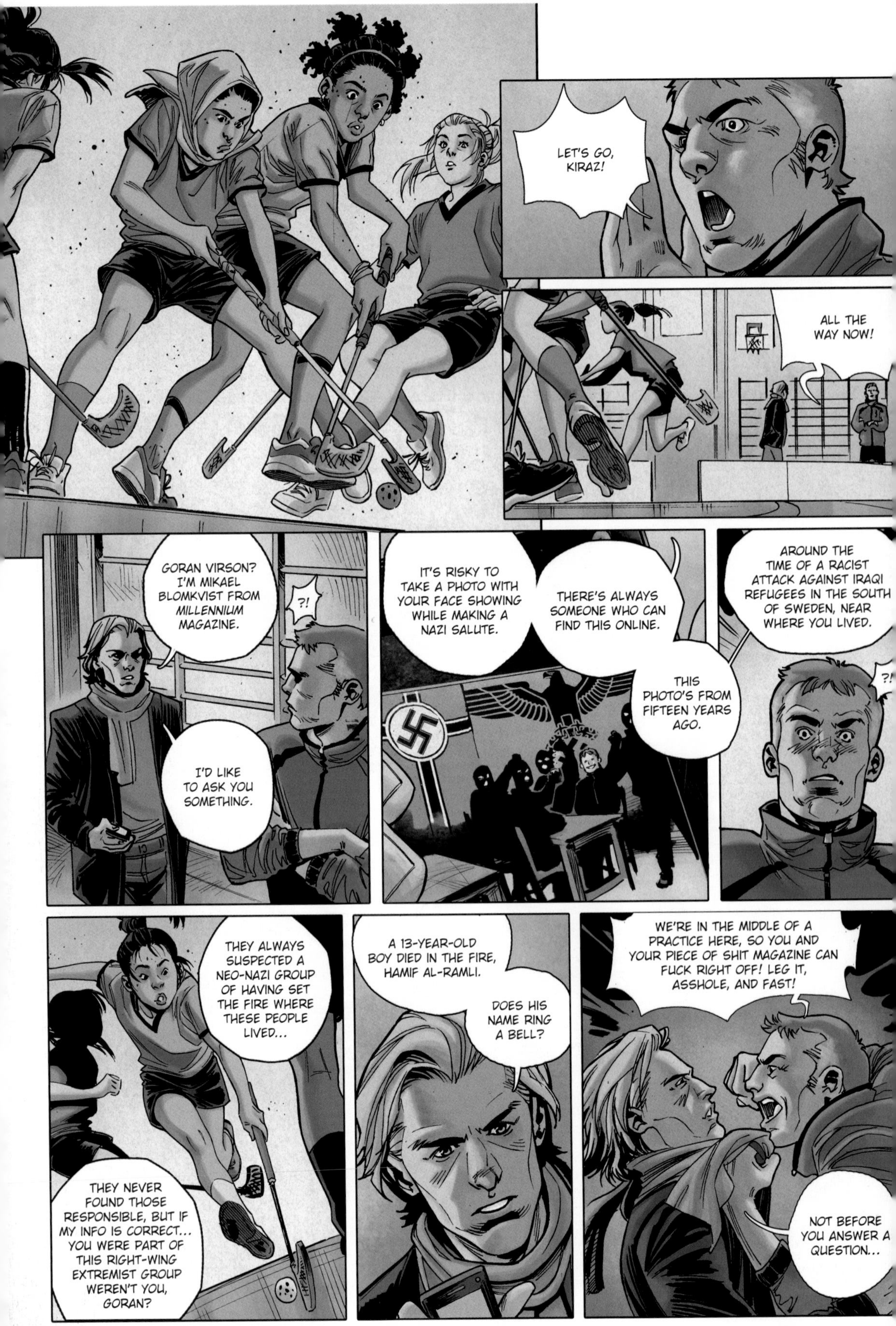
LET'S GO, KIRAZ!
ALL THE WAY NOW!
GORAN VIRSON? I'M MIKAEL BLOMKVIST FROM MILLENNIUM MAGAZINE.
?!
I'D LIKE TO ASK YOU SOMETHING.
IT'S RISKY TO TAKE A PHOTO WITH YOUR FACE SHOWING WHILE MAKING A NAZI SALUTE.
THERE'S ALWAYS SOMEONE WHO CAN FIND THIS ONLINE.
THIS PHOTO'S FROM FIFTEEN YEARS AGO.
AROUND THE TIME OF A RACIST ATTACK AGAINST IRAQI REFUGEES IN THE SOUTH OF SWEDEN, NEAR WHERE YOU LIVED.
?!
THEY ALWAYS SUSPECTED A NEO-NAZI GROUP OF HAVING SET THE FIRE WHERE THESE PEOPLE LIVED...
THEY NEVER FOUND THOSE RESPONSIBLE, BUT IF MY INFO IS CORRECT... YOU WERE PART OF THIS RIGHT-WING EXTREMIST GROUP WEREN'T YOU, GORAN?
A 13-YEAR-OLD BOY DIED IN THE FIRE, HAMIF AL-RAMLI.
DOES HIS NAME RING A BELL?
WE'RE IN THE MIDDLE OF A PRACTICE HERE, SO YOU AND YOUR PIECE OF SHIT MAGAZINE CAN FUCK RIGHT OFF! LEG IT, ASSHOLE, AND FAST!
NOT BEFORE YOU ANSWER A QUESTION...

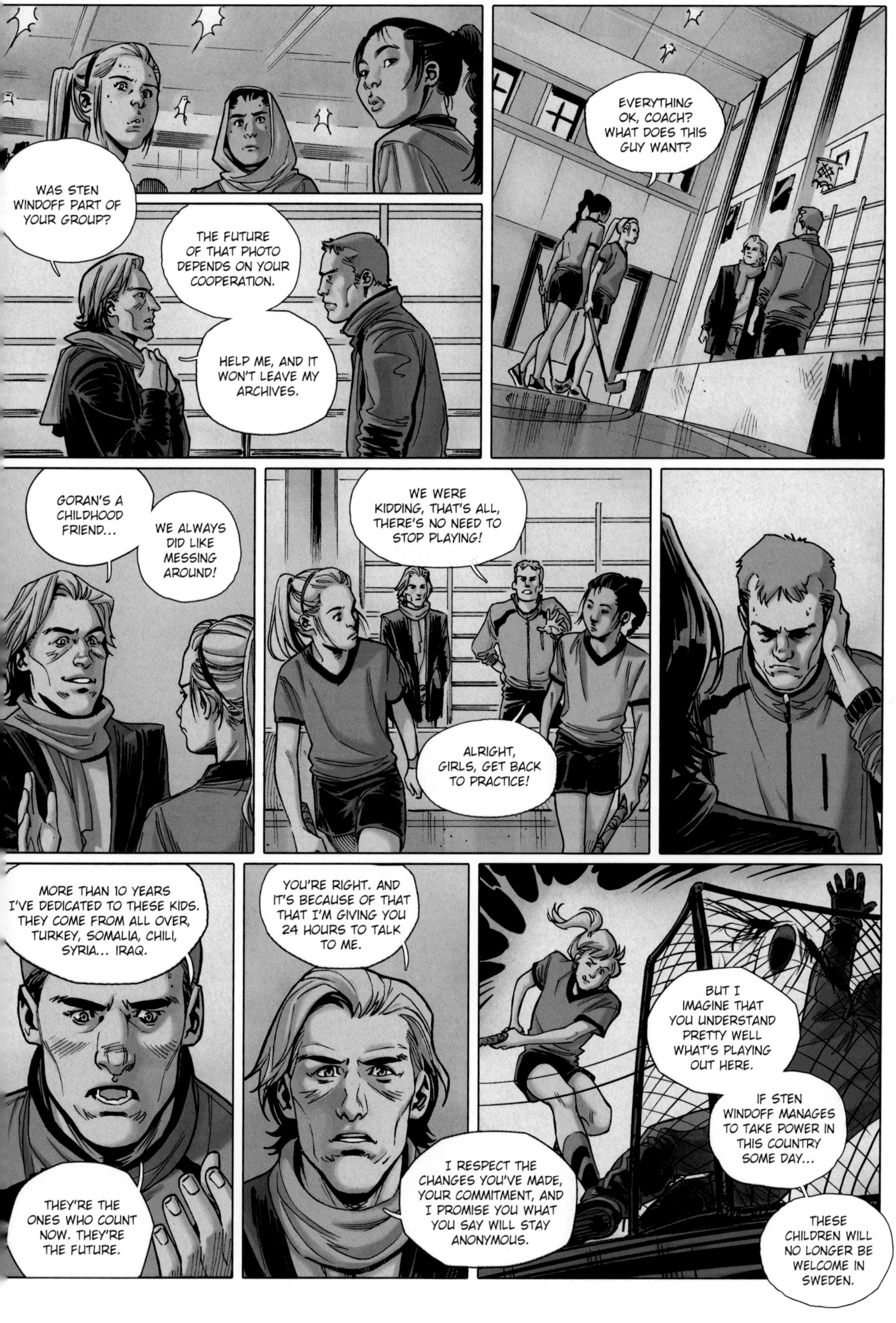
WAS STEN WINDOFF PART OF YOUR GROUP?
THE FUTURE OF THAT PHOTO DEPENDS ON YOUR COOPERATION.
HELP ME, AND IT WON'T LEAVE MY ARCHIVES.
EVERYTHING OK, COACH? WHAT DOES THIS GUY WANT?
GORAN'S A CHILDHOOD FRIEND...
WE ALWAYS DID LIKE MESSING AROUND!
WE WERE KIDDING, THAT'S ALL, THERE'S NO NEED TO STOP PLAYING!
ALRIGHT, GIRLS, GET BACK TO PRACTICE!
MORE THAN 10 YEARS I'VE DEDICATED TO THESE KIDS. THEY COME FROM ALL OVER, TURKEY, SOMALIA, CHILI, SYRIA... IRAQ.
THEY'RE THE ONES WHO COUNT NOW. THEY'RE THE FUTURE.
YOU'RE RIGHT. AND IT'S BECAUSE OF THAT THAT I'M GIVING YOU 24 HOURS TO TALK TO ME.
I RESPECT THE CHANGES YOU'VE MADE, YOUR COMMITMENT, AND I PROMISE YOU WHAT YOU SAY WILL STAY ANONYMOUS.
BUT I IMAGINE THAT YOU UNDERSTAND PRETTY WELL WHAT'S PLAYING OUT HERE.
IF STEN WINDOFF MANAGES TO TAKE POWER IN THIS COUNTRY SOME DAY...
THESE CHILDREN WILL NO LONGER BE WELCOME IN SWEDEN.

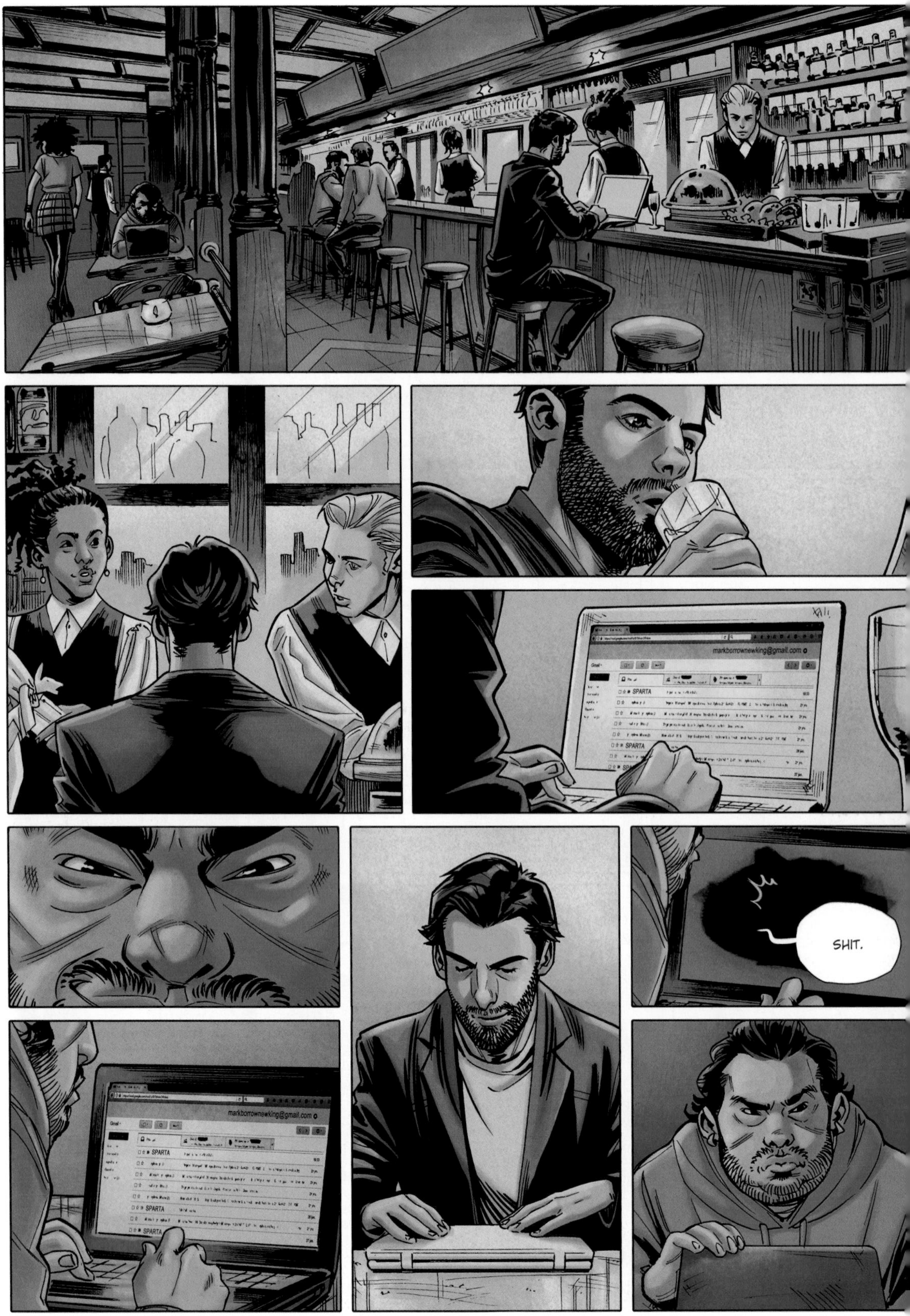
markborrownewking@gmail.com
SPARTA
SPARTA
SHIT.
markborrownewking@gmail.com
SPARTA
SPARTA
SPARTA

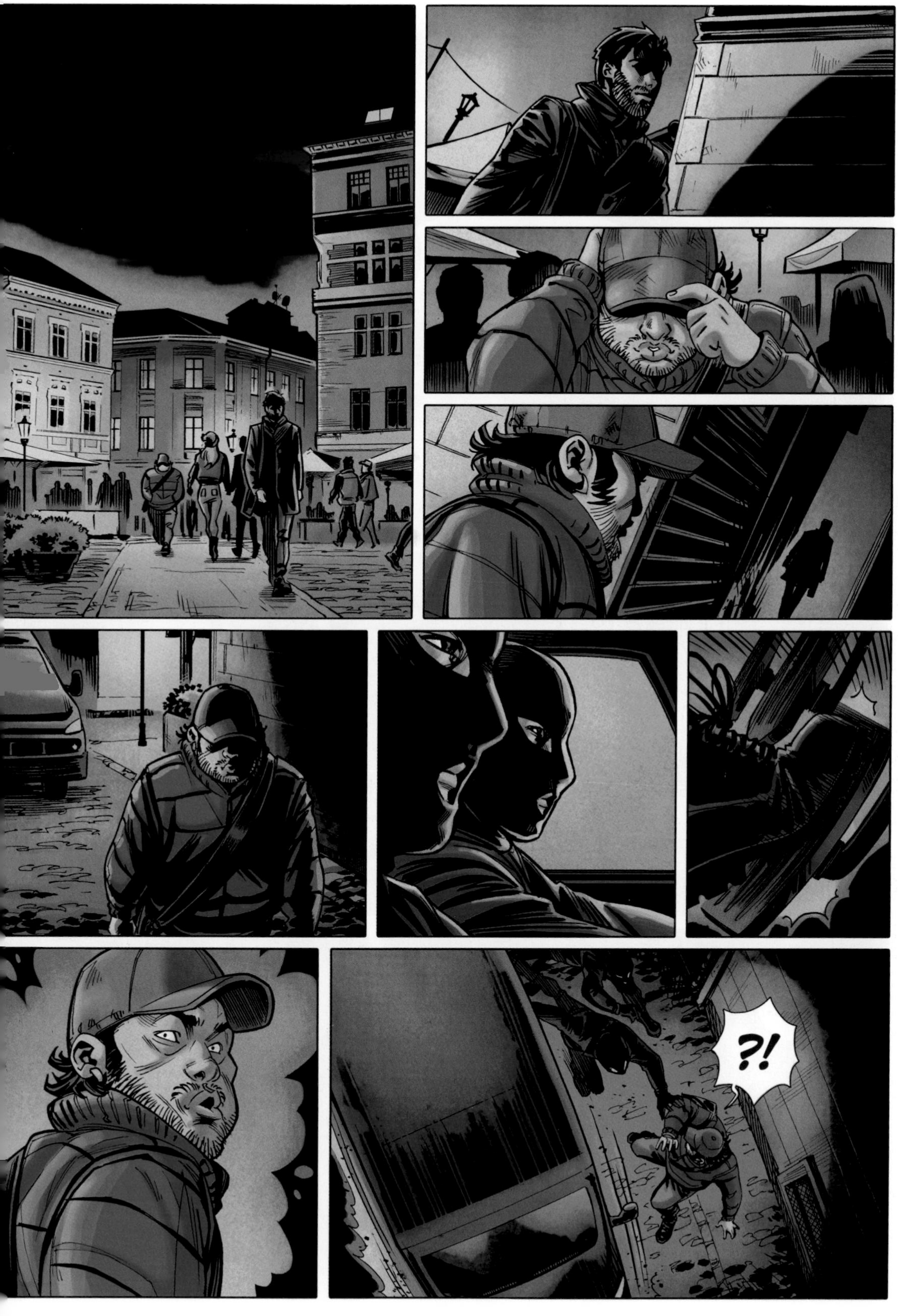
?!

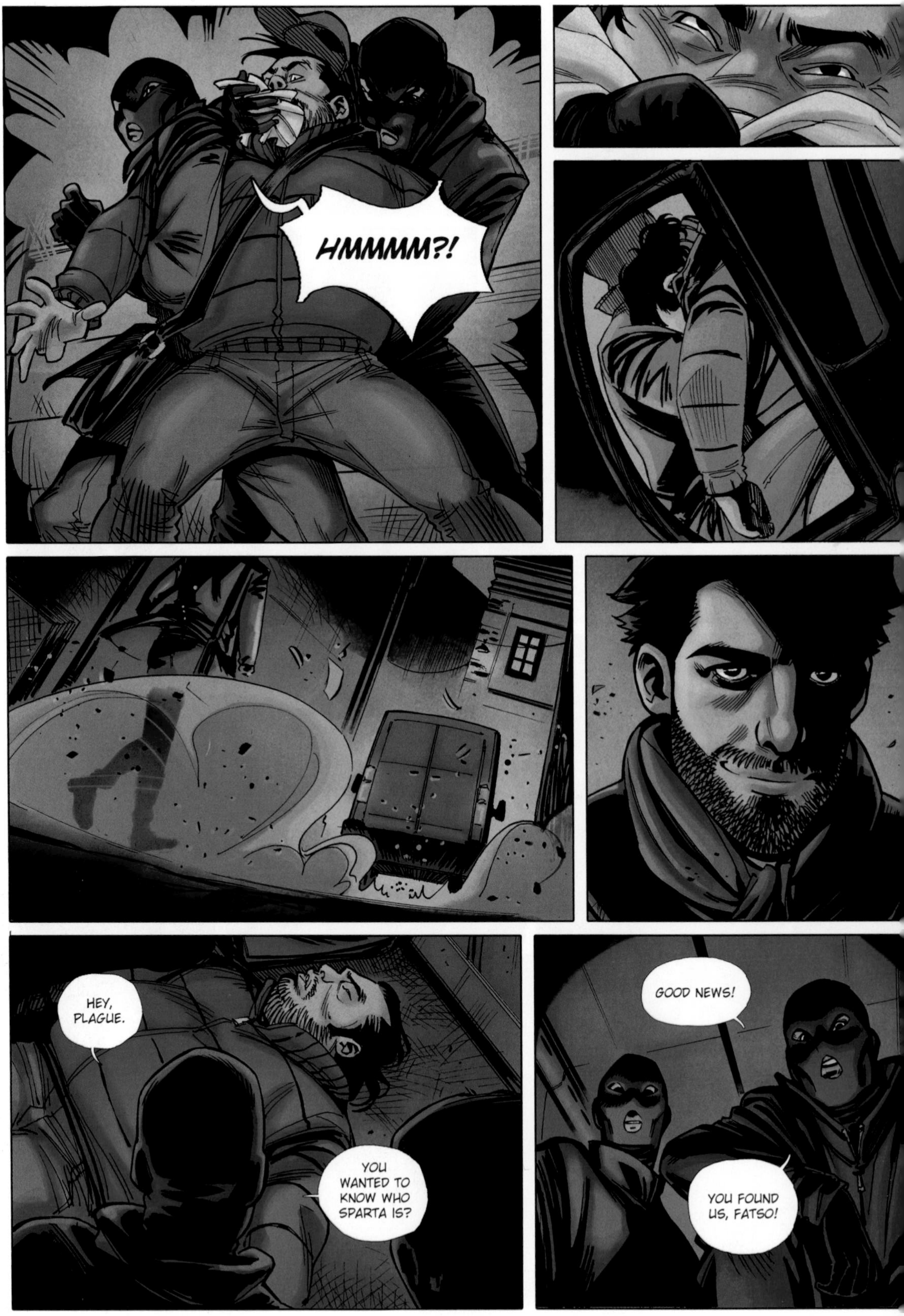
HMMMM?!
HEY, PLAGUE.
YOU WANTED TO KNOW WHO SPARTA IS?
GOOD NEWS!
YOU FOUND US, FATSO!

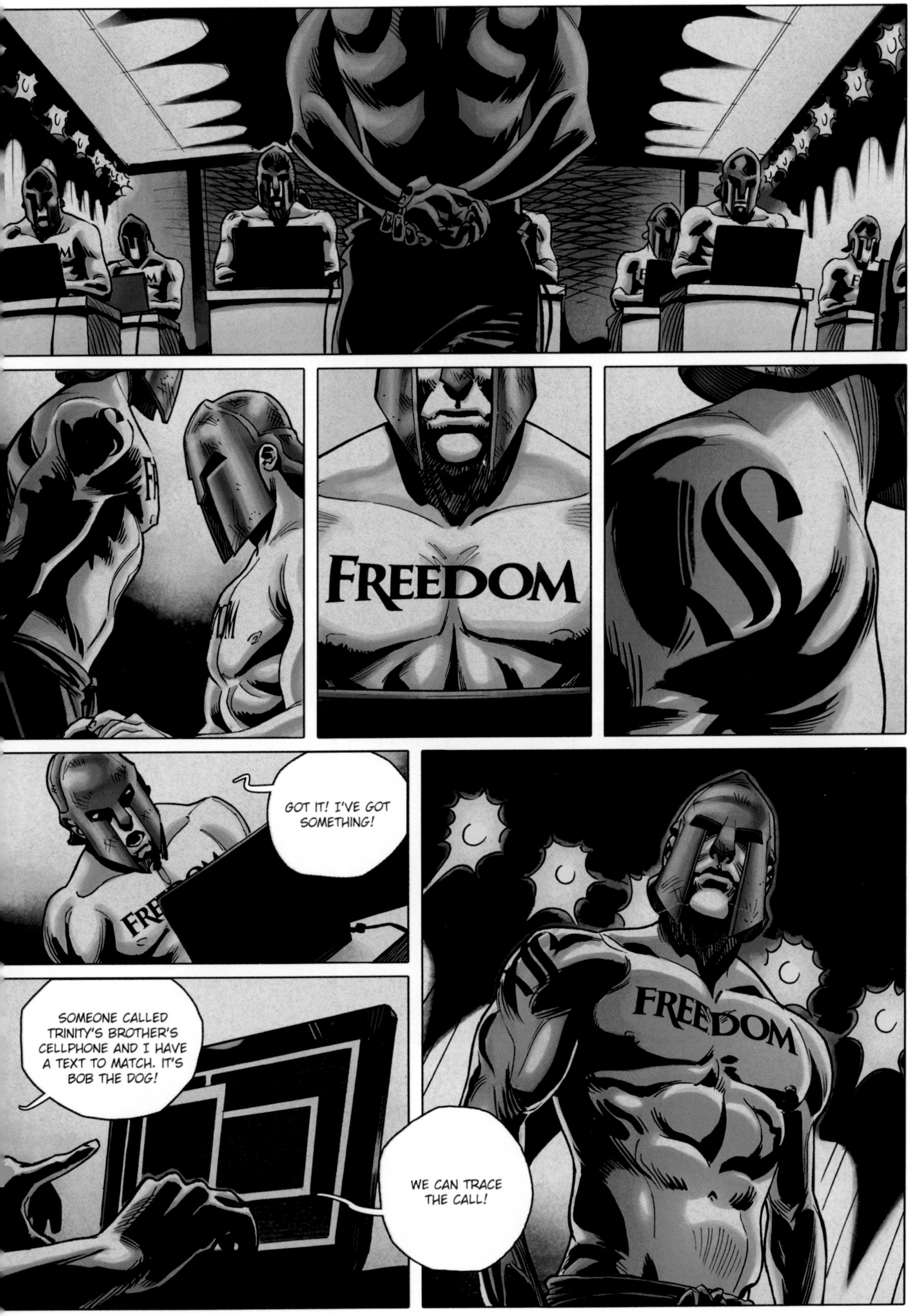
FREEDOM
FREEDOM
GOT IT! I'VE GOT SOMETHING!
FREEDOM
SOMEONE CALLED TRINITY'S BROTHER'S CELLPHONE AND I HAVE A TEXT TO MATCH. IT'S BOB THE DOG!
WE CAN TRACE THE CALL!

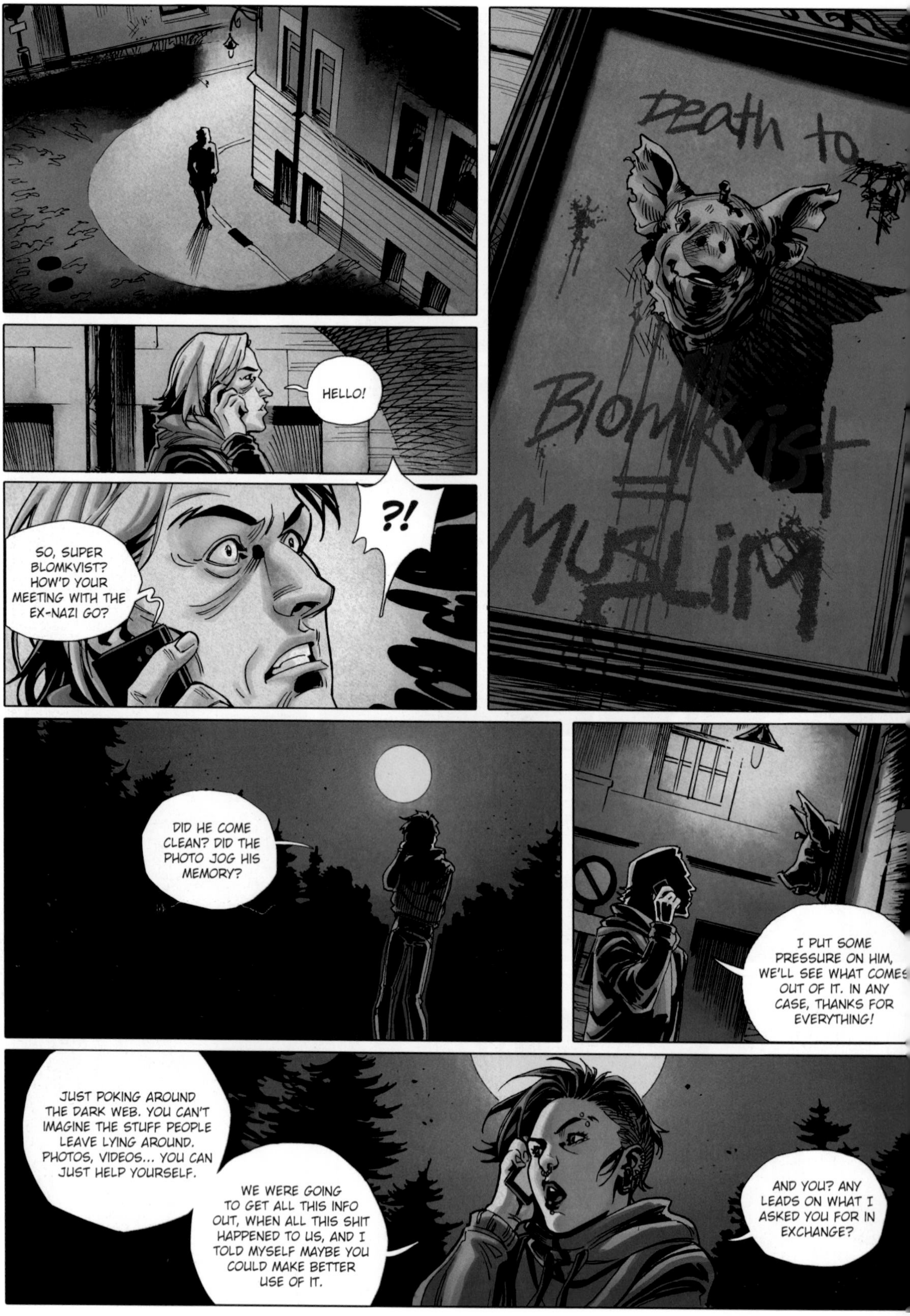
HELLO!
?!
SO, SUPER BLOMKVIST? HOW'D YOUR MEETING WITH THE EX-NAZI GO?
Death to
BLOMKVIST = MUSLIM
DID HE COME CLEAN? DID THE PHOTO JOG HIS MEMORY?
I PUT SOME PRESSURE ON HIM, WE'LL SEE WHAT COMES OUT OF IT. IN ANY CASE, THANKS FOR EVERYTHING!
JUST POKING AROUND THE DARK WEB. YOU CAN'T IMAGINE THE STUFF PEOPLE LEAVE LYING AROUND. PHOTOS, VIDEOS... YOU CAN JUST HELP YOURSELF.
WE WERE GOING TO GET ALL THIS INFO OUT, WHEN ALL THIS SHIT HAPPENED TO US, AND I TOLD MYSELF MAYBE YOU COULD MAKE BETTER USE OF IT.
AND YOU? ANY LEADS ON WHAT I ASKED YOU FOR IN EXCHANGE?

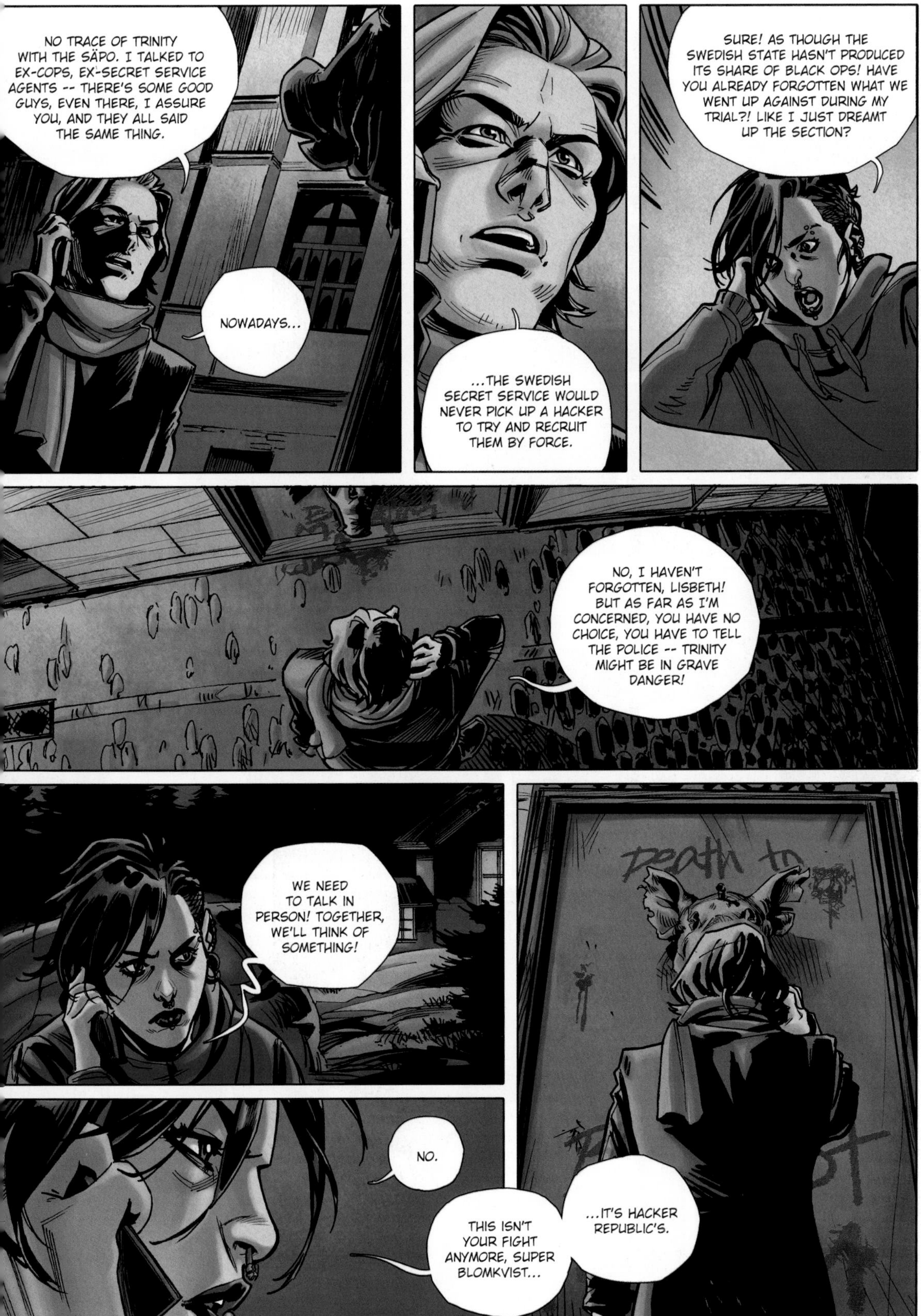
NO TRACE OF TRINITY WITH THE SÄPO. I TALKED TO EX-COPS, EX-SECRET SERVICE AGENTS -- THERE'S SOME GOOD GUYS, EVEN THERE, I ASSURE YOU, AND THEY ALL SAID THE SAME THING.
NOWADAYS...
...THE SWEDISH SECRET SERVICE WOULD NEVER PICK UP A HACKER TO TRY AND RECRUIT THEM BY FORCE.
SURE! AS THOUGH THE SWEDISH STATE HASN'T PRODUCED ITS SHARE OF BLACK OPS! HAVE YOU ALREADY FORGOTTEN WHAT WE WENT UP AGAINST DURING MY TRIAL?! LIKE I JUST DREAMT UP THE SECTION?
NO, I HAVEN'T FORGOTTEN, LISBETH! BUT AS FAR AS I'M CONCERNED, YOU HAVE NO CHOICE, YOU HAVE TO TELL THE POLICE -- TRINITY MIGHT BE IN GRAVE DANGER!
WE NEED TO TALK IN PERSON! TOGETHER, WE'LL THINK OF SOMETHING!
NO.
THIS ISN'T YOUR FIGHT ANYMORE, SUPER BLOMKVIST...
...IT'S HACKER REPUBLIC'S.

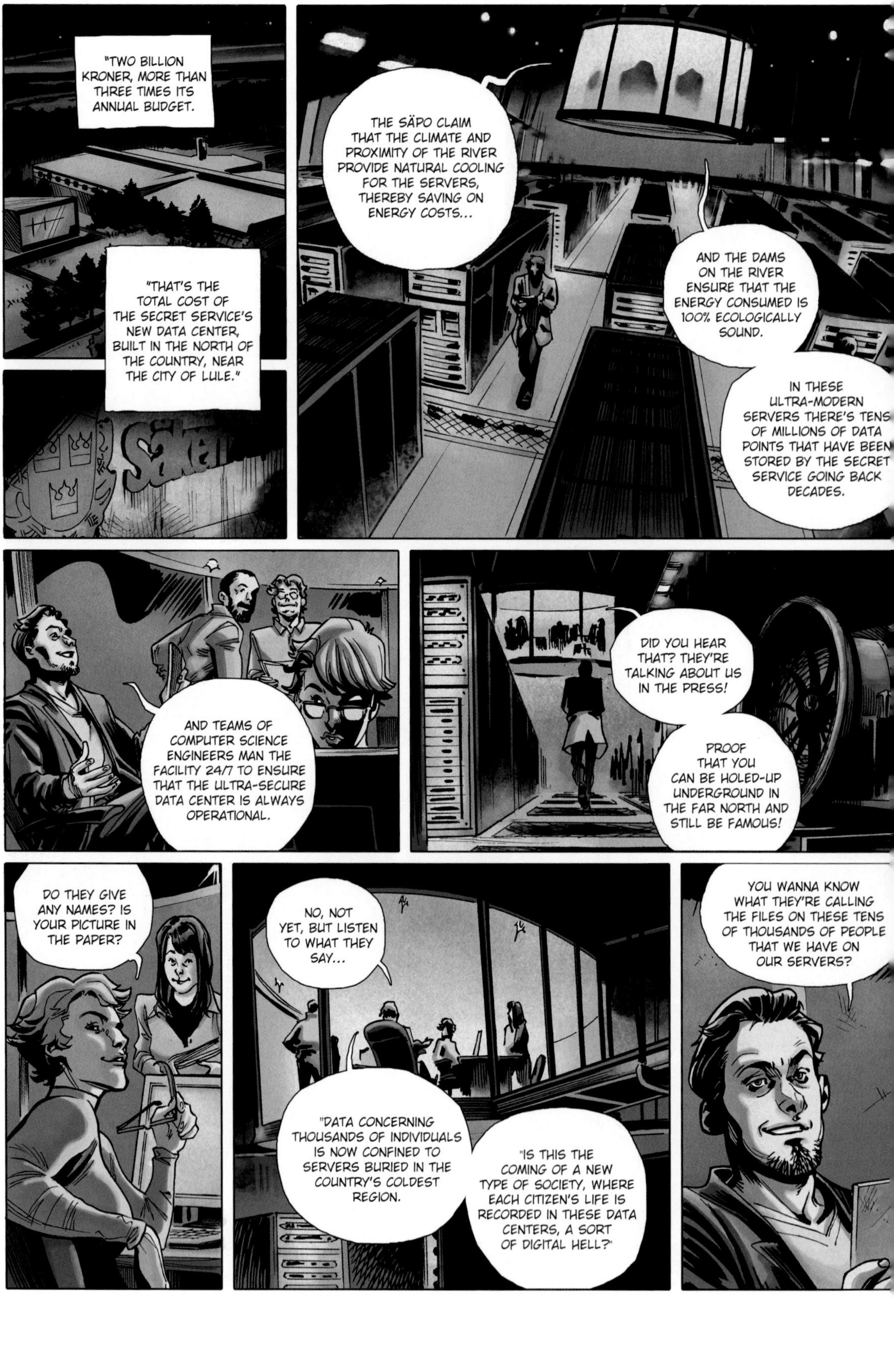
"TWO BILLION KRONER, MORE THAN THREE TIMES ITS ANNUAL BUDGET.
"THAT'S THE TOTAL COST OF THE SECRET SERVICE'S NEW DATA CENTER, BUILT IN THE NORTH OF THE COUNTRY, NEAR THE CITY OF LULE."
THE SÄPO CLAIM THAT THE CLIMATE AND PROXIMITY OF THE RIVER PROVIDE NATURAL COOLING FOR THE SERVERS, THEREBY SAVING ON ENERGY COSTS...
AND THE DAMS ON THE RIVER ENSURE THAT THE ENERGY CONSUMED IS 100% ECOLOGICALLY SOUND.
IN THESE ULTRA-MODERN SERVERS THERE'S TENS OF MILLIONS OF DATA POINTS THAT HAVE BEEN STORED BY THE SECRET SERVICE GOING BACK DECADES.
AND TEAMS OF COMPUTER SCIENCE ENGINEERS MAN THE FACILITY 24/7 TO ENSURE THAT THE ULTRA-SECURE DATA CENTER IS ALWAYS OPERATIONAL.
DID YOU HEAR THAT? THEY'RE TALKING ABOUT US IN THE PRESS!
PROOF THAT YOU CAN BE HOLED-UP UNDERGROUND IN THE FAR NORTH AND STILL BE FAMOUS!
DO THEY GIVE ANY NAMES? IS YOUR PICTURE IN THE PAPER?
NO, NOT YET, BUT LISTEN TO WHAT THEY SAY...
"DATA CONCERNING THOUSANDS OF INDIVIDUALS IS NOW CONFINED TO SERVERS BURIED IN THE COUNTRY'S COLDEST REGION.
"IS THIS THE COMING OF A NEW TYPE OF SOCIETY, WHERE EACH CITIZEN'S LIFE IS RECORDED IN THESE DATA CENTERS, A SORT OF DIGITAL HELL?"
YOU WANNA KNOW WHAT THEY'RE CALLING THE FILES ON THESE TENS OF THOUSANDS OF PEOPLE THAT WE HAVE ON OUR SERVERS?

THERE WE GO...

I'M IN!!

ARE YOU KIDDING?

"COLD SOULS".

YOU'RE IN THEIR DATA CENTER?

TOTALLY INSIDE! SÄPO WON'T HAVE ANY SECRETS FROM US, OR FROM ANYONE!

WE SHOULD WARN ALL THE OTHER HACKER REPUBLIC MEMBERS, SHARE THE DATA, SORT IT, REFERENCE IT, THIS IS HUGE!

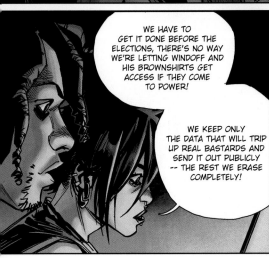

WE HAVE TO GET IT DONE BEFORE THE ELECTIONS, THERE'S NO WAY WE'RE LETTING WINDOFF AND HIS BROWNSHIRTS GET ACCESS IF THEY COME TO POWER!

WE KEEP ONLY THE DATA THAT WILL TRIP UP REAL BASTARDS AND SEND IT OUT PUBLICLY -- THE REST WE ERASE COMPLETELY!

WHAT'S THAT FOLDER "HUGIN" -- IT LOOKS MORE LIKE A PROGRAM THAN A FILE?

HUGIN

HOLY SHIT...

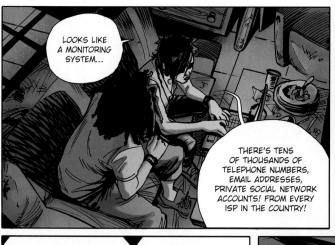

LOOKS LIKE A MONITORING SYSTEM...

THERE'S TENS OF THOUSANDS OF TELEPHONE NUMBERS, EMAIL ADDRESSES, PRIVATE SOCIAL NETWORK ACCOUNTS! FROM EVERY ISP IN THE COUNTRY!

THERE, LOOK, LOOK! IT'S NOT JUST SWEDEN, DENMARK, NORWAY, FRANCE, GREAT BRITAIN, GERMANY, RUSSIA...?

THESE CREEPS HAVE PUT TOGETHER A GENERAL SURVEILLANCE SYSTEM, COVERING THE WHOLE OF EUROPE?! I DOUBT THAT COMPLIES WITH THE CONSTITUTION!

PARLIAMENT WOULD NEVER AUTHORIZE THIS. IT'LL TRIGGER A MAJOR CRISIS! IMAGINE IF THE RUSSIANS GOT HOLD OF THIS?

AND THAT NAME... HUGIN...?

IN NORSE MYTHOLOGY, IT'S THE NAME OF ONE OF ODIN'S RAVENS.

THE ONE THE GOD SENT OUT INTO THE WORLD TO SPY...

...AND WHO WOULD RETURN TO WHISPER IN ITS MASTER'S EAR ALL THE SECRETS IT HAD LEARNED!

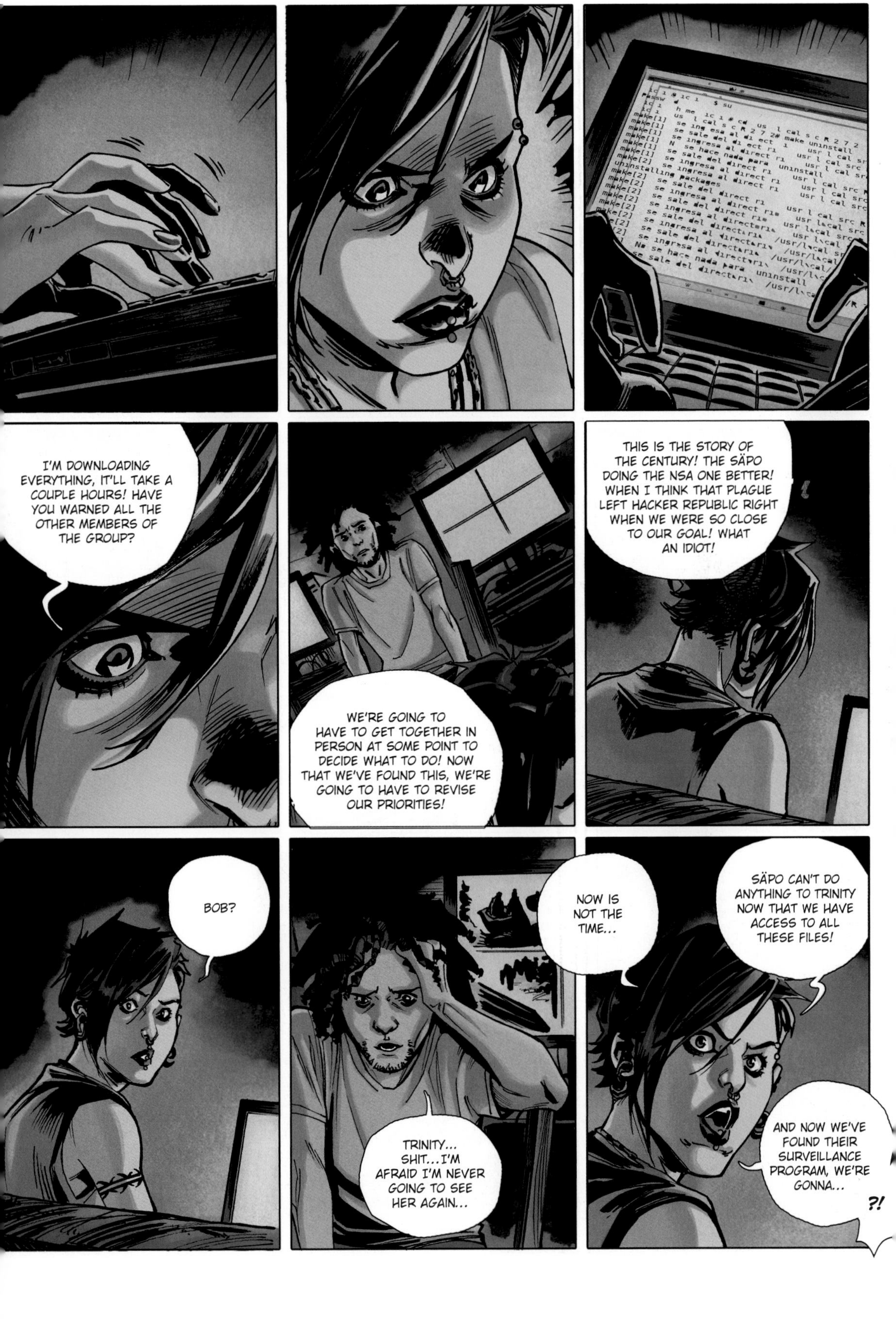
I'M DOWNLOADING EVERYTHING, IT'LL TAKE A COUPLE HOURS! HAVE YOU WARNED ALL THE OTHER MEMBERS OF THE GROUP?
WE'RE GOING TO HAVE TO GET TOGETHER IN PERSON AT SOME POINT TO DECIDE WHAT TO DO! NOW THAT WE'VE FOUND THIS, WE'RE GOING TO HAVE TO REVISE OUR PRIORITIES!
THIS IS THE STORY OF THE CENTURY! THE SÄPO DOING THE NSA ONE BETTER! WHEN I THINK THAT PLAGUE LEFT HACKER REPUBLIC RIGHT WHEN WE WERE SO CLOSE TO OUR GOAL! WHAT AN IDIOT!
BOB?
TRINITY... SHIT...I'M AFRAID I'M NEVER GOING TO SEE HER AGAIN...
NOW IS NOT THE TIME...
SÄPO CAN'T DO ANYTHING TO TRINITY NOW THAT WE HAVE ACCESS TO ALL THESE FILES!
AND NOW WE'VE FOUND THEIR SURVEILLANCE PROGRAM, WE'RE GONNA...
?!

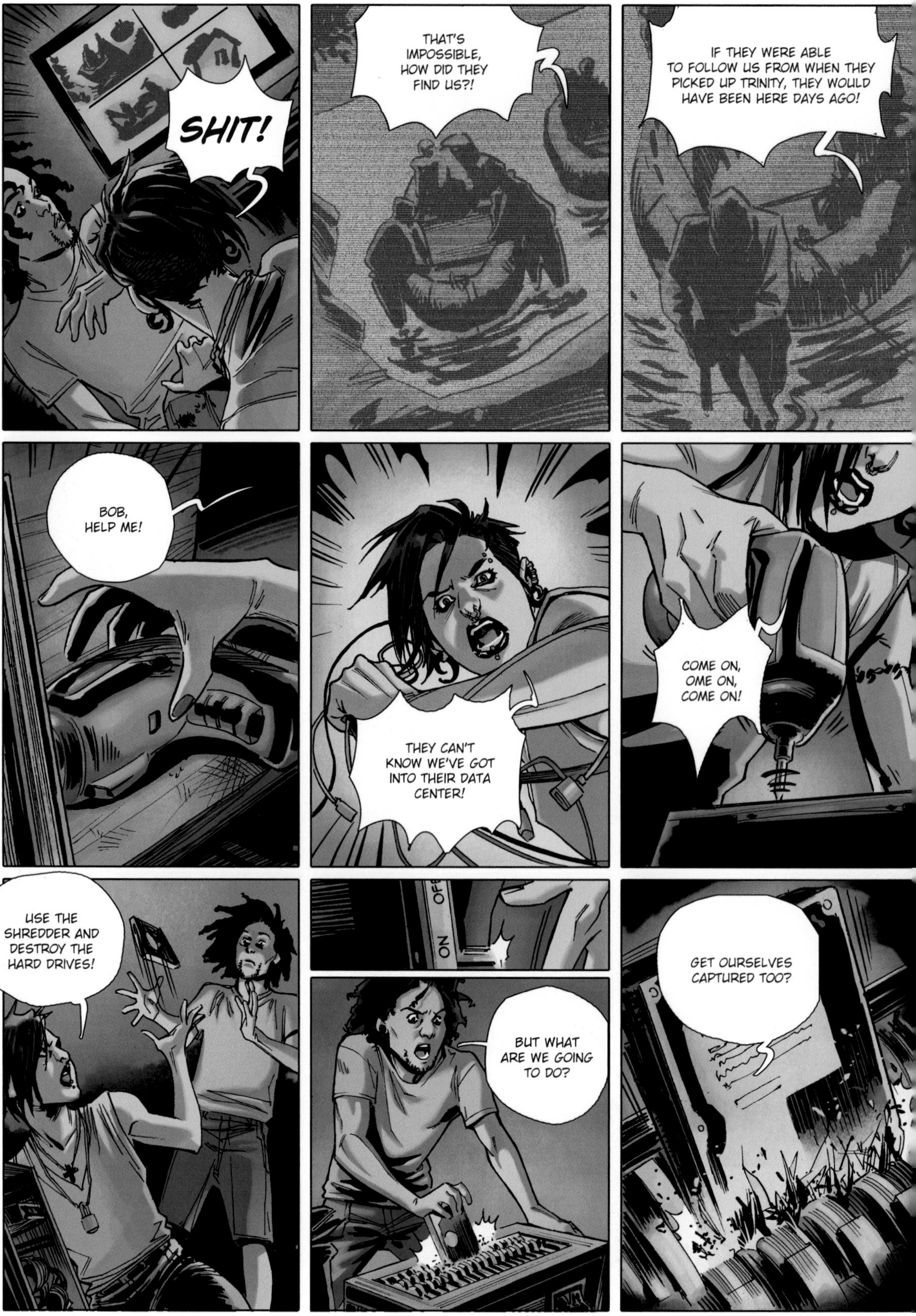
SHIT!
THAT'S IMPOSSIBLE, HOW DID THEY FIND US?!
IF THEY WERE ABLE TO FOLLOW US FROM WHEN THEY PICKED UP TRINITY, THEY WOULD HAVE BEEN HERE DAYS AGO!
BOB, HELP ME!
THEY CAN'T KNOW WE'VE GOT INTO THEIR DATA CENTER!
COME ON, OME ON, COME ON!
USE THE SHREDDER AND DESTROY THE HARD DRIVES!
ON
OFF
BUT WHAT ARE WE GOING TO DO?
GET OURSELVES CAPTURED TOO?

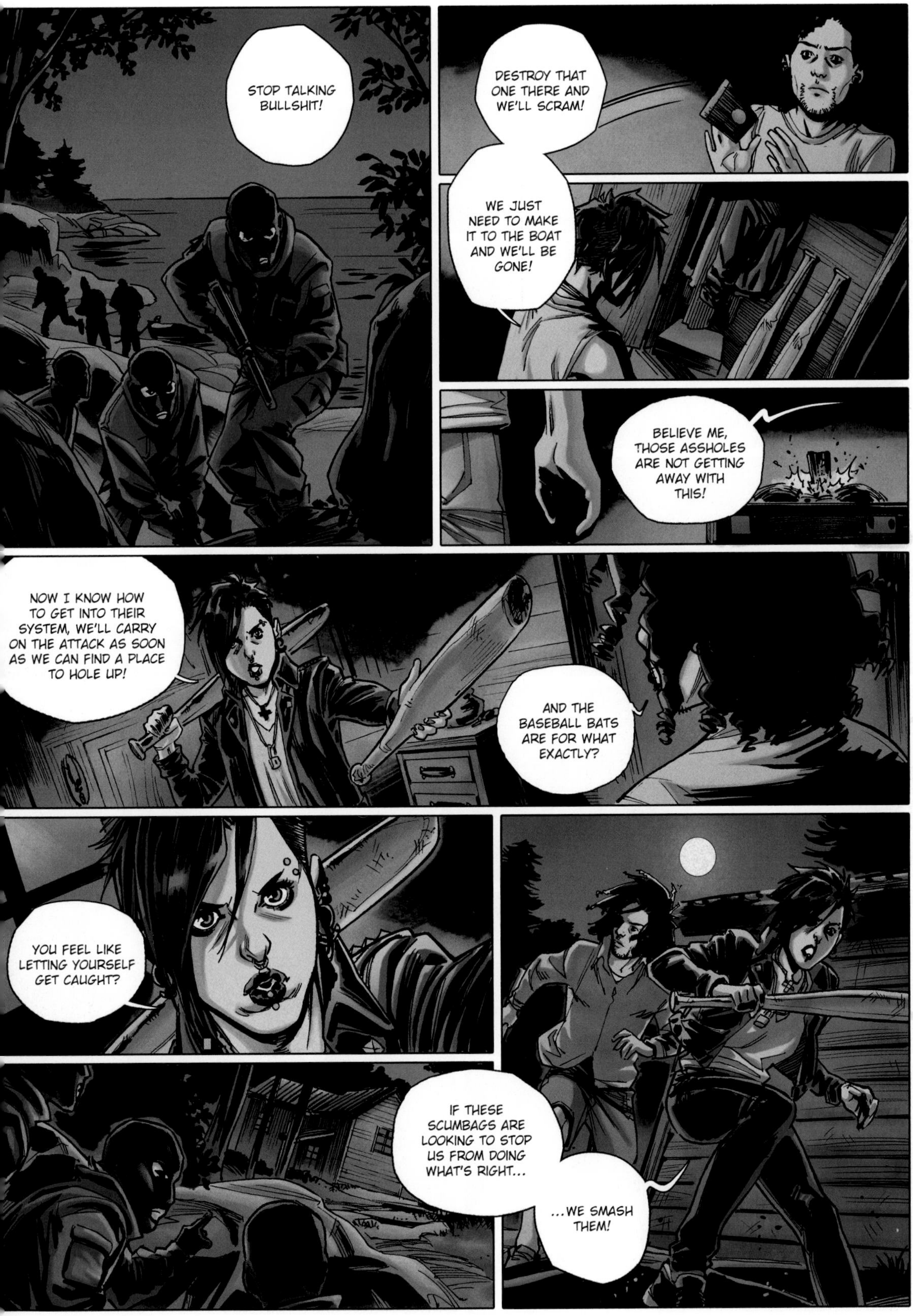
STOP TALKING BULLSHIT!
DESTROY THAT ONE THERE AND WE'LL SCRAM!
WE JUST NEED TO MAKE IT TO THE BOAT AND WE'LL BE GONE!
BELIEVE ME, THOSE ASSHOLES ARE NOT GETTING AWAY WITH THIS!
NOW I KNOW HOW TO GET INTO THEIR SYSTEM, WE'LL CARRY ON THE ATTACK AS SOON AS WE CAN FIND A PLACE TO HOLE UP!
AND THE BASEBALL BATS ARE FOR WHAT EXACTLY?
YOU FEEL LIKE LETTING YOURSELF GET CAUGHT?
IF THESE SCUMBAGS ARE LOOKING TO STOP US FROM DOING WHAT'S RIGHT...
...WE SMASH THEM!

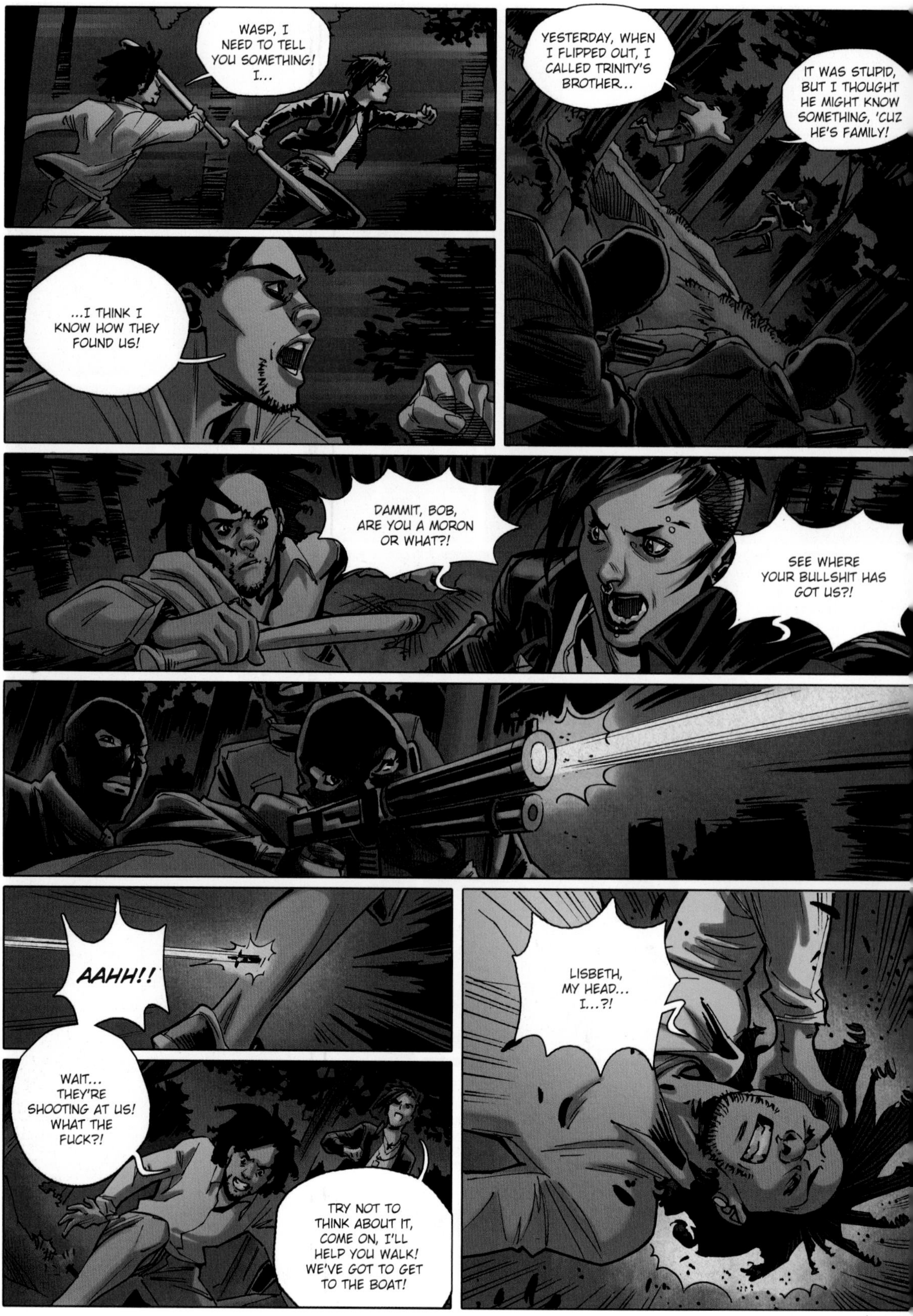
WASP, I NEED TO TELL YOU SOMETHING! I...
YESTERDAY, WHEN I FLIPPED OUT, I CALLED TRINITY'S BROTHER...
IT WAS STUPID, BUT I THOUGHT HE MIGHT KNOW SOMETHING, 'CUZ HE'S FAMILY!
...I THINK I KNOW HOW THEY FOUND US!
DAMMIT, BOB, ARE YOU A MORON OR WHAT?!
SEE WHERE YOUR BULLSHIT HAS GOT US?!
AAHH!!
LISBETH, MY HEAD... I...?!
WAIT... THEY'RE SHOOTING AT US! WHAT THE FUCK?!
TRY NOT TO THINK ABOUT IT, COME ON, I'LL HELP YOU WALK! WE'VE GOT TO GET TO THE BOAT!

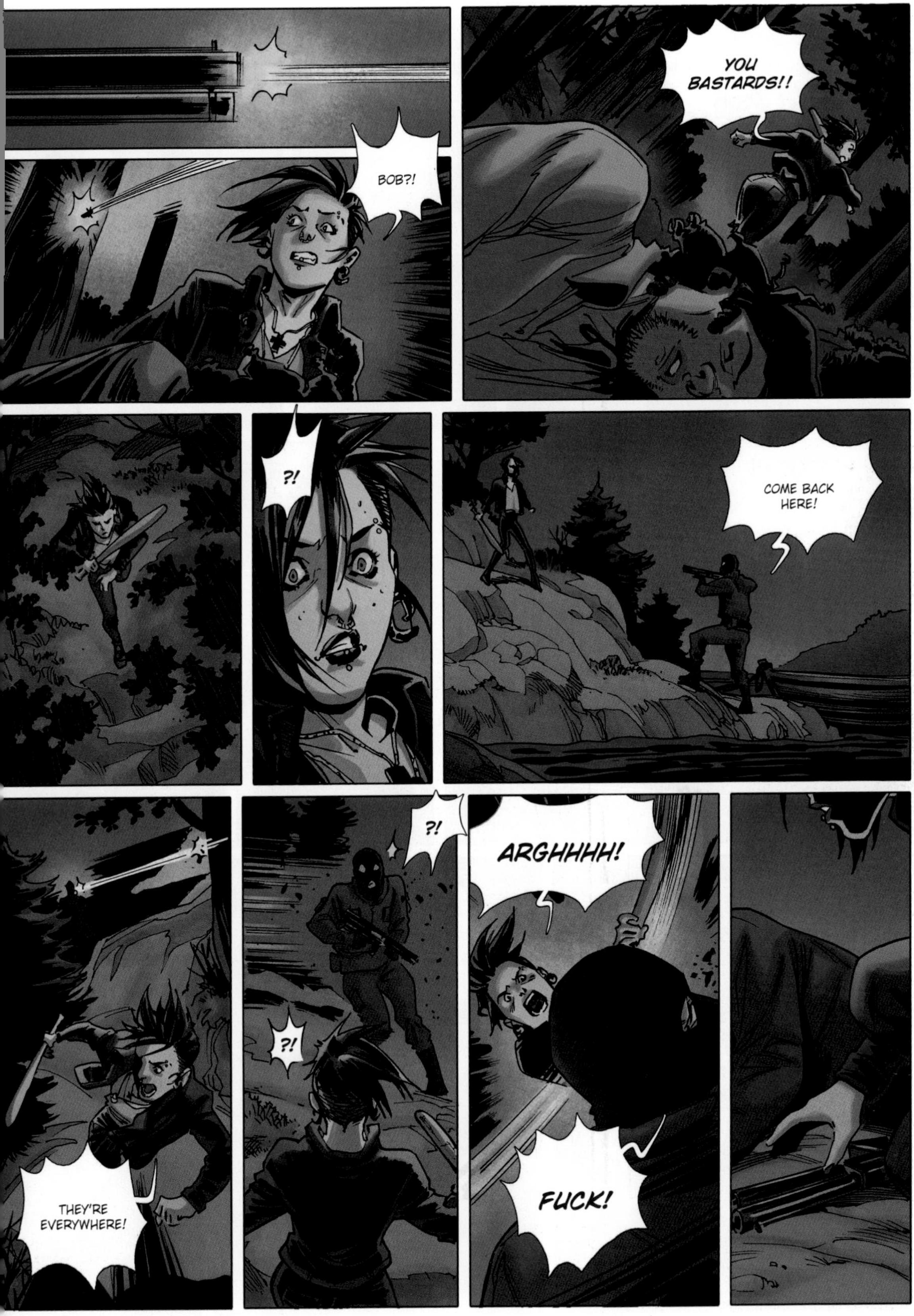
BOB?!
YOU BASTARDS!!
?!
COME BACK HERE!
THEY'RE EVERYWHERE!
?!
?!
ARGHHHH!
FUCK!

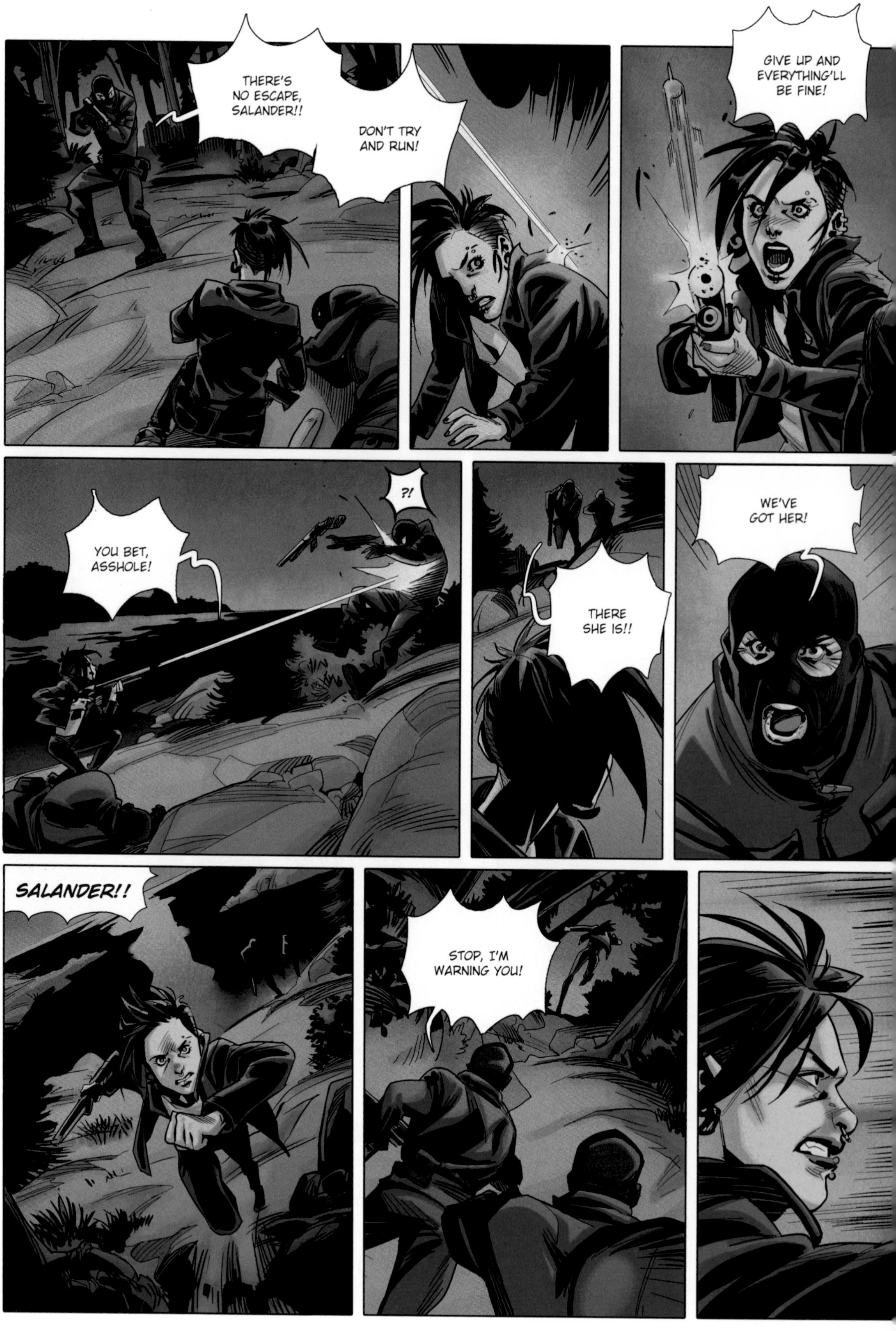
THERE'S NO ESCAPE, SALANDER!!
DON'T TRY AND RUN!
GIVE UP AND EVERYTHING'LL BE FINE!
YOU BET, ASSHOLE!
?!
THERE SHE IS!!
WE'VE GOT HER!
SALANDER!!
STOP, I'M WARNING YOU!

YOU'VE GOT NOWHERE ELSE TO GO!!

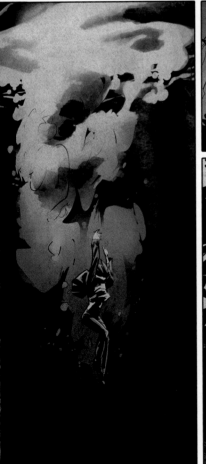

DO YOU SEE HER?!

SHE JUMPED, THE CRAZY BITCH!

NO... NO SIGN OF HER...

FROM THAT HEIGHT...

SHE'LL SINK LIKE A STONE!

TOO BAD FOR HER...

AT LEAST WE HAVE BOB THE DOG!

AND HOPEFULLY HE'S AS TALENTED AS SHE IS!

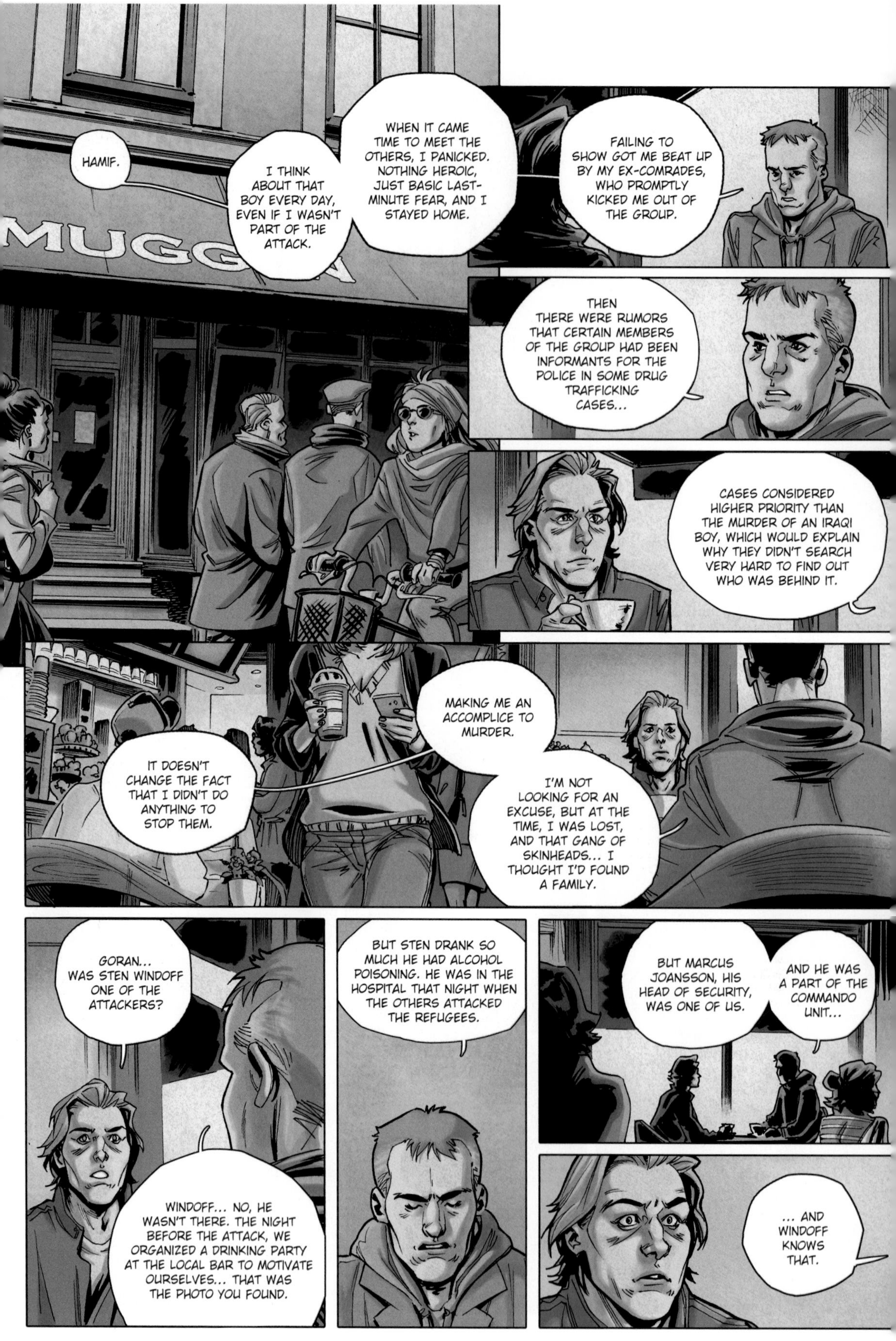
HAMIF.
I THINK ABOUT THAT BOY EVERY DAY, EVEN IF I WASN'T PART OF THE ATTACK.
WHEN IT CAME TIME TO MEET THE OTHERS, I PANICKED. NOTHING HEROIC, JUST BASIC LAST-MINUTE FEAR, AND I STAYED HOME.
FAILING TO SHOW GOT ME BEAT UP BY MY EX-COMRADES, WHO PROMPTLY KICKED ME OUT OF THE GROUP.
THEN THERE WERE RUMORS THAT CERTAIN MEMBERS OF THE GROUP HAD BEEN INFORMANTS FOR THE POLICE IN SOME DRUG TRAFFICKING CASES...
CASES CONSIDERED HIGHER PRIORITY THAN THE MURDER OF AN IRAQI BOY, WHICH WOULD EXPLAIN WHY THEY DIDN'T SEARCH VERY HARD TO FIND OUT WHO WAS BEHIND IT.
IT DOESN'T CHANGE THE FACT THAT I DIDN'T DO ANYTHING TO STOP THEM.
MAKING ME AN ACCOMPLICE TO MURDER.
I'M NOT LOOKING FOR AN EXCUSE, BUT AT THE TIME, I WAS LOST, AND THAT GANG OF SKINHEADS... I THOUGHT I'D FOUND A FAMILY.
GORAN... WAS STEN WINDOFF ONE OF THE ATTACKERS?
WINDOFF... NO, HE WASN'T THERE. THE NIGHT BEFORE THE ATTACK, WE ORGANIZED A DRINKING PARTY AT THE LOCAL BAR TO MOTIVATE OURSELVES... THAT WAS THE PHOTO YOU FOUND.
BUT STEN DRANK SO MUCH HE HAD ALCOHOL POISONING. HE WAS IN THE HOSPITAL THAT NIGHT WHEN THE OTHERS ATTACKED THE REFUGEES.
BUT MARCUS JOANSSON, HIS HEAD OF SECURITY, WAS ONE OF US.
AND HE WAS A PART OF THE COMMANDO UNIT...
... AND WINDOFF KNOWS THAT.

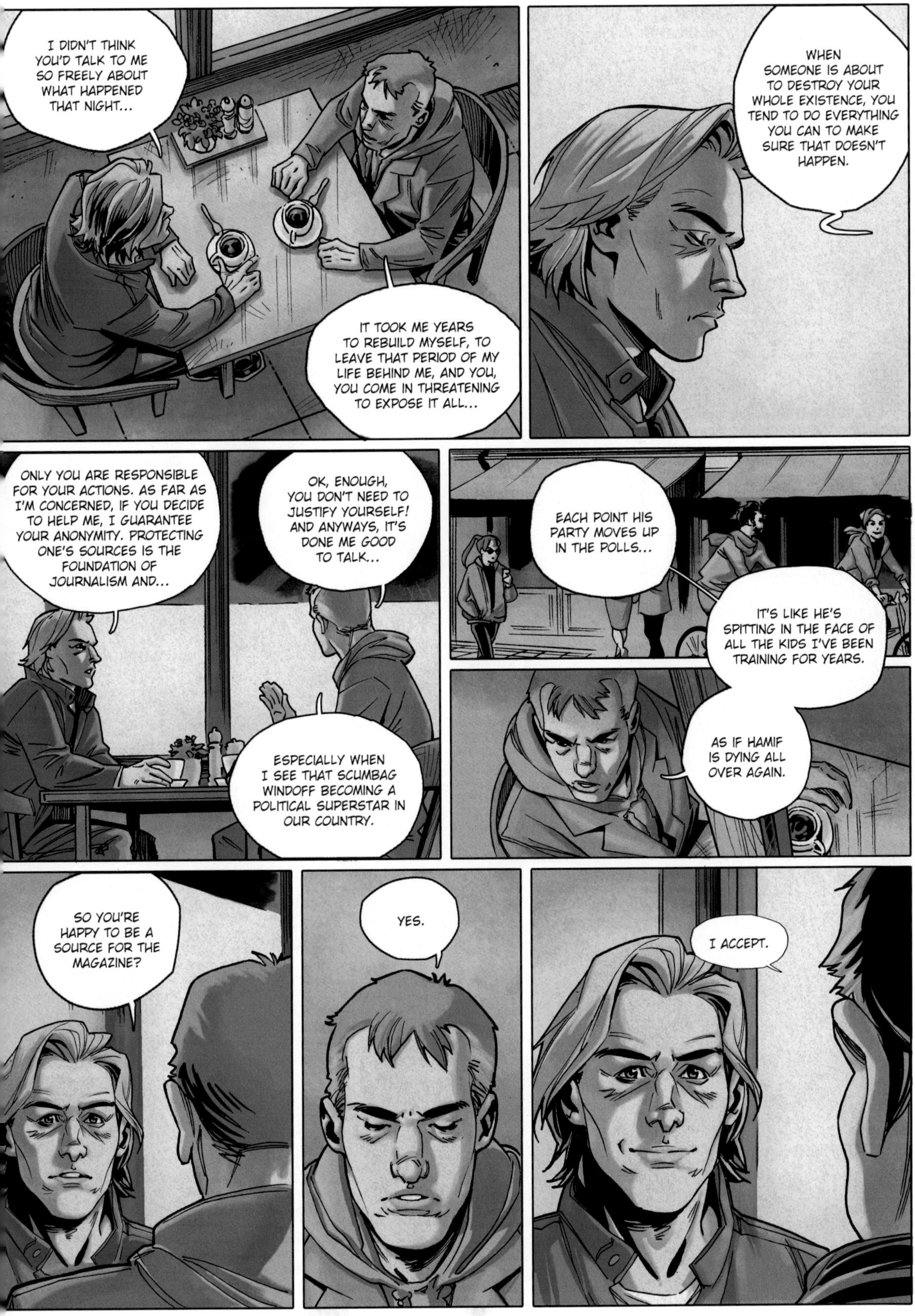
I DIDN'T THINK YOU'D TALK TO ME SO FREELY ABOUT WHAT HAPPENED THAT NIGHT...
IT TOOK ME YEARS TO REBUILD MYSELF, TO LEAVE THAT PERIOD OF MY LIFE BEHIND ME, AND YOU, YOU COME IN THREATENING TO EXPOSE IT ALL...
WHEN SOMEONE IS ABOUT TO DESTROY YOUR WHOLE EXISTENCE, YOU TEND TO DO EVERYTHING YOU CAN TO MAKE SURE THAT DOESN'T HAPPEN.
ONLY YOU ARE RESPONSIBLE FOR YOUR ACTIONS. AS FAR AS I'M CONCERNED, IF YOU DECIDE TO HELP ME, I GUARANTEE YOUR ANONYMITY. PROTECTING ONE'S SOURCES IS THE FOUNDATION OF JOURNALISM AND...
OK, ENOUGH, YOU DON'T NEED TO JUSTIFY YOURSELF! AND ANYWAYS, IT'S DONE ME GOOD TO TALK...
ESPECIALLY WHEN I SEE THAT SCUMBAG WINDOFF BECOMING A POLITICAL SUPERSTAR IN OUR COUNTRY.
EACH POINT HIS PARTY MOVES UP IN THE POLLS...
IT'S LIKE HE'S SPITTING IN THE FACE OF ALL THE KIDS I'VE BEEN TRAINING FOR YEARS.
AS IF HAMIF IS DYING ALL OVER AGAIN.
SO YOU'RE HAPPY TO BE A SOURCE FOR THE MAGAZINE?
YES.
I ACCEPT.

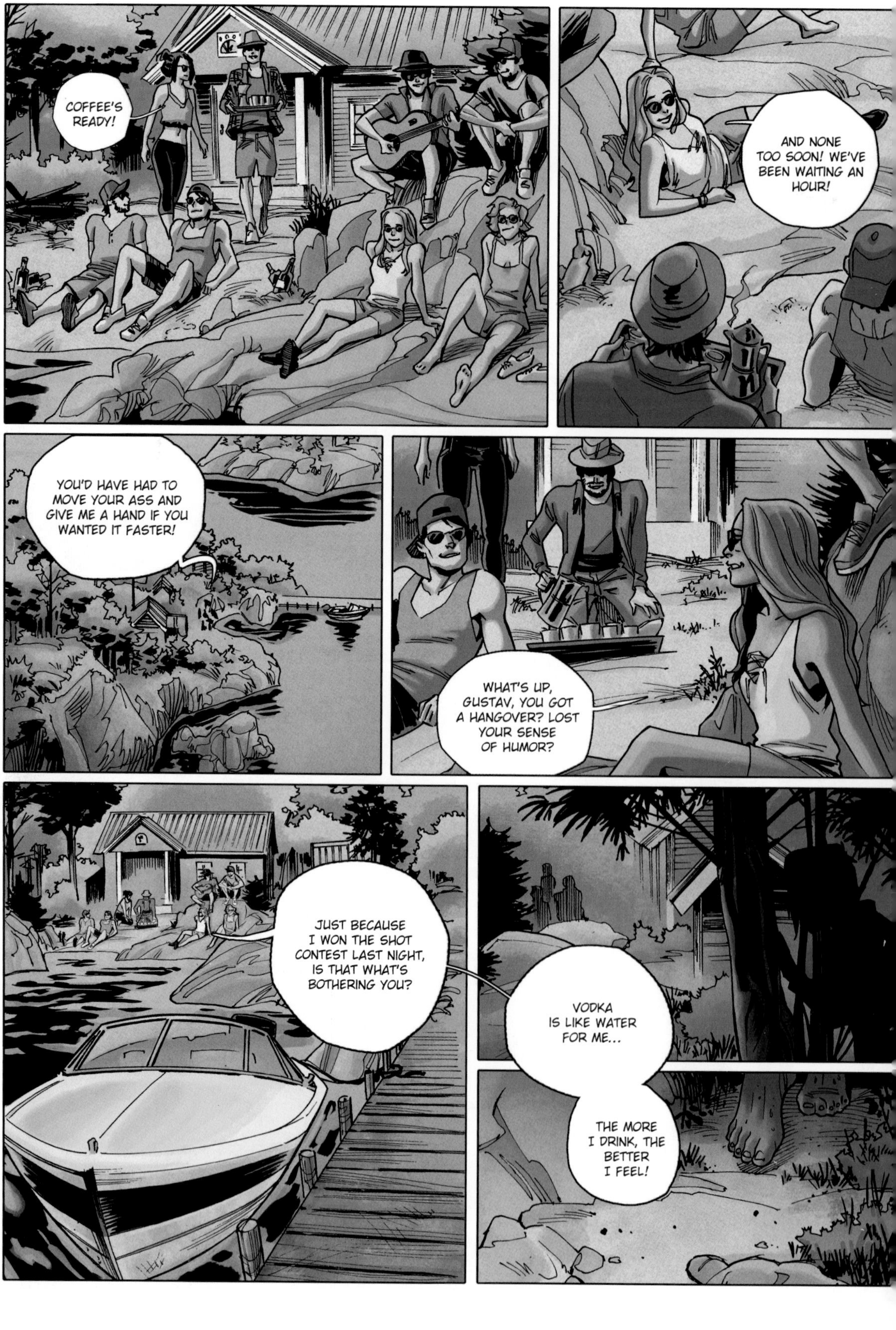
COFFEE'S READY!
AND NONE TOO SOON! WE'VE BEEN WAITING AN HOUR!
YOU'D HAVE HAD TO MOVE YOUR ASS AND GIVE ME A HAND IF YOU WANTED IT FASTER!
WHAT'S UP, GUSTAV, YOU GOT A HANGOVER? LOST YOUR SENSE OF HUMOR?
JUST BECAUSE I WON THE SHOT CONTEST LAST NIGHT, IS THAT WHAT'S BOTHERING YOU?
VODKA IS LIKE WATER FOR ME...
THE MORE I DRINK, THE BETTER I FEEL!

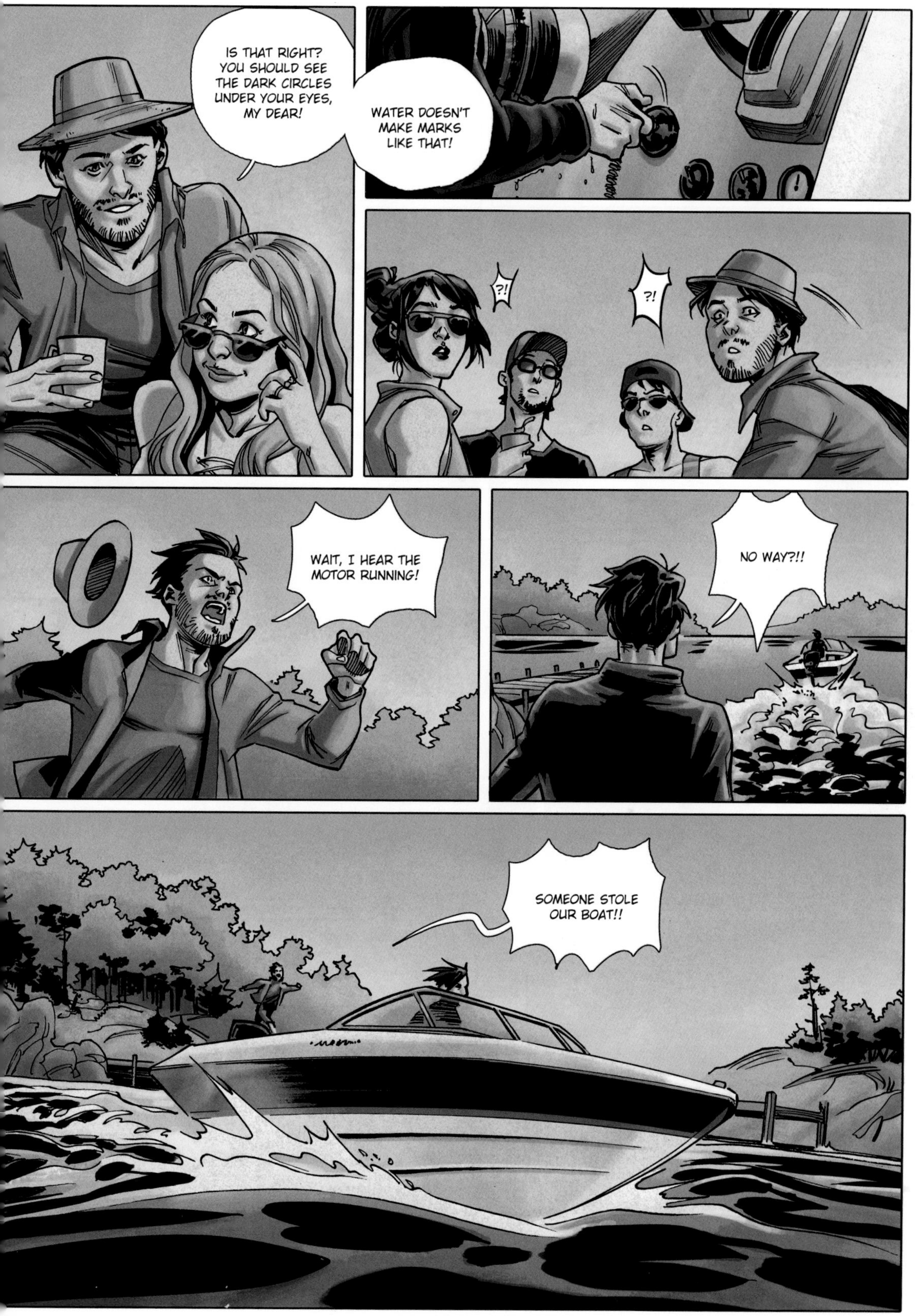
IS THAT RIGHT? YOU SHOULD SEE THE DARK CIRCLES UNDER YOUR EYES, MY DEAR!
WATER DOESN'T MAKE MARKS LIKE THAT!
?!
?!
WAIT, I HEAR THE MOTOR RUNNING!
NO WAY?!!
SOMEONE STOLE OUR BOAT!!

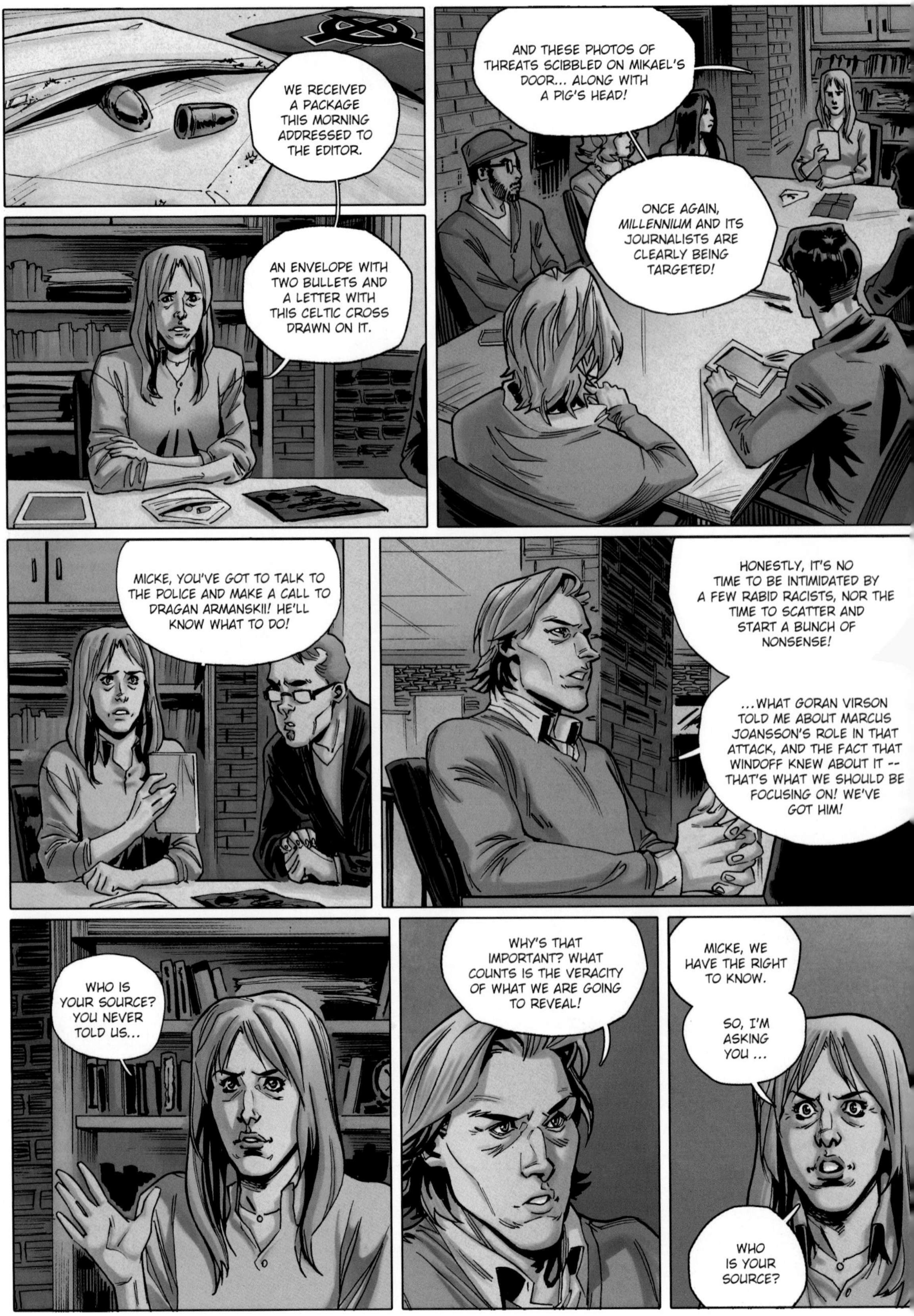
WE RECEIVED A PACKAGE THIS MORNING ADDRESSED TO THE EDITOR.
AN ENVELOPE WITH TWO BULLETS AND A LETTER WITH THIS CELTIC CROSS DRAWN ON IT.
AND THESE PHOTOS OF THREATS SCIBBLED ON MIKAEL'S DOOR... ALONG WITH A PIG'S HEAD!
ONCE AGAIN, MILLENNIUM AND ITS JOURNALISTS ARE CLEARLY BEING TARGETED!
MICKE, YOU'VE GOT TO TALK TO THE POLICE AND MAKE A CALL TO DRAGAN ARMANSKII! HE'LL KNOW WHAT TO DO!
HONESTLY, IT'S NO TIME TO BE INTIMIDATED BY A FEW RABID RACISTS, NOR THE TIME TO SCATTER AND START A BUNCH OF NONSENSE!
...WHAT GORAN VIRSON TOLD ME ABOUT MARCUS JOANSSON'S ROLE IN THAT ATTACK, AND THE FACT THAT WINDOFF KNEW ABOUT IT -- THAT'S WHAT WE SHOULD BE FOCUSING ON! WE'VE GOT HIM!
WHO IS YOUR SOURCE? YOU NEVER TOLD US...
WHY'S THAT IMPORTANT? WHAT COUNTS IS THE VERACITY OF WHAT WE ARE GOING TO REVEAL!
MICKE, WE HAVE THE RIGHT TO KNOW.
SO, I'M ASKING YOU ...
WHO IS YOUR SOURCE?

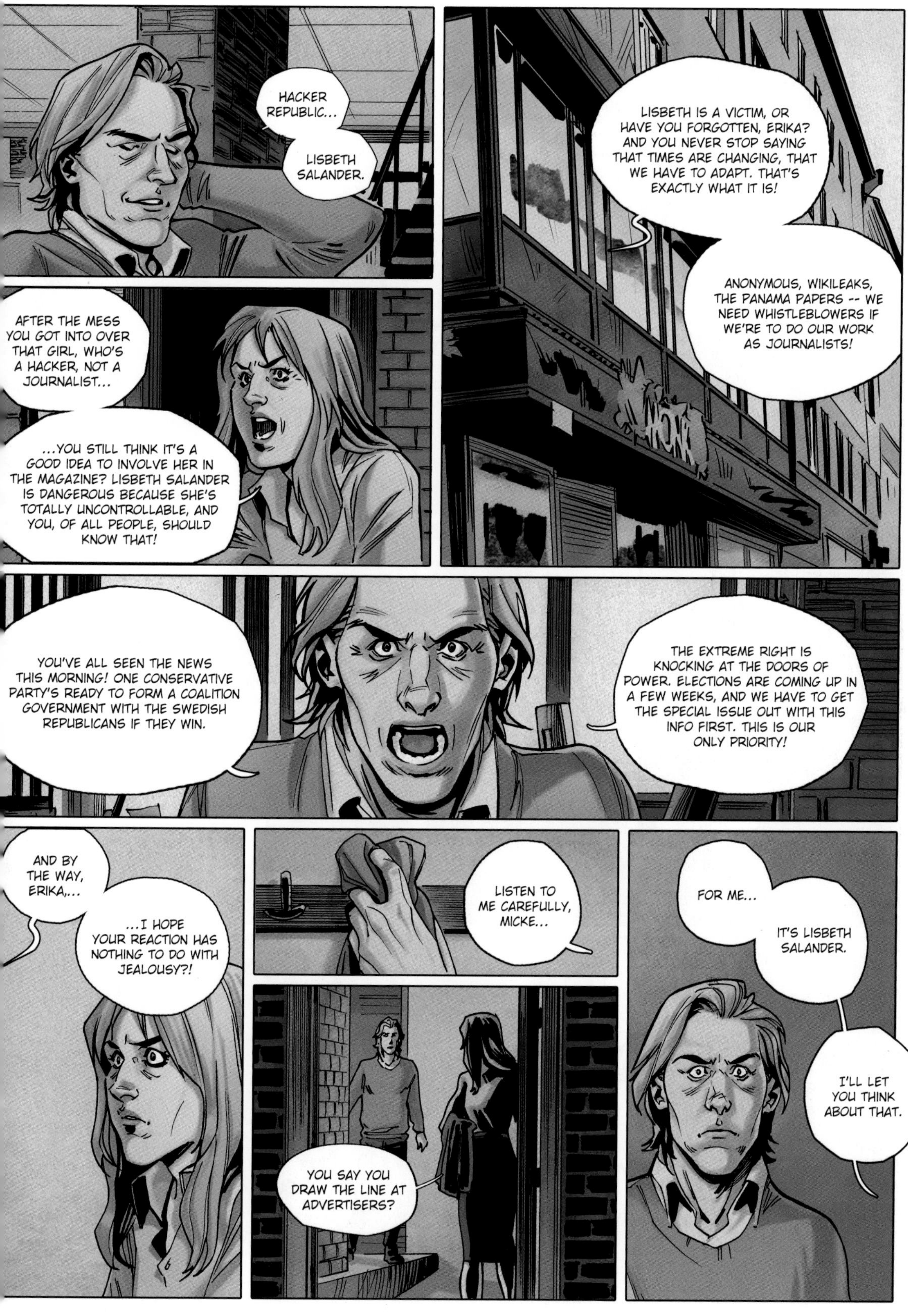
HACKER REPUBLIC...
LISBETH SALANDER.
LISBETH IS A VICTIM, OR HAVE YOU FORGOTTEN, ERIKA? AND YOU NEVER STOP SAYING THAT TIMES ARE CHANGING, THAT WE HAVE TO ADAPT. THAT'S EXACTLY WHAT IT IS!
ANONYMOUS, WIKILEAKS, THE PANAMA PAPERS -- WE NEED WHISTLEBLOWERS IF WE'RE TO DO OUR WORK AS JOURNALISTS!
AFTER THE MESS YOU GOT INTO OVER THAT GIRL, WHO'S A HACKER, NOT A JOURNALIST...
...YOU STILL THINK IT'S A GOOD IDEA TO INVOLVE HER IN THE MAGAZINE? LISBETH SALANDER IS DANGEROUS BECAUSE SHE'S TOTALLY UNCONTROLLABLE, AND YOU, OF ALL PEOPLE, SHOULD KNOW THAT!
YOU'VE ALL SEEN THE NEWS THIS MORNING! ONE CONSERVATIVE PARTY'S READY TO FORM A COALITION GOVERNMENT WITH THE SWEDISH REPUBLICANS IF THEY WIN.
THE EXTREME RIGHT IS KNOCKING AT THE DOORS OF POWER. ELECTIONS ARE COMING UP IN A FEW WEEKS, AND WE HAVE TO GET THE SPECIAL ISSUE OUT WITH THIS INFO FIRST. THIS IS OUR ONLY PRIORITY!
AND BY THE WAY, ERIKA,...
...I HOPE YOUR REACTION HAS NOTHING TO DO WITH JEALOUSY?!
LISTEN TO ME CAREFULLY, MICKE...
YOU SAY YOU DRAW THE LINE AT ADVERTISERS?
FOR ME...
IT'S LISBETH SALANDER.
I'LL LET YOU THINK ABOUT THAT.

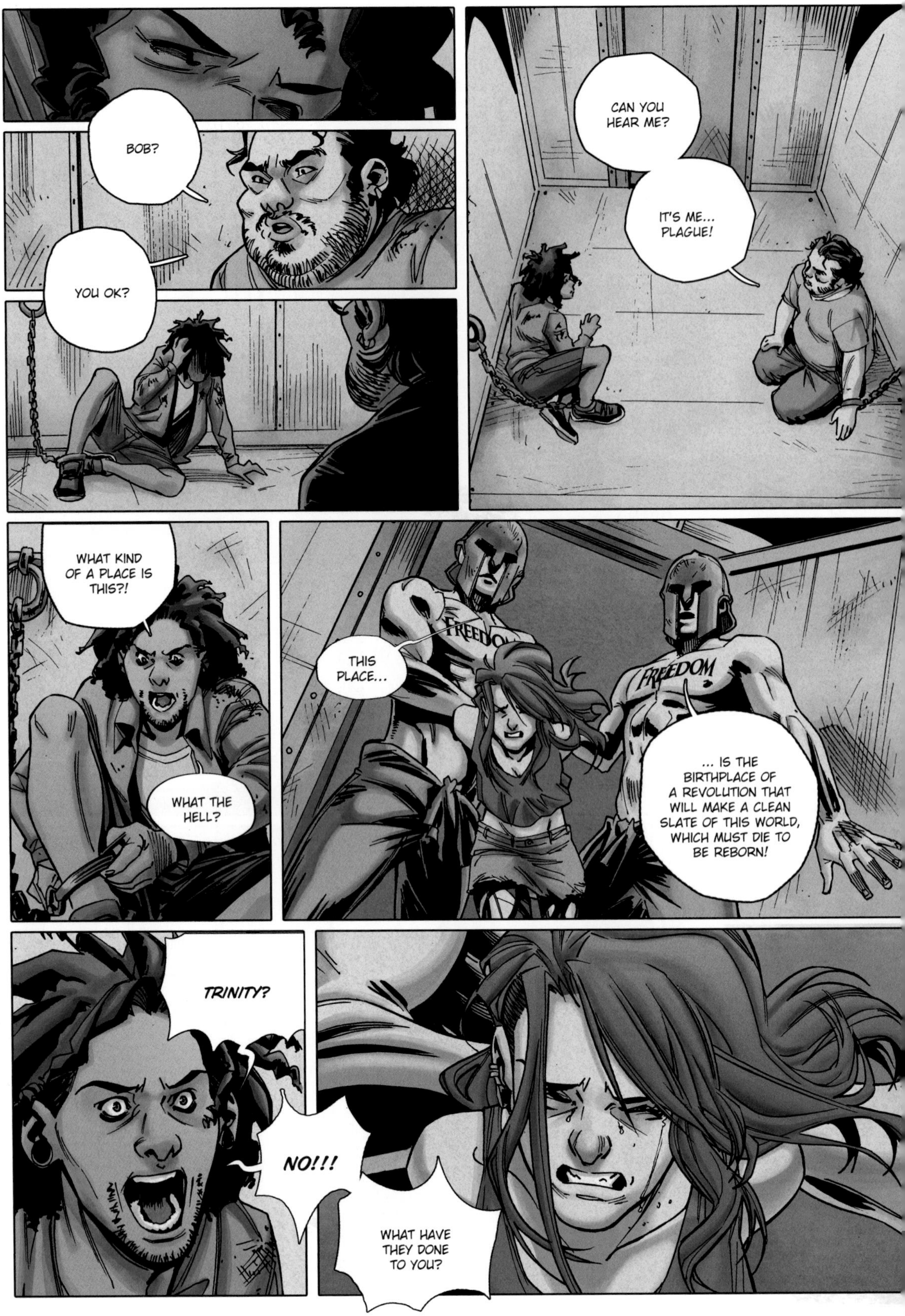
BOB?
YOU OK?
CAN YOU HEAR ME?
IT'S ME... PLAGUE!
WHAT KIND OF A PLACE IS THIS?!
WHAT THE HELL?
THIS PLACE...
... IS THE BIRTHPLACE OF A REVOLUTION THAT WILL MAKE A CLEAN SLATE OF THIS WORLD, WHICH MUST DIE TO BE REBORN!
FREEDOM
FREEDOM
TRINITY?
NO!!!
WHAT HAVE THEY DONE TO YOU?

YOUR GIRLFRIEND HAS FAILED IN HER MISSION...

...HACKING INTO THE NEW DATA CENTER OF THE SECRET SERVICE.

APPARENTLY, IT EXCEEDED HER CAPABILITIES. WE SHOULD'VE KNOWN. THIS IS WHAT HAPPENS WHEN YOU GET A WOMAN TO DO A MAN'S JOB

THEN PLAGUE HERE DECIDED TO PLAY THE LONE HERO AND TRACK US DOWN, AT WHICH HE SUCCEEDED IN PART.

SO WE DECIDED TO OPEN OUR DOORS TO HIM AS WELL.

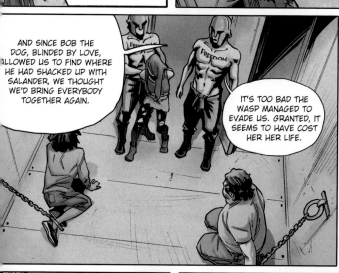

AND SINCE BOB THE DOG, BLINDED BY LOVE, ALLOWED US TO FIND WHERE HE HAD SHACKED UP WITH SALANDER, WE THOUGHT WE'D BRING EVERYBODY TOGETHER AGAIN.

IT'S TOO BAD THE WASP MANAGED TO EVADE US. GRANTED, IT SEEMS TO HAVE COST HER HER LIFE.

LISBETH IS DEAD?!

YOU FUCKERS! WHAT DID YOU DO TO HER?

US? NOTHING. SHE DROWNED HERSELF, LIKE A BIG GIRL.

BUT TRINITY, ON THE OTHER HAND, WE COULD DO SOMETHING TO HER!

SO YOU'RE GOING TO HELP US HACK INTO THE SÄPO DATA CENTER!

TO BUILD A WORLD WHERE INDIVIDUALS WILL BE TRULY LIBERATED, FREE OF THE STATE, FREE OF TAXES, FREE OF COERCION...

WITHOUT STUPID RULES THAT PROHIBIT THE BEST OF US FROM FULFILLING OUR DESTINY, WHERE INDIVIDUAL LIBERTY AND NATURAL LAW WILL FINALLY BE THE PILLARS OF OUR NEW SOCIETY!

AND YOU WILL HELP US.

OR YOU CAN WATCH TRINITY DIE.

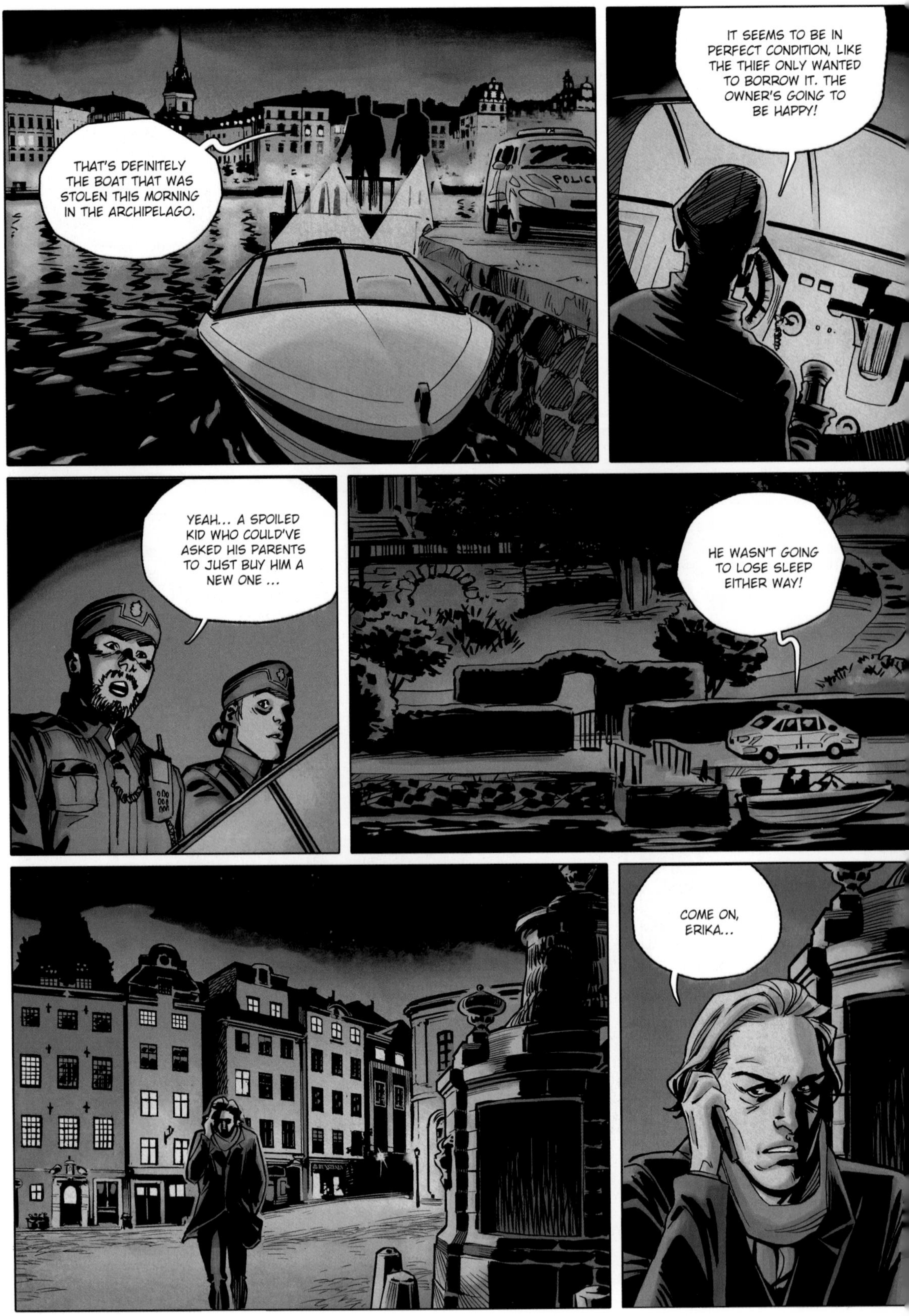
THAT'S DEFINITELY THE BOAT THAT WAS STOLEN THIS MORNING IN THE ARCHIPELAGO.
POLICE
IT SEEMS TO BE IN PERFECT CONDITION, LIKE THE THIEF ONLY WANTED TO BORROW IT. THE OWNER'S GOING TO BE HAPPY!
YEAH... A SPOILED KID WHO COULD'VE ASKED HIS PARENTS TO JUST BUY HIM A NEW ONE ...
HE WASN'T GOING TO LOSE SLEEP EITHER WAY!
COME ON, ERIKA...

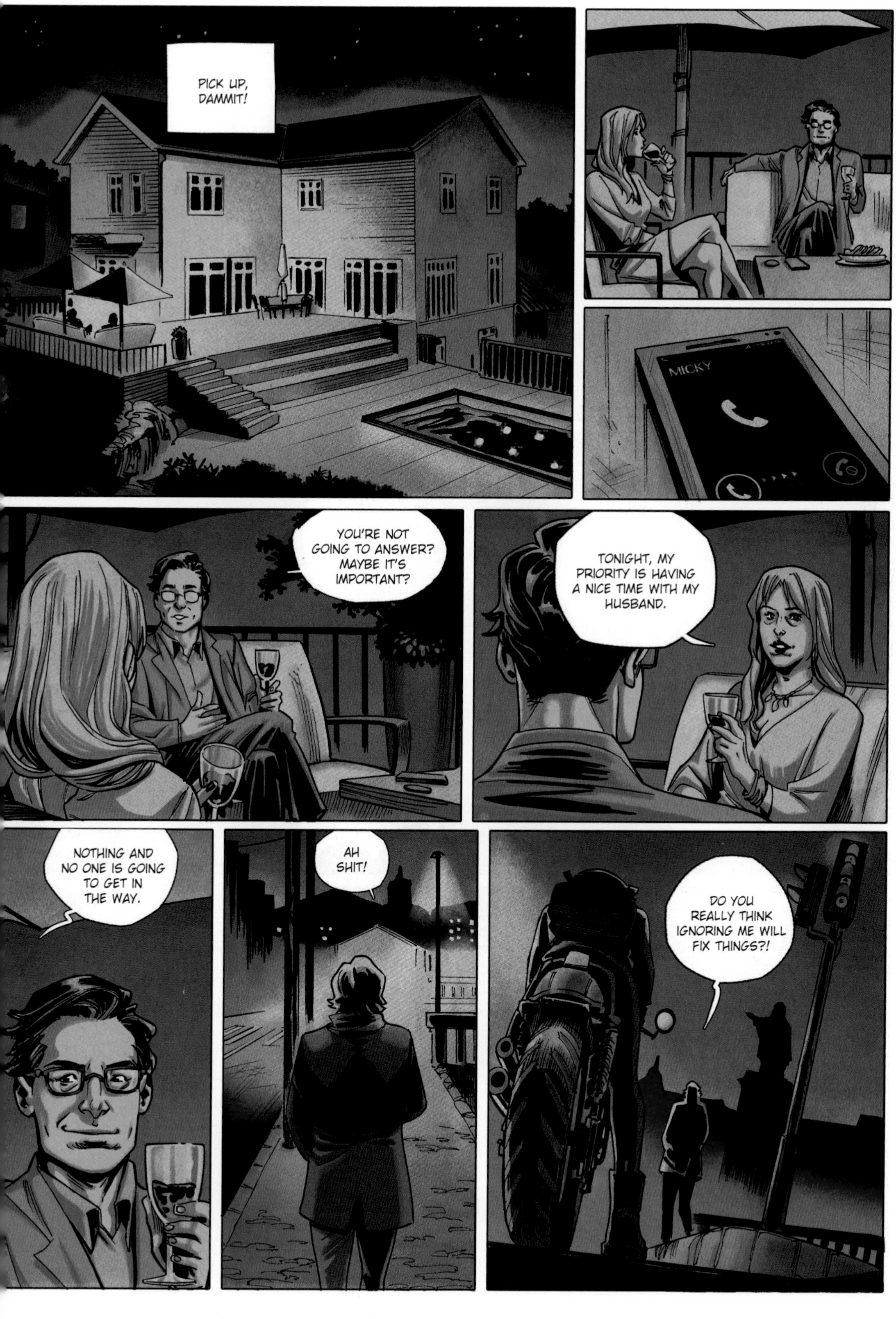
PICK UP, DAMMIT!
MICKY
YOU'RE NOT GOING TO ANSWER? MAYBE IT'S IMPORTANT?
TONIGHT, MY PRIORITY IS HAVING A NICE TIME WITH MY HUSBAND.
NOTHING AND NO ONE IS GOING TO GET IN THE WAY.
AH SHIT!
DO YOU REALLY THINK IGNORING ME WILL FIX THINGS?!

IT'S HIM. LIKE CLOCKWORK...

HE'S ON HIS LITTLE NIGHTTIME STROLL AROUND THE OLD CITY.

SO BLOMKVIST, RUN INTO MANY OF YOUR ARAB BUDDIES TONIGHT?

YEAH, YOU GONNA BRING OVER THOUSANDS OF RAGHEADS?

YOU THINK THERE AREN'T ENOUGH ALREADY, EH? YOU SHOULD GROW YOUR BEARD OUT SO YOU CAN GO PRAY AT THE MOSQUE WITH YOUR PALS!

I DON'T KNOW WHO YO ARE, BUT YOU' MISTAKEN. I'M AN ATHEIST.

SHUT THE FUCK UP, FUCKER!!

I REALLY DON'T WANT TO FIGHT YOU... VIOLENCE IS NEVER THE SOLUTION!

WE'RE GOING TO FUCK YOU UP, FUCKING MARXIST BITCH!

VIOLENCE IS ALWAYS THE SOLUTION!!

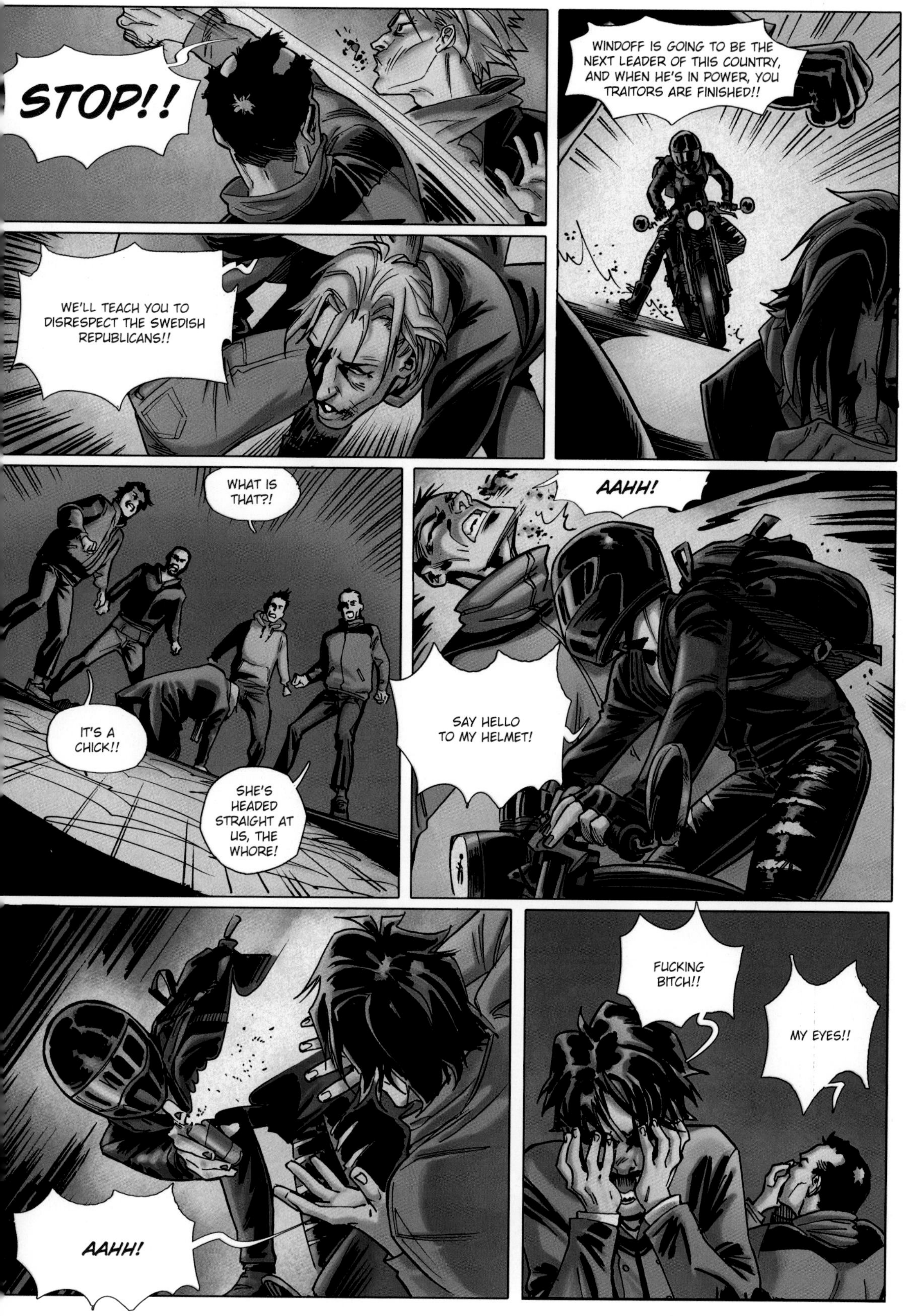
STOP!!
WINDOFF IS GOING TO BE THE NEXT LEADER OF THIS COUNTRY, AND WHEN HE'S IN POWER, YOU TRAITORS ARE FINISHED!!
WE'LL TEACH YOU TO DISRESPECT THE SWEDISH REPUBLICANS!!
WHAT IS THAT?!
IT'S A CHICK!!
SHE'S HEADED STRAIGHT AT US, THE WHORE!
AAHH!
SAY HELLO TO MY HELMET!
AAHH!
FUCKING BITCH!!
MY EYES!!

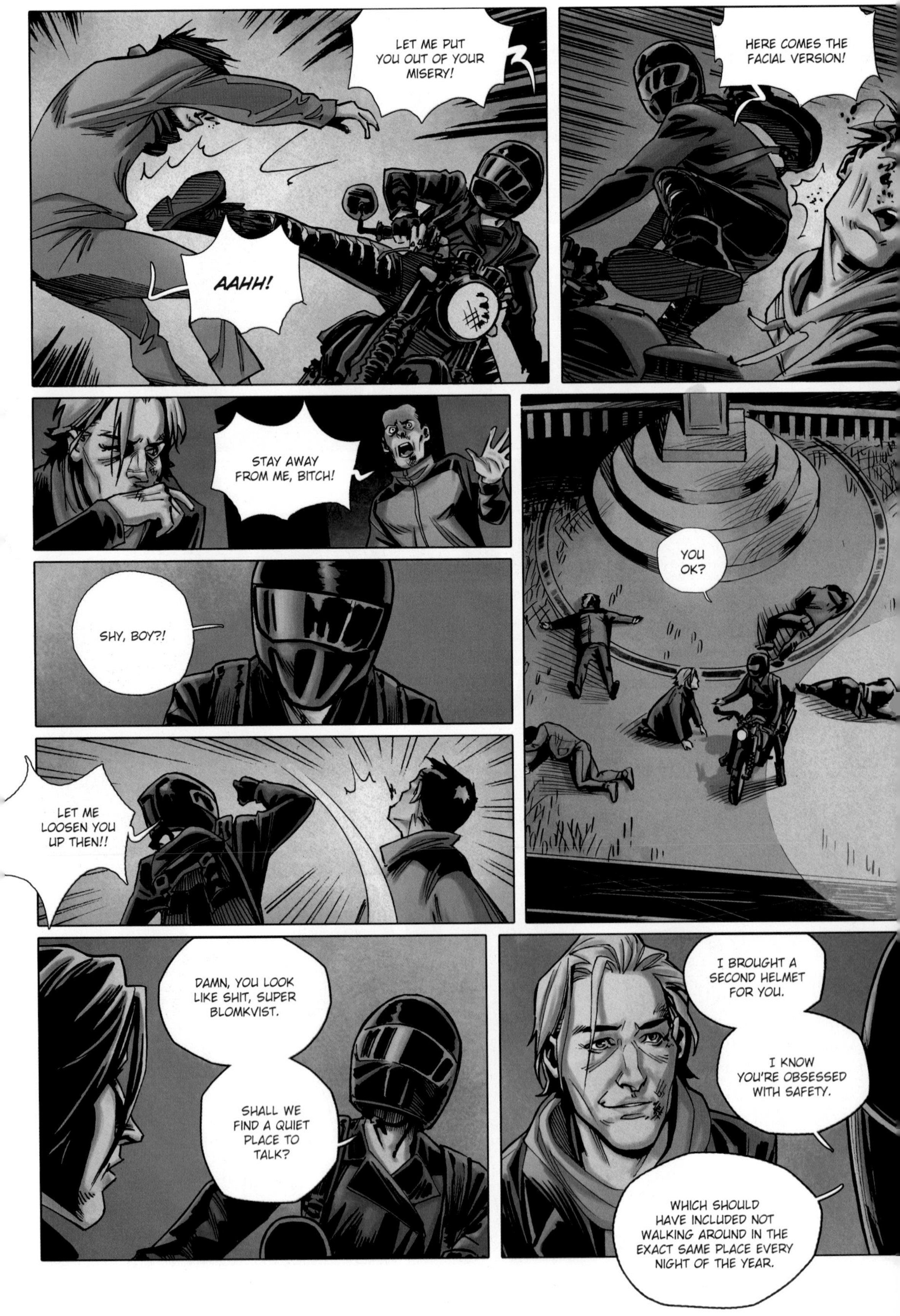
LET ME PUT YOU OUT OF YOUR MISERY!
AAHH!
HERE COMES THE FACIAL VERSION!
STAY AWAY FROM ME, BITCH!
SHY, BOY?!
LET ME LOOSEN YOU UP THEN!!
YOU OK?
DAMN, YOU LOOK LIKE SHIT, SUPER BLOMKVIST.
SHALL WE FIND A QUIET PLACE TO TALK?
I BROUGHT A SECOND HELMET FOR YOU.
I KNOW YOU'RE OBSESSED WITH SAFETY.
WHICH SHOULD HAVE INCLUDED NOT WALKING AROUND IN THE EXACT SAME PLACE EVERY NIGHT OF THE YEAR.

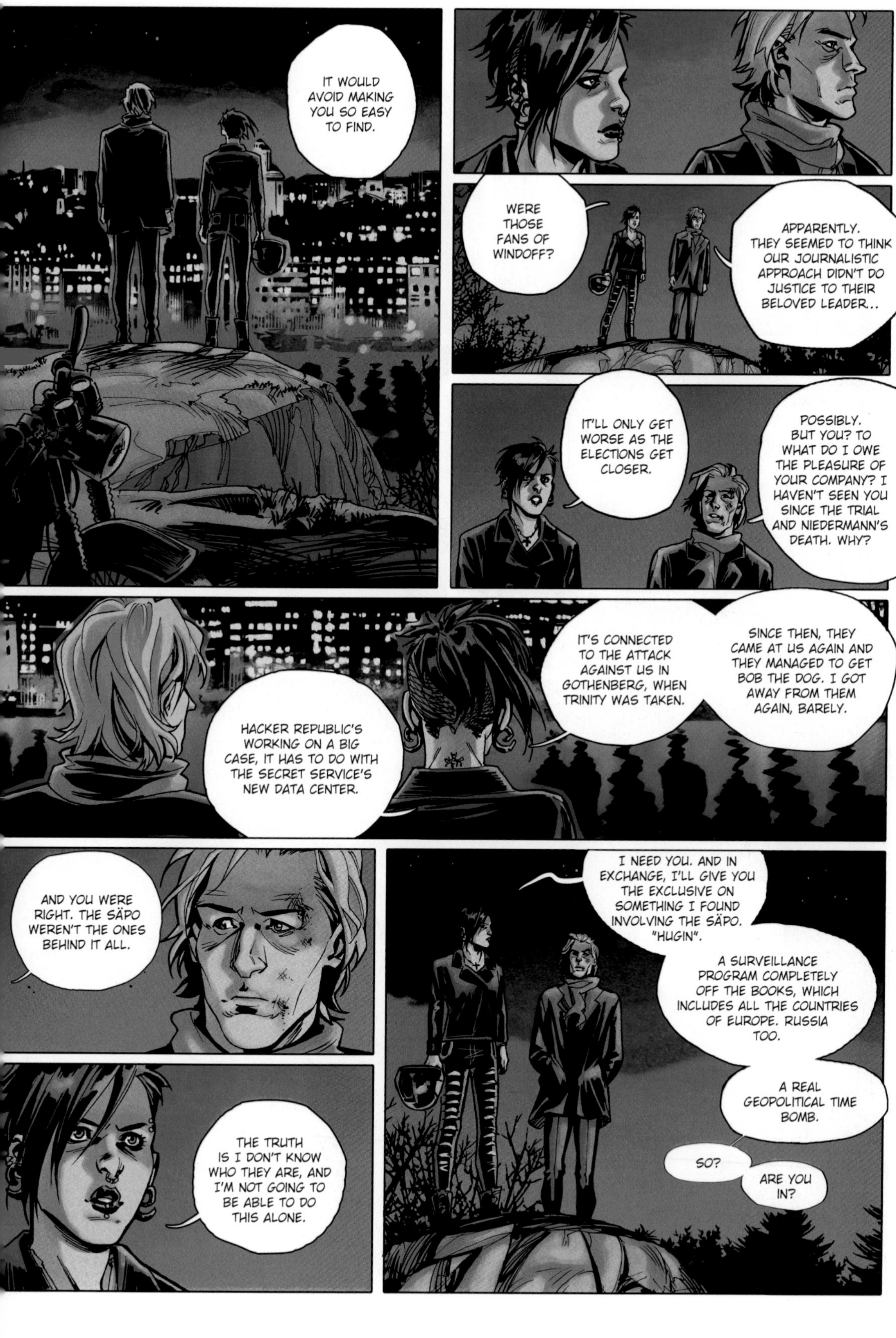
IT WOULD AVOID MAKING YOU SO EASY TO FIND.
WERE THOSE FANS OF WINDOFF?
APPARENTLY. THEY SEEMED TO THINK OUR JOURNALISTIC APPROACH DIDN'T DO JUSTICE TO THEIR BELOVED LEADER...
IT'LL ONLY GET WORSE AS THE ELECTIONS GET CLOSER.
POSSIBLY. BUT YOU? TO WHAT DO I OWE THE PLEASURE OF YOUR COMPANY? I HAVEN'T SEEN YOU SINCE THE TRIAL AND NIEDERMANN'S DEATH. WHY?
HACKER REPUBLIC'S WORKING ON A BIG CASE, IT HAS TO DO WITH THE SECRET SERVICE'S NEW DATA CENTER.
IT'S CONNECTED TO THE ATTACK AGAINST US IN GOTHENBERG, WHEN TRINITY WAS TAKEN.
SINCE THEN, THEY CAME AT US AGAIN AND THEY MANAGED TO GET BOB THE DOG. I GOT AWAY FROM THEM AGAIN, BARELY.
AND YOU WERE RIGHT. THE SÄPO WEREN'T THE ONES BEHIND IT ALL.
THE TRUTH IS I DON'T KNOW WHO THEY ARE, AND I'M NOT GOING TO BE ABLE TO DO THIS ALONE.
I NEED YOU. AND IN EXCHANGE, I'LL GIVE YOU THE EXCLUSIVE ON SOMETHING I FOUND INVOLVING THE SÄPO. "HUGIN".
A SURVEILLANCE PROGRAM COMPLETELY OFF THE BOOKS, WHICH INCLUDES ALL THE COUNTRIES OF EUROPE. RUSSIA TOO.
A REAL GEOPOLITICAL TIME BOMB.
SO?
ARE YOU IN?

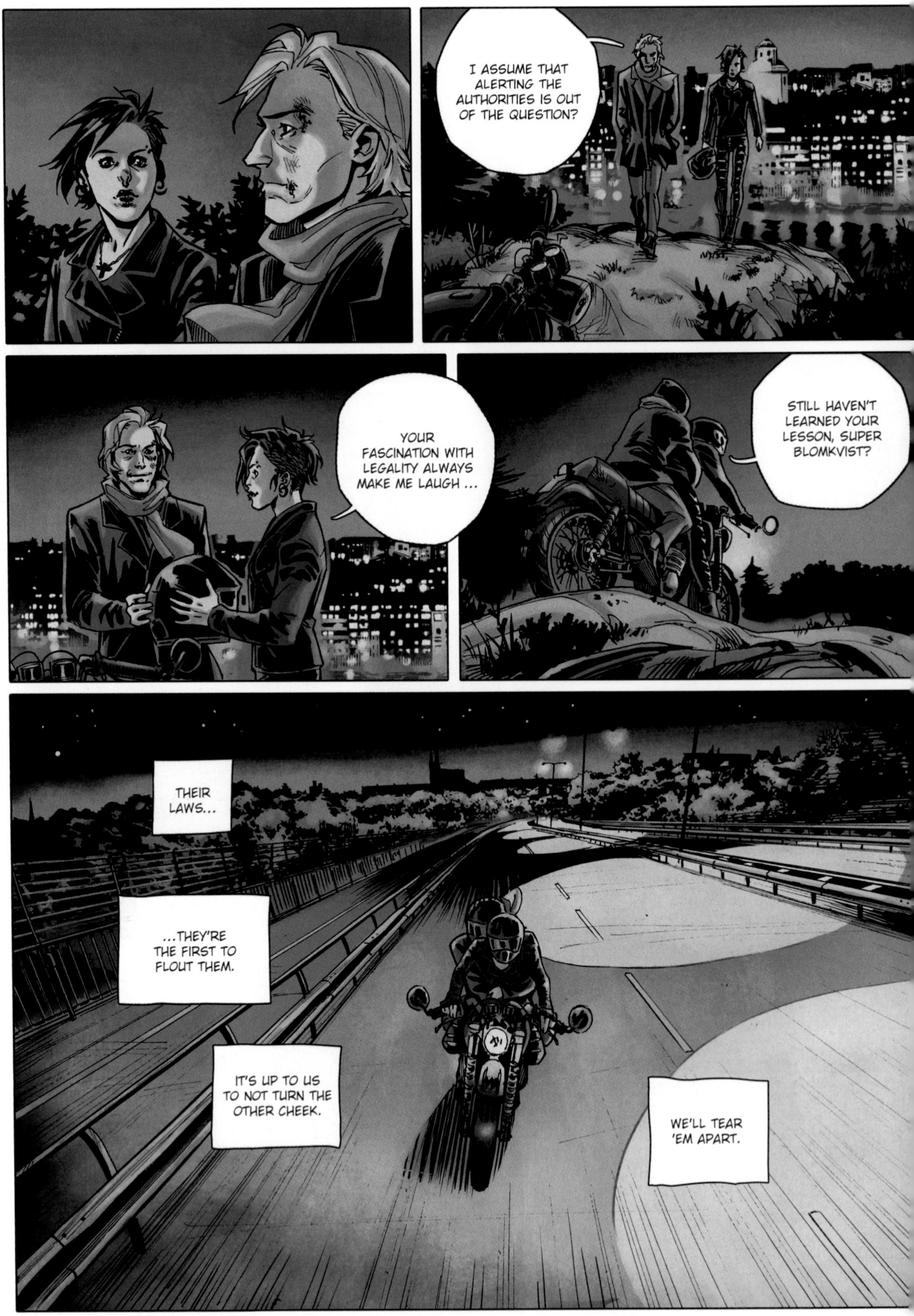
I ASSUME THAT ALERTING THE AUTHORITIES IS OUT OF THE QUESTION?
YOUR FASCINATION WITH LEGALITY ALWAYS MAKE ME LAUGH ...
STILL HAVEN'T LEARNED YOUR LESSON, SUPER BLOMKVIST?
THEIR LAWS...
...THEY'RE THE FIRST TO FLOUT THEM.
IT'S UP TO US TO NOT TURN THE OTHER CHEEK.
WE'LL TEAR 'EM APART.

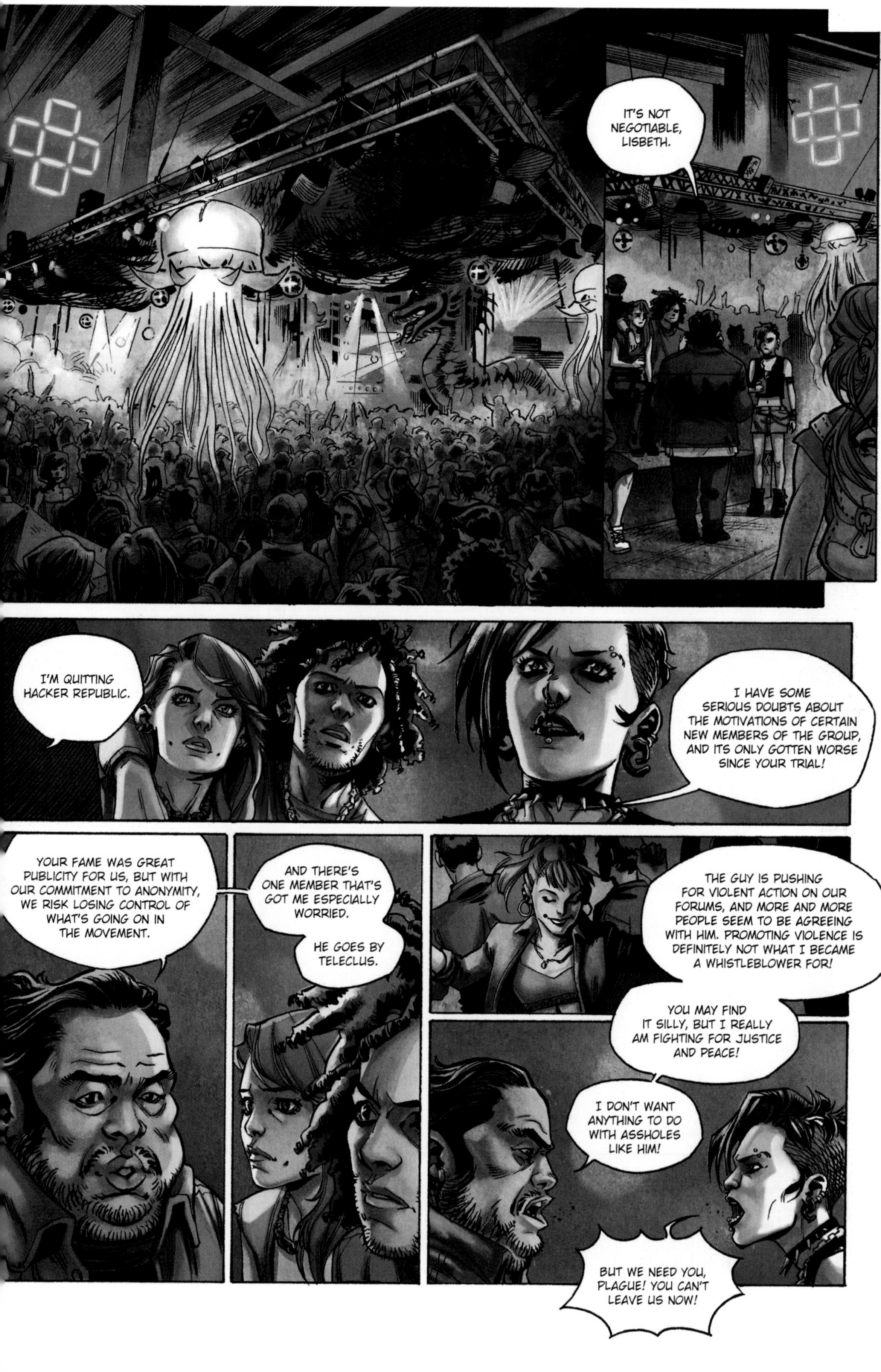
IT'S NOT NEGOTIABLE, LISBETH.
I'M QUITTING HACKER REPUBLIC.
I HAVE SOME SERIOUS DOUBTS ABOUT THE MOTIVATIONS OF CERTAIN NEW MEMBERS OF THE GROUP, AND ITS ONLY GOTTEN WORSE SINCE YOUR TRIAL!
YOUR FAME WAS GREAT PUBLICITY FOR US, BUT WITH OUR COMMITMENT TO ANONYMITY, WE RISK LOSING CONTROL OF WHAT'S GOING ON IN THE MOVEMENT.
AND THERE'S ONE MEMBER THAT'S GOT ME ESPECIALLY WORRIED.
HE GOES BY TELECLUS.
THE GUY IS PUSHING FOR VIOLENT ACTION ON OUR FORUMS, AND MORE AND MORE PEOPLE SEEM TO BE AGREEING WITH HIM. PROMOTING VIOLENCE IS DEFINITELY NOT WHAT I BECAME A WHISTLEBLOWER FOR!
YOU MAY FIND IT SILLY, BUT I REALLY AM FIGHTING FOR JUSTICE AND PEACE!
I DON'T WANT ANYTHING TO DO WITH ASSHOLES LIKE HIM!
BUT WE NEED YOU, PLAGUE! YOU CAN'T LEAVE US NOW!

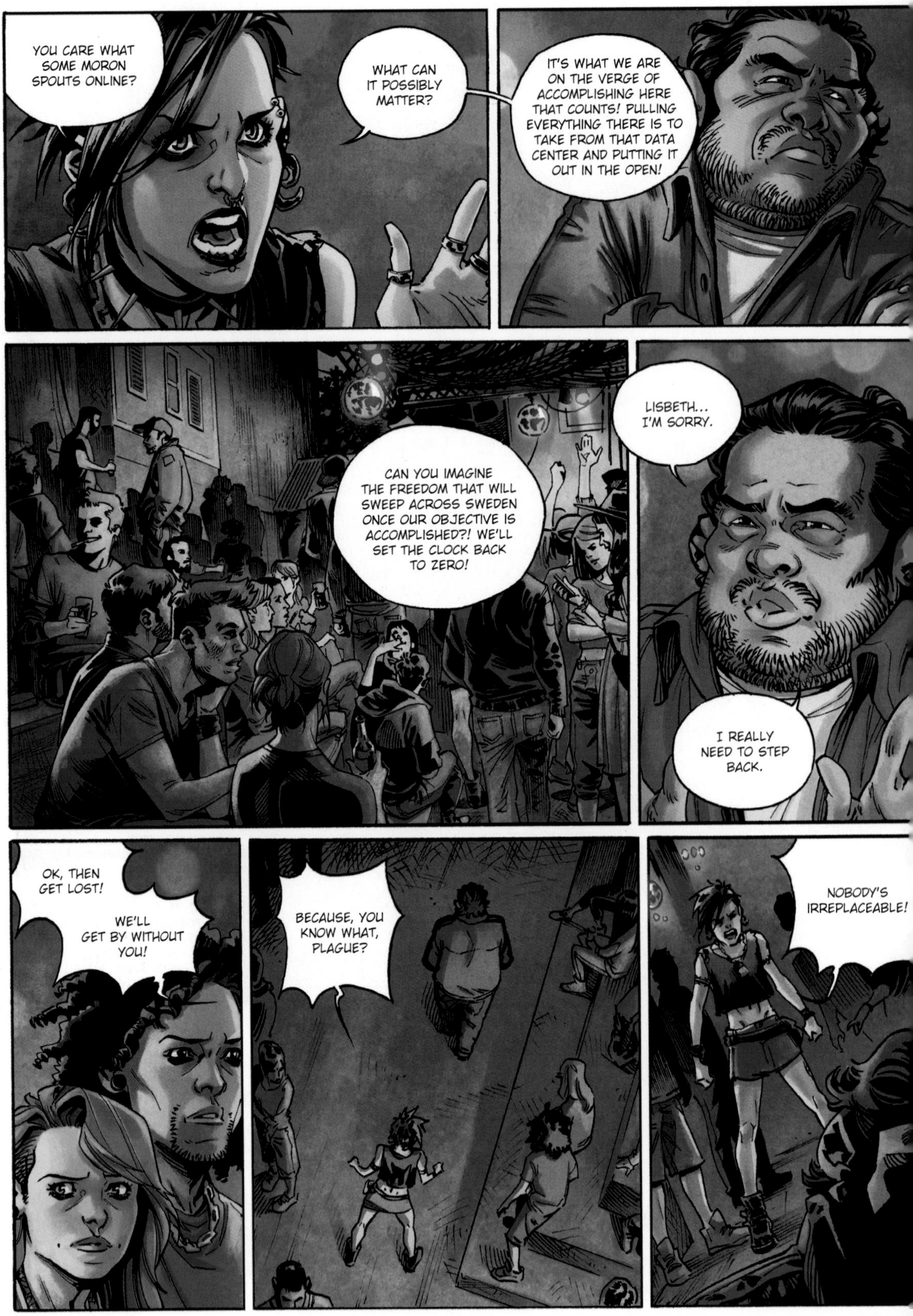
YOU CARE WHAT SOME MORON SPOUTS ONLINE?
WHAT CAN IT POSSIBLY MATTER?
IT'S WHAT WE ARE ON THE VERGE OF ACCOMPLISHING HERE THAT COUNTS! PULLING EVERYTHING THERE IS TO TAKE FROM THAT DATA CENTER AND PUTTING IT OUT IN THE OPEN!
CAN YOU IMAGINE THE FREEDOM THAT WILL SWEEP ACROSS SWEDEN ONCE OUR OBJECTIVE IS ACCOMPLISHED?! WE'LL SET THE CLOCK BACK TO ZERO!
LISBETH... I'M SORRY.
I REALLY NEED TO STEP BACK.
OK, THEN GET LOST!
WE'LL GET BY WITHOUT YOU!
BECAUSE, YOU KNOW WHAT, PLAGUE?
NOBODY'S IRREPLACEABLE!

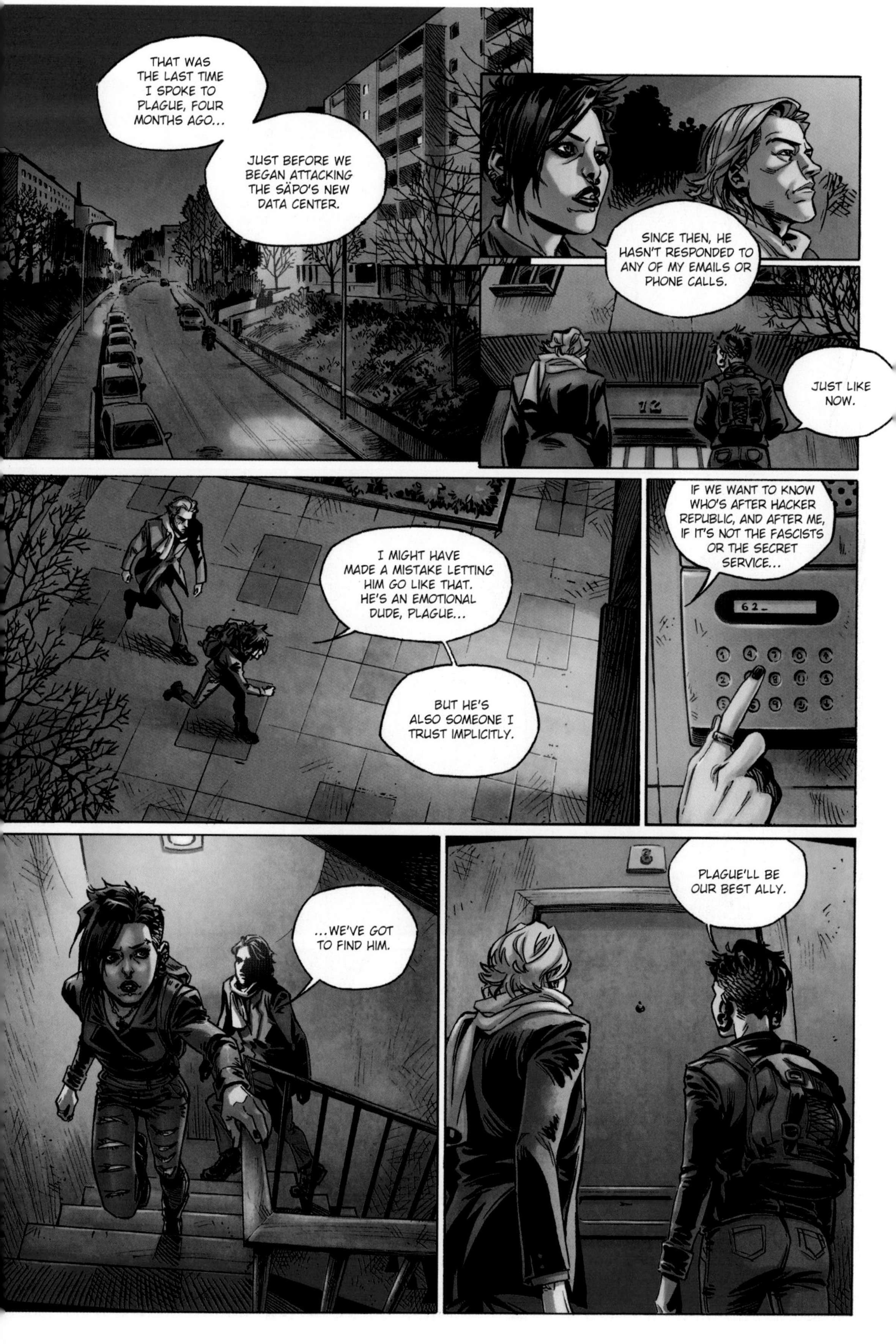
THAT WAS THE LAST TIME I SPOKE TO PLAGUE, FOUR MONTHS AGO...
JUST BEFORE WE BEGAN ATTACKING THE SÄPO'S NEW DATA CENTER.
SINCE THEN, HE HASN'T RESPONDED TO ANY OF MY EMAILS OR PHONE CALLS.
12
JUST LIKE NOW.
I MIGHT HAVE MADE A MISTAKE LETTING HIM GO LIKE THAT. HE'S AN EMOTIONAL DUDE, PLAGUE...
BUT HE'S ALSO SOMEONE I TRUST IMPLICITLY.
IF WE WANT TO KNOW WHO'S AFTER HACKER REPUBLIC, AND AFTER ME, IF IT'S NOT THE FASCISTS OR THE SECRET SERVICE...
62_
...WE'VE GOT TO FIND HIM.
PLAGUE'LL BE OUR BEST ALLY.

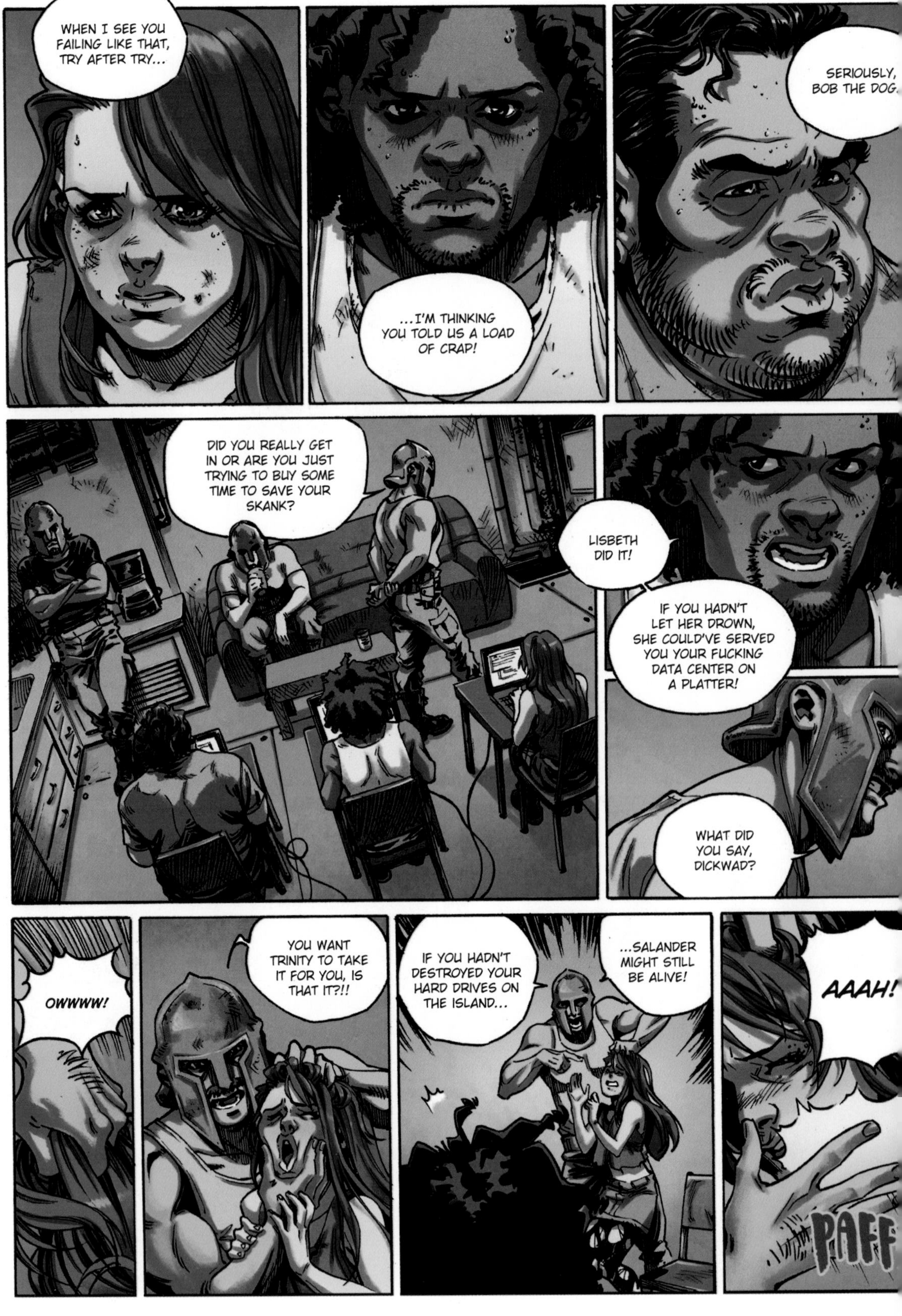
WHEN I SEE YOU FAILING LIKE THAT, TRY AFTER TRY...
...I'M THINKING YOU TOLD US A LOAD OF CRAP!
SERIOUSLY, BOB THE DOG.
DID YOU REALLY GET IN OR ARE YOU JUST TRYING TO BUY SOME TIME TO SAVE YOUR SKANK?
LISBETH DID IT!
IF YOU HADN'T LET HER DROWN, SHE COULD'VE SERVED YOU YOUR FUCKING DATA CENTER ON A PLATTER!
WHAT DID YOU SAY, DICKWAD?
OWWWW!
YOU WANT TRINITY TO TAKE IT FOR YOU, IS THAT IT?!!
IF YOU HADN'T DESTROYED YOUR HARD DRIVES ON THE ISLAND...
...SALANDER MIGHT STILL BE ALIVE!
AAAH!
PAFF

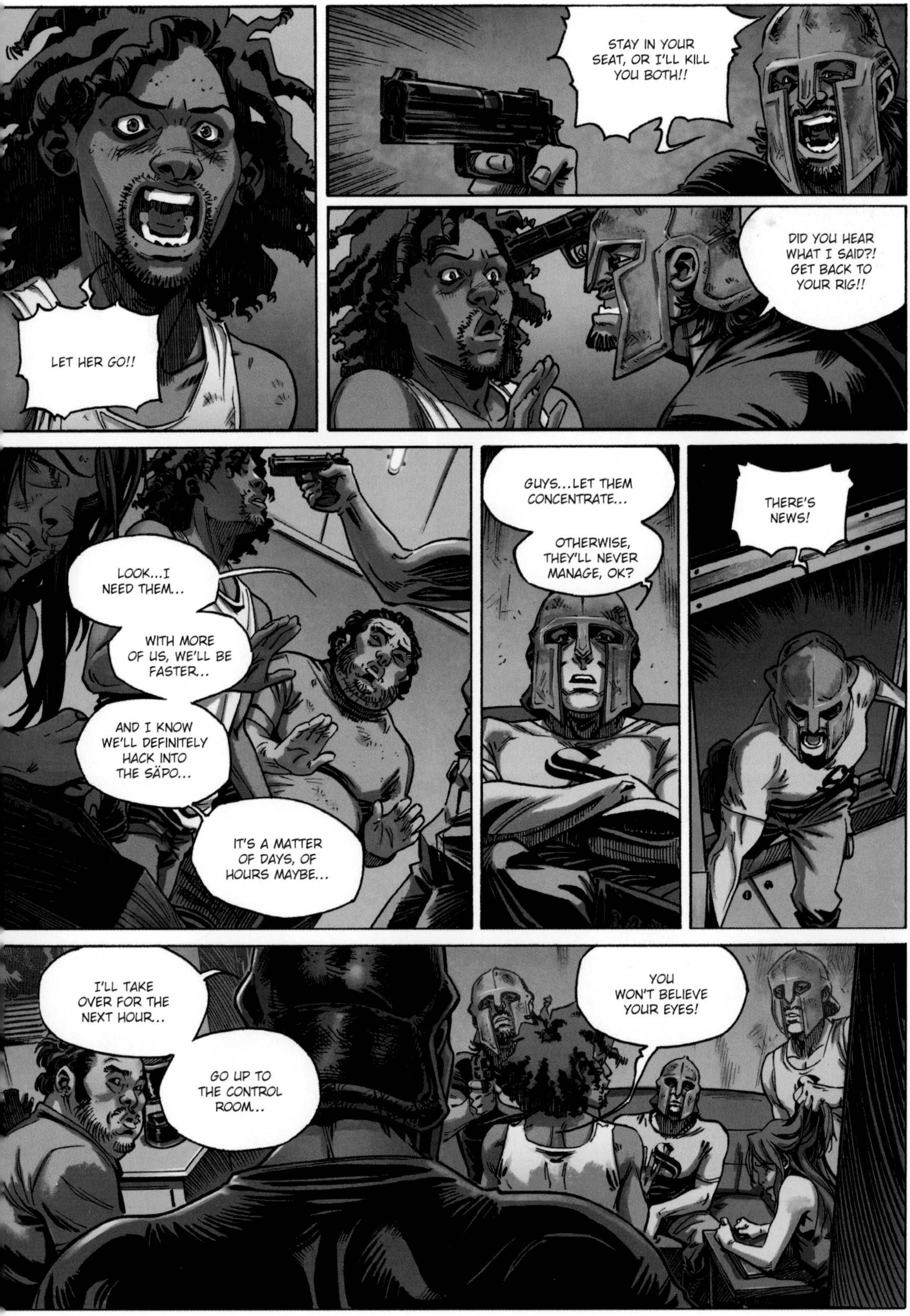
LET HER GO!!
STAY IN YOUR SEAT, OR I'LL KILL YOU BOTH!!
DID YOU HEAR WHAT I SAID?! GET BACK TO YOUR RIG!!
LOOK...I NEED THEM..
WITH MORE OF US, WE'LL BE FASTER..
AND I KNOW WE'LL DEFINITELY HACK INTO THE SÄPO...
IT'S A MATTER OF DAYS, OF HOURS MAYBE...
GUYS...LET THEM CONCENTRATE...
OTHERWISE, THEY'LL NEVER MANAGE, OK?
THERE'S NEWS!
I'LL TAKE OVER FOR THE NEXT HOUR..
GO UP TO THE CONTROL ROOM..
YOU WON'T BELIEVE YOUR EYES!

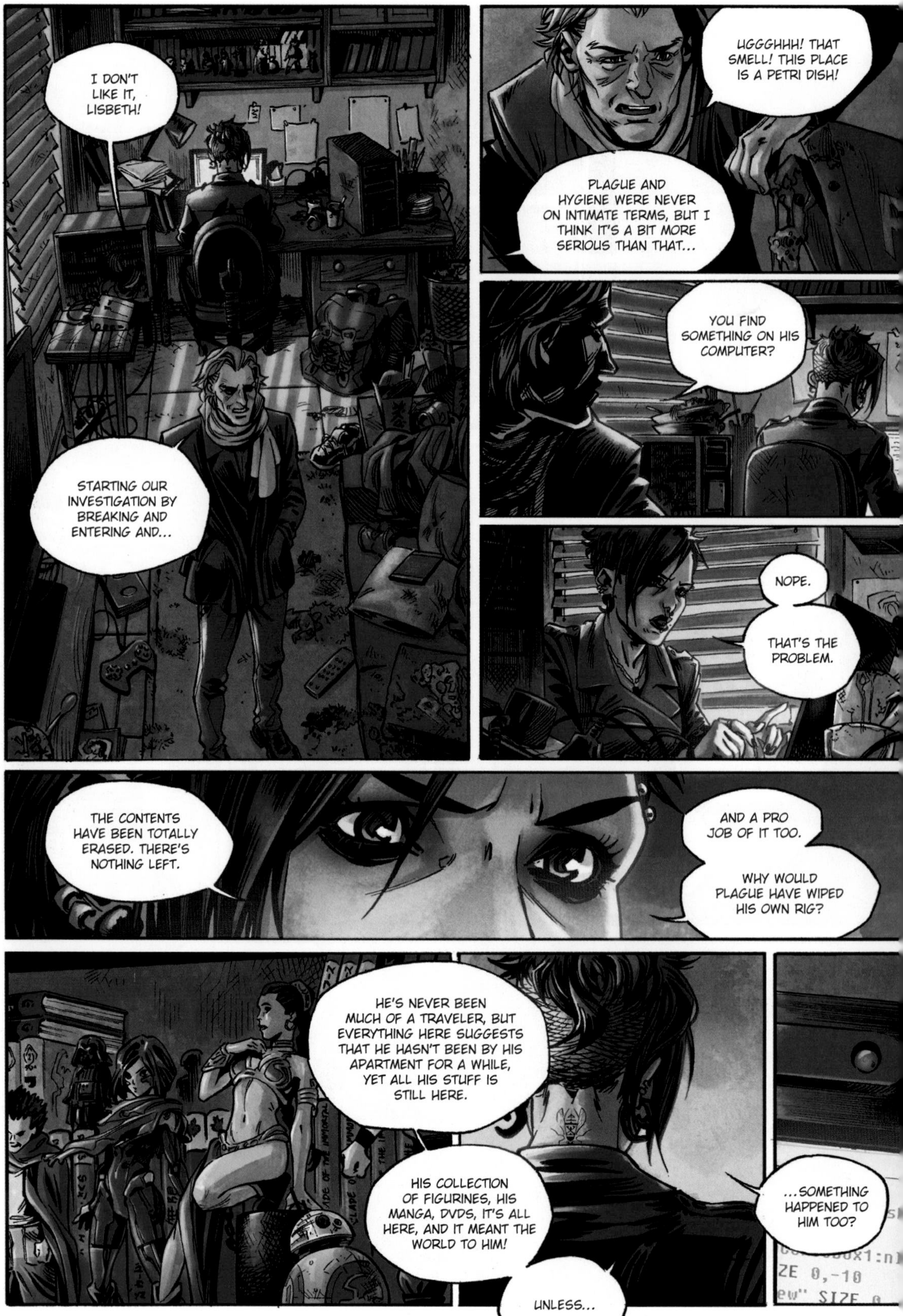
I DON'T LIKE IT, LISBETH!
STARTING OUR INVESTIGATION BY BREAKING AND ENTERING AND...
UGGGHHH! THAT SMELL! THIS PLACE IS A PETRI DISH!
PLAGUE AND HYGIENE WERE NEVER ON INTIMATE TERMS, BUT I THINK IT'S A BIT MORE SERIOUS THAN THAT...
YOU FIND SOMETHING ON HIS COMPUTER?
NOPE.
THAT'S THE PROBLEM.
THE CONTENTS HAVE BEEN TOTALLY ERASED. THERE'S NOTHING LEFT.
AND A PRO JOB OF IT TOO.
WHY WOULD PLAGUE HAVE WIPED HIS OWN RIG?
HE'S NEVER BEEN MUCH OF A TRAVELER, BUT EVERYTHING HERE SUGGESTS THAT HE HASN'T BEEN BY HIS APARTMENT FOR A WHILE, YET ALL HIS STUFF IS STILL HERE.
HIS COLLECTION OF FIGURINES, HIS MANGA, DVDS, IT'S ALL HERE, AND IT MEANT THE WORLD TO HIM!
UNLESS...
...SOMETHING HAPPENED TO HIM TOO?

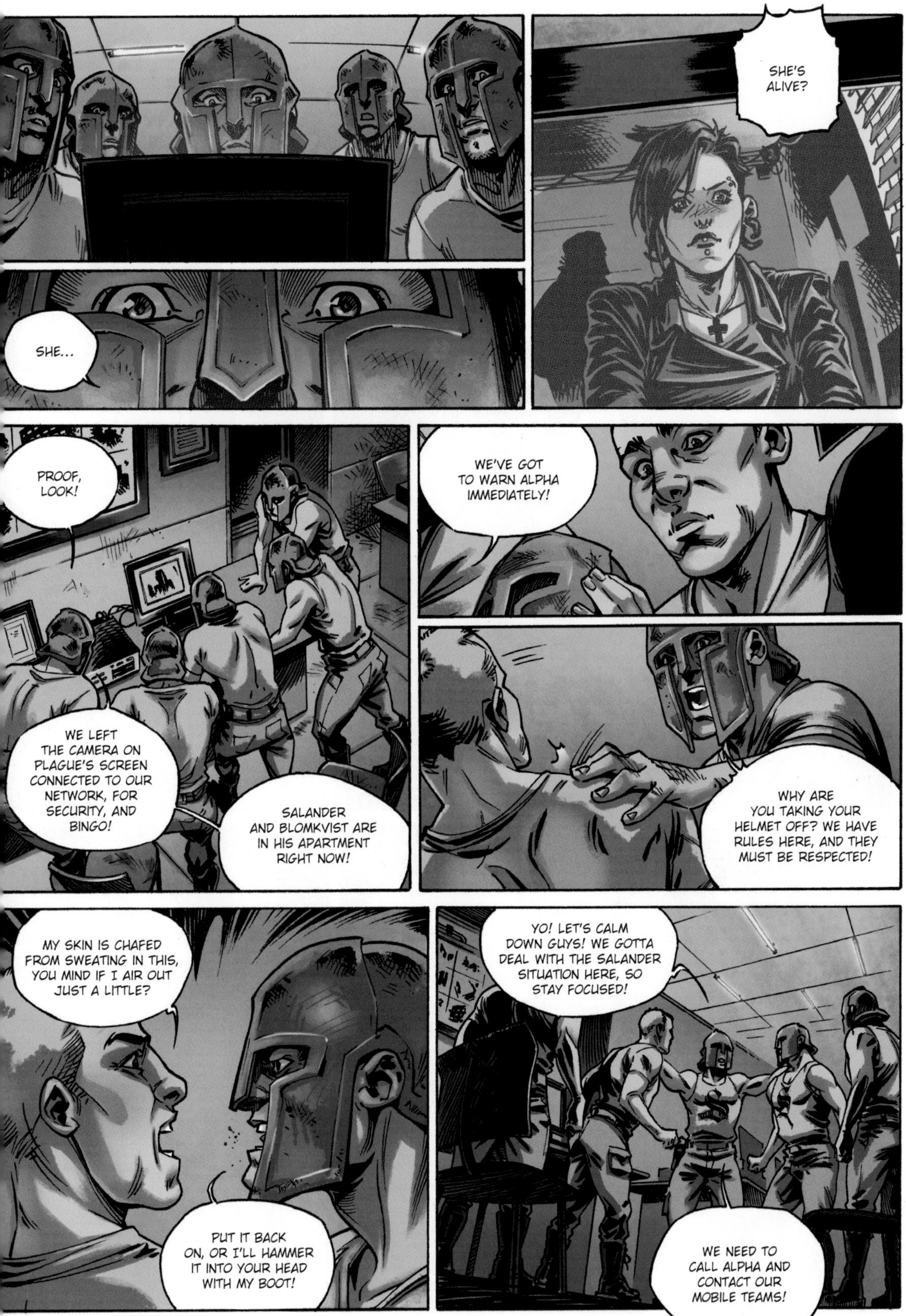
SHE...
SHE'S ALIVE?
PROOF, LOOK!
WE LEFT THE CAMERA ON PLAGUE'S SCREEN CONNECTED TO OUR NETWORK, FOR SECURITY, AND BINGO!
SALANDER AND BLOMKVIST ARE IN HIS APARTMENT RIGHT NOW!
WE'VE GOT TO WARN ALPHA IMMEDIATELY!
WHY ARE YOU TAKING YOUR HELMET OFF? WE HAVE RULES HERE, AND THEY MUST BE RESPECTED!
MY SKIN IS CHAFED FROM SWEATING IN THIS, YOU MIND IF I AIR OUT JUST A LITTLE?
PUT IT BACK ON, OR I'LL HAMMER IT INTO YOUR HEAD WITH MY BOOT!
YO! LET'S CALM DOWN GUYS! WE GOTTA DEAL WITH THE SALANDER SITUATION HERE, SO STAY FOCUSED!
WE NEED TO CALL ALPHA AND CONTACT OUR MOBILE TEAMS!

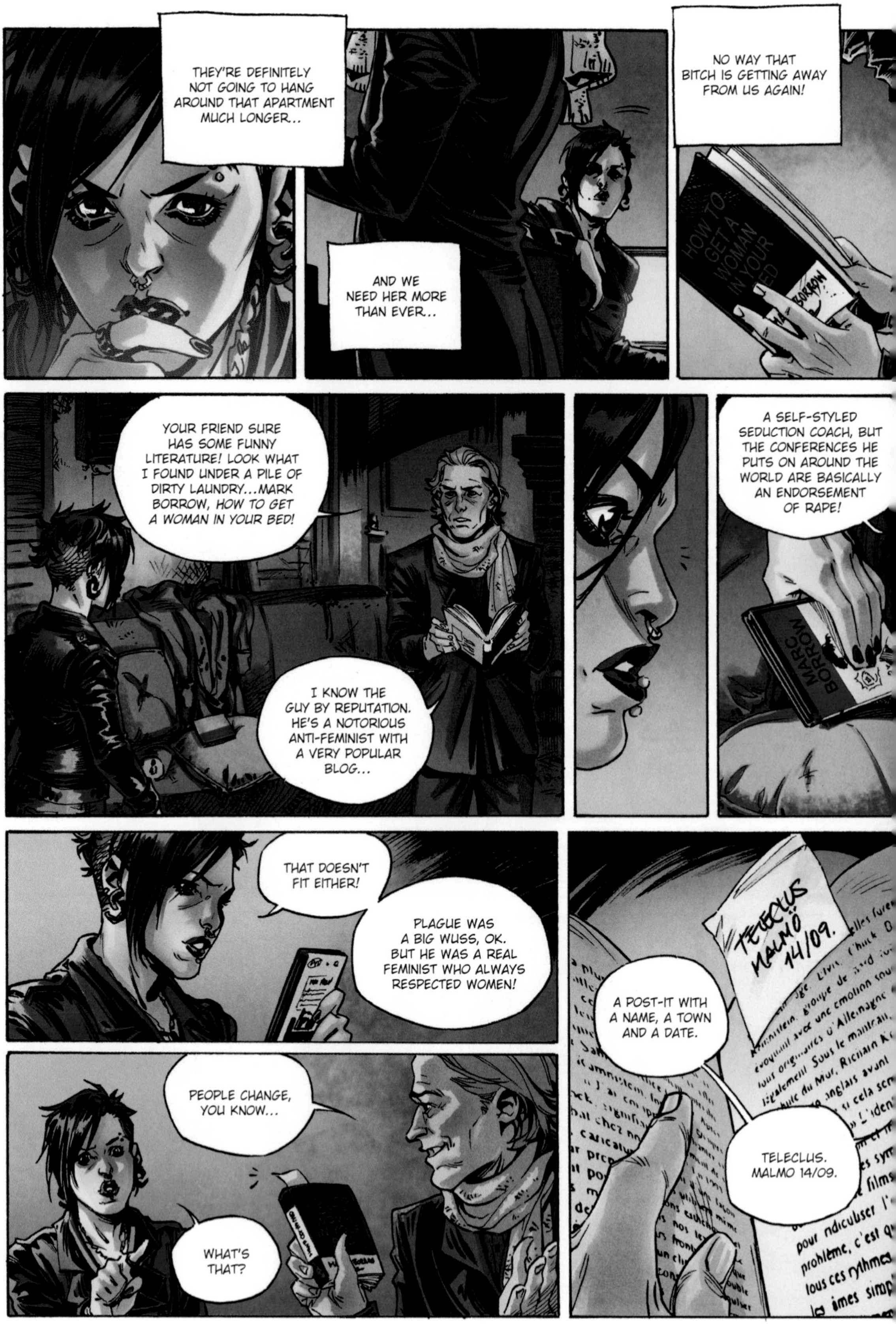
THEY'RE DEFINITELY NOT GOING TO HANG AROUND THAT APARTMENT MUCH LONGER...
AND WE NEED HER MORE THAN EVER...
NO WAY THAT BITCH IS GETTING AWAY FROM US AGAIN!
HOW TO GET A WOMAN IN YOUR BED
YOUR FRIEND SURE HAS SOME FUNNY LITERATURE! LOOK WHAT I FOUND UNDER A PILE OF DIRTY LAUNDRY...MARK BORROW, HOW TO GET A WOMAN IN YOUR BED!
I KNOW THE GUY BY REPUTATION. HE'S A NOTORIOUS ANTI-FEMINIST WITH A VERY POPULAR BLOG...
A SELF-STYLED SEDUCTION COACH, BUT THE CONFERENCES HE PUTS ON AROUND THE WORLD ARE BASICALLY AN ENDORSEMENT OF RAPE!
MARC BORROW
THAT DOESN'T FIT EITHER!
PLAGUE WAS A BIG WUSS, OK. BUT HE WAS A REAL FEMINIST WHO ALWAYS RESPECTED WOMEN!
PEOPLE CHANGE, YOU KNOW...
WHAT'S THAT?
TELECLUS MALMÖ 14/09.
A POST-IT WITH A NAME, A TOWN AND A DATE.
TELECLUS. MALMO 14/09.

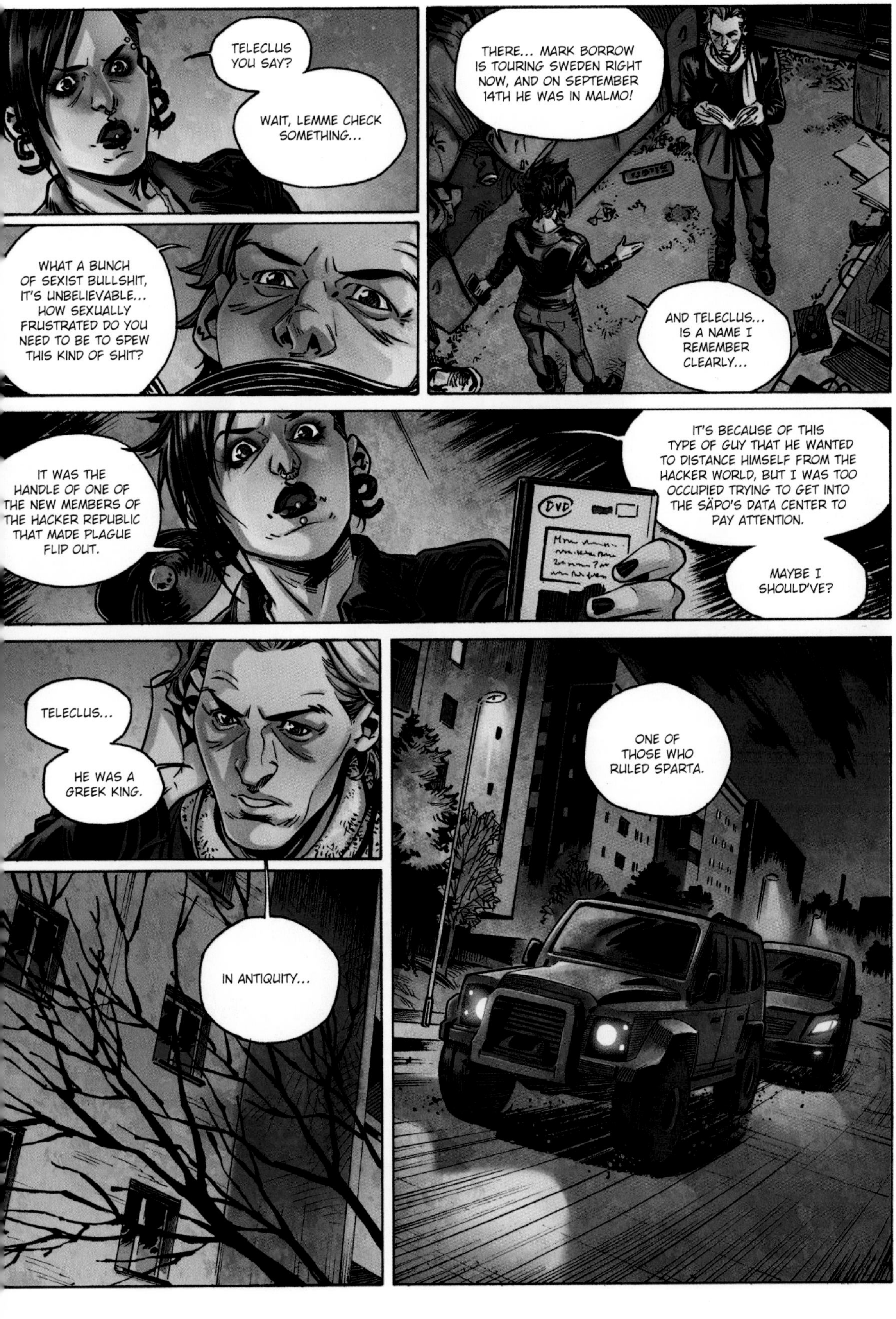
TELECLUS YOU SAY?
WAIT, LEMME CHECK SOMETHING...
THERE... MARK BORROW IS TOURING SWEDEN RIGHT NOW, AND ON SEPTEMBER 14TH HE WAS IN MALMO!
WHAT A BUNCH OF SEXIST BULLSHIT, IT'S UNBELIEVABLE... HOW SEXUALLY FRUSTRATED DO YOU NEED TO BE TO SPEW THIS KIND OF SHIT?
AND TELECLUS... IS A NAME I REMEMBER CLEARLY...
IT WAS THE HANDLE OF ONE OF THE NEW MEMBERS OF THE HACKER REPUBLIC THAT MADE PLAGUE FLIP OUT.
DVD
IT'S BECAUSE OF THIS TYPE OF GUY THAT HE WANTED TO DISTANCE HIMSELF FROM THE HACKER WORLD, BUT I WAS TOO OCCUPIED TRYING TO GET INTO THE SÄPO'S DATA CENTER TO PAY ATTENTION.
MAYBE I SHOULD'VE?
TELECLUS...
HE WAS A GREEK KING.
ONE OF THOSE WHO RULED SPARTA.
IN ANTIQUITY...

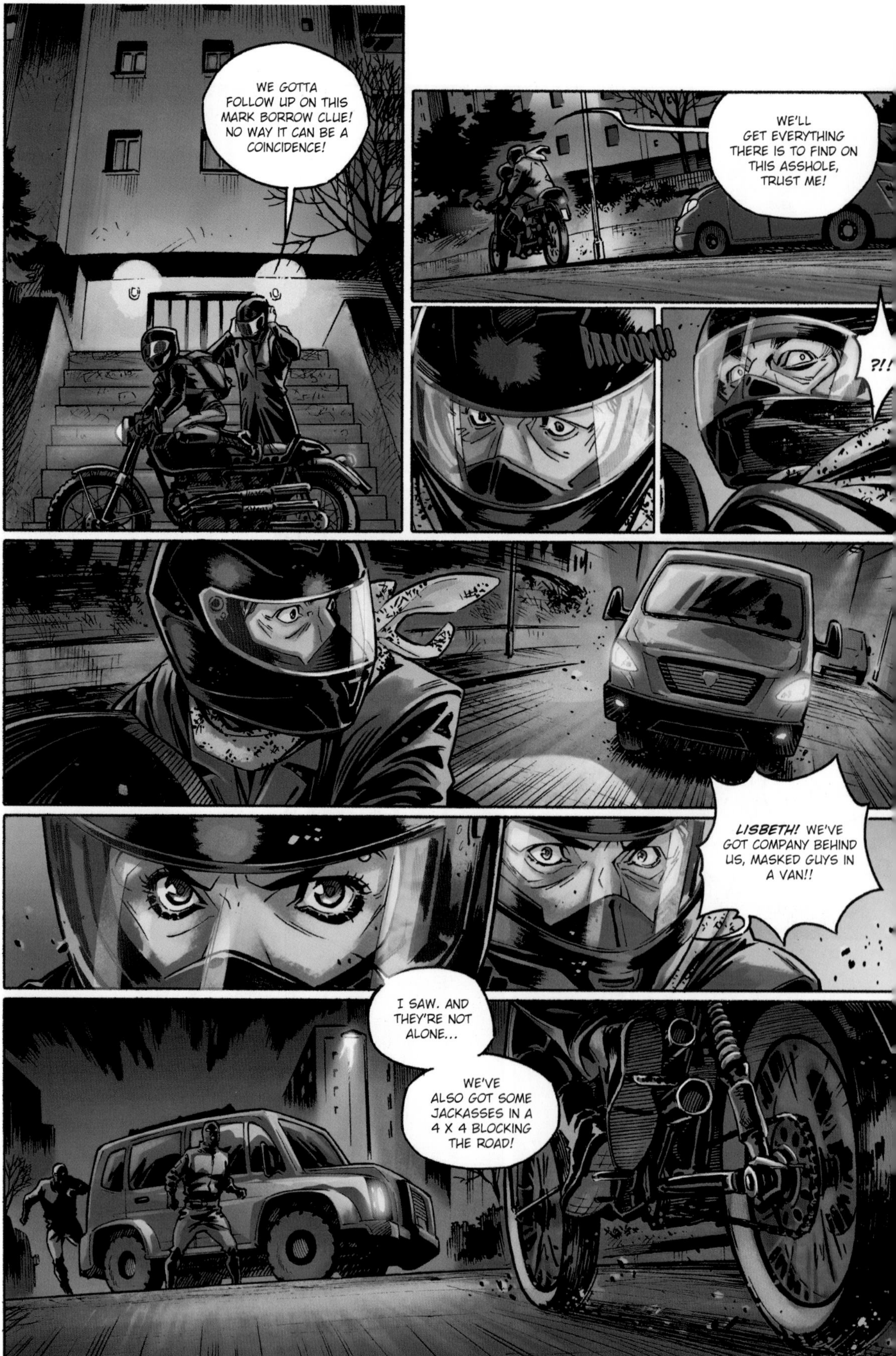
WE GOTTA FOLLOW UP ON THIS MARK BORROW CLUE! NO WAY IT CAN BE A COINCIDENCE!
WE'LL GET EVERYTHING THERE IS TO FIND ON THIS ASSHOLE, TRUST ME!
BRROOM!!
?!!
LISBETH! WE'VE GOT COMPANY BEHIND US, MASKED GUYS IN A VAN!!
I SAW. AND THEY'RE NOT ALONE...
WE'VE ALSO GOT SOME JACKASSES IN A 4 X 4 BLOCKING THE ROAD!

HANG ON!!

WHAT'RE YOU GOING TO DO?!

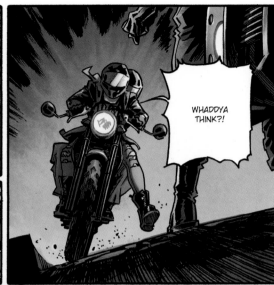

WHADDYA THINK?!

PAK!

WE'RE GOING TO LOSE THESE GUYS AND GET BORROW!!

GET BACK IN, DAMMIT!!

DON'T LOSE THEM!

AND BRING HER IN ALIVE!

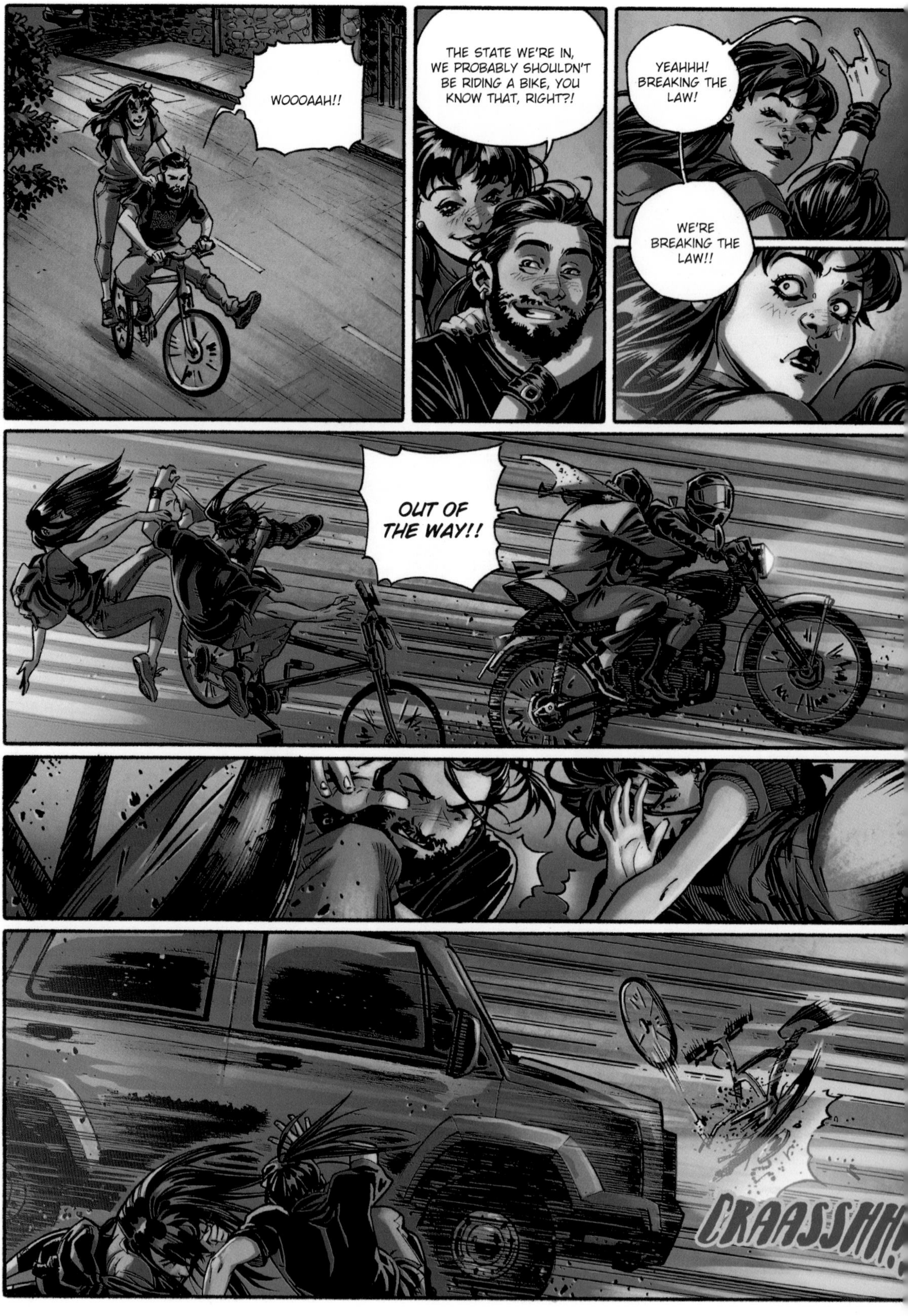
WOOOAAH!!
THE STATE WE'RE IN, WE PROBABLY SHOULDN'T BE RIDING A BIKE, YOU KNOW THAT, RIGHT?!
YEAHHH! BREAKING THE LAW!
WE'RE BREAKING THE LAW!!
OUT OF THE WAY!!
CRAASSHH!

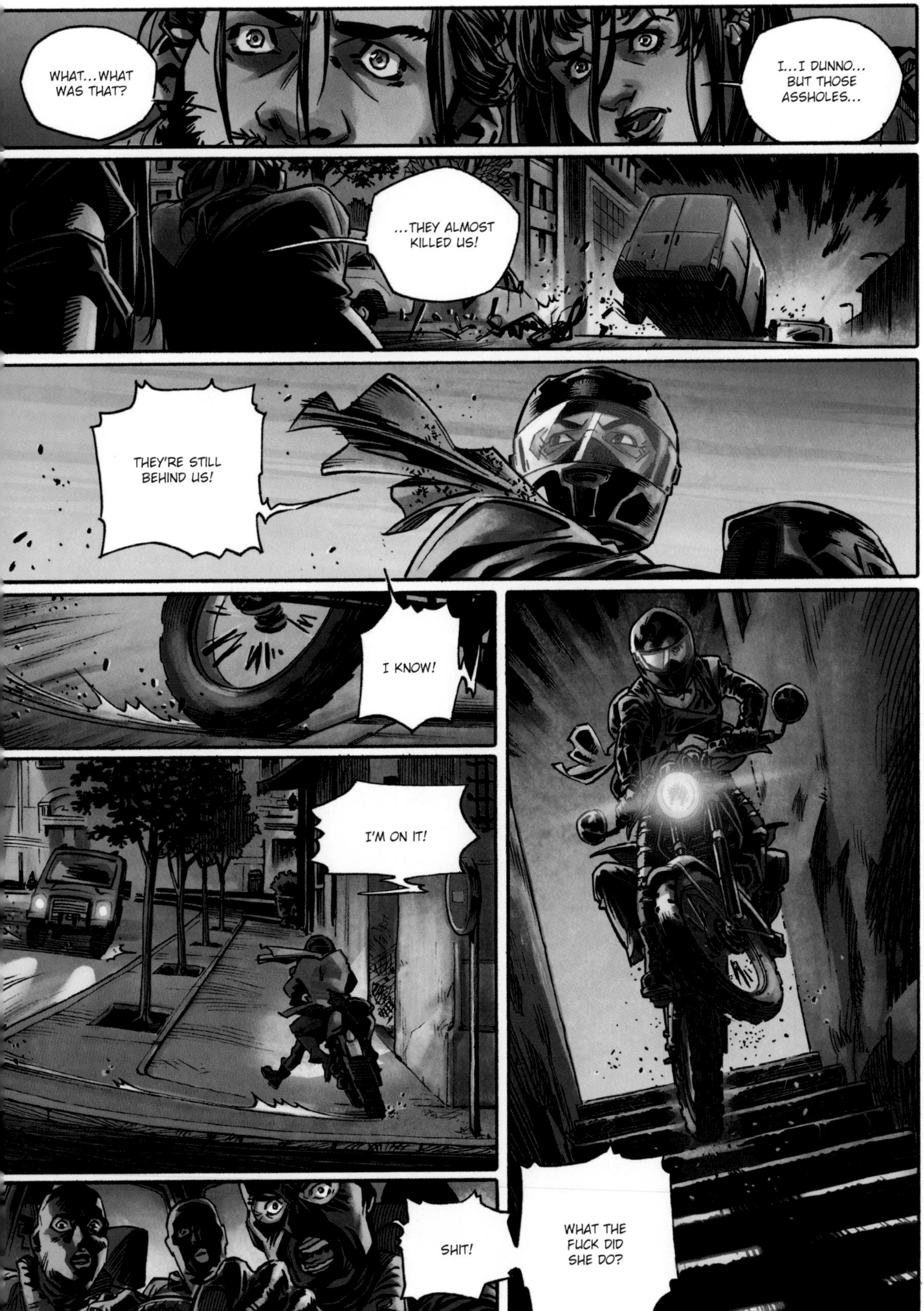
WHAT...WHAT WAS THAT?
I...I DUNNO... BUT THOSE ASSHOLES...
...THEY ALMOST KILLED US!
THEY'RE STILL BEHIND US!
I KNOW!
I'M ON IT!
SHIT!
WHAT THE FUCK DID SHE DO?

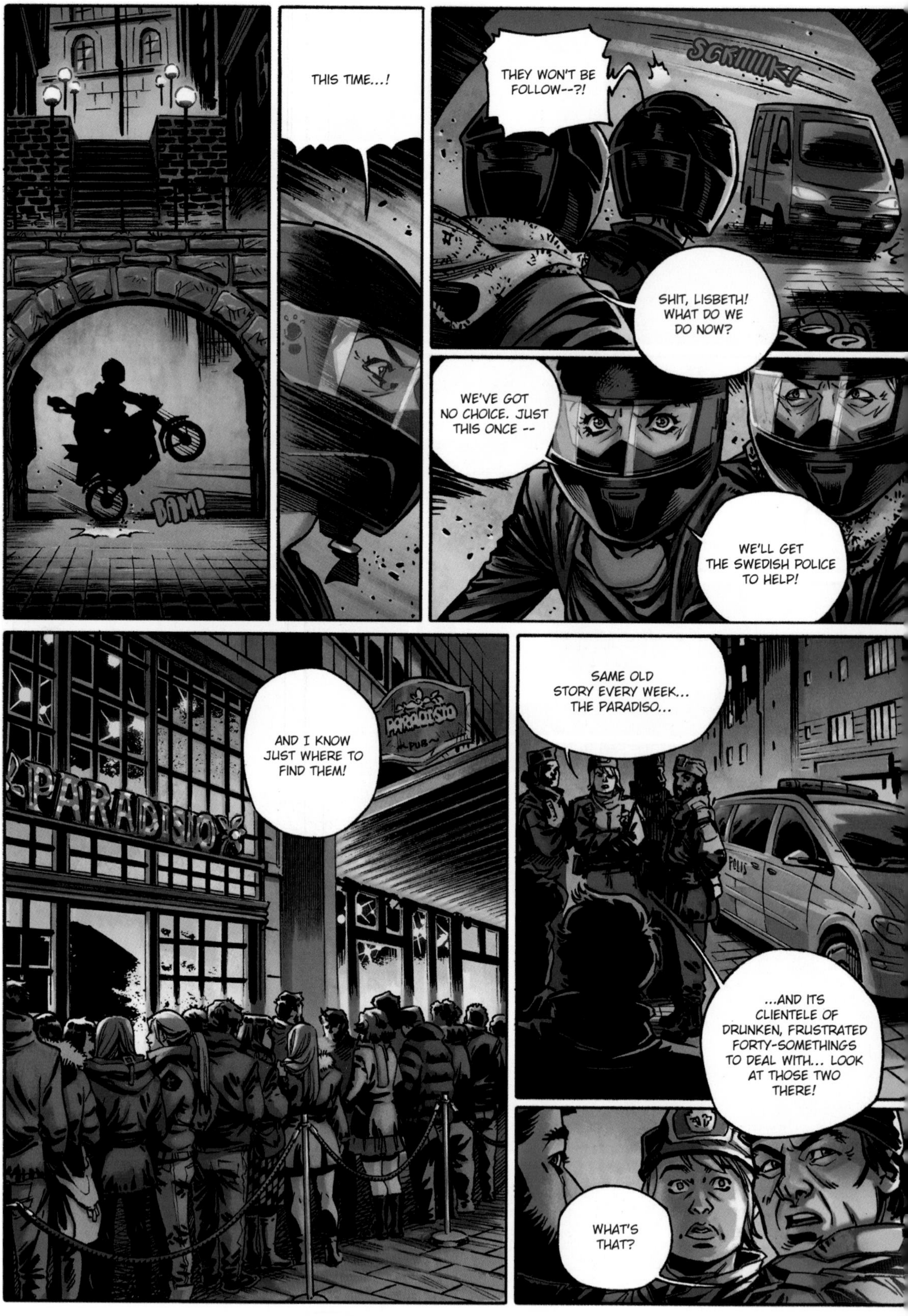

BAM!
THIS TIME...!
THEY WON'T BE FOLLOW--?!
SCRIIIIIK!
SHIT, LISBETH! WHAT DO WE DO NOW?
WE'VE GOT NO CHOICE. JUST THIS ONCE --
WE'LL GET THE SWEDISH POLICE TO HELP!
PARADISO
AND I KNOW JUST WHERE TO FIND THEM!
SAME OLD STORY EVERY WEEK... THE PARADISO...
POLIS
...AND ITS CLIENTELE OF DRUNKEN, FRUSTRATED FORTY-SOMETHINGS TO DEAL WITH... LOOK AT THOSE TWO THERE!
WHAT'S THAT?

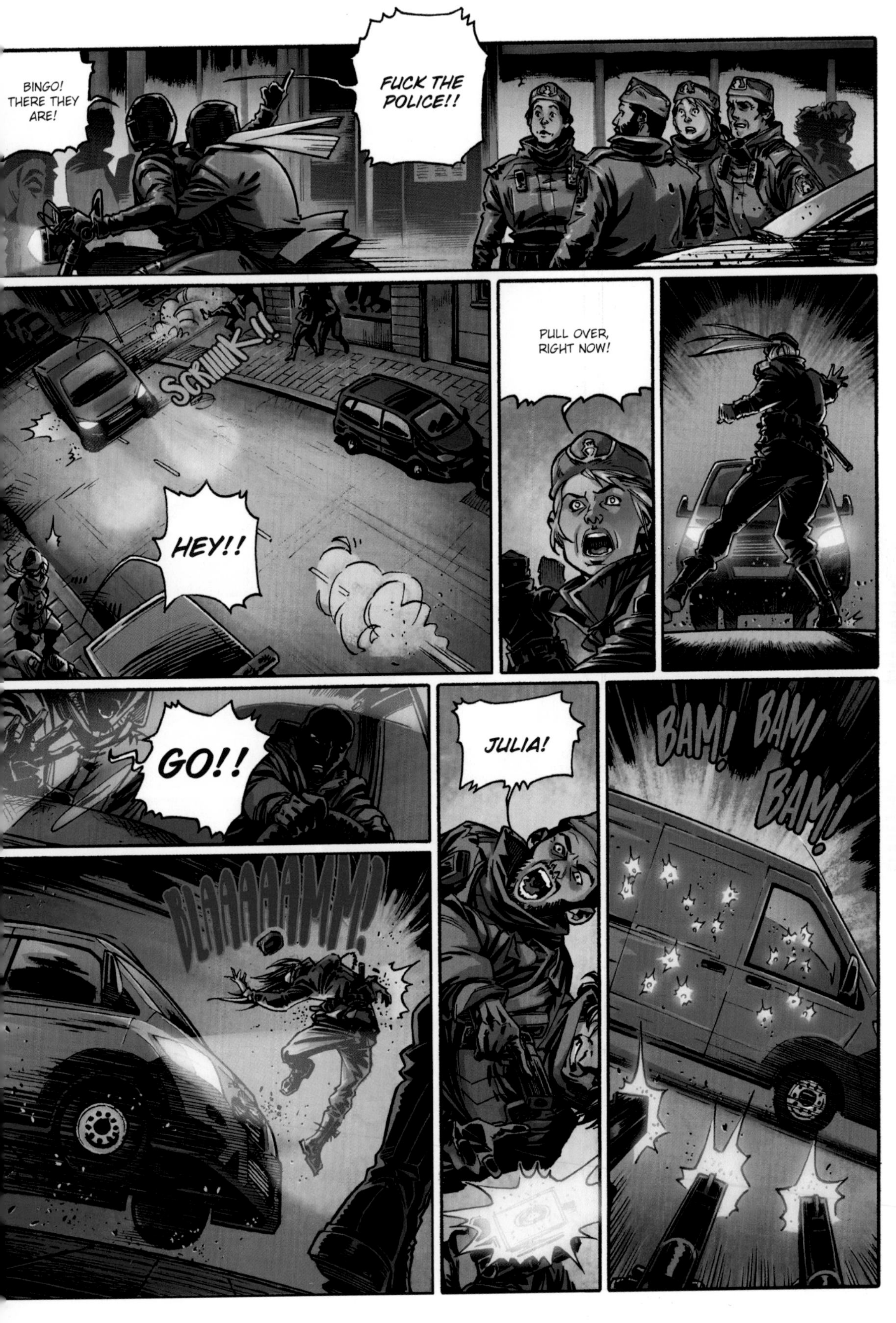
BINGO! THERE THEY ARE!
FUCK THE POLICE!!
SCRIIIIK!
HEY!!
PULL OVER, RIGHT NOW!
GO!!
JULIA!
BAM! BAM! BAM!
BLAAAAAMM!

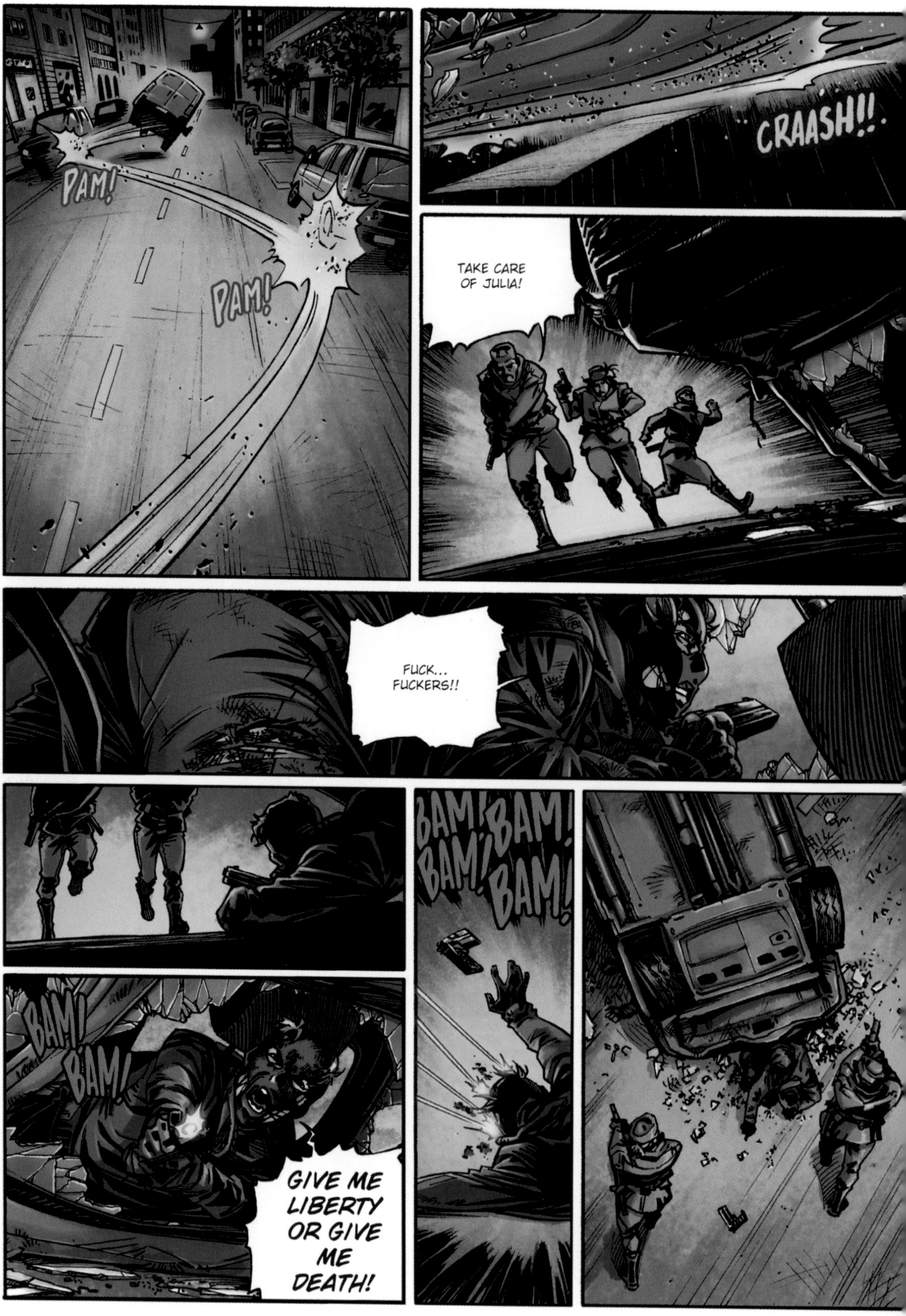
PAM!
PAM!
CRAASH!!
TAKE CARE OF JULIA!
FUCK... FUCKERS!!
BAM!
BAM!
GIVE ME LIBERTY OR GIVE ME DEATH!
BAM! BAM! BAM! BAM!

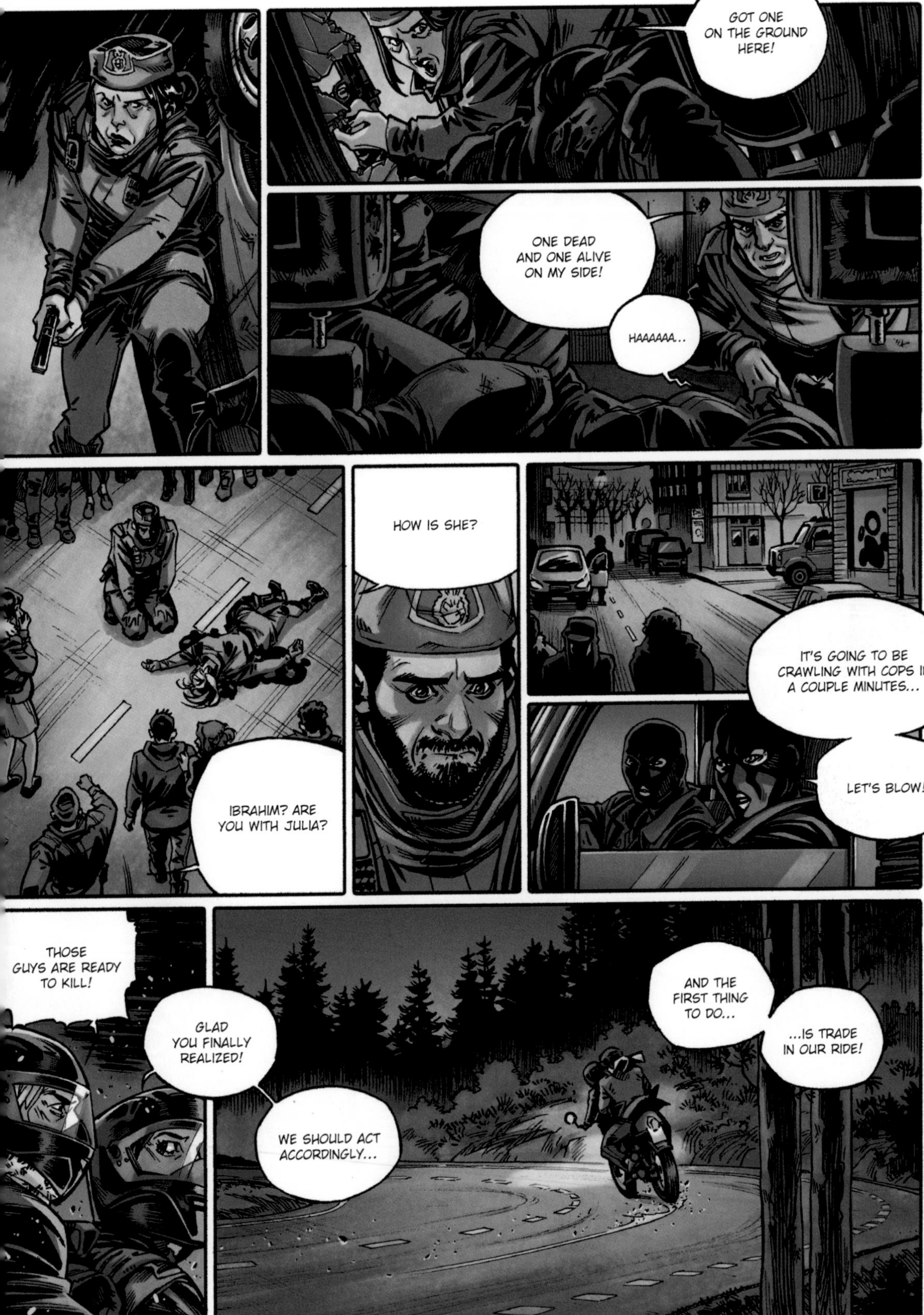
GOT ONE ON THE GROUND HERE!
ONE DEAD AND ONE ALIVE ON MY SIDE!
HAAAAAA...
IBRAHIM? ARE YOU WITH JULIA?
HOW IS SHE?
IT'S GOING TO BE CRAWLING WITH COPS IN A COUPLE MINUTES...
LET'S BLOW!
THOSE GUYS ARE READY TO KILL!
GLAD YOU FINALLY REALIZED!
WE SHOULD ACT ACCORDINGLY...
AND THE FIRST THING TO DO...
...IS TRADE IN OUR RIDE!

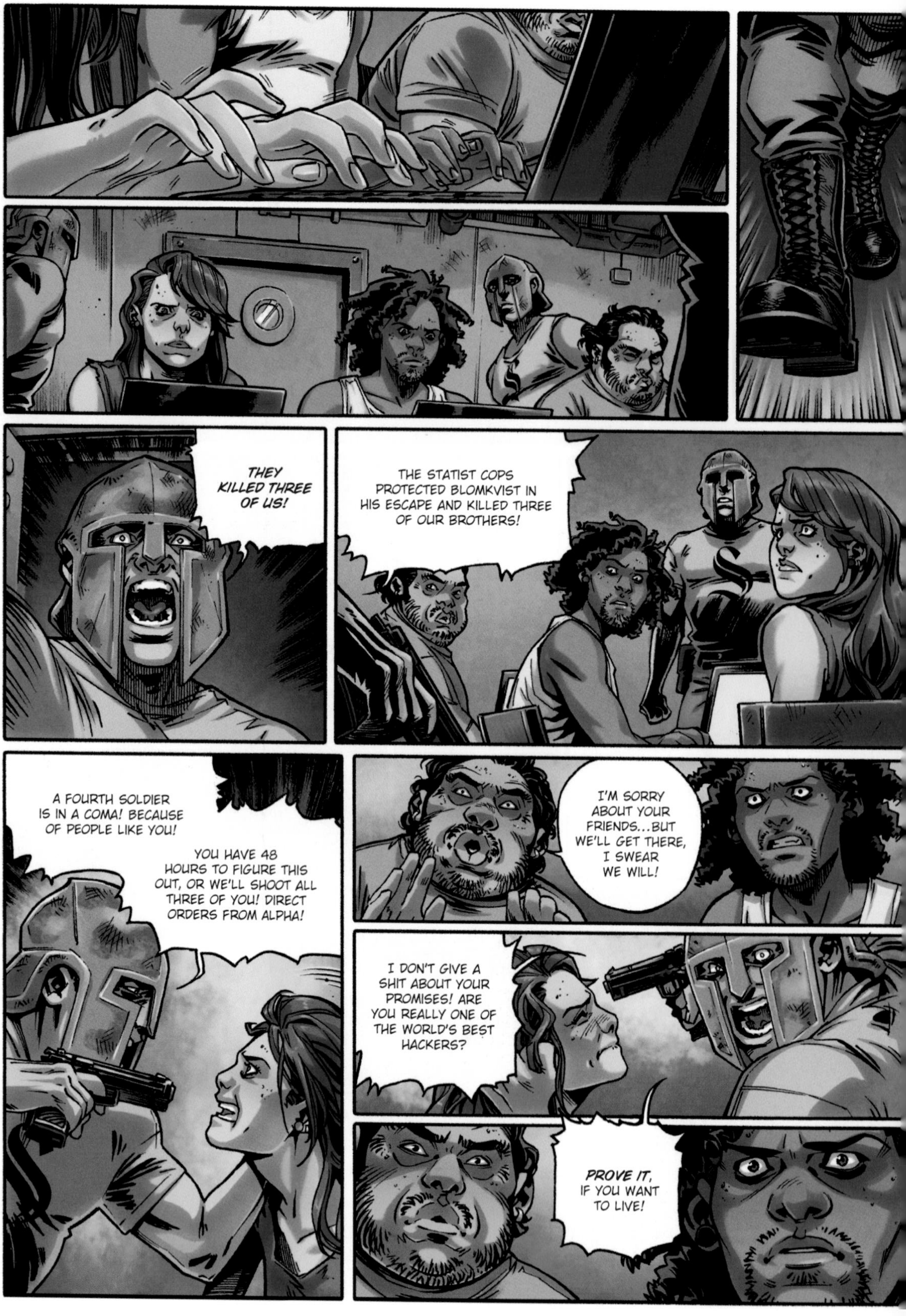
THEY KILLED THREE OF US!
THE STATIST COPS PROTECTED BLOMKVIST IN HIS ESCAPE AND KILLED THREE OF OUR BROTHERS!
A FOURTH SOLDIER IS IN A COMA! BECAUSE OF PEOPLE LIKE YOU!
YOU HAVE 48 HOURS TO FIGURE THIS OUT, OR WE'LL SHOOT ALL THREE OF YOU! DIRECT ORDERS FROM ALPHA!
I'M SORRY ABOUT YOUR FRIENDS...BUT WE'LL GET THERE, I SWEAR WE WILL!
I DON'T GIVE A SHIT ABOUT YOUR PROMISES! ARE YOU REALLY ONE OF THE WORLD'S BEST HACKERS?
PROVE IT, IF YOU WANT TO LIVE!

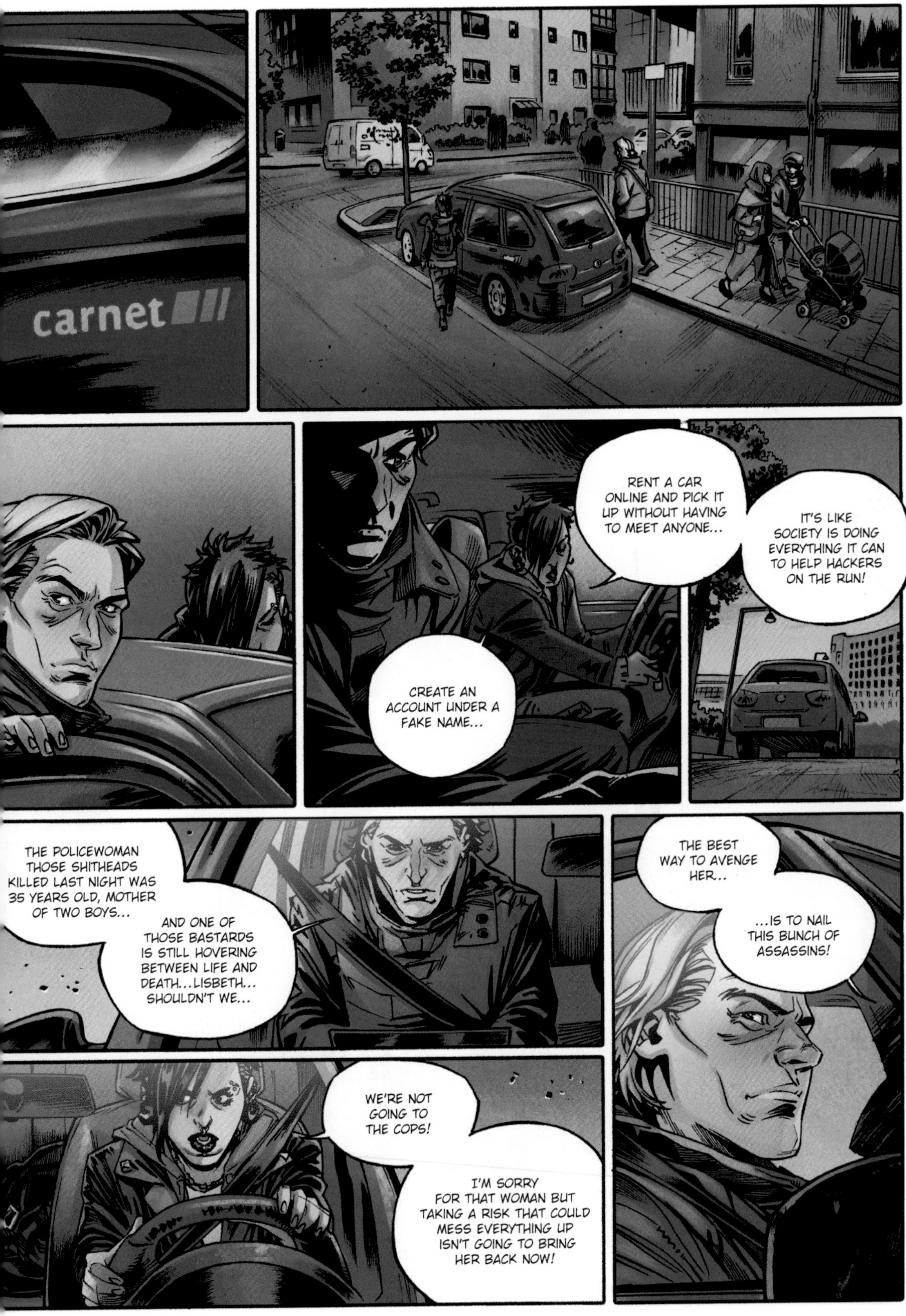
carnet
RENT A CAR ONLINE AND PICK IT UP WITHOUT HAVING TO MEET ANYONE...
CREATE AN ACCOUNT UNDER A FAKE NAME...
IT'S LIKE SOCIETY IS DOING EVERYTHING IT CAN TO HELP HACKERS ON THE RUN!
THE POLICEWOMAN THOSE SHITHEADS KILLED LAST NIGHT WAS 35 YEARS OLD, MOTHER OF TWO BOYS...
AND ONE OF THOSE BASTARDS IS STILL HOVERING BETWEEN LIFE AND DEATH...LISBETH... SHOULDN'T WE...
THE BEST WAY TO AVENGE HER..
...IS TO NAIL THIS BUNCH OF ASSASSINS!
WE'RE NOT GOING TO THE COPS!
I'M SORRY FOR THAT WOMAN BUT TAKING A RISK THAT COULD MESS EVERYTHING UP ISN'T GOING TO BRING HER BACK NOW!

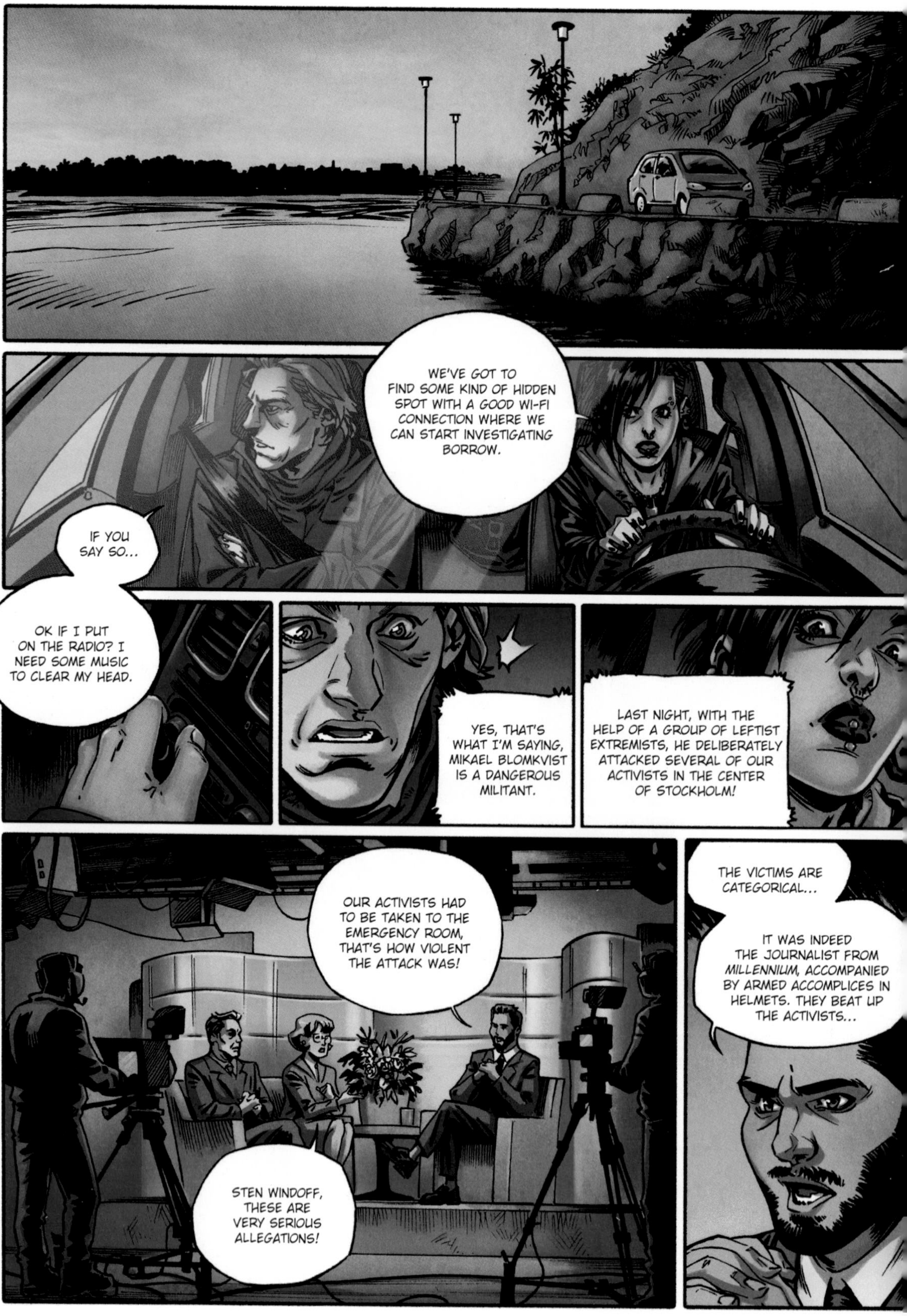
WE'VE GOT TO FIND SOME KIND OF HIDDEN SPOT WITH A GOOD WI-FI CONNECTION WHERE WE CAN START INVESTIGATING BORROW.
IF YOU SAY SO...
OK IF I PUT ON THE RADIO? I NEED SOME MUSIC TO CLEAR MY HEAD.
YES, THAT'S WHAT I'M SAYING, MIKAEL BLOMKVIST IS A DANGEROUS MILITANT.
LAST NIGHT, WITH THE HELP OF A GROUP OF LEFTIST EXTREMISTS, HE DELIBERATELY ATTACKED SEVERAL OF OUR ACTIVISTS IN THE CENTER OF STOCKHOLM!
OUR ACTIVISTS HAD TO BE TAKEN TO THE EMERGENCY ROOM, THAT'S HOW VIOLENT THE ATTACK WAS!
STEN WINDOFF, THESE ARE VERY SERIOUS ALLEGATIONS!
THE VICTIMS ARE CATEGORICAL...
IT WAS INDEED THE JOURNALIST FROM MILLENNIUM, ACCOMPANIED BY ARMED ACCOMPLICES IN HELMETS. THEY BEAT UP THE ACTIVISTS...

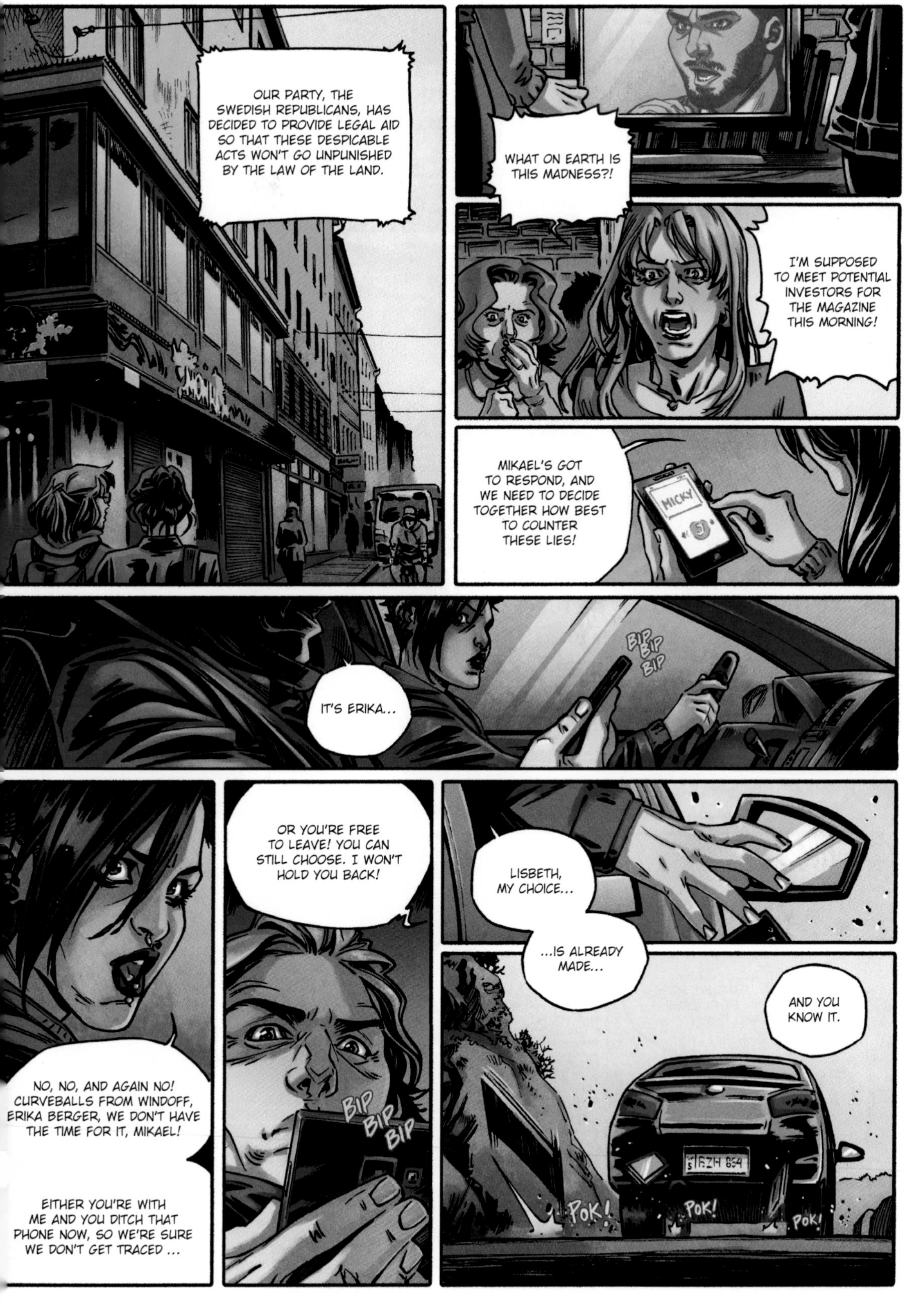
OUR PARTY, THE SWEDISH REPUBLICANS, HAS DECIDED TO PROVIDE LEGAL AID SO THAT THESE DESPICABLE ACTS WON'T GO UNPUNISHED BY THE LAW OF THE LAND.
WHAT ON EARTH IS THIS MADNESS?!
I'M SUPPOSED TO MEET POTENTIAL INVESTORS FOR THE MAGAZINE THIS MORNING!
MIKAEL'S GOT TO RESPOND, AND WE NEED TO DECIDE TOGETHER HOW BEST TO COUNTER THESE LIES!
MICKY
BIP BIP BIP
IT'S ERIKA...
NO, NO, AND AGAIN NO! CURVEBALLS FROM WINDOFF, ERIKA BERGER, WE DON'T HAVE THE TIME FOR IT, MIKAEL!
EITHER YOU'RE WITH ME AND YOU DITCH THAT PHONE NOW, SO WE'RE SURE WE DON'T GET TRACED ...
OR YOU'RE FREE TO LEAVE! YOU CAN STILL CHOOSE. I WON'T HOLD YOU BACK!
BIP BIP BIP
LISBETH, MY CHOICE...
...IS ALREADY MADE...
AND YOU KNOW IT.
POK! POK! POK!

THESE BEAT-UP ACTIVISTS, IT'S LIKE MANNA FROM HEAVEN!

BLESS YOU, MIKAEL BLOMKVIST!

STILL NO IDEA WHO WAS DRIVING THE MOTORCYCLE THAT SLAMMED THEM?

NO, IT HAPPENED TOO FAST, THE GUYS DON'T KNOW. SOME THINK IT WAS A WOMAN, OTHERS DON'T. WITH THE HELMET, IT'S IMPOSSIBLE TO PUT A FACE TOGETHER.

NO MATTER.

THIS ASSAULT, THE POLLS SHOWING US IN THE LEAD...

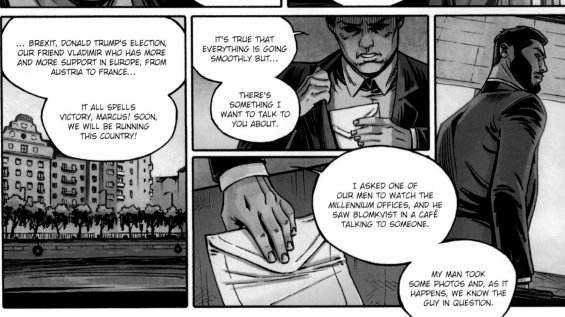

... BREXIT, DONALD TRUMP'S ELECTION, OUR FRIEND VLADIMIR WHO HAS MORE AND MORE SUPPORT IN EUROPE, FROM AUSTRIA TO FRANCE...

IT ALL SPELLS VICTORY, MARCUS! SOON, WE WILL BE RUNNING THIS COUNTRY!

IT'S TRUE THAT EVERYTHING IS GOING SMOOTHLY BUT...

THERE'S SOMETHING I WANT TO TALK TO YOU ABOUT.

I ASKED ONE OF OUR MEN TO WATCH THE MILLENNIUM OFFICES, AND HE SAW BLOMKVIST IN A CAFÉ TALKING TO SOMEONE.

MY MAN TOOK SOME PHOTOS AND, AS IT HAPPENS, WE KNOW THE GUY IN QUESTION.

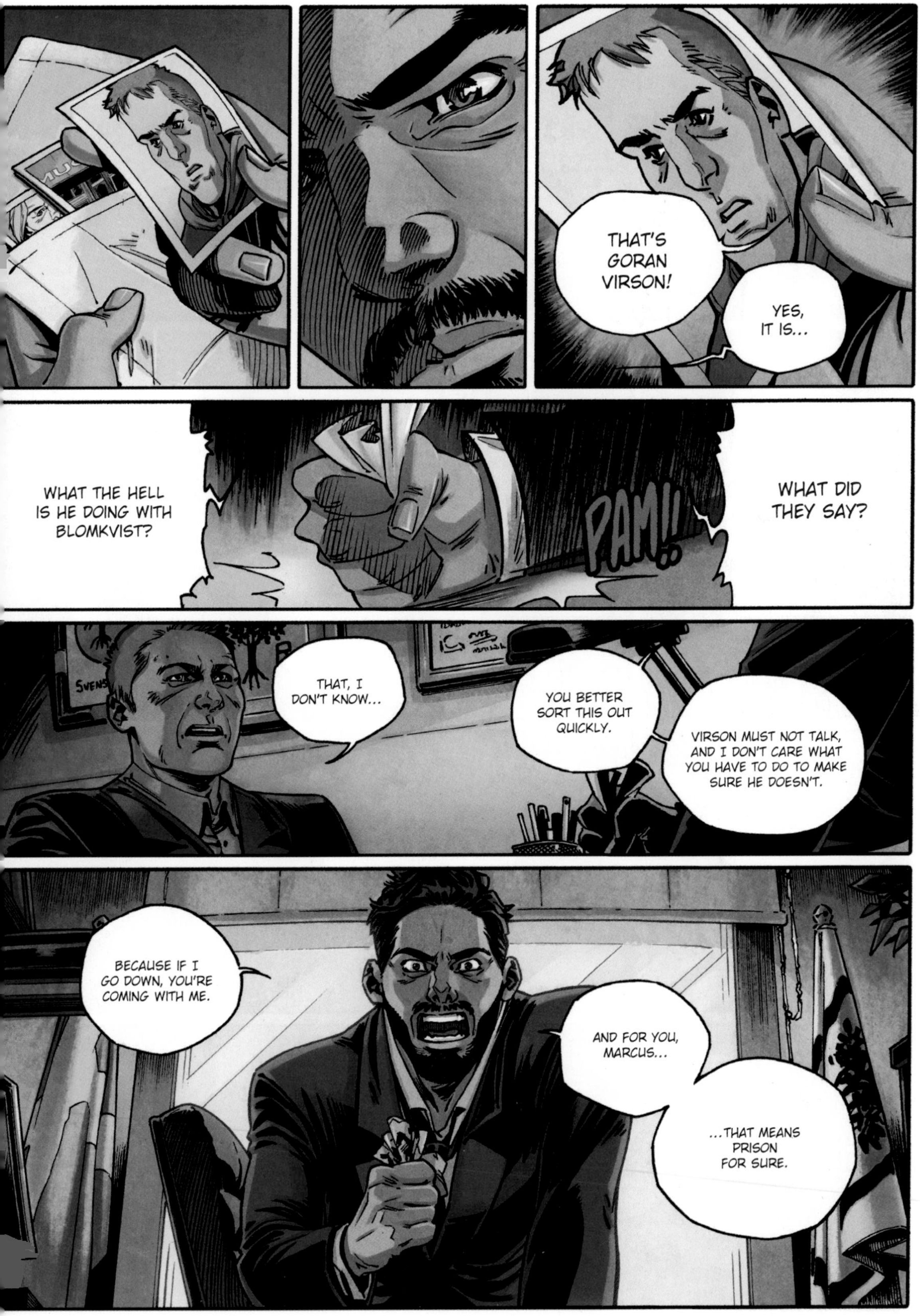
THAT'S GORAN VIRSON!
YES, IT IS...
WHAT THE HELL IS HE DOING WITH BLOMKVIST?
PAM!!
WHAT DID THEY SAY?
THAT, I DON'T KNOW...
YOU BETTER SORT THIS OUT QUICKLY.
VIRSON MUST NOT TALK, AND I DON'T CARE WHAT YOU HAVE TO DO TO MAKE SURE HE DOESN'T.
BECAUSE IF I GO DOWN, YOU'RE COMING WITH ME.
AND FOR YOU, MARCUS...
...THAT MEANS PRISON FOR SURE.

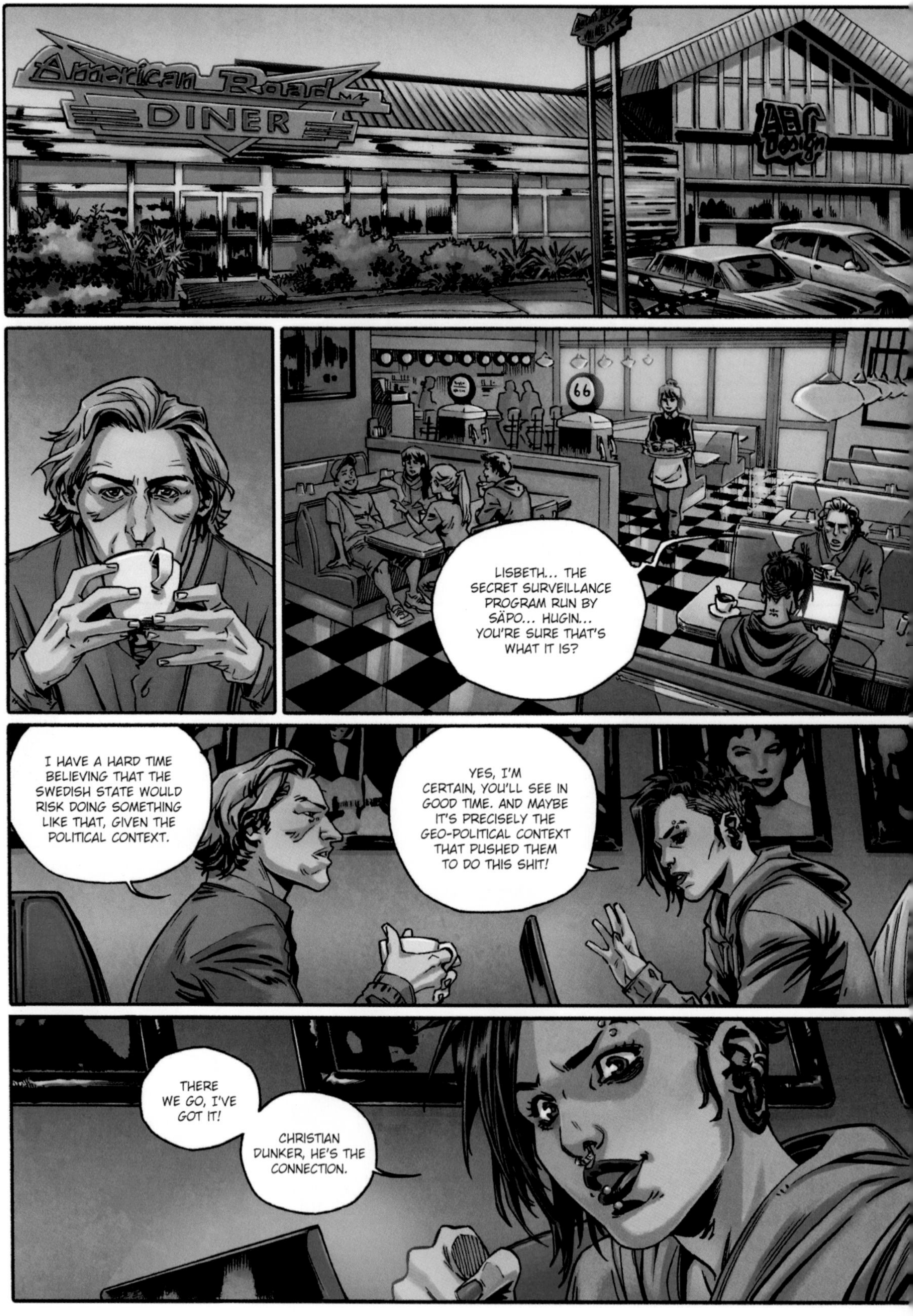
American Road
DINER
LISBETH... THE SECRET SURVEILLANCE PROGRAM RUN BY SÄPO... HUGIN... YOU'RE SURE THAT'S WHAT IT IS?
I HAVE A HARD TIME BELIEVING THAT THE SWEDISH STATE WOULD RISK DOING SOMETHING LIKE THAT, GIVEN THE POLITICAL CONTEXT.
YES, I'M CERTAIN, YOU'LL SEE IN GOOD TIME. AND MAYBE IT'S PRECISELY THE GEO-POLITICAL CONTEXT THAT PUSHED THEM TO DO THIS SHIT!
THERE WE GO, I'VE GOT IT!
CHRISTIAN DUNKER, HE'S THE CONNECTION.

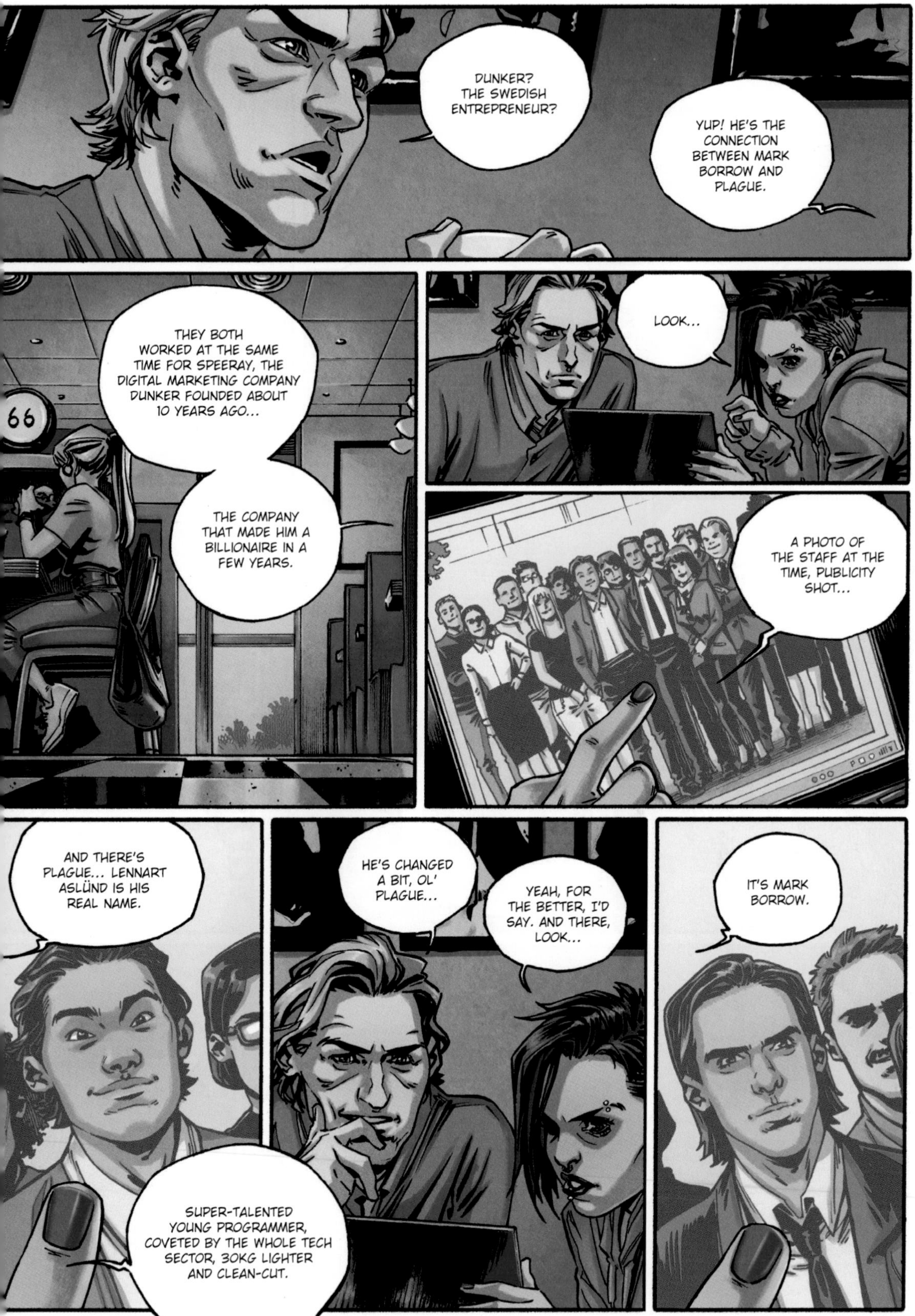
DUNKER? THE SWEDISH ENTREPRENEUR?
YUP! HE'S THE CONNECTION BETWEEN MARK BORROW AND PLAGUE.
THEY BOTH WORKED AT THE SAME TIME FOR SPEERAY, THE DIGITAL MARKETING COMPANY DUNKER FOUNDED ABOUT 10 YEARS AGO...
THE COMPANY THAT MADE HIM A BILLIONAIRE IN A FEW YEARS.
66
LOOK...
A PHOTO OF THE STAFF AT THE TIME, PUBLICITY SHOT...
AND THERE'S PLAGUE... LENNART ASLÜND IS HIS REAL NAME.
SUPER-TALENTED YOUNG PROGRAMMER, COVETED BY THE WHOLE TECH SECTOR, 30KG LIGHTER AND CLEAN-CUT.
HE'S CHANGED A BIT, OL' PLAGUE...
YEAH, FOR THE BETTER, I'D SAY. AND THERE, LOOK...
IT'S MARK BORROW.

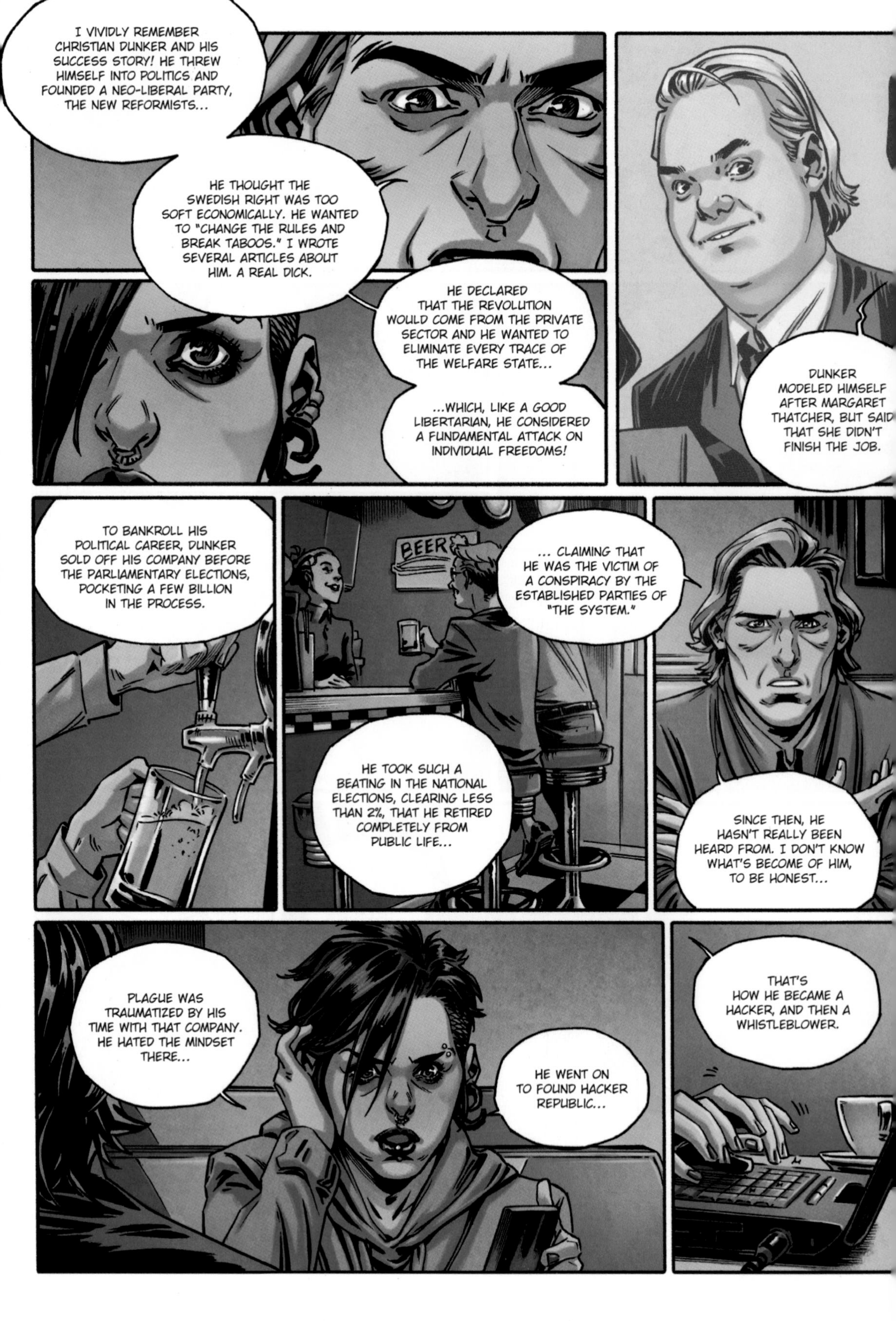
I VIVIDLY REMEMBER CHRISTIAN DUNKER AND HIS SUCCESS STORY! HE THREW HIMSELF INTO POLITICS AND FOUNDED A NEO-LIBERAL PARTY, THE NEW REFORMISTS...
HE THOUGHT THE SWEDISH RIGHT WAS TOO SOFT ECONOMICALLY. HE WANTED TO "CHANGE THE RULES AND BREAK TABOOS." I WROTE SEVERAL ARTICLES ABOUT HIM. A REAL DICK.
HE DECLARED THAT THE REVOLUTION WOULD COME FROM THE PRIVATE SECTOR AND HE WANTED TO ELIMINATE EVERY TRACE OF THE WELFARE STATE...
...WHICH, LIKE A GOOD LIBERTARIAN, HE CONSIDERED A FUNDAMENTAL ATTACK ON INDIVIDUAL FREEDOMS!
DUNKER MODELED HIMSELF AFTER MARGARET THATCHER, BUT SAID THAT SHE DIDN'T FINISH THE JOB.
TO BANKROLL HIS POLITICAL CAREER, DUNKER SOLD OFF HIS COMPANY BEFORE THE PARLIAMENTARY ELECTIONS, POCKETING A FEW BILLION IN THE PROCESS.
BEER
HE TOOK SUCH A BEATING IN THE NATIONAL ELECTIONS, CLEARING LESS THAN 2%, THAT HE RETIRED COMPLETELY FROM PUBLIC LIFE...
... CLAIMING THAT HE WAS THE VICTIM OF A CONSPIRACY BY THE ESTABLISHED PARTIES OF "THE SYSTEM."
SINCE THEN, HE HASN'T REALLY BEEN HEARD FROM. I DON'T KNOW WHAT'S BECOME OF HIM, TO BE HONEST...
PLAGUE WAS TRAUMATIZED BY HIS TIME WITH THAT COMPANY. HE HATED THE MINDSET THERE...
HE WENT ON TO FOUND HACKER REPUBLIC...
THAT'S HOW HE BECAME A HACKER, AND THEN A WHISTLEBLOWER.

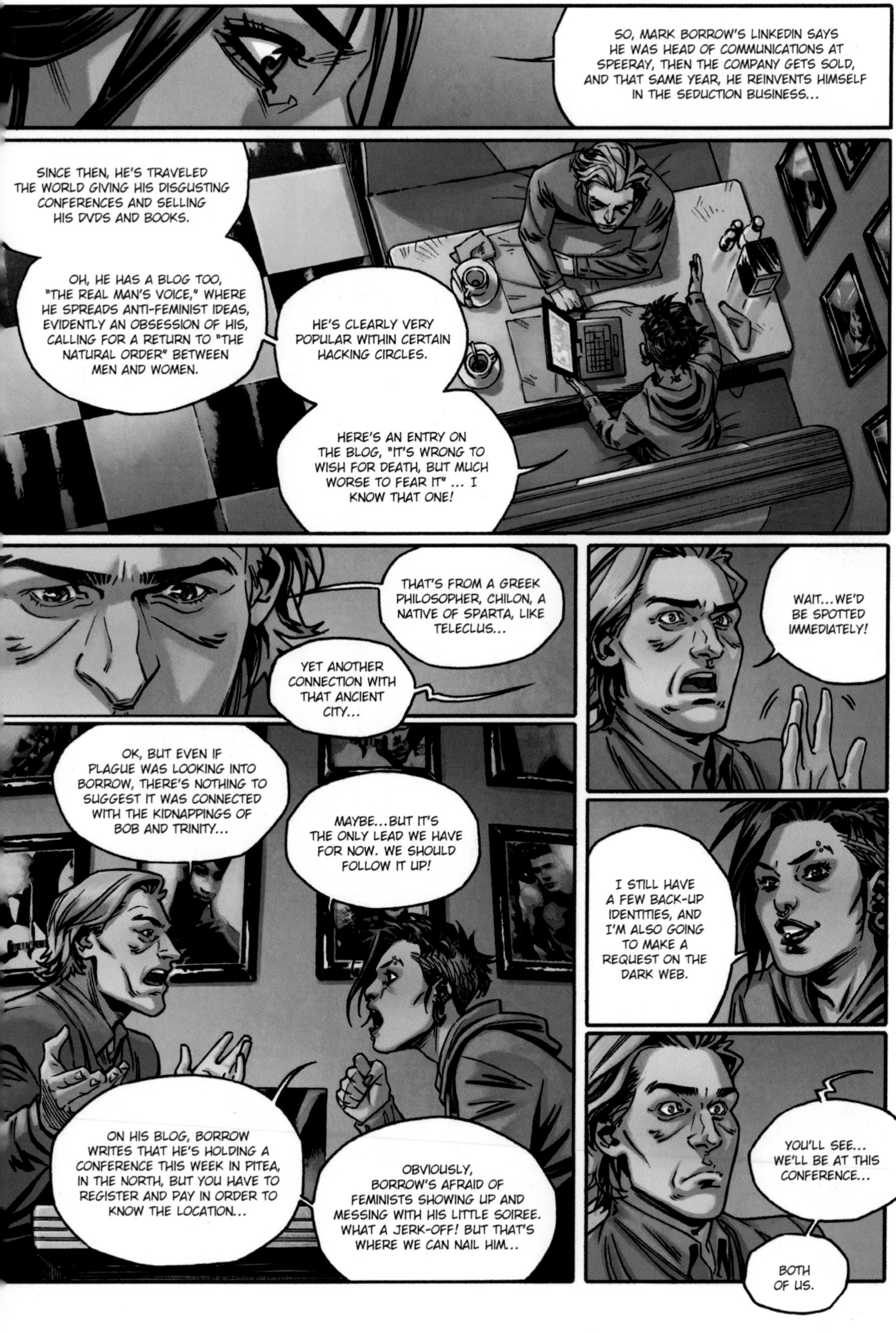

SO, MARK BORROW'S LINKEDIN SAYS HE WAS HEAD OF COMMUNICATIONS AT SPEERAY, THEN THE COMPANY GETS SOLD, AND THAT SAME YEAR, HE REINVENTS HIMSELF IN THE SEDUCTION BUSINESS...
SINCE THEN, HE'S TRAVELED THE WORLD GIVING HIS DISGUSTING CONFERENCES AND SELLING HIS DVDS AND BOOKS.
OH, HE HAS A BLOG TOO, "THE REAL MAN'S VOICE," WHERE HE SPREADS ANTI-FEMINIST IDEAS, EVIDENTLY AN OBSESSION OF HIS, CALLING FOR A RETURN TO "THE NATURAL ORDER" BETWEEN MEN AND WOMEN.
HE'S CLEARLY VERY POPULAR WITHIN CERTAIN HACKING CIRCLES.
HERE'S AN ENTRY ON THE BLOG, "IT'S WRONG TO WISH FOR DEATH, BUT MUCH WORSE TO FEAR IT" ... I KNOW THAT ONE!
THAT'S FROM A GREEK PHILOSOPHER, CHILON, A NATIVE OF SPARTA, LIKE TELECLUS...
YET ANOTHER CONNECTION WITH THAT ANCIENT CITY...
OK, BUT EVEN IF PLAGUE WAS LOOKING INTO BORROW, THERE'S NOTHING TO SUGGEST IT WAS CONNECTED WITH THE KIDNAPPINGS OF BOB AND TRINITY...
MAYBE...BUT IT'S THE ONLY LEAD WE HAVE FOR NOW. WE SHOULD FOLLOW IT UP!
ON HIS BLOG, BORROW WRITES THAT HE'S HOLDING A CONFERENCE THIS WEEK IN PITEA, IN THE NORTH, BUT YOU HAVE TO REGISTER AND PAY IN ORDER TO KNOW THE LOCATION...
OBVIOUSLY, BORROW'S AFRAID OF FEMINISTS SHOWING UP AND MESSING WITH HIS LITTLE SOIREE. WHAT A JERK-OFF! BUT THAT'S WHERE WE CAN NAIL HIM...
WAIT...WE'D BE SPOTTED IMMEDIATELY!
I STILL HAVE A FEW BACK-UP IDENTITIES, AND I'M ALSO GOING TO MAKE A REQUEST ON THE DARK WEB.
YOU'LL SEE... WE'LL BE AT THIS CONFERENCE...
BOTH OF US.

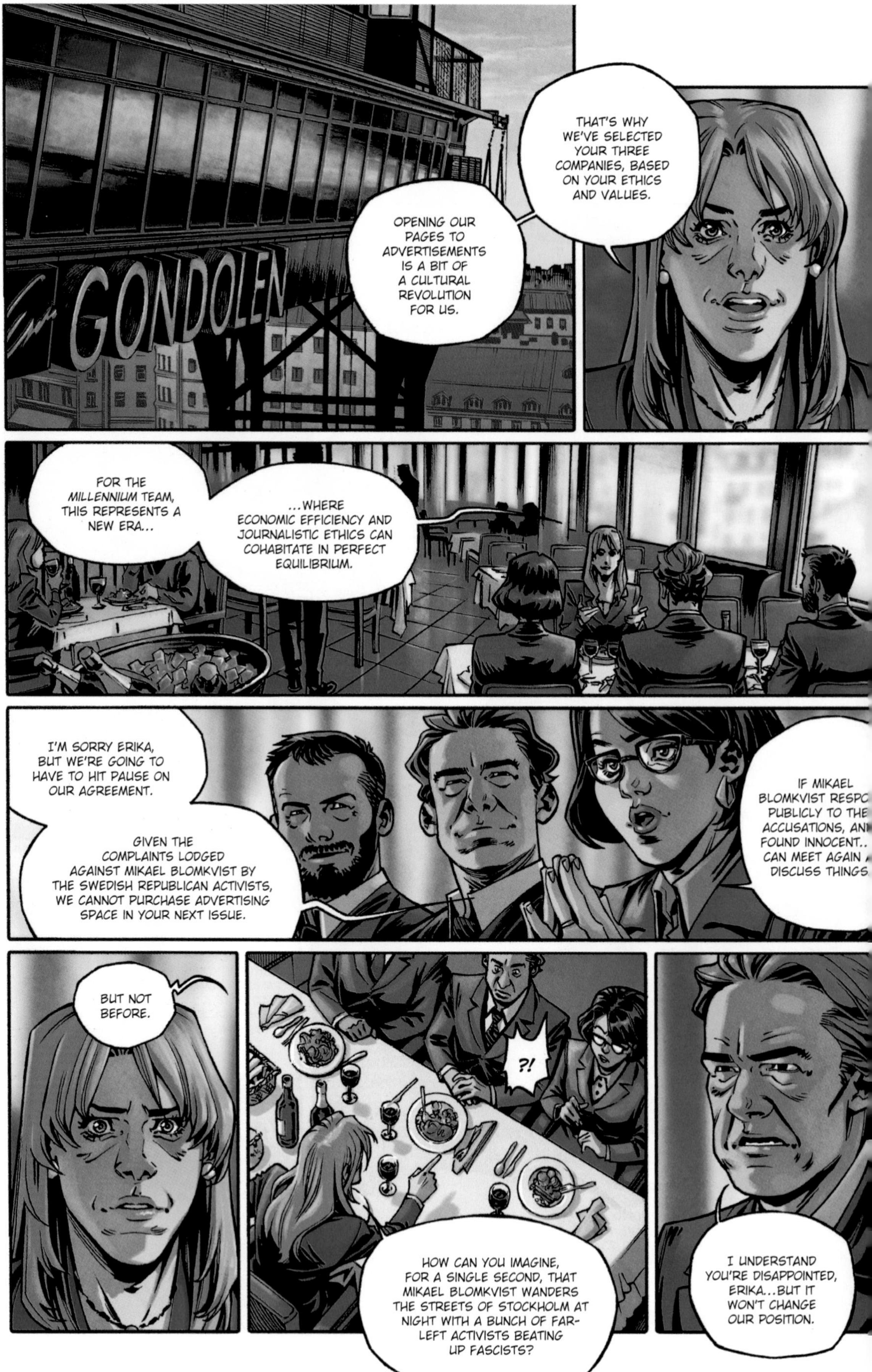

GONDOLEN
OPENING OUR PAGES TO ADVERTISEMENTS IS A BIT OF A CULTURAL REVOLUTION FOR US.
THAT'S WHY WE'VE SELECTED YOUR THREE COMPANIES, BASED ON YOUR ETHICS AND VALUES.
FOR THE MILLENNIUM TEAM, THIS REPRESENTS A NEW ERA...
...WHERE ECONOMIC EFFICIENCY AND JOURNALISTIC ETHICS CAN COHABITATE IN PERFECT EQUILIBRIUM.
I'M SORRY ERIKA, BUT WE'RE GOING TO HAVE TO HIT PAUSE ON OUR AGREEMENT.
GIVEN THE COMPLAINTS LODGED AGAINST MIKAEL BLOMKVIST BY THE SWEDISH REPUBLICAN ACTIVISTS, WE CANNOT PURCHASE ADVERTISING SPACE IN YOUR NEXT ISSUE.
IF MIKAEL BLOMKVIST RESPO PUBLICLY TO THE ACCUSATIONS, AN FOUND INNOCENT.. CAN MEET AGAIN DISCUSS THINGS.
BUT NOT BEFORE.
?!
HOW CAN YOU IMAGINE, FOR A SINGLE SECOND, THAT MIKAEL BLOMKVIST WANDERS THE STREETS OF STOCKHOLM AT NIGHT WITH A BUNCH OF FAR-LEFT ACTIVISTS BEATING UP FASCISTS?
I UNDERSTAND YOU'RE DISAPPOINTED, ERIKA...BUT IT WON'T CHANGE OUR POSITION.

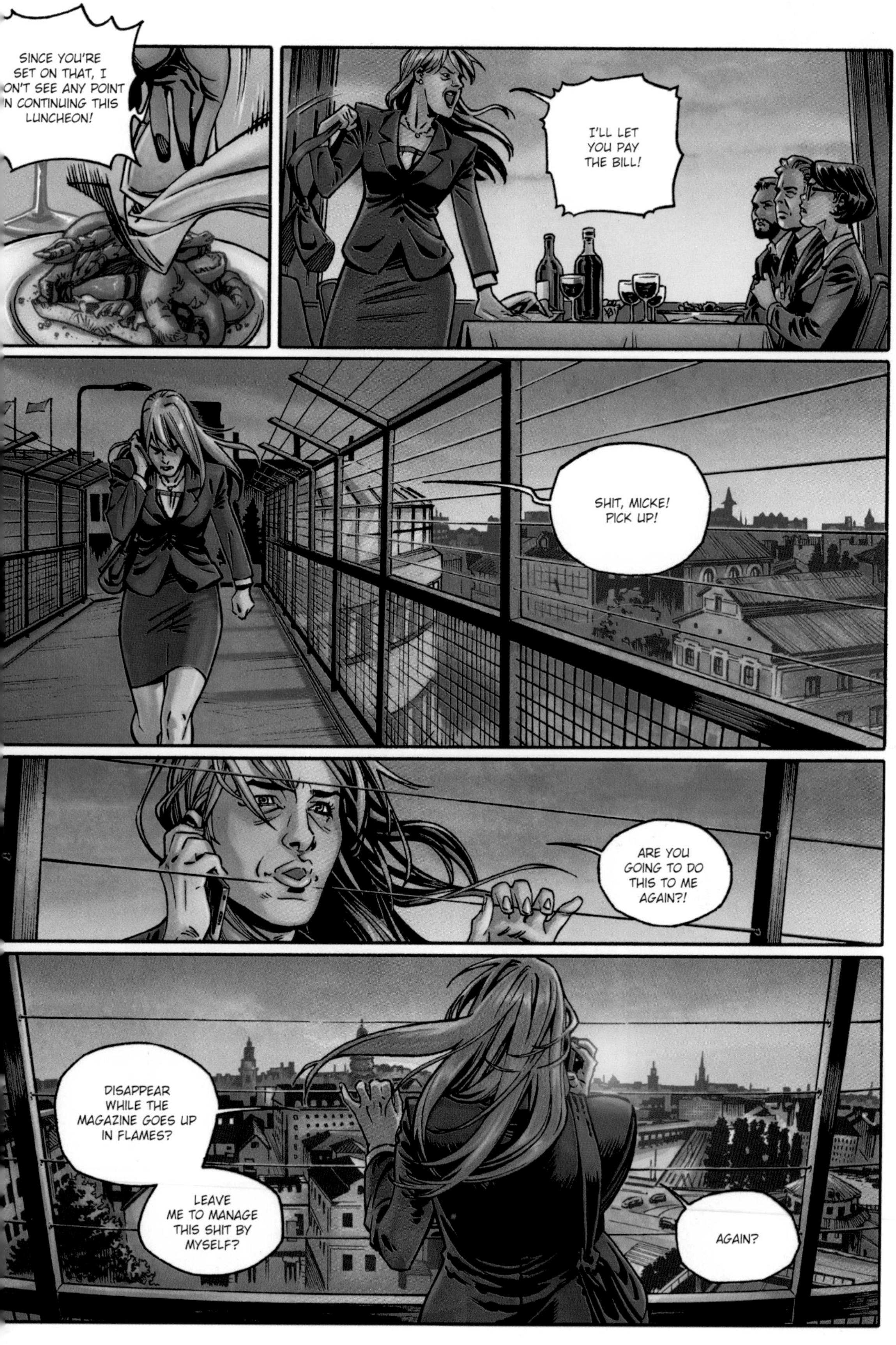
SINCE YOU'RE SET ON THAT, I ON'T SEE ANY POINT N CONTINUING THIS LUNCHEON!
I'LL LET YOU PAY THE BILL!
SHIT, MICKE! PICK UP!
ARE YOU GOING TO DO THIS TO ME AGAIN?!
DISAPPEAR WHILE THE MAGAZINE GOES UP IN FLAMES?
LEAVE ME TO MANAGE THIS SHIT BY MYSELF?
AGAIN?

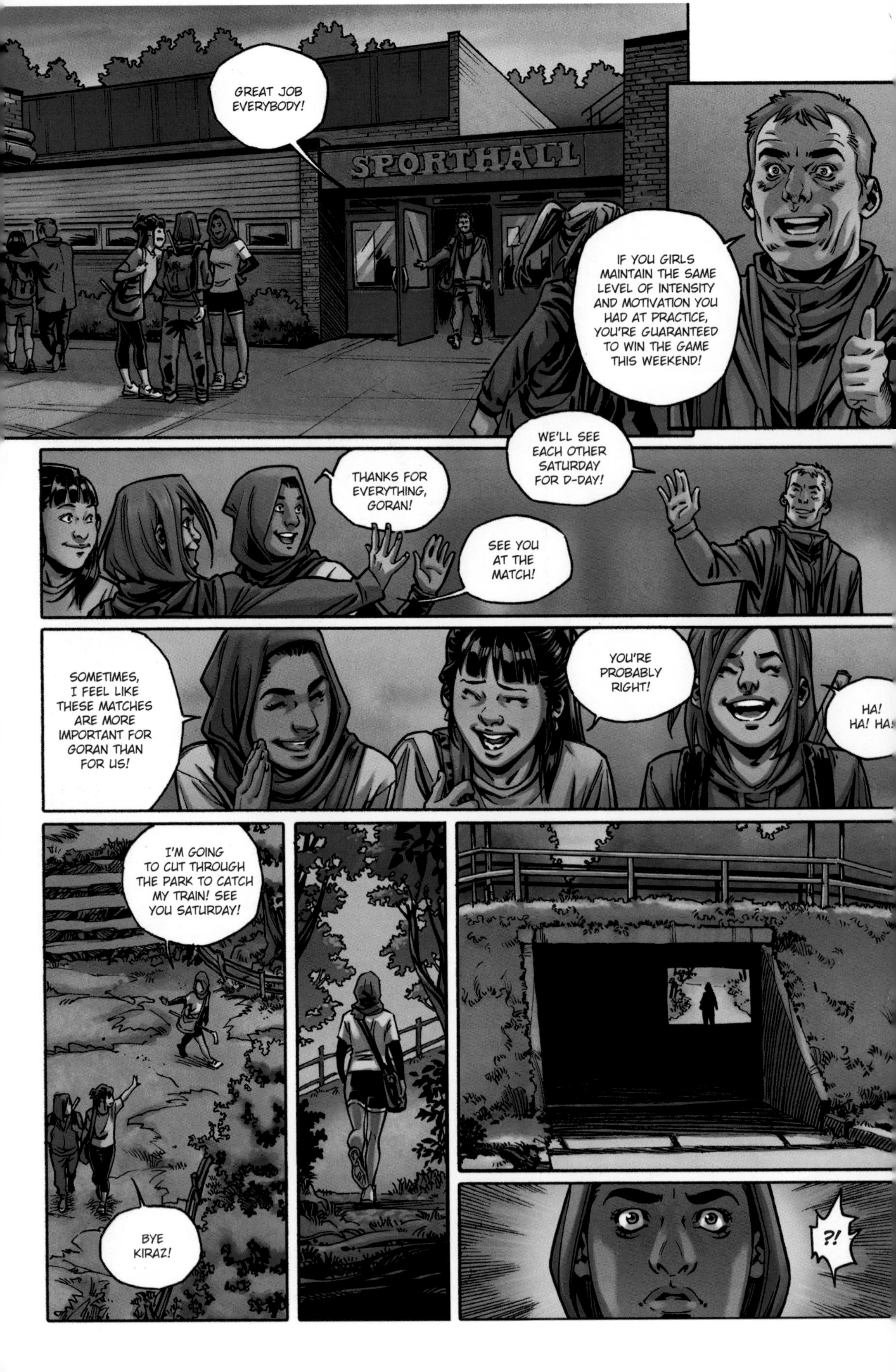
SPORTHALL
GREAT JOB EVERYBODY!
IF YOU GIRLS MAINTAIN THE SAME LEVEL OF INTENSITY AND MOTIVATION YOU HAD AT PRACTICE, YOU'RE GUARANTEED TO WIN THE GAME THIS WEEKEND!
THANKS FOR EVERYTHING, GORAN!
WE'LL SEE EACH OTHER SATURDAY FOR D-DAY!
SEE YOU AT THE MATCH!
SOMETIMES, I FEEL LIKE THESE MATCHES ARE MORE IMPORTANT FOR GORAN THAN FOR US!
YOU'RE PROBABLY RIGHT!
HA! HA! HA!
I'M GOING TO CUT THROUGH THE PARK TO CATCH MY TRAIN! SEE YOU SATURDAY!
BYE KIRAZ!
?!

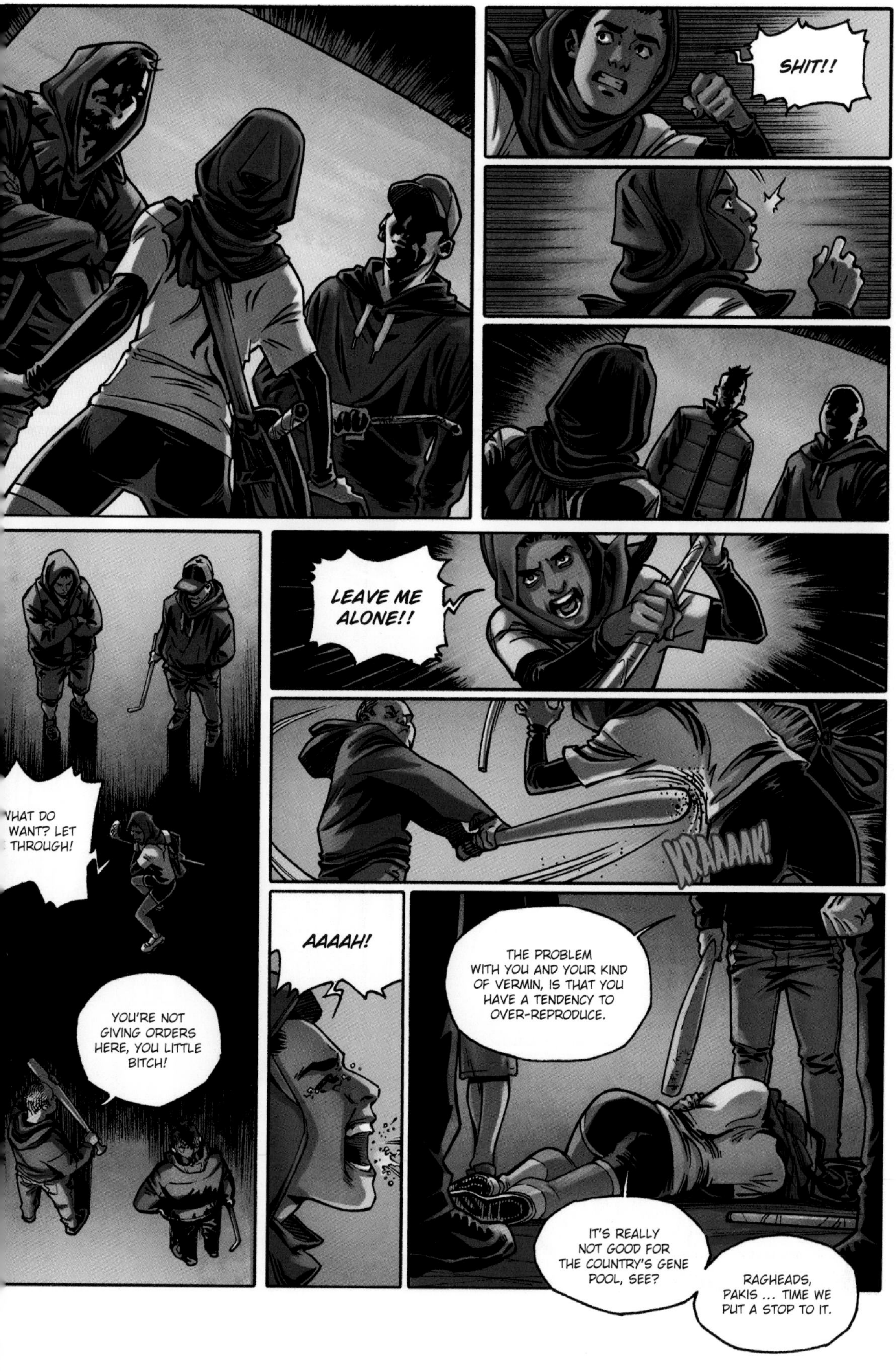
SHIT!!
WHAT DO WANT? LET THROUGH!
YOU'RE NOT GIVING ORDERS HERE, YOU LITTLE BITCH!
LEAVE ME ALONE!!
KRAAAAK!
AAAAH!
THE PROBLEM WITH YOU AND YOUR KIND OF VERMIN, IS THAT YOU HAVE A TENDENCY TO OVER-REPRODUCE.
IT'S REALLY NOT GOOD FOR THE COUNTRY'S GENE POOL, SEE?
RAGHEADS, PAKIS ... TIME WE PUT A STOP TO IT.

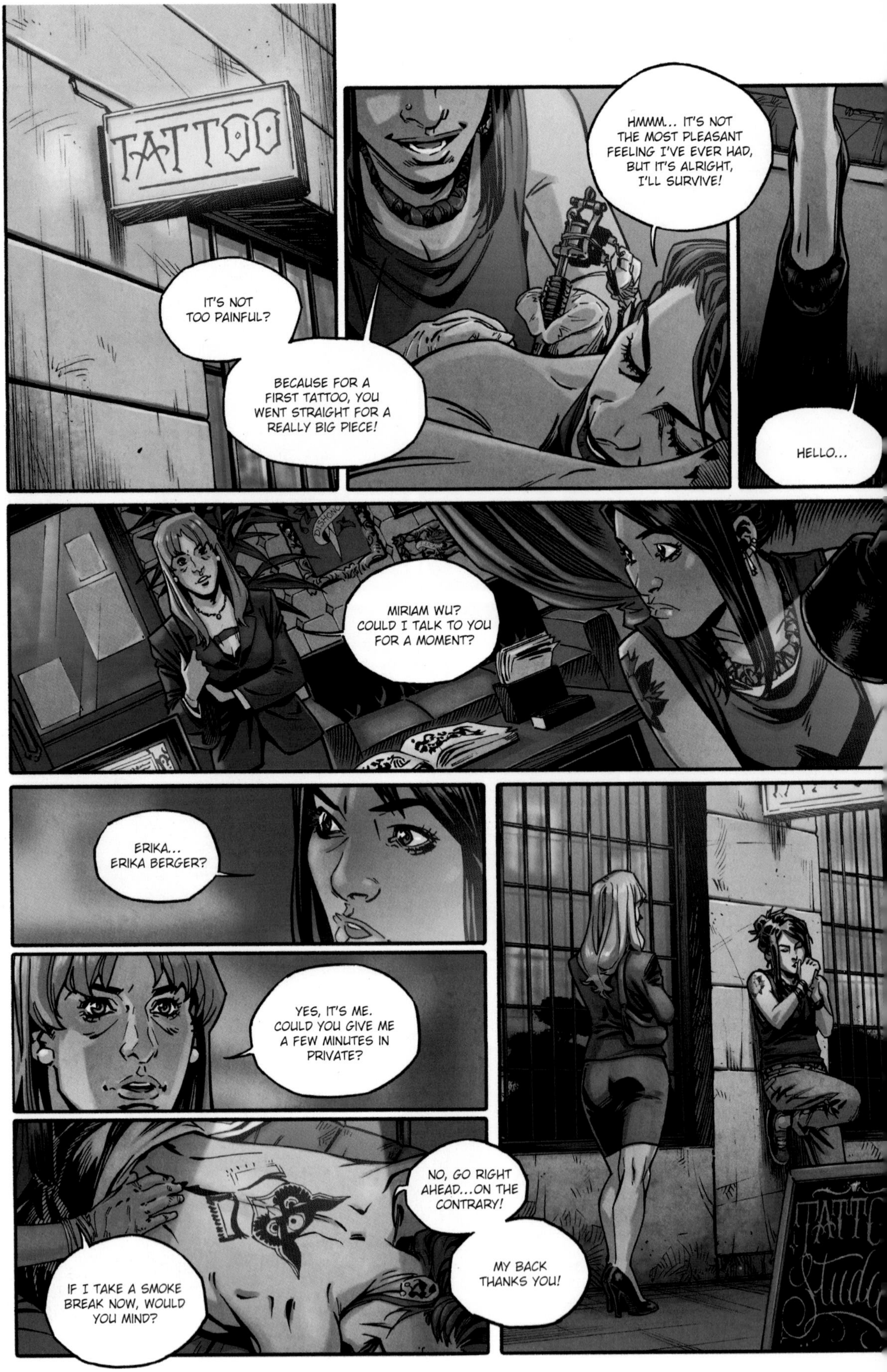
TATTOO
IT'S NOT TOO PAINFUL?
BECAUSE FOR A FIRST TATTOO, YOU WENT STRAIGHT FOR A REALLY BIG PIECE!
HMMM... IT'S NOT THE MOST PLEASANT FEELING I'VE EVER HAD, BUT IT'S ALRIGHT, I'LL SURVIVE!
HELLO...
MIRIAM WU? COULD I TALK TO YOU FOR A MOMENT?
ERIKA... ERIKA BERGER?
YES, IT'S ME. COULD YOU GIVE ME A FEW MINUTES IN PRIVATE?
IF I TAKE A SMOKE BREAK NOW, WOULD YOU MIND?
NO, GO RIGHT AHEAD...ON THE CONTRARY!
MY BACK THANKS YOU!

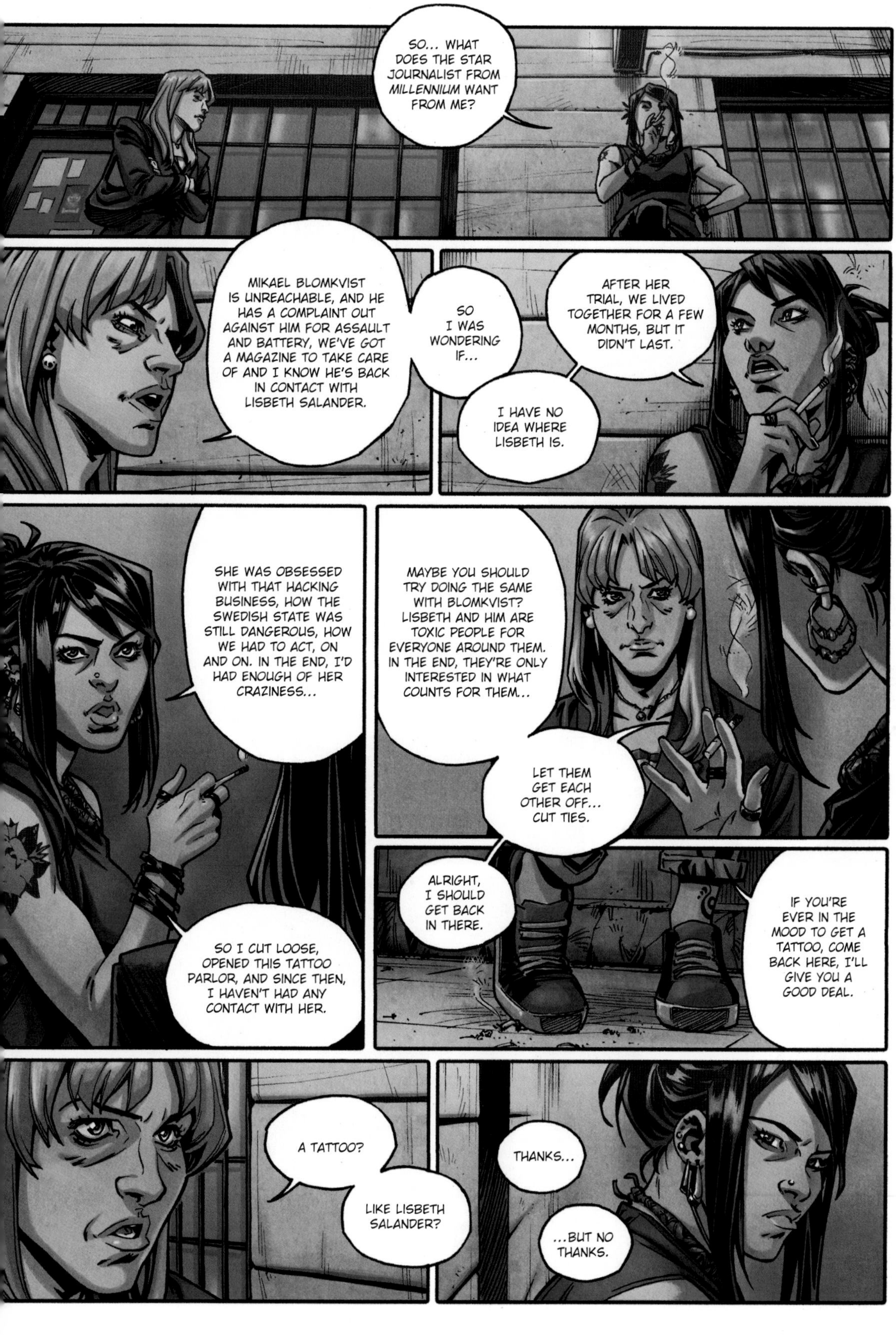
SO... WHAT DOES THE STAR JOURNALIST FROM *MILLENNIUM* WANT FROM ME?
MIKAEL BLOMKVIST IS UNREACHABLE, AND HE HAS A COMPLAINT OUT AGAINST HIM FOR ASSAULT AND BATTERY, WE'VE GOT A MAGAZINE TO TAKE CARE OF AND I KNOW HE'S BACK IN CONTACT WITH LISBETH SALANDER.
SO I WAS WONDERING IF...
I HAVE NO IDEA WHERE LISBETH IS.
AFTER HER TRIAL, WE LIVED TOGETHER FOR A FEW MONTHS, BUT IT DIDN'T LAST.
SHE WAS OBSESSED WITH THAT HACKING BUSINESS, HOW THE SWEDISH STATE WAS STILL DANGEROUS, HOW WE HAD TO ACT, ON AND ON. IN THE END, I'D HAD ENOUGH OF HER CRAZINESS...
SO I CUT LOOSE, OPENED THIS TATTOO PARLOR, AND SINCE THEN, I HAVEN'T HAD ANY CONTACT WITH HER.
MAYBE YOU SHOULD TRY DOING THE SAME WITH BLOMKVIST? LISBETH AND HIM ARE TOXIC PEOPLE FOR EVERYONE AROUND THEM. IN THE END, THEY'RE ONLY INTERESTED IN WHAT COUNTS FOR THEM...
LET THEM GET EACH OTHER OFF... CUT TIES.
ALRIGHT, I SHOULD GET BACK IN THERE.
IF YOU'RE EVER IN THE MOOD TO GET A TATTOO, COME BACK HERE, I'LL GIVE YOU A GOOD DEAL.
A TATTOO?
LIKE LISBETH SALANDER?
THANKS...
...BUT NO THANKS.

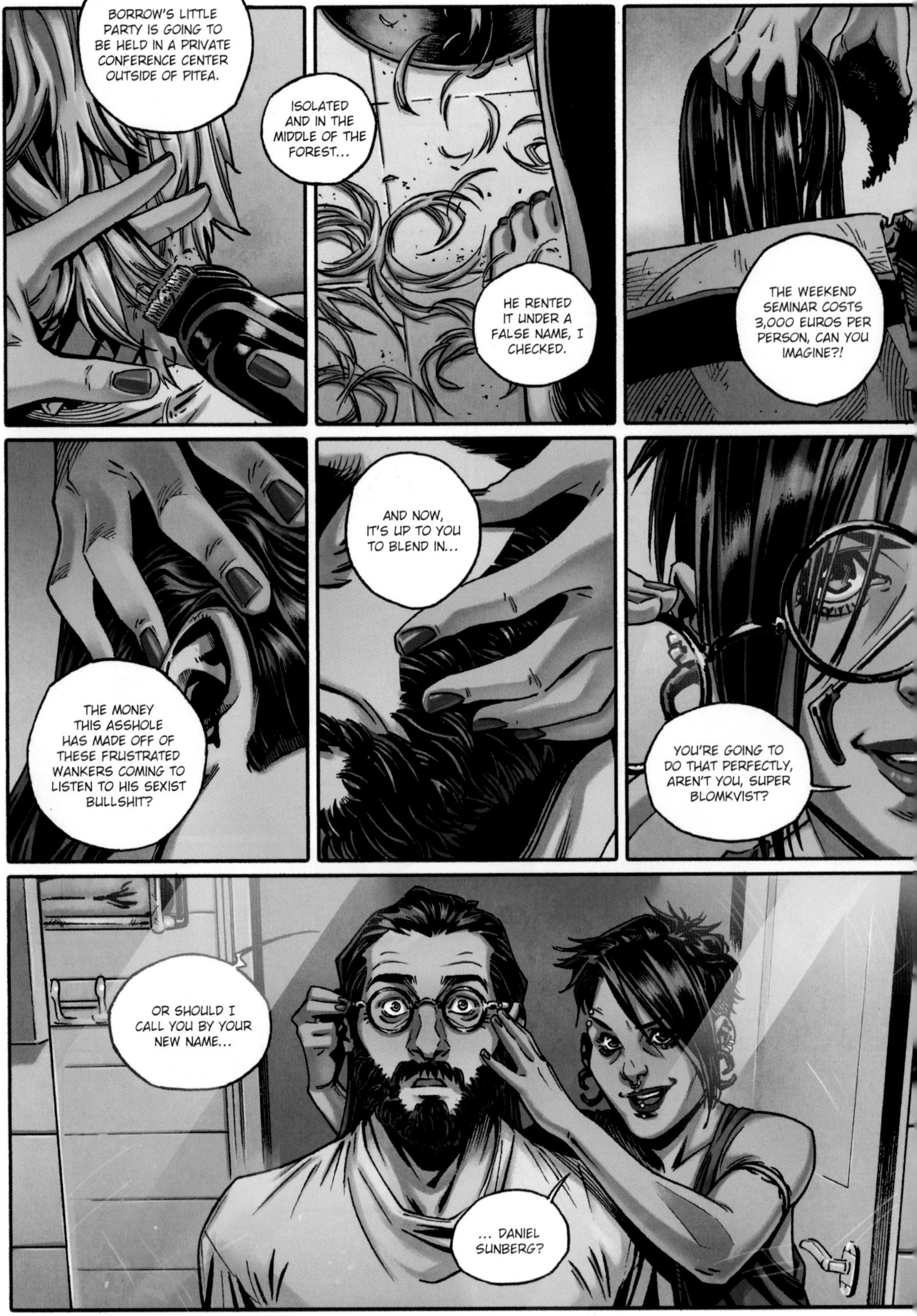
BORROW'S LITTLE PARTY IS GOING TO BE HELD IN A PRIVATE CONFERENCE CENTER OUTSIDE OF PITEA.
ISOLATED AND IN THE MIDDLE OF THE FOREST...
HE RENTED IT UNDER A FALSE NAME, I CHECKED.
THE WEEKEND SEMINAR COSTS 3,000 EUROS PER PERSON, CAN YOU IMAGINE?!
THE MONEY THIS ASSHOLE HAS MADE OFF OF THESE FRUSTRATED WANKERS COMING TO LISTEN TO HIS SEXIST BULLSHIT?
AND NOW, IT'S UP TO YOU TO BLEND IN...
YOU'RE GOING TO DO THAT PERFECTLY, AREN'T YOU, SUPER BLOMKVIST?
OR SHOULD I CALL YOU BY YOUR NEW NAME...
... DANIEL SUNBERG?

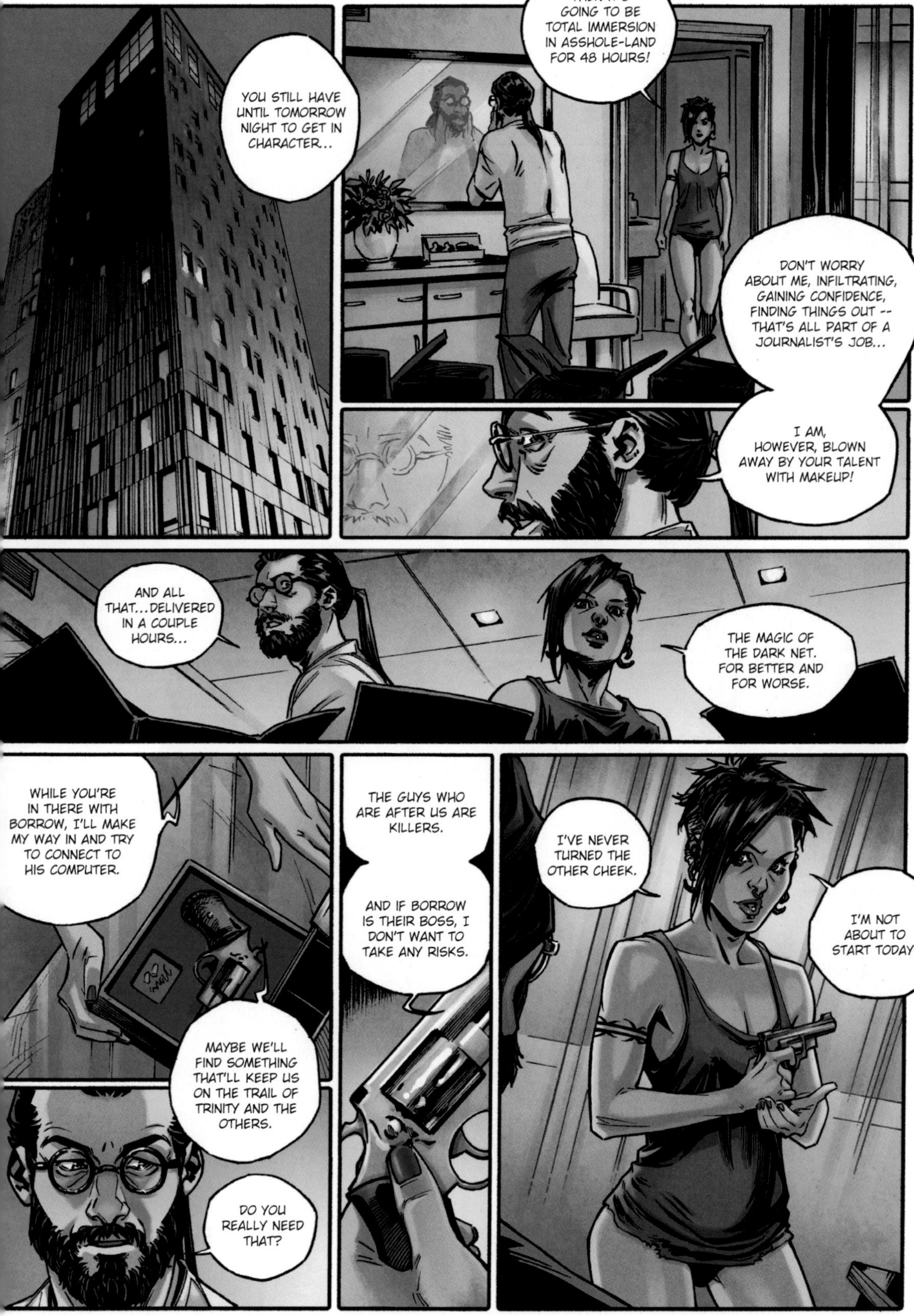
YOU STILL HAVE UNTIL TOMORROW NIGHT TO GET IN CHARACTER...
THEN IT'S GOING TO BE TOTAL IMMERSION IN ASSHOLE-LAND FOR 48 HOURS!
DON'T WORRY ABOUT ME, INFILTRATING, GAINING CONFIDENCE, FINDING THINGS OUT -- THAT'S ALL PART OF A JOURNALIST'S JOB...
I AM, HOWEVER, BLOWN AWAY BY YOUR TALENT WITH MAKEUP!
AND ALL THAT...DELIVERED IN A COUPLE HOURS...
THE MAGIC OF THE DARK NET. FOR BETTER AND FOR WORSE.
WHILE YOU'RE IN THERE WITH BORROW, I'LL MAKE MY WAY IN AND TRY TO CONNECT TO HIS COMPUTER.
MAYBE WE'LL FIND SOMETHING THAT'LL KEEP US ON THE TRAIL OF TRINITY AND THE OTHERS.
DO YOU REALLY NEED THAT?
THE GUYS WHO ARE AFTER US ARE KILLERS.
AND IF BORROW IS THEIR BOSS, I DON'T WANT TO TAKE ANY RISKS.
I'VE NEVER TURNED THE OTHER CHEEK.
I'M NOT ABOUT TO START TODAY.

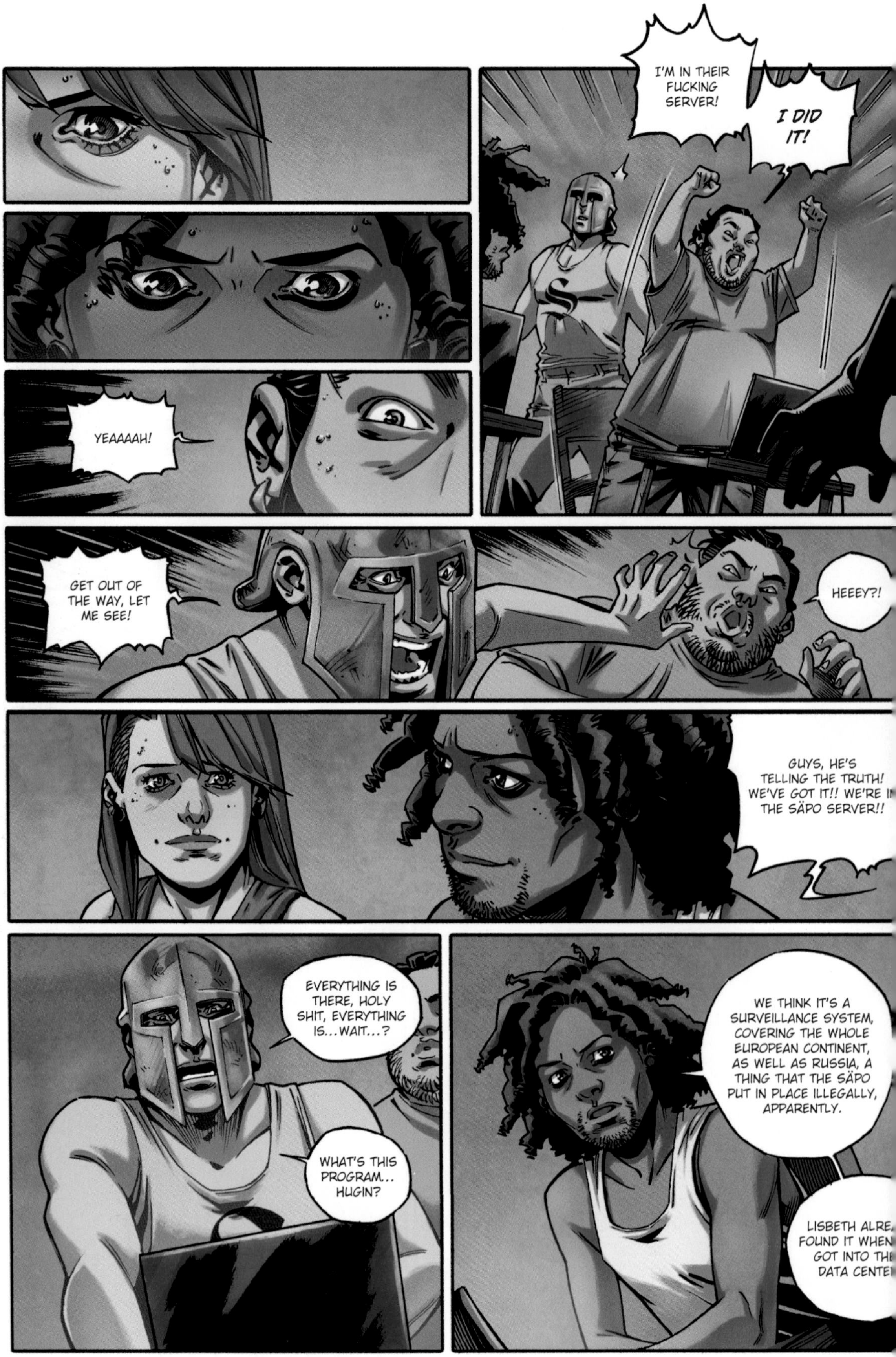

I'M IN THEIR FUCKING SERVER!
I DID IT!
YEAAAAH!
GET OUT OF THE WAY, LET ME SEE!
HEEEY?!
GUYS, HE'S TELLING THE TRUTH! WE'VE GOT IT!! WE'RE I
THE SÄPO SERVER!!
EVERYTHING IS THERE, HOLY SHIT, EVERYTHING IS...WAIT...?
WHAT'S THIS PROGRAM... HUGIN?
WE THINK IT'S A SURVEILLANCE SYSTEM, COVERING THE WHOLE EUROPEAN CONTINENT, AS WELL AS RUSSIA, A THING THAT THE SÄPO PUT IN PLACE ILLEGALLY, APPARENTLY.
LISBETH ALRE FOUND IT WHEN GOT INTO THE DATA CENTE

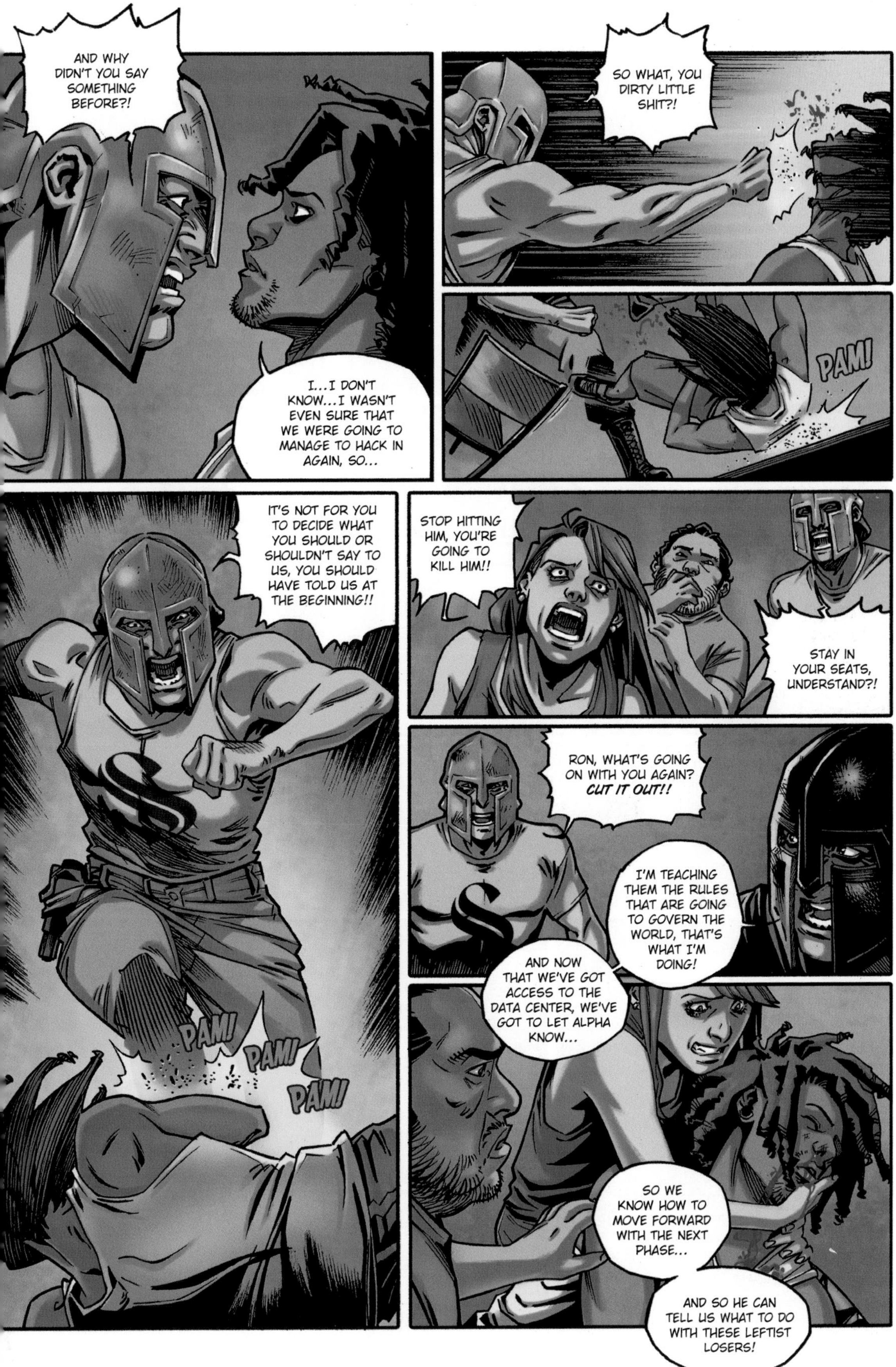
AND WHY DIDN'T YOU SAY SOMETHING BEFORE?!
I...I DON'T KNOW...I WASN'T EVEN SURE THAT WE WERE GOING TO MANAGE TO HACK IN AGAIN, SO...
SO WHAT, YOU DIRTY LITTLE SHIT?!
PAM!
IT'S NOT FOR YOU TO DECIDE WHAT YOU SHOULD OR SHOULDN'T SAY TO US, YOU SHOULD HAVE TOLD US AT THE BEGINNING!!
PAM!
PAM!
PAM!
STOP HITTING HIM, YOU'RE GOING TO KILL HIM!!
STAY IN YOUR SEATS, UNDERSTAND?!
RON, WHAT'S GOING ON WITH YOU AGAIN? ***CUT IT OUT!!***
I'M TEACHING THEM THE RULES THAT ARE GOING TO GOVERN THE WORLD, THAT'S WHAT I'M DOING!
AND NOW THAT WE'VE GOT ACCESS TO THE DATA CENTER, WE'VE GOT TO LET ALPHA KNOW...
SO WE KNOW HOW TO MOVE FORWARD WITH THE NEXT PHASE...
AND SO HE CAN TELL US WHAT TO DO WITH THESE LEFTIST LOSERS!

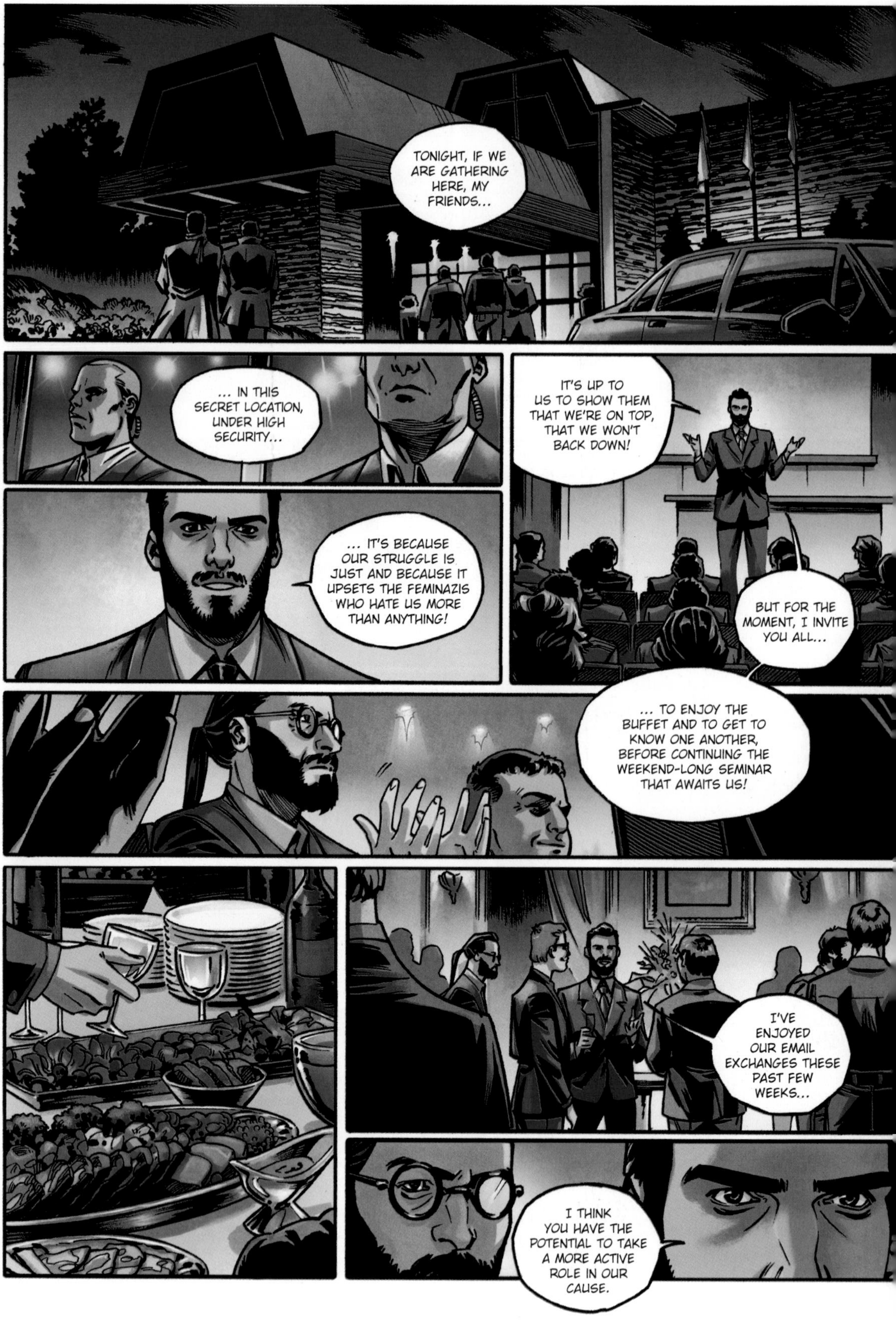
TONIGHT, IF WE ARE GATHERING HERE, MY FRIENDS...
... IN THIS SECRET LOCATION, UNDER HIGH SECURITY...
... IT'S BECAUSE OUR STRUGGLE IS JUST AND BECAUSE IT UPSETS THE FEMINAZIS WHO HATE US MORE THAN ANYTHING!
IT'S UP TO US TO SHOW THEM THAT WE'RE ON TOP, THAT WE WON'T BACK DOWN!
BUT FOR THE MOMENT, I INVITE YOU ALL...
... TO ENJOY THE BUFFET AND TO GET TO KNOW ONE ANOTHER, BEFORE CONTINUING THE WEEKEND-LONG SEMINAR THAT AWAITS US!
I'VE ENJOYED OUR EMAIL EXCHANGES THESE PAST FEW WEEKS...
I THINK YOU HAVE THE POTENTIAL TO TAKE A MORE ACTIVE ROLE IN OUR CAUSE.

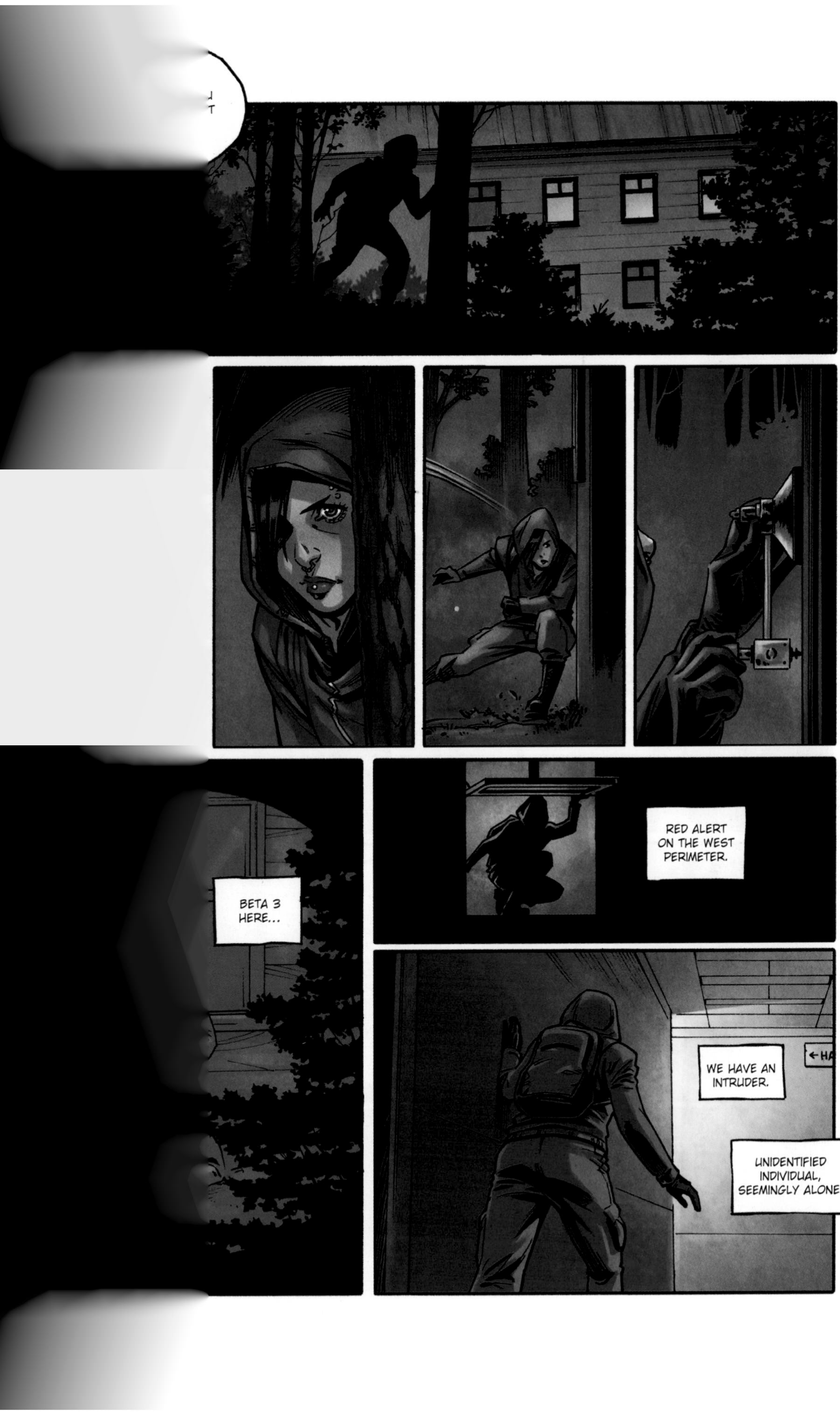
BETA 3 HERE...
RED ALERT ON THE WEST PERIMETER.
WE HAVE AN INTRUDER.
UNIDENTIFIED INDIVIDUAL, SEEMINGLY ALONE.

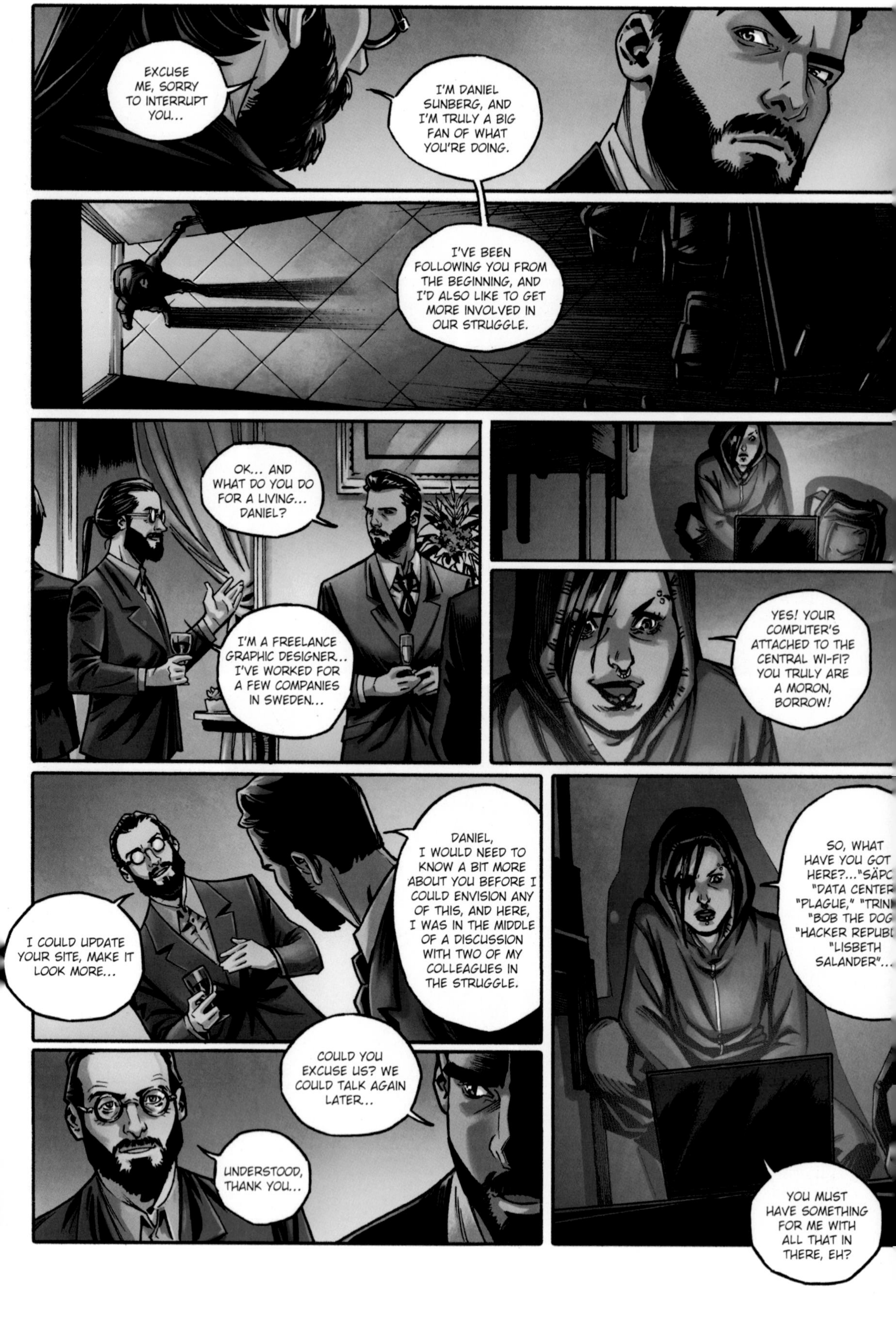

EXCUSE ME, SORRY TO INTERRUPT YOU...
I'M DANIEL SUNBERG, AND I'M TRULY A BIG FAN OF WHAT YOU'RE DOING.
I'VE BEEN FOLLOWING YOU FROM THE BEGINNING, AND I'D ALSO LIKE TO GET MORE INVOLVED IN OUR STRUGGLE.
OK... AND WHAT DO YOU DO FOR A LIVING... DANIEL?
I'M A FREELANCE GRAPHIC DESIGNER... I'VE WORKED FOR A FEW COMPANIES IN SWEDEN...
YES! YOUR COMPUTER'S ATTACHED TO THE CENTRAL WI-FI? YOU TRULY ARE A MORON, BORROW!
I COULD UPDATE YOUR SITE, MAKE IT LOOK MORE...
DANIEL, I WOULD NEED TO KNOW A BIT MORE ABOUT YOU BEFORE I COULD ENVISION ANY OF THIS, AND HERE, I WAS IN THE MIDDLE OF A DISCUSSION WITH TWO OF MY COLLEAGUES IN THE STRUGGLE.
COULD YOU EXCUSE US? WE COULD TALK AGAIN LATER..
UNDERSTOOD, THANK YOU...
YOU MUST HAVE SOMETHING FOR ME WITH ALL THAT IN THERE, EH?

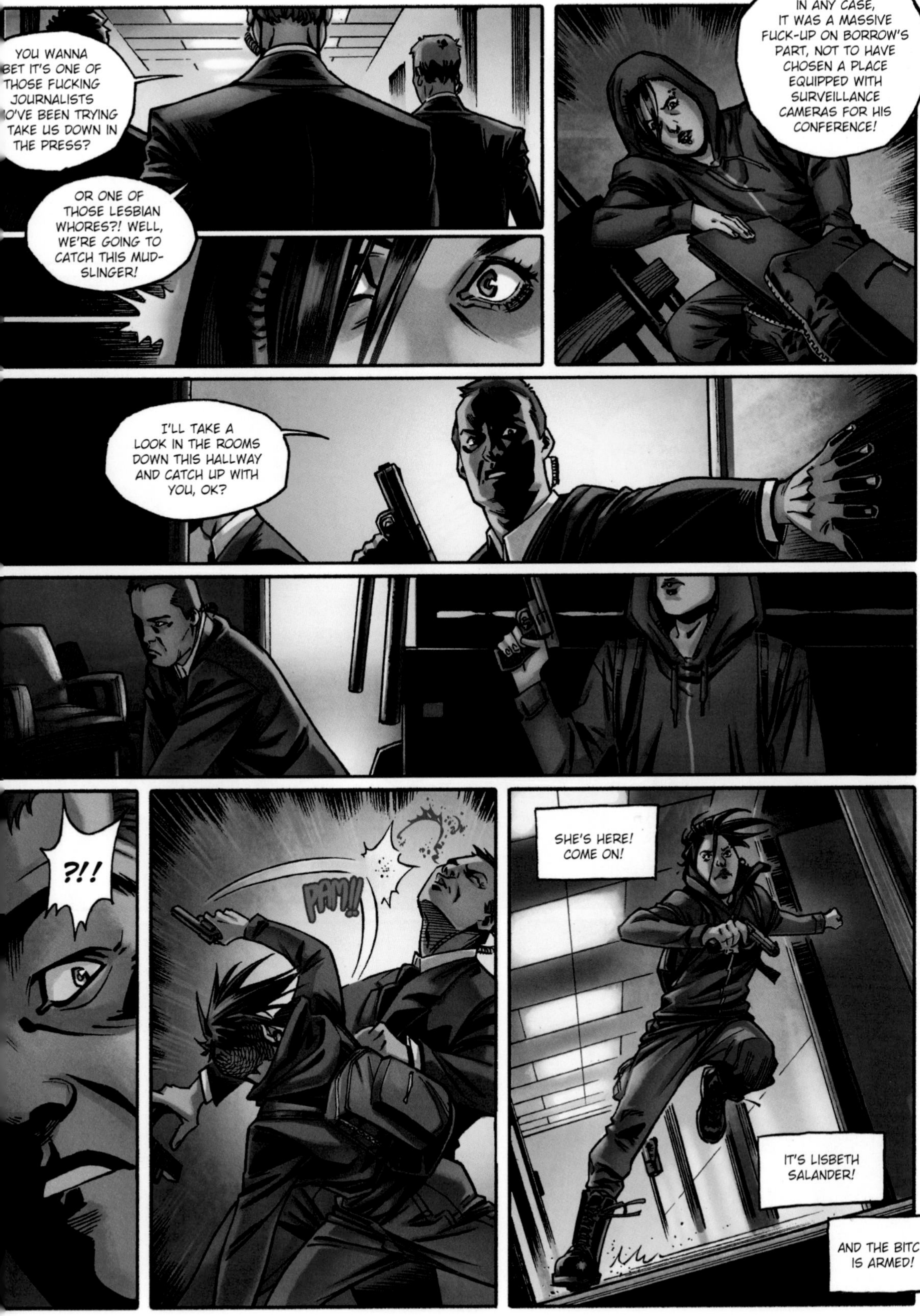
YOU WANNA BET IT'S ONE OF THOSE FUCKING JOURNALISTS O'VE BEEN TRYING TAKE US DOWN IN THE PRESS?
OR ONE OF THOSE LESBIAN WHORES?! WELL, WE'RE GOING TO CATCH THIS MUD-SLINGER!
IN ANY CASE, IT WAS A MASSIVE FUCK-UP ON BORROW'S PART, NOT TO HAVE CHOSEN A PLACE EQUIPPED WITH SURVEILLANCE CAMERAS FOR HIS CONFERENCE!
I'LL TAKE A LOOK IN THE ROOMS DOWN THIS HALLWAY AND CATCH UP WITH YOU, OK?
?!!
PAM!!
SHE'S HERE! COME ON!
IT'S LISBETH SALANDER!
AND THE BITCH IS ARMED!

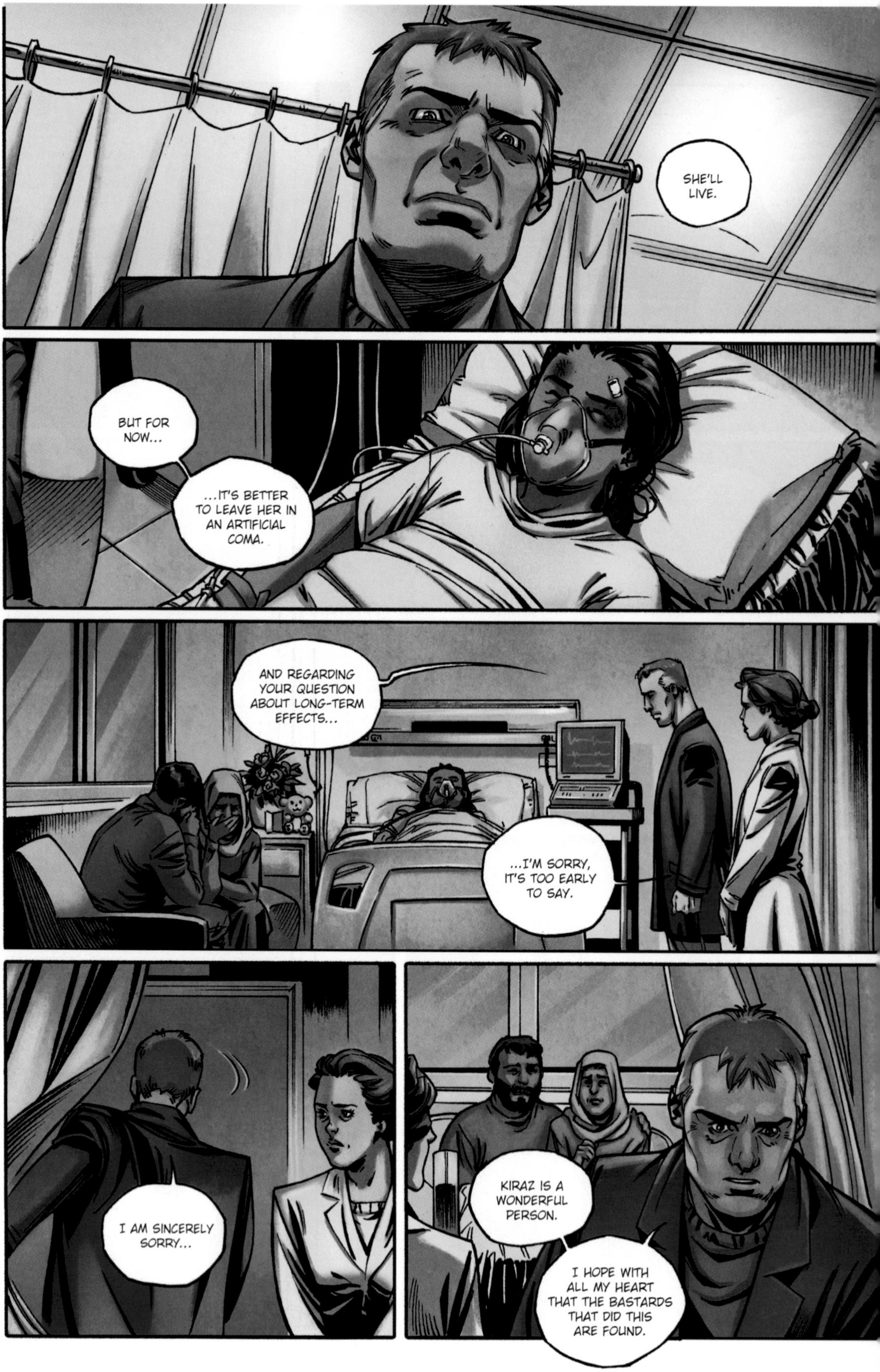
SHE'LL LIVE.
BUT FOR NOW...
...IT'S BETTER TO LEAVE HER IN AN ARTIFICIAL COMA.
AND REGARDING YOUR QUESTION ABOUT LONG-TERM EFFECTS...
...I'M SORRY, IT'S TOO EARLY TO SAY.
I AM SINCERELY SORRY...
KIRAZ IS A WONDERFUL PERSON.
I HOPE WITH ALL MY HEART THAT THE BASTARDS THAT DID THIS ARE FOUND.

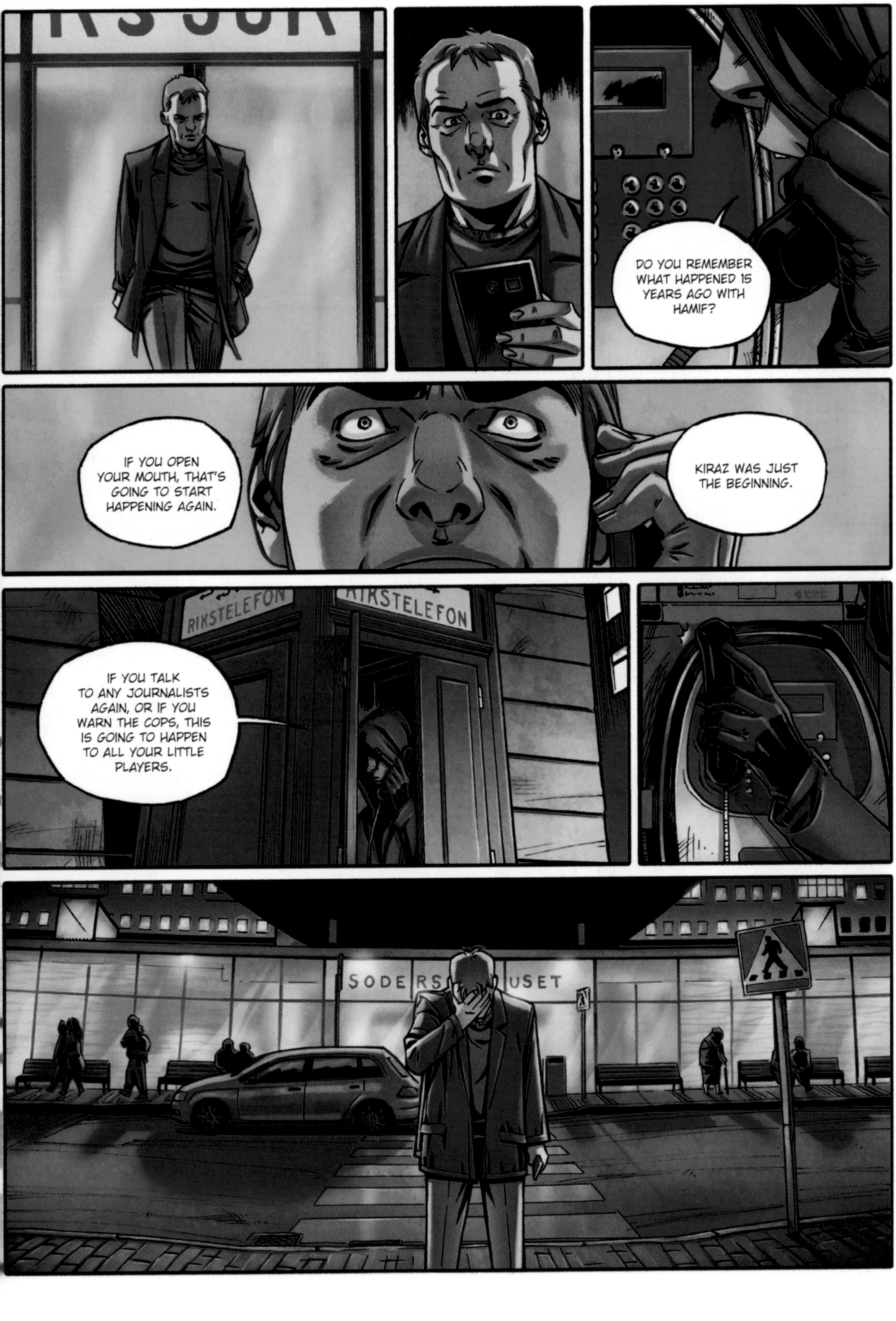
RS SÖK
DO YOU REMEMBER WHAT HAPPENED 15 YEARS AGO WITH HAMIF?
IF YOU OPEN YOUR MOUTH, THAT'S GOING TO START HAPPENING AGAIN.
KIRAZ WAS JUST THE BEGINNING.
RIKSTELEFON
RIKSTELEFON
IF YOU TALK TO ANY JOURNALISTS AGAIN, OR IF YOU WARN THE COPS, THIS IS GOING TO HAPPEN TO ALL YOUR LITTLE PLAYERS.
SODERS USET

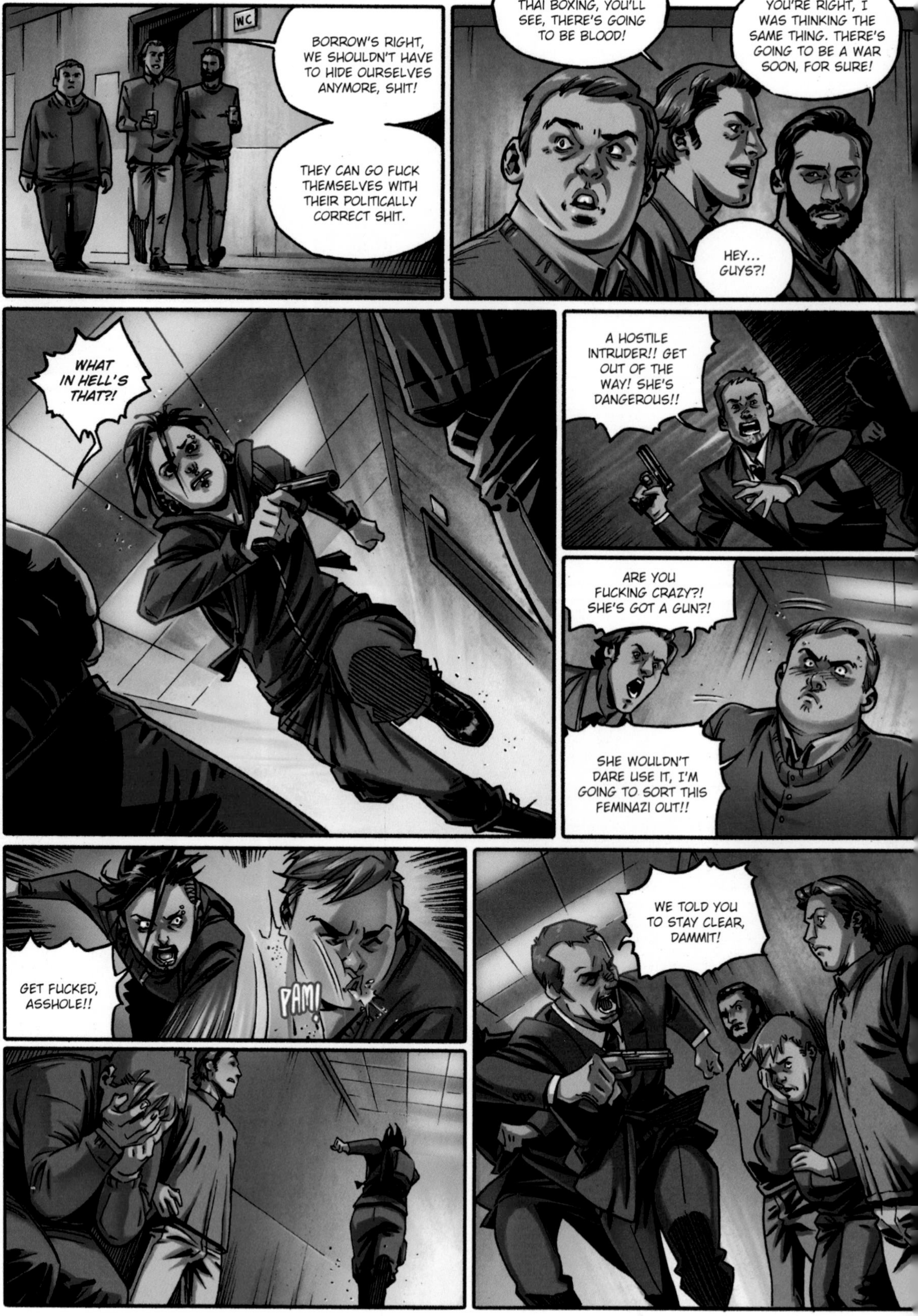
BORROW'S RIGHT, WE SHOULDN'T HAVE TO HIDE OURSELVES ANYMORE, SHIT!
THEY CAN GO FUCK THEMSELVES WITH THEIR POLITICALLY CORRECT SHIT.
I'VE BEEN DOING THAI BOXING, YOU'LL SEE, THERE'S GOING TO BE BLOOD!
YOU'RE RIGHT, I WAS THINKING THE SAME THING. THERE'S GOING TO BE A WAR SOON, FOR SURE!
HEY... GUYS?!
WHAT IN HELL'S THAT?!
A HOSTILE INTRUDER!! GET OUT OF THE WAY! SHE'S DANGEROUS!!
ARE YOU FUCKING CRAZY?! SHE'S GOT A GUN?!
SHE WOULDN'T DARE USE IT, I'M GOING TO SORT THIS FEMINAZI OUT!!
GET FUCKED, ASSHOLE!!
PAM!
WE TOLD YOU TO STAY CLEAR, DAMMIT!

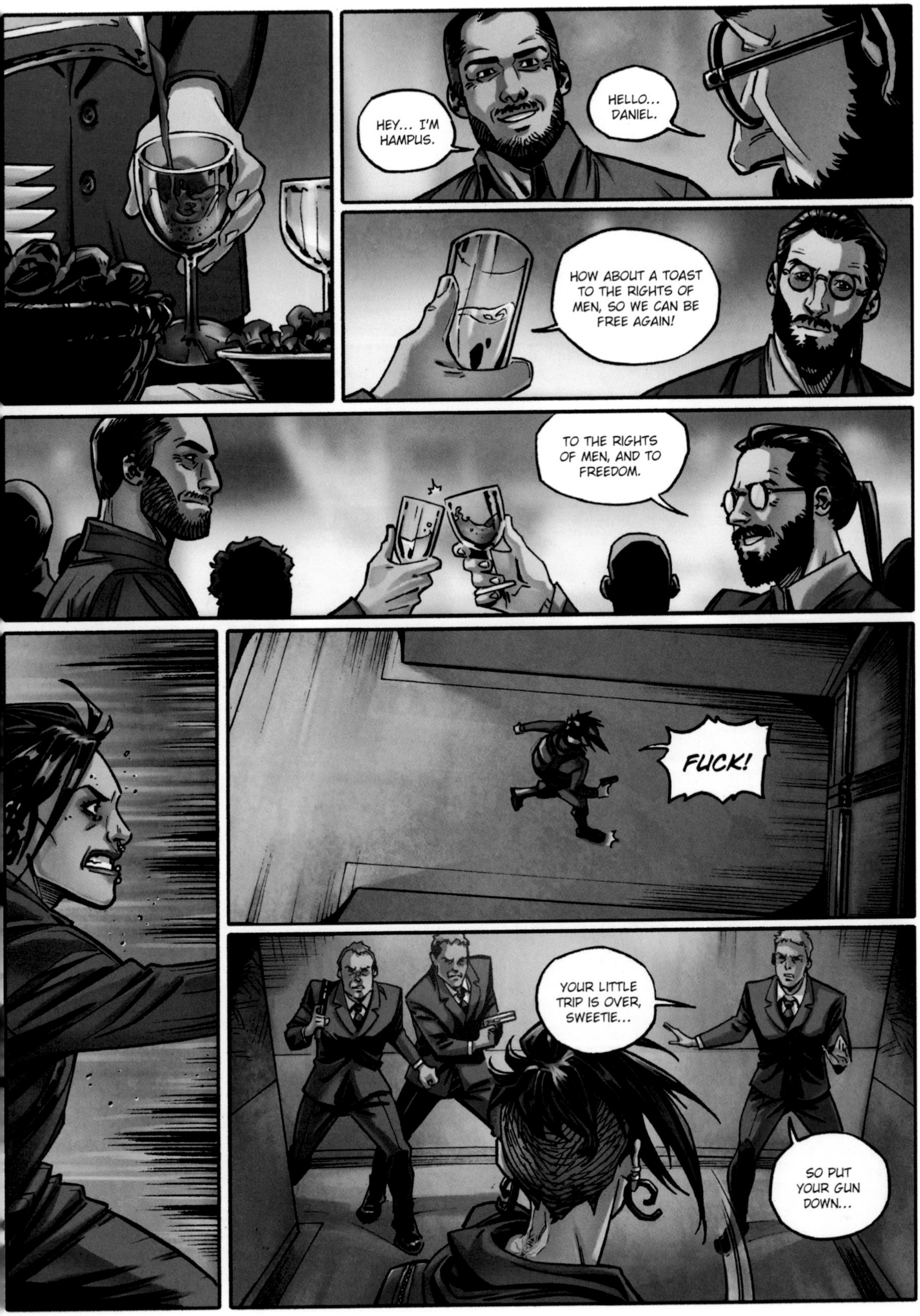
HEY... I'M HAMPUS.
HELLO... DANIEL.
HOW ABOUT A TOAST TO THE RIGHTS OF MEN, SO WE CAN BE FREE AGAIN!
TO THE RIGHTS OF MEN, AND TO FREEDOM.
FUCK!
YOUR LITTLE TRIP IS OVER, SWEETIE...
SO PUT YOUR GUN DOWN...

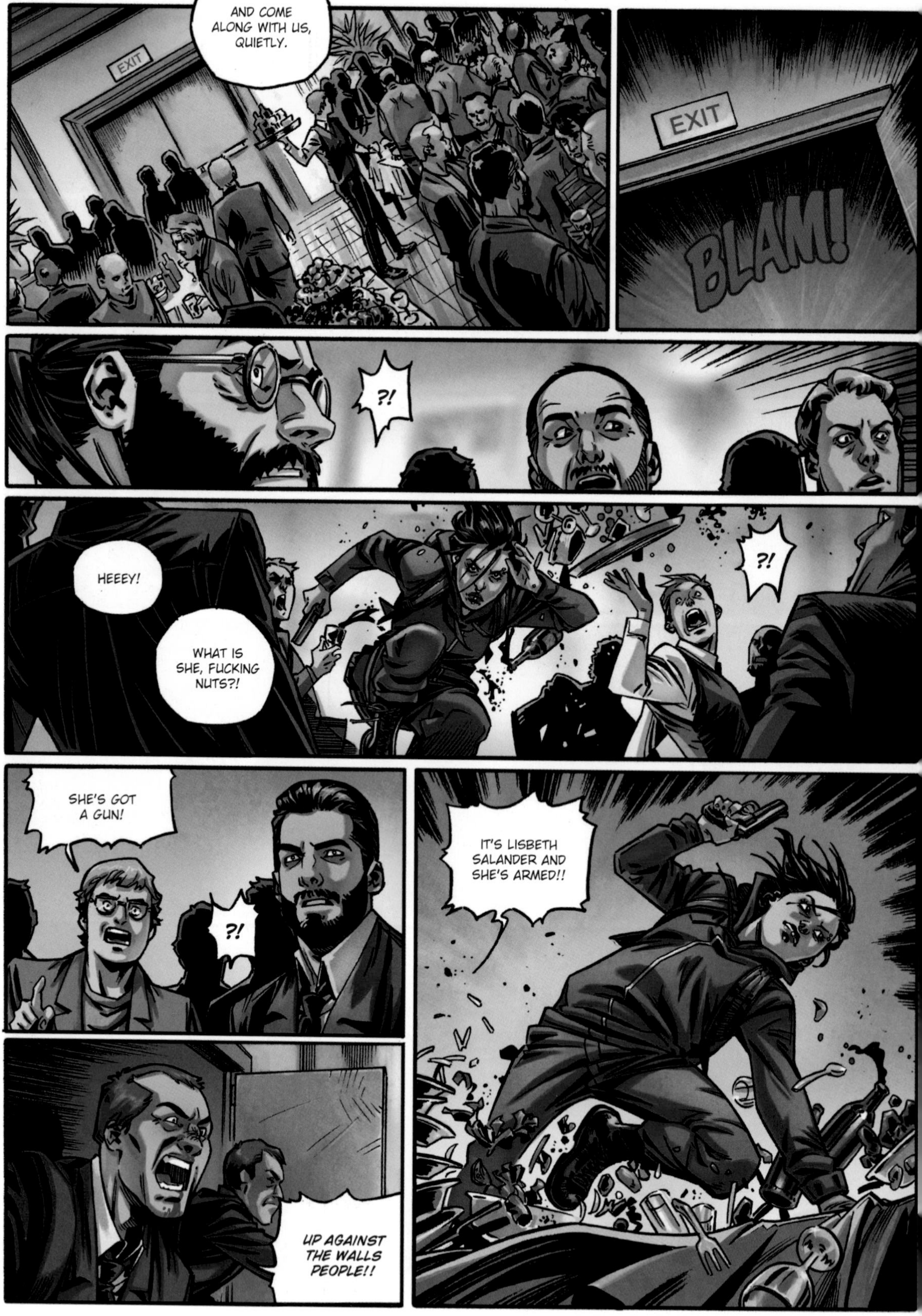
AND COME ALONG WITH US, QUIETLY.
EXIT
EXIT
BLAM!
?!
HEEEY!
WHAT IS SHE, FUCKING NUTS?!
?!
SHE'S GOT A GUN!
?!
UP AGAINST THE WALLS PEOPLE!!
IT'S LISBETH SALANDER AND SHE'S ARMED!!

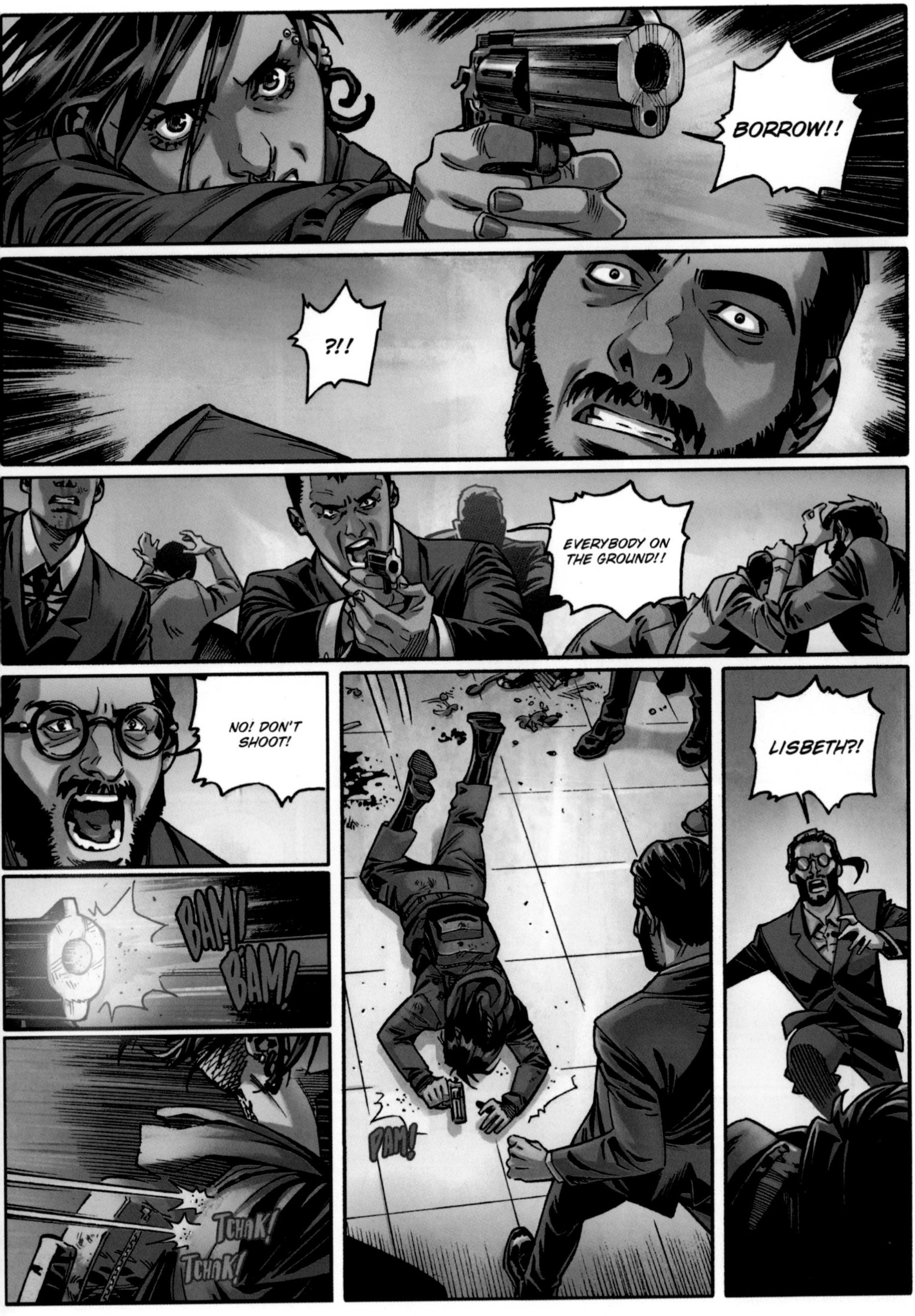
BORROW!!
?!!
EVERYBODY ON THE GROUND!!
NO! DON'T SHOOT!
BAM!
BAM!
TCHAK!
TCHAK!
PAM!
LISBETH?!

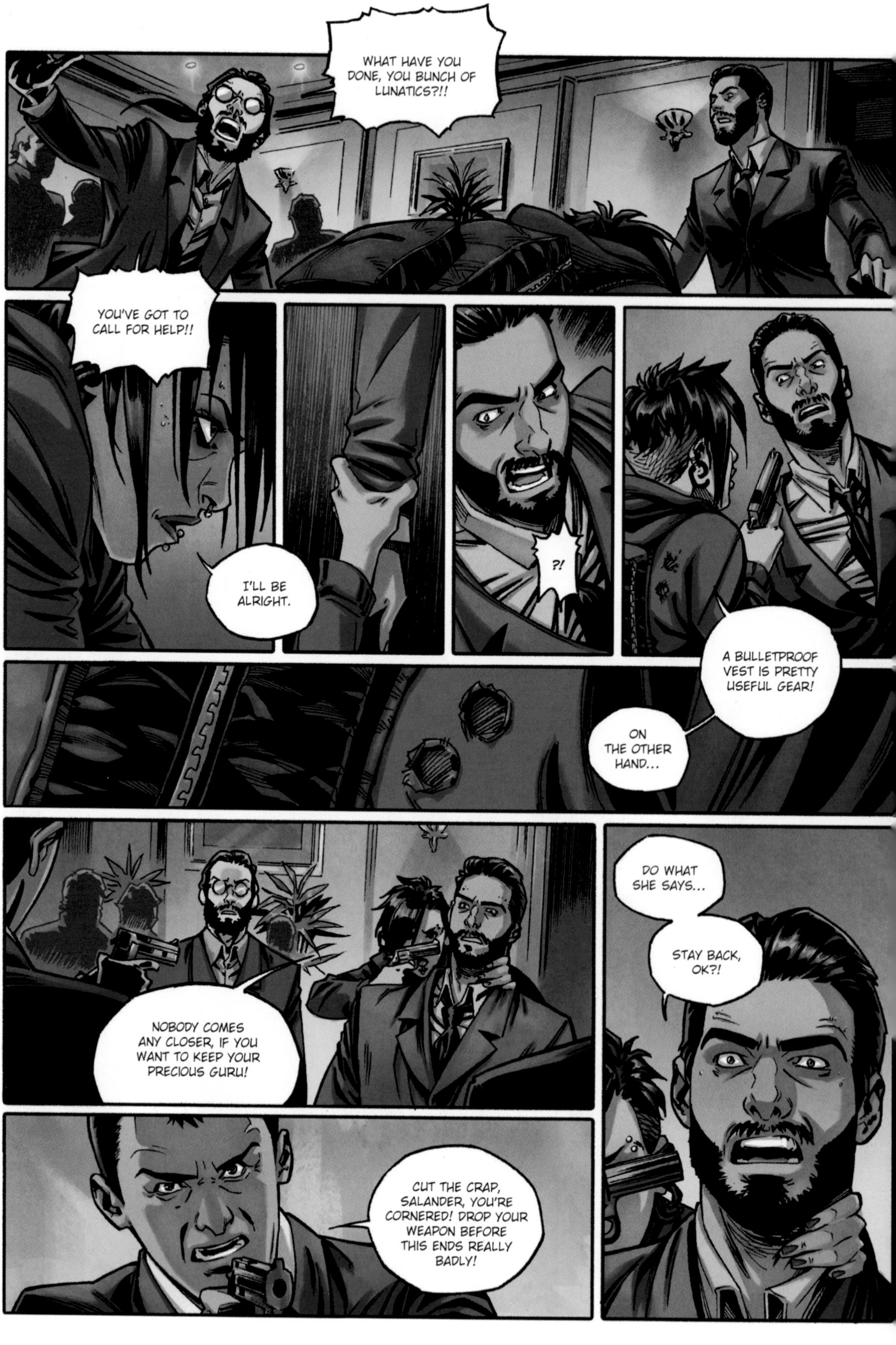
WHAT HAVE YOU DONE, YOU BUNCH OF LUNATICS?!!
YOU'VE GOT TO CALL FOR HELP!!
I'LL BE ALRIGHT.
?!
A BULLETPROOF VEST IS PRETTY USEFUL GEAR!
ON THE OTHER HAND...
NOBODY COMES ANY CLOSER, IF YOU WANT TO KEEP YOUR PRECIOUS GURU!
DO WHAT SHE SAYS...
STAY BACK, OK?!
CUT THE CRAP, SALANDER, YOU'RE CORNERED! DROP YOUR WEAPON BEFORE THIS ENDS REALLY BADLY!

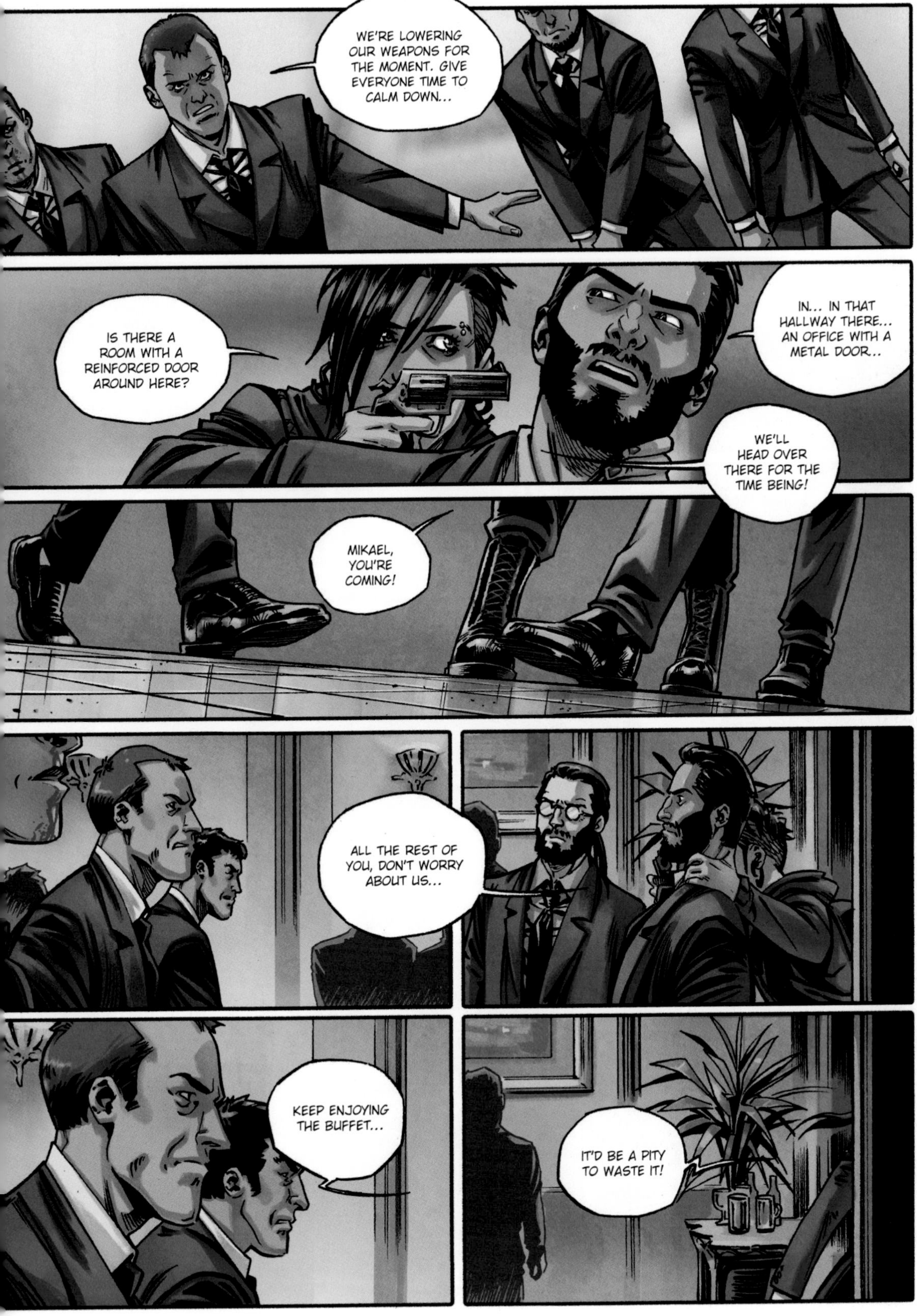
WE'RE LOWERING OUR WEAPONS FOR THE MOMENT. GIVE EVERYONE TIME TO CALM DOWN...
IS THERE A ROOM WITH A REINFORCED DOOR AROUND HERE?
IN... IN THAT HALLWAY THERE... AN OFFICE WITH A METAL DOOR...
WE'LL HEAD OVER THERE FOR THE TIME BEING!
MIKAEL, YOU'RE COMING!
ALL THE REST OF YOU, DON'T WORRY ABOUT US...
KEEP ENJOYING THE BUFFET...
IT'D BE A PITY TO WASTE IT!

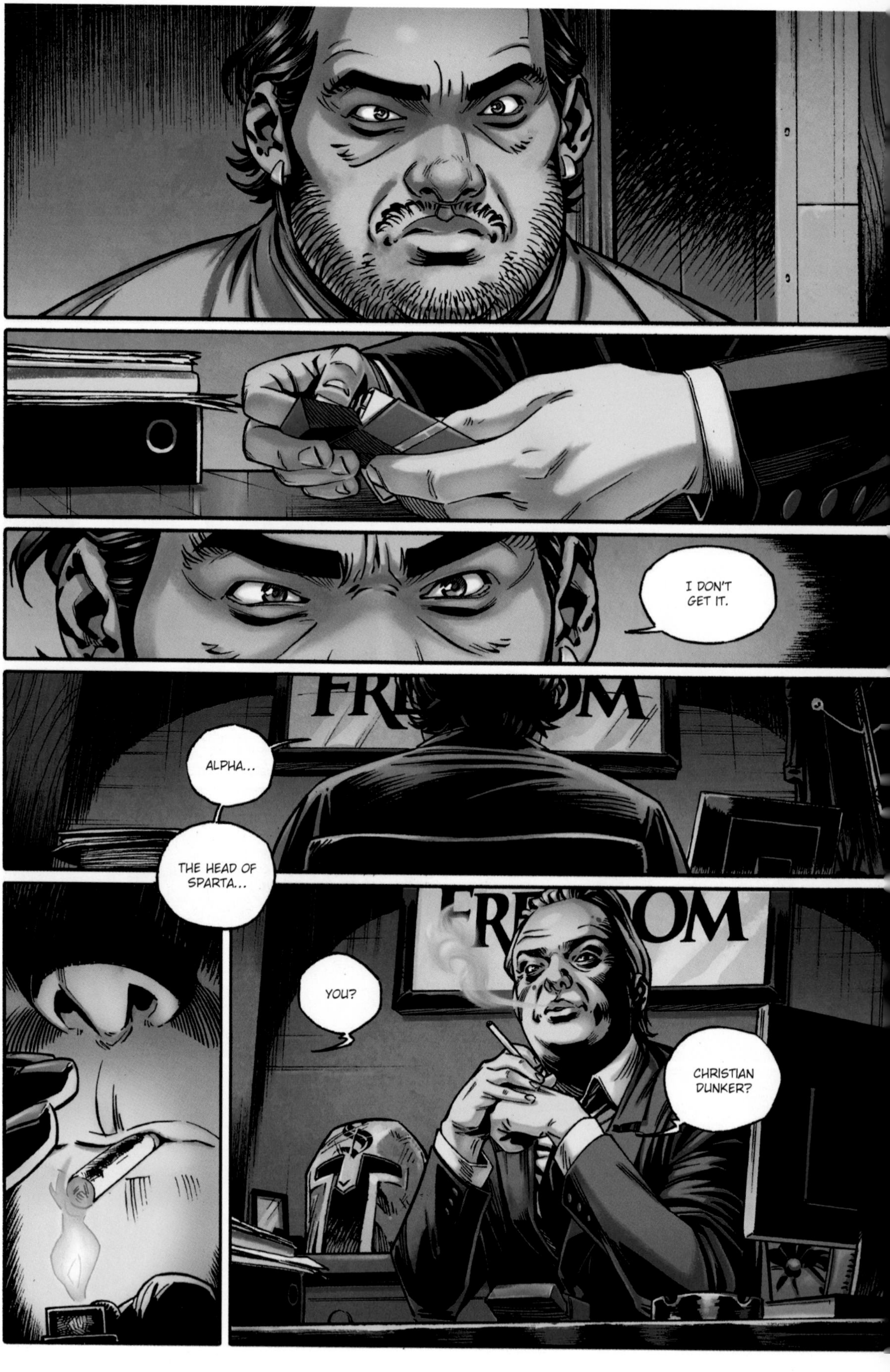
I DON'T GET IT.
ALPHA...
THE HEAD OF SPARTA...
FREEDOM
YOU?
CHRISTIAN DUNKER?

WHY DO YOU SEEM SO SURPRISED, LENNART ASL... AH... SORRY...

I FORGOT.

IT'S PLAGUE NOW.

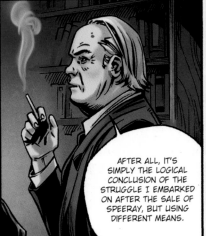

AFTER ALL, IT'S SIMPLY THE LOGICAL CONCLUSION OF THE STRUGGLE I EMBARKED ON AFTER THE SALE OF SPEERAY, BUT USING DIFFERENT MEANS.

DIFFERENT MEANS? A BUNCH OF DELINQUENTS DRESSED UP AS SPARTANS? I'D CALL IT CHEAP COSPLAY, EXCEPT YOU GUYS HAVE REAL BLOOD ON YOUR HANDS!!

YOU'RE BEING A BIT UNFAIR. WHEN YOUR LEFTIST PALS FROM ANONYMOUS CAUSED A SCENE WITH THEIR RIDICULOUS MASKS...

... I DON'T RECALL HACKER REPUBLIC RAISING ANY OBJECTIONS.

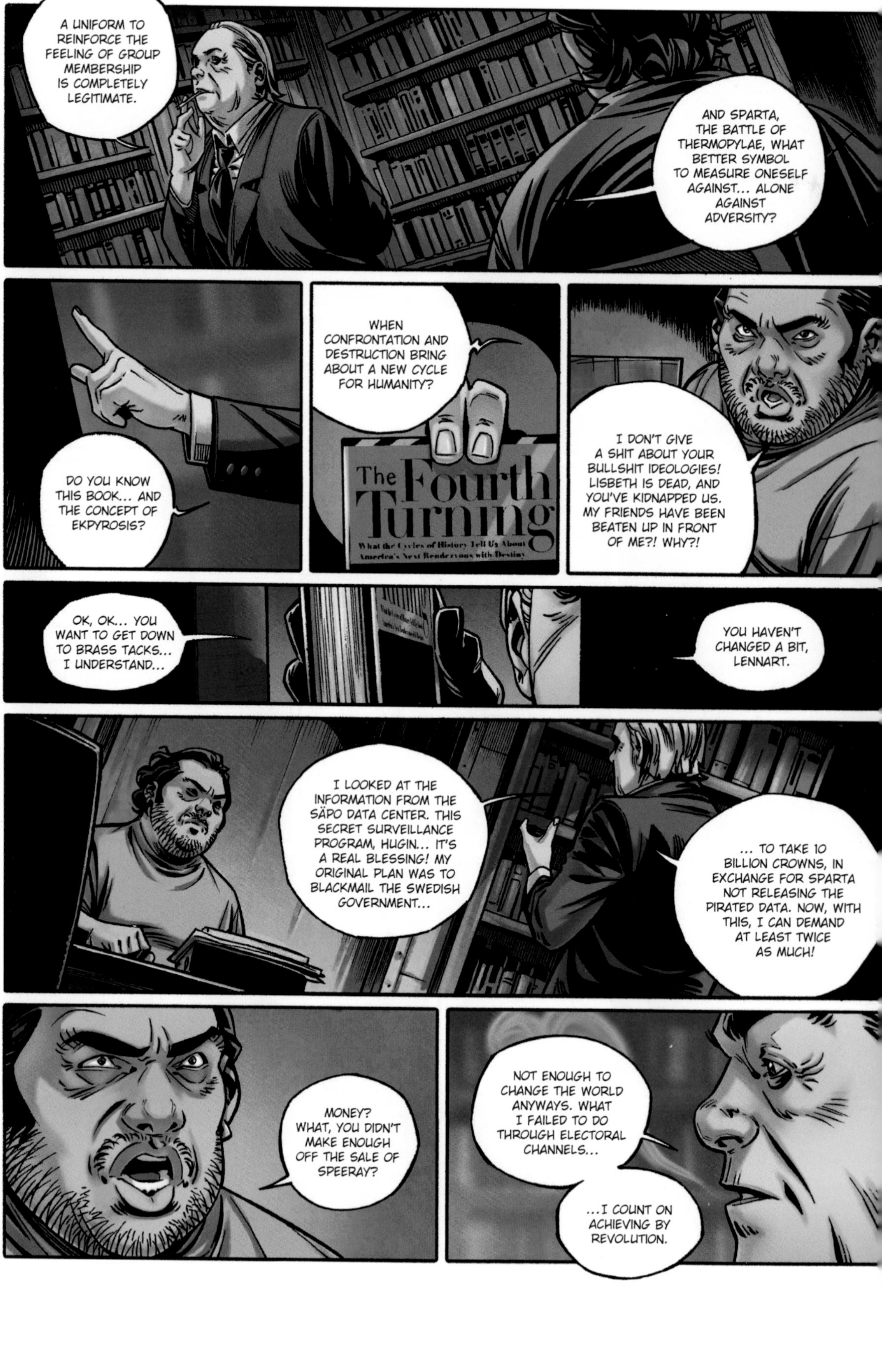
A UNIFORM TO REINFORCE THE FEELING OF GROUP MEMBERSHIP IS COMPLETELY LEGITIMATE.
AND SPARTA, THE BATTLE OF THERMOPYLAE, WHAT BETTER SYMBOL TO MEASURE ONESELF AGAINST... ALONE AGAINST ADVERSITY?
DO YOU KNOW THIS BOOK... AND THE CONCEPT OF EKPYROSIS?
WHEN CONFRONTATION AND DESTRUCTION BRING ABOUT A NEW CYCLE FOR HUMANITY?
The Fourth Turning
I DON'T GIVE A SHIT ABOUT YOUR BULLSHIT IDEOLOGIES! LISBETH IS DEAD, AND YOU'VE KIDNAPPED US. MY FRIENDS HAVE BEEN BEATEN UP IN FRONT OF ME?! WHY?!
OK, OK... YOU WANT TO GET DOWN TO BRASS TACKS... I UNDERSTAND...
YOU HAVEN'T CHANGED A BIT, LENNART.
I LOOKED AT THE INFORMATION FROM THE SÄPO DATA CENTER. THIS SECRET SURVEILLANCE PROGRAM, HUGIN... IT'S A REAL BLESSING! MY ORIGINAL PLAN WAS TO BLACKMAIL THE SWEDISH GOVERNMENT...
... TO TAKE 10 BILLION CROWNS, IN EXCHANGE FOR SPARTA NOT RELEASING THE PIRATED DATA. NOW, WITH THIS, I CAN DEMAND AT LEAST TWICE AS MUCH!
MONEY? WHAT, YOU DIDN'T MAKE ENOUGH OFF THE SALE OF SPEERAY?
NOT ENOUGH TO CHANGE THE WORLD ANYWAYS. WHAT I FAILED TO DO THROUGH ELECTORAL CHANNELS...
...I COUNT ON ACHIEVING BY REVOLUTION.

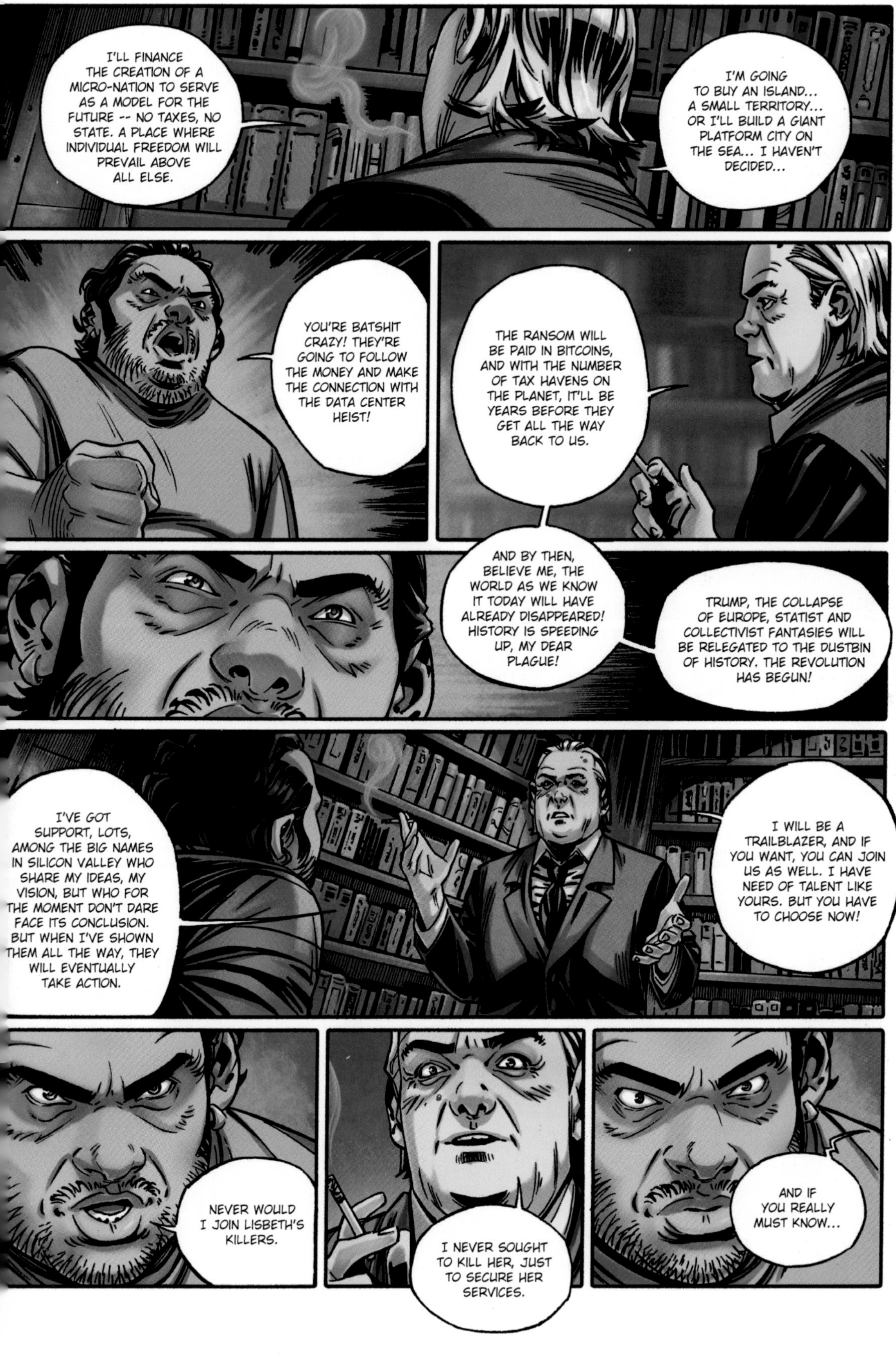
I'LL FINANCE THE CREATION OF A MICRO-NATION TO SERVE AS A MODEL FOR THE FUTURE -- NO TAXES, NO STATE. A PLACE WHERE INDIVIDUAL FREEDOM WILL PREVAIL ABOVE ALL ELSE.
I'M GOING TO BUY AN ISLAND... A SMALL TERRITORY... OR I'LL BUILD A GIANT PLATFORM CITY ON THE SEA... I HAVEN'T DECIDED...
YOU'RE BATSHIT CRAZY! THEY'RE GOING TO FOLLOW THE MONEY AND MAKE THE CONNECTION WITH THE DATA CENTER HEIST!
THE RANSOM WILL BE PAID IN BITCOINS, AND WITH THE NUMBER OF TAX HAVENS ON THE PLANET, IT'LL BE YEARS BEFORE THEY GET ALL THE WAY BACK TO US.
AND BY THEN, BELIEVE ME, THE WORLD AS WE KNOW IT TODAY WILL HAVE ALREADY DISAPPEARED! HISTORY IS SPEEDING UP, MY DEAR PLAGUE!
TRUMP, THE COLLAPSE OF EUROPE, STATIST AND COLLECTIVIST FANTASIES WILL BE RELEGATED TO THE DUSTBIN OF HISTORY. THE REVOLUTION HAS BEGUN!
I'VE GOT SUPPORT, LOTS, AMONG THE BIG NAMES IN SILICON VALLEY WHO SHARE MY IDEAS, MY VISION, BUT WHO FOR THE MOMENT DON'T DARE FACE ITS CONCLUSION. BUT WHEN I'VE SHOWN THEM ALL THE WAY, THEY WILL EVENTUALLY TAKE ACTION.
I WILL BE A TRAILBLAZER, AND IF YOU WANT, YOU CAN JOIN US AS WELL. I HAVE NEED OF TALENT LIKE YOURS. BUT YOU HAVE TO CHOOSE NOW!
NEVER WOULD I JOIN LISBETH'S KILLERS.
I NEVER SOUGHT TO KILL HER, JUST TO SECURE HER SERVICES.
AND IF YOU REALLY MUST KNOW...

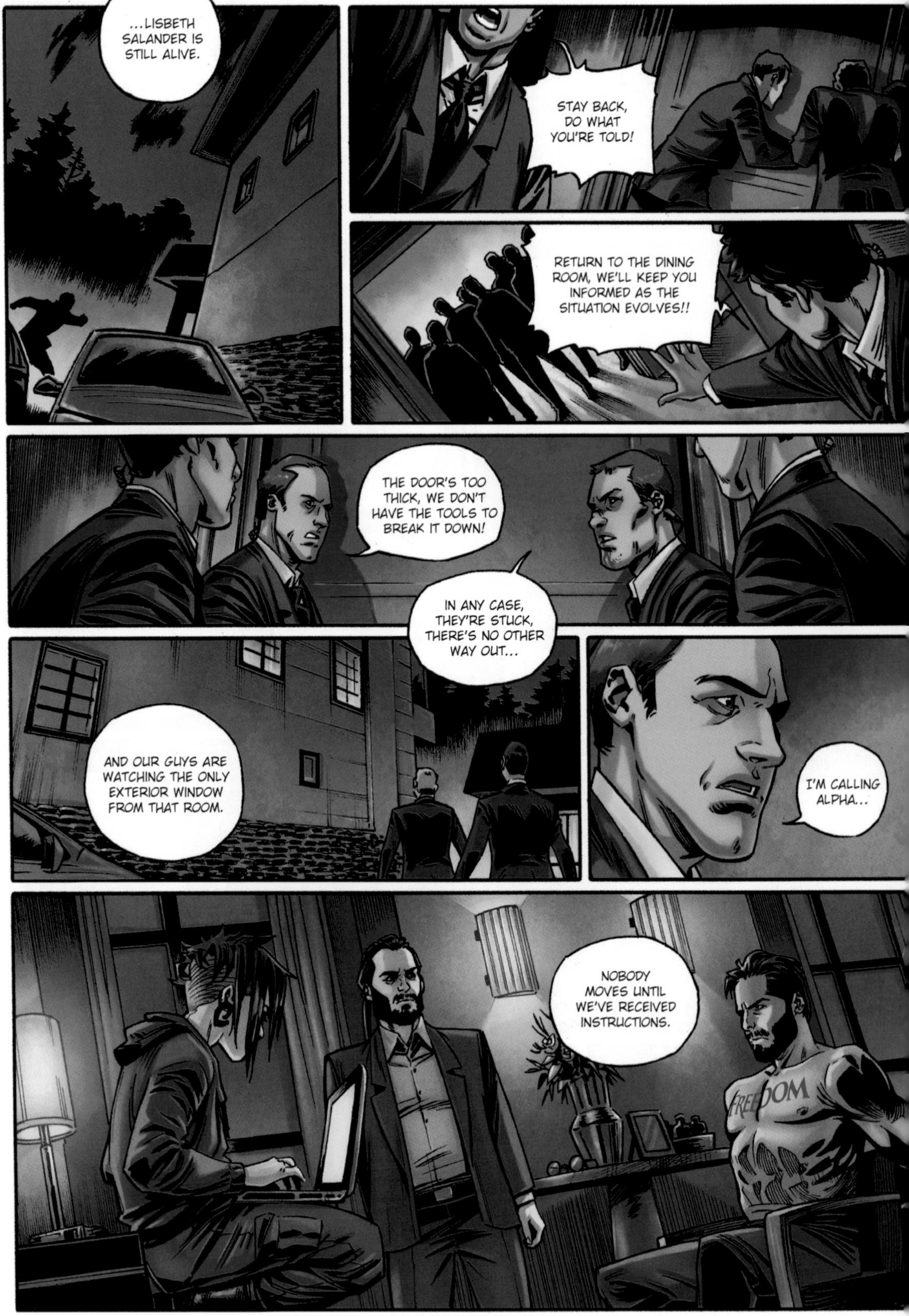
...LISBETH SALANDER IS STILL ALIVE.
STAY BACK, DO WHAT YOU'RE TOLD!
RETURN TO THE DINING ROOM, WE'LL KEEP YOU INFORMED AS THE SITUATION EVOLVES!!
THE DOOR'S TOO THICK, WE DON'T HAVE THE TOOLS TO BREAK IT DOWN!
IN ANY CASE, THEY'RE STUCK, THERE'S NO OTHER WAY OUT...
AND OUR GUYS ARE WATCHING THE ONLY EXTERIOR WINDOW FROM THAT ROOM.
I'M CALLING ALPHA...
NOBODY MOVES UNTIL WE'VE RECEIVED INSTRUCTIONS.
FREEDOM

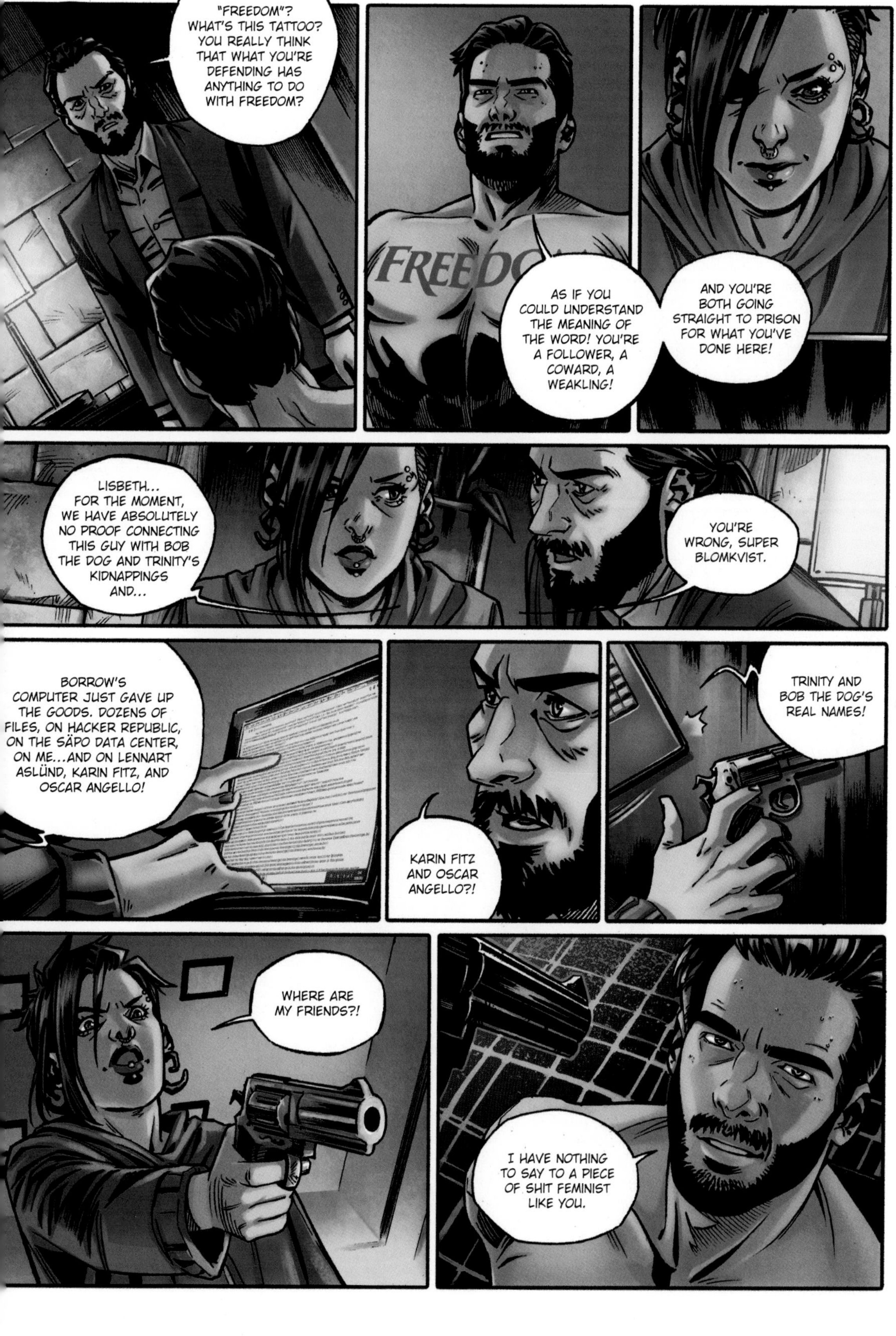
"FREEDOM"? WHAT'S THIS TATTOO? YOU REALLY THINK THAT WHAT YOU'RE DEFENDING HAS ANYTHING TO DO WITH FREEDOM?
FREEDO
AS IF YOU COULD UNDERSTAND THE MEANING OF THE WORD! YOU'RE A FOLLOWER, A COWARD, A WEAKLING!
AND YOU'RE BOTH GOING STRAIGHT TO PRISON FOR WHAT YOU'VE DONE HERE!
LISBETH... FOR THE MOMENT, WE HAVE ABSOLUTELY NO PROOF CONNECTING THIS GUY WITH BOB THE DOG AND TRINITY'S KIDNAPPINGS AND...
YOU'RE WRONG, SUPER BLOMKVIST.
BORROW'S COMPUTER JUST GAVE UP THE GOODS. DOZENS OF FILES, ON HACKER REPUBLIC, ON THE SÄPO DATA CENTER, ON ME...AND ON LENNART ASLÜND, KARIN FITZ, AND OSCAR ANGELLO!
KARIN FITZ AND OSCAR ANGELLO?!
TRINITY AND BOB THE DOG'S REAL NAMES!
WHERE ARE MY FRIENDS?!
I HAVE NOTHING TO SAY TO A PIECE OF SHIT FEMINIST LIKE YOU.

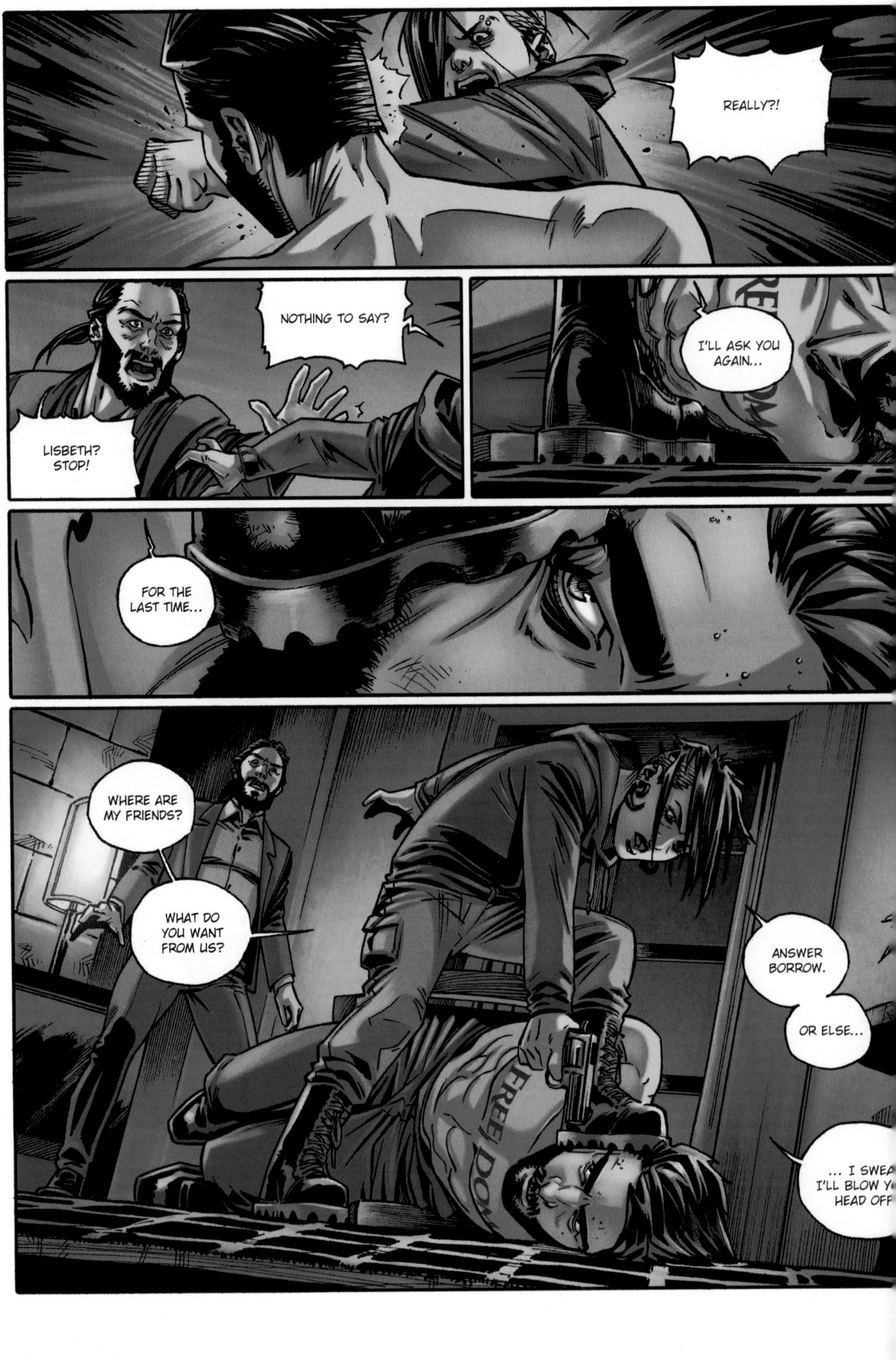
REALLY?!
NOTHING TO SAY?
LISBETH? STOP!
I'LL ASK YOU AGAIN...
FOR THE LAST TIME...
WHERE ARE MY FRIENDS?
WHAT DO YOU WANT FROM US?
ANSWER BORROW.
OR ELSE...
... I SWEA
I'LL BLOW Y
HEAD OFF

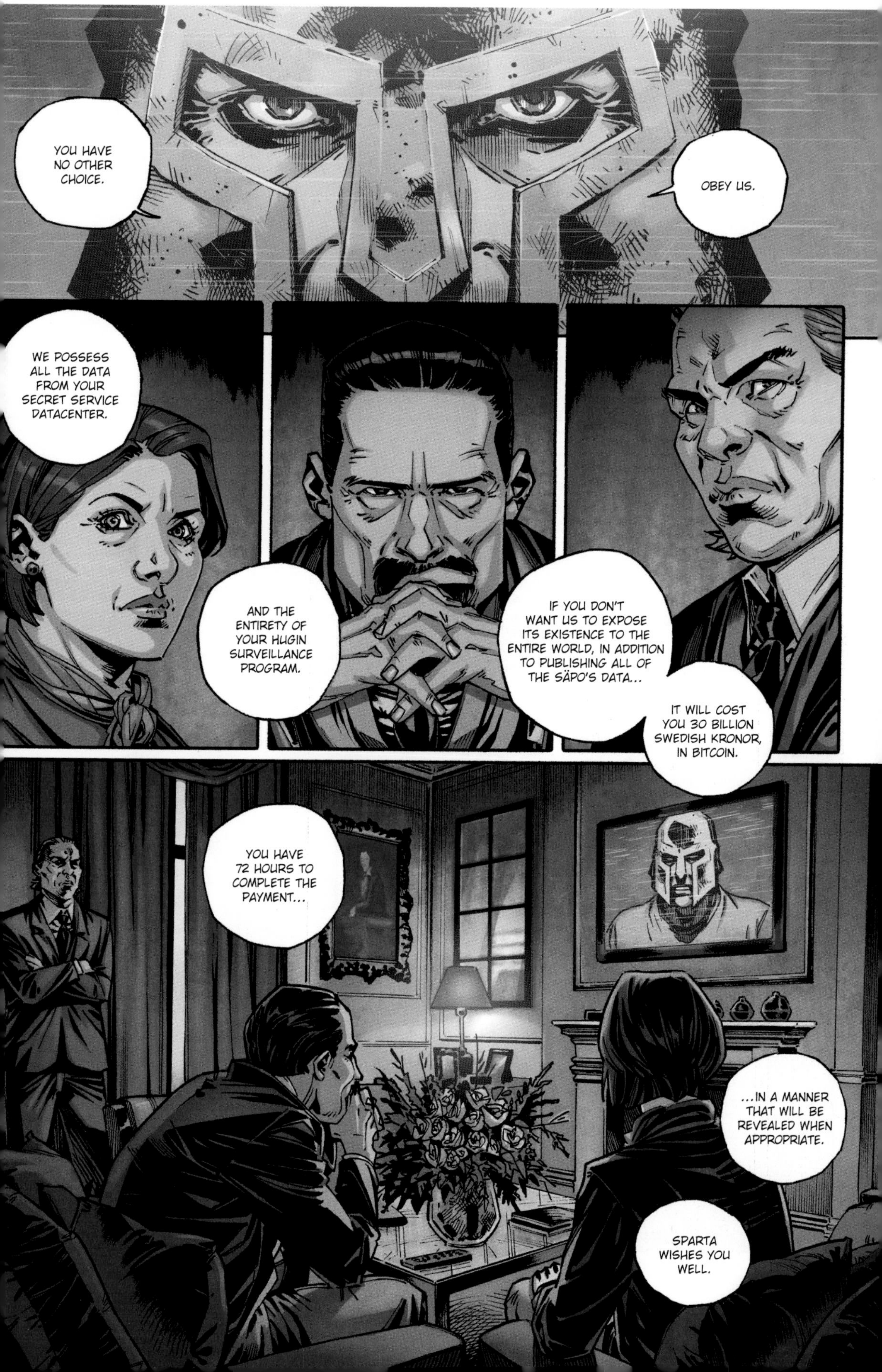
YOU HAVE NO OTHER CHOICE.
OBEY US.
WE POSSESS ALL THE DATA FROM YOUR SECRET SERVICE DATACENTER.
AND THE ENTIRETY OF YOUR HUGIN SURVEILLANCE PROGRAM.
IF YOU DON'T WANT US TO EXPOSE ITS EXISTENCE TO THE ENTIRE WORLD, IN ADDITION TO PUBLISHING ALL OF THE SÄPO'S DATA...
IT WILL COST YOU 30 BILLION SWEDISH KRONOR, IN BITCOIN.
YOU HAVE 72 HOURS TO COMPLETE THE PAYMENT...
...IN A MANNER THAT WILL BE REVEALED WHEN APPROPRIATE.
SPARTA WISHES YOU WELL.

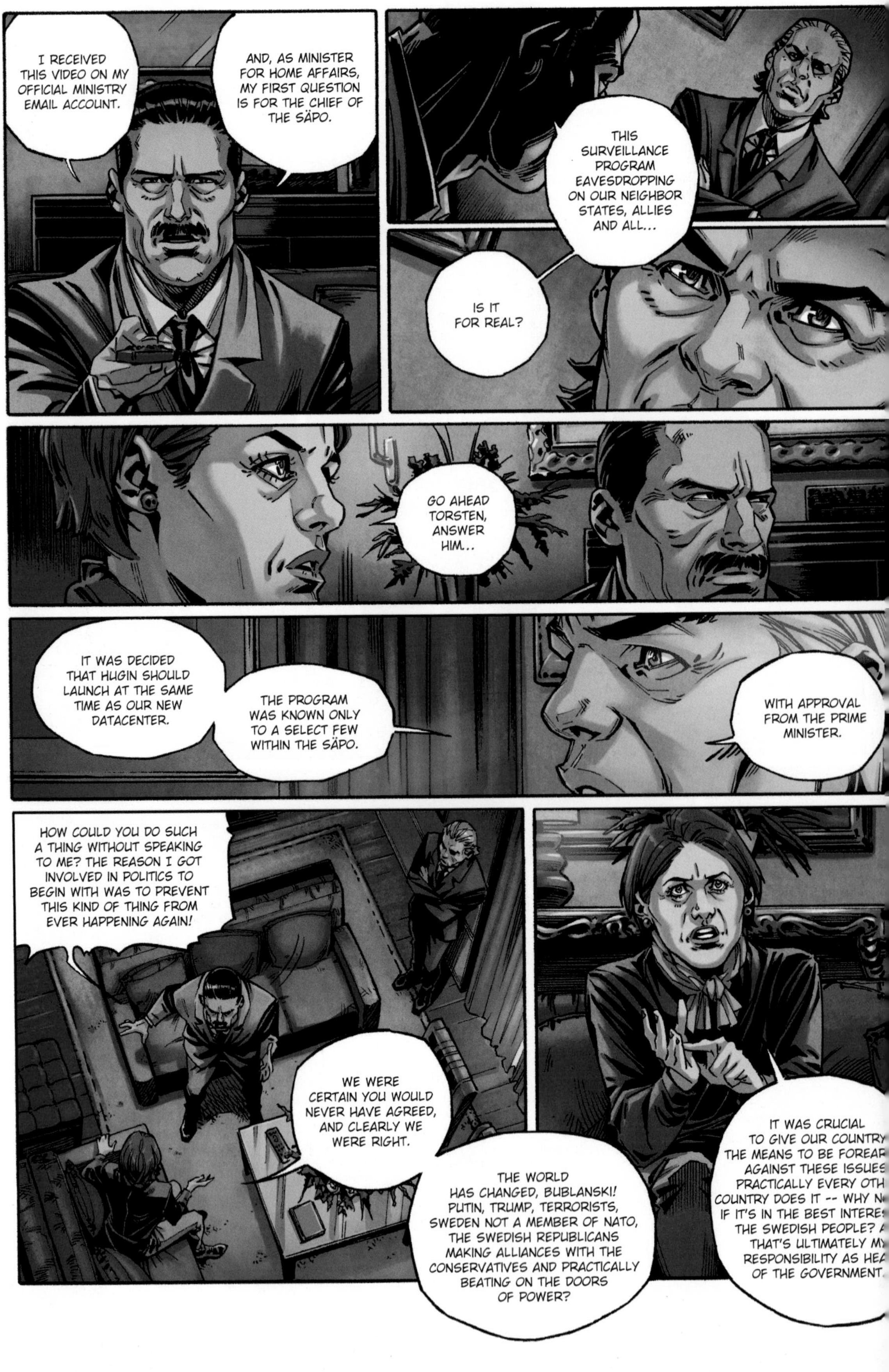

I RECEIVED THIS VIDEO ON MY OFFICIAL MINISTRY EMAIL ACCOUNT.
AND, AS MINISTER FOR HOME AFFAIRS, MY FIRST QUESTION IS FOR THE CHIEF OF THE SÄPO.
THIS SURVEILLANCE PROGRAM EAVESDROPPING ON OUR NEIGHBOR STATES, ALLIES AND ALL...
IS IT FOR REAL?
GO AHEAD TORSTEN, ANSWER HIM...
IT WAS DECIDED THAT HUGIN SHOULD LAUNCH AT THE SAME TIME AS OUR NEW DATACENTER.
THE PROGRAM WAS KNOWN ONLY TO A SELECT FEW WITHIN THE SÄPO.
WITH APPROVAL FROM THE PRIME MINISTER.
HOW COULD YOU DO SUCH A THING WITHOUT SPEAKING TO ME? THE REASON I GOT INVOLVED IN POLITICS TO BEGIN WITH WAS TO PREVENT THIS KIND OF THING FROM EVER HAPPENING AGAIN!
WE WERE CERTAIN YOU WOULD NEVER HAVE AGREED, AND CLEARLY WE WERE RIGHT.
THE WORLD HAS CHANGED, BUBLANSKI! PUTIN, TRUMP, TERRORISTS, SWEDEN NOT A MEMBER OF NATO, THE SWEDISH REPUBLICANS MAKING ALLIANCES WITH THE CONSERVATIVES AND PRACTICALLY BEATING ON THE DOORS OF POWER?
IT WAS CRUCIAL TO GIVE OUR COUNTRY THE MEANS TO BE FOREAR AGAINST THESE ISSUES PRACTICALLY EVERY OTH COUNTRY DOES IT -- WHY N IF IT'S IN THE BEST INTERES THE SWEDISH PEOPLE? THAT'S ULTIMATELY M RESPONSIBILITY AS HEA OF THE GOVERNMENT.

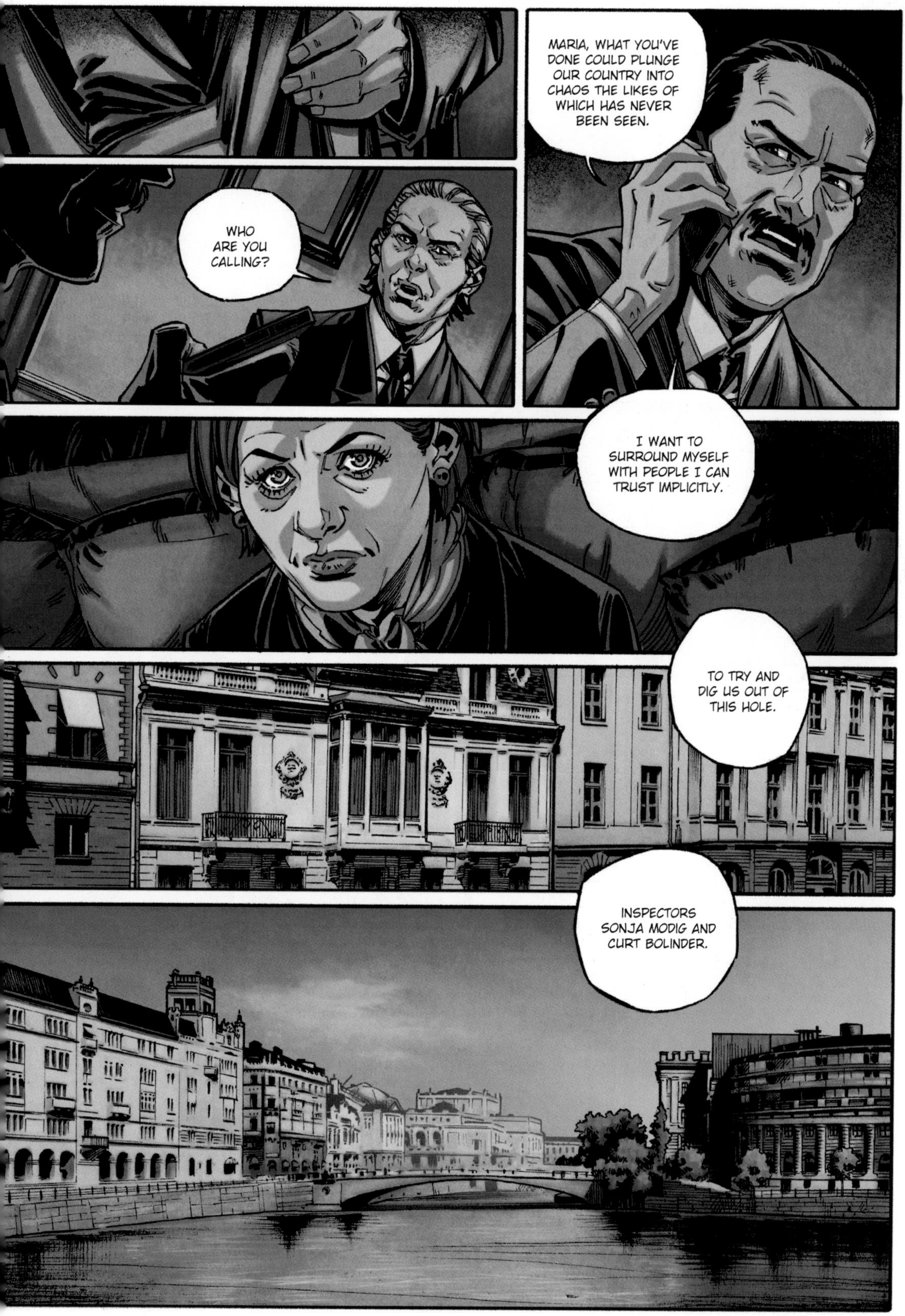
MARIA, WHAT YOU'VE DONE COULD PLUNGE OUR COUNTRY INTO CHAOS THE LIKES OF WHICH HAS NEVER BEEN SEEN.
WHO ARE YOU CALLING?
I WANT TO SURROUND MYSELF WITH PEOPLE I CAN TRUST IMPLICITLY.
TO TRY AND DIG US OUT OF THIS HOLE.
INSPECTORS SONJA MODIG AND CURT BOLINDER.

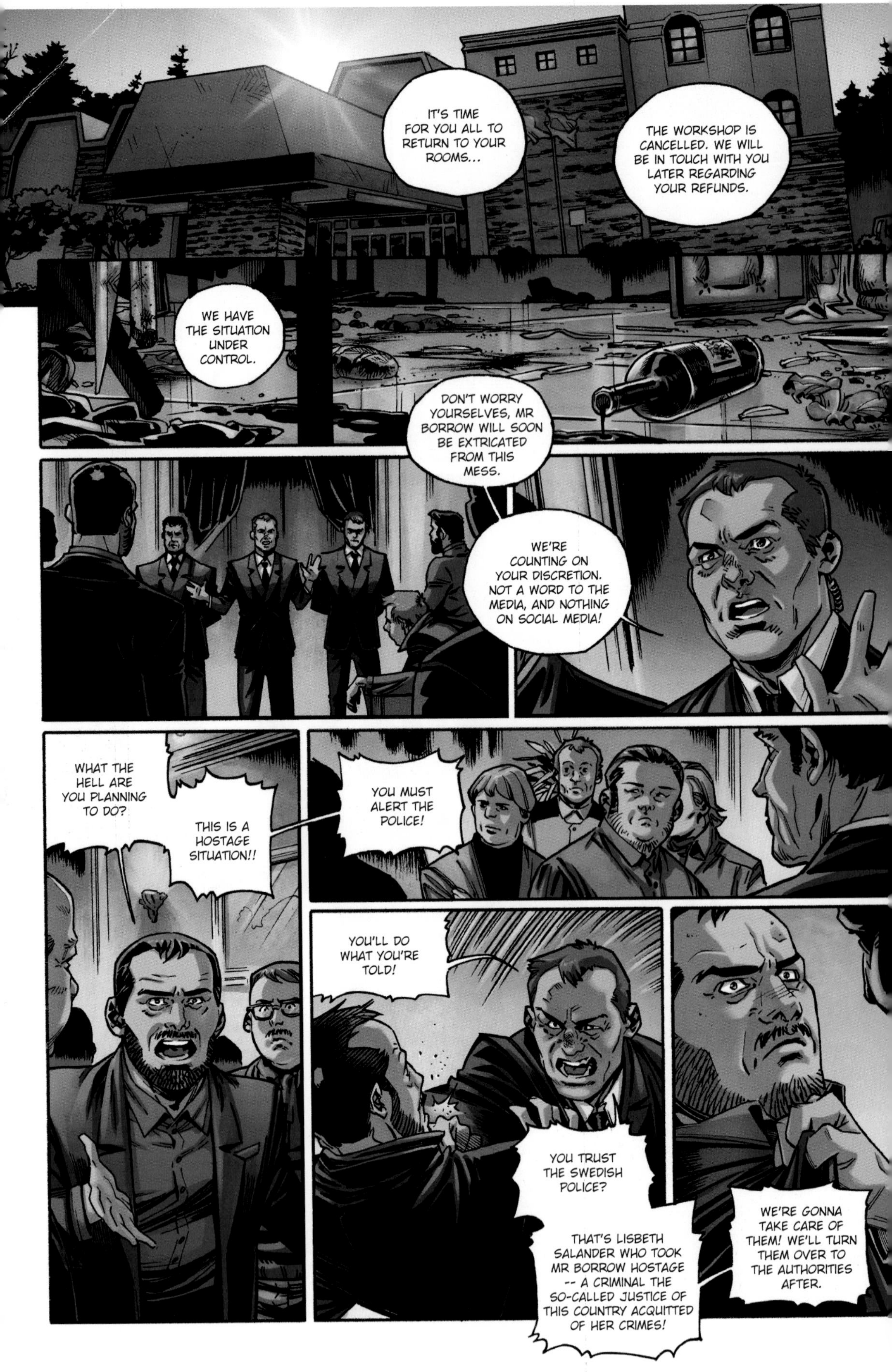
IT'S TIME FOR YOU ALL TO RETURN TO YOUR ROOMS...
THE WORKSHOP IS CANCELLED. WE WILL BE IN TOUCH WITH YOU LATER REGARDING YOUR REFUNDS.
WE HAVE THE SITUATION UNDER CONTROL.
DON'T WORRY YOURSELVES, MR BORROW WILL SOON BE EXTRICATED FROM THIS MESS.
WE'RE COUNTING ON YOUR DISCRETION. NOT A WORD TO THE MEDIA, AND NOTHING ON SOCIAL MEDIA!
WHAT THE HELL ARE YOU PLANNING TO DO?
THIS IS A HOSTAGE SITUATION!!
YOU MUST ALERT THE POLICE!
YOU'LL DO WHAT YOU'RE TOLD!
YOU TRUST THE SWEDISH POLICE?
THAT'S LISBETH SALANDER WHO TOOK MR BORROW HOSTAGE -- A CRIMINAL THE SO-CALLED JUSTICE OF THIS COUNTRY ACQUITTED OF HER CRIMES!
WE'RE GONNA TAKE CARE OF THEM! WE'LL TURN THEM OVER TO THE AUTHORITIES AFTER.

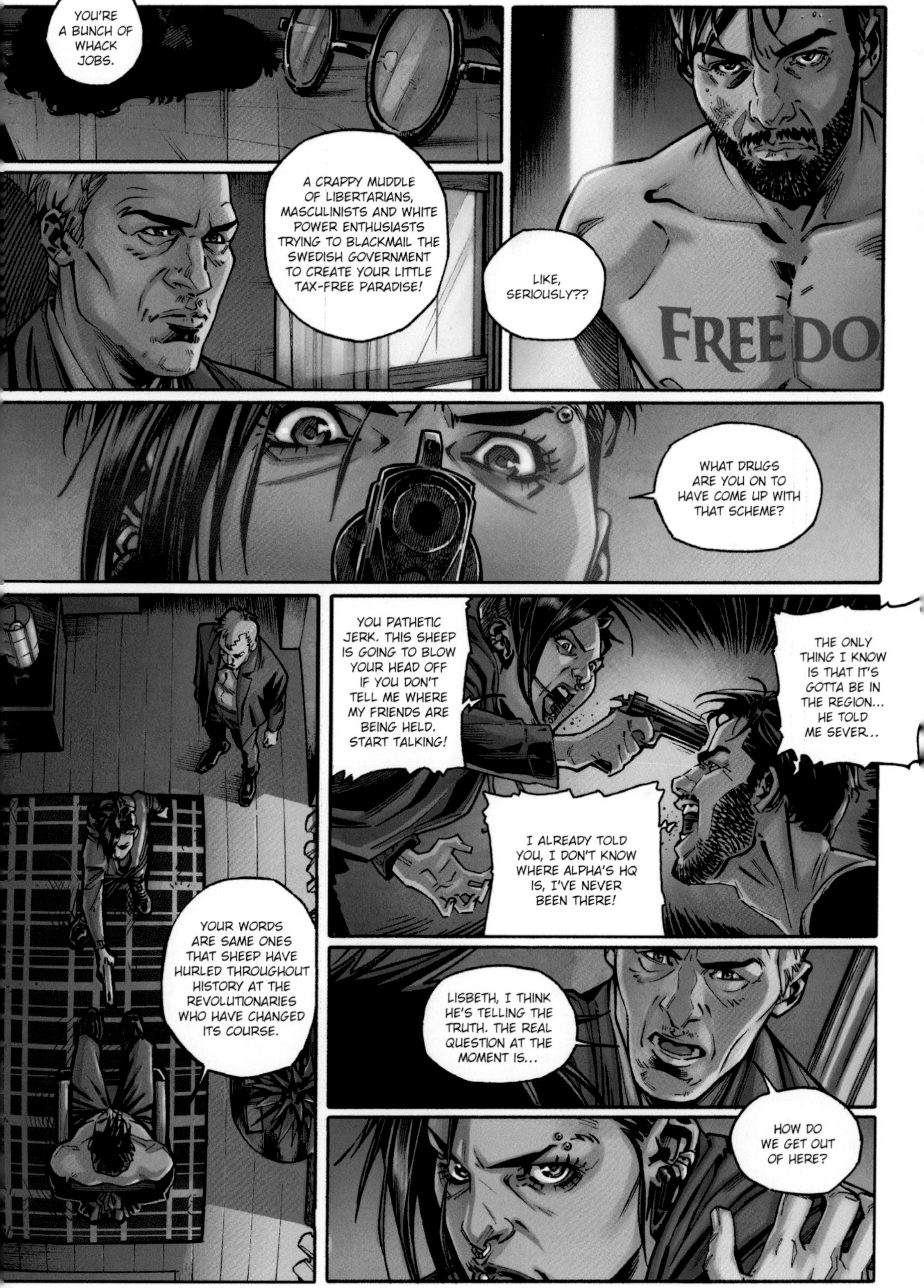
YOU'RE A BUNCH OF WHACK JOBS.
A CRAPPY MUDDLE OF LIBERTARIANS, MASCULINISTS AND WHITE POWER ENTHUSIASTS TRYING TO BLACKMAIL THE SWEDISH GOVERNMENT TO CREATE YOUR LITTLE TAX-FREE PARADISE!
LIKE, SERIOUSLY??
FREEDO
WHAT DRUGS ARE YOU ON TO HAVE COME UP WITH THAT SCHEME?
YOU PATHETIC JERK. THIS SHEEP IS GOING TO BLOW YOUR HEAD OFF IF YOU DON'T TELL ME WHERE MY FRIENDS ARE BEING HELD. START TALKING!
I ALREADY TOLD YOU, I DON'T KNOW WHERE ALPHA'S HQ IS, I'VE NEVER BEEN THERE!
THE ONLY THING I KNOW IS THAT IT'S GOTTA BE IN THE REGION... HE TOLD ME SEVER..
YOUR WORDS ARE SAME ONES THAT SHEEP HAVE HURLED THROUGHOUT HISTORY AT THE REVOLUTIONARIES WHO HAVE CHANGED ITS COURSE.
LISBETH, I THINK HE'S TELLING THE TRUTH. THE REAL QUESTION AT THE MOMENT IS...
HOW DO WE GET OUT OF HERE?

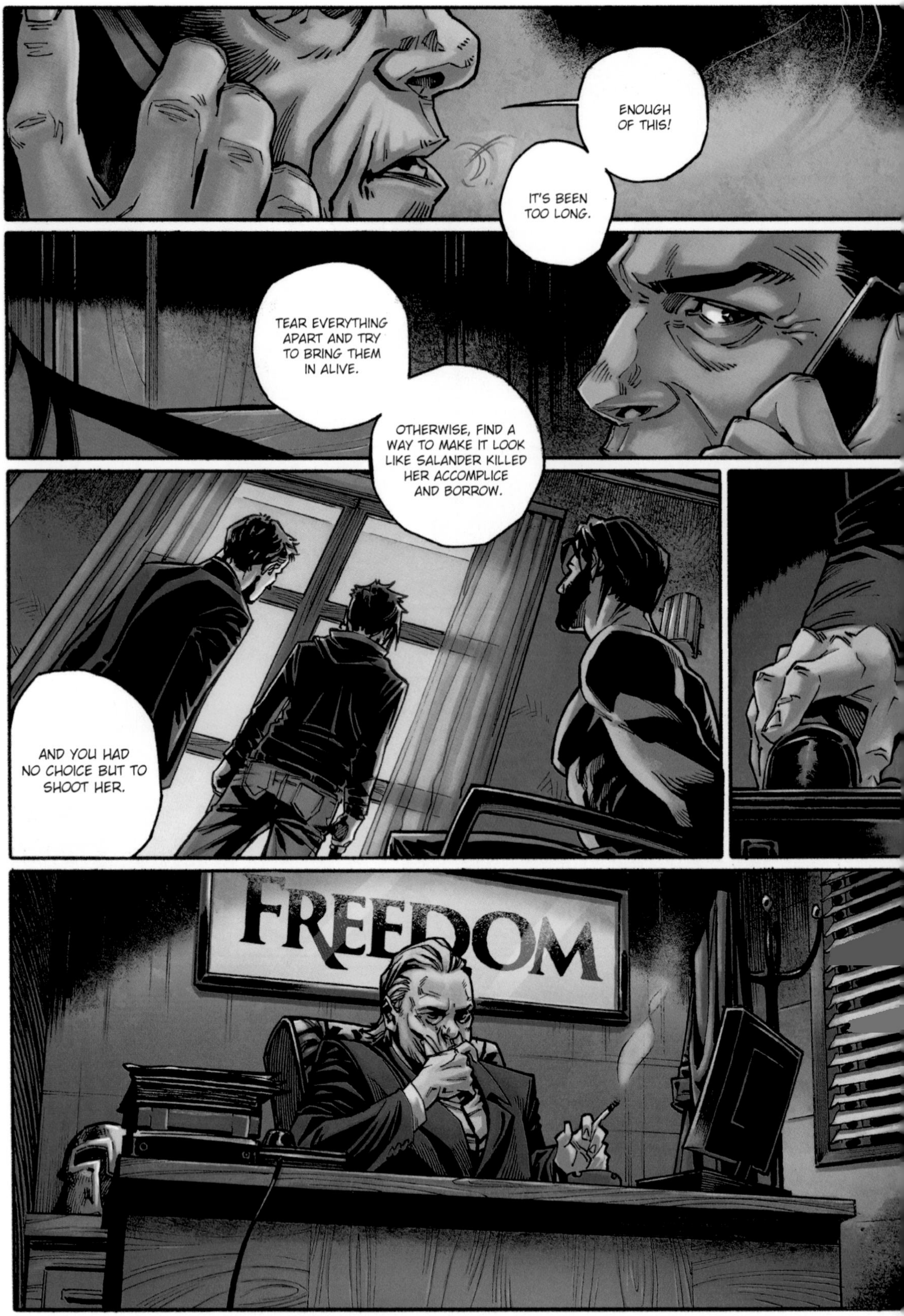
ENOUGH OF THIS!
IT'S BEEN TOO LONG.
TEAR EVERYTHING APART AND TRY TO BRING THEM IN ALIVE.
OTHERWISE, FIND A WAY TO MAKE IT LOOK LIKE SALANDER KILLED HER ACCOMPLICE AND BORROW.
AND YOU HAD NO CHOICE BUT TO SHOOT HER.
FREEDOM

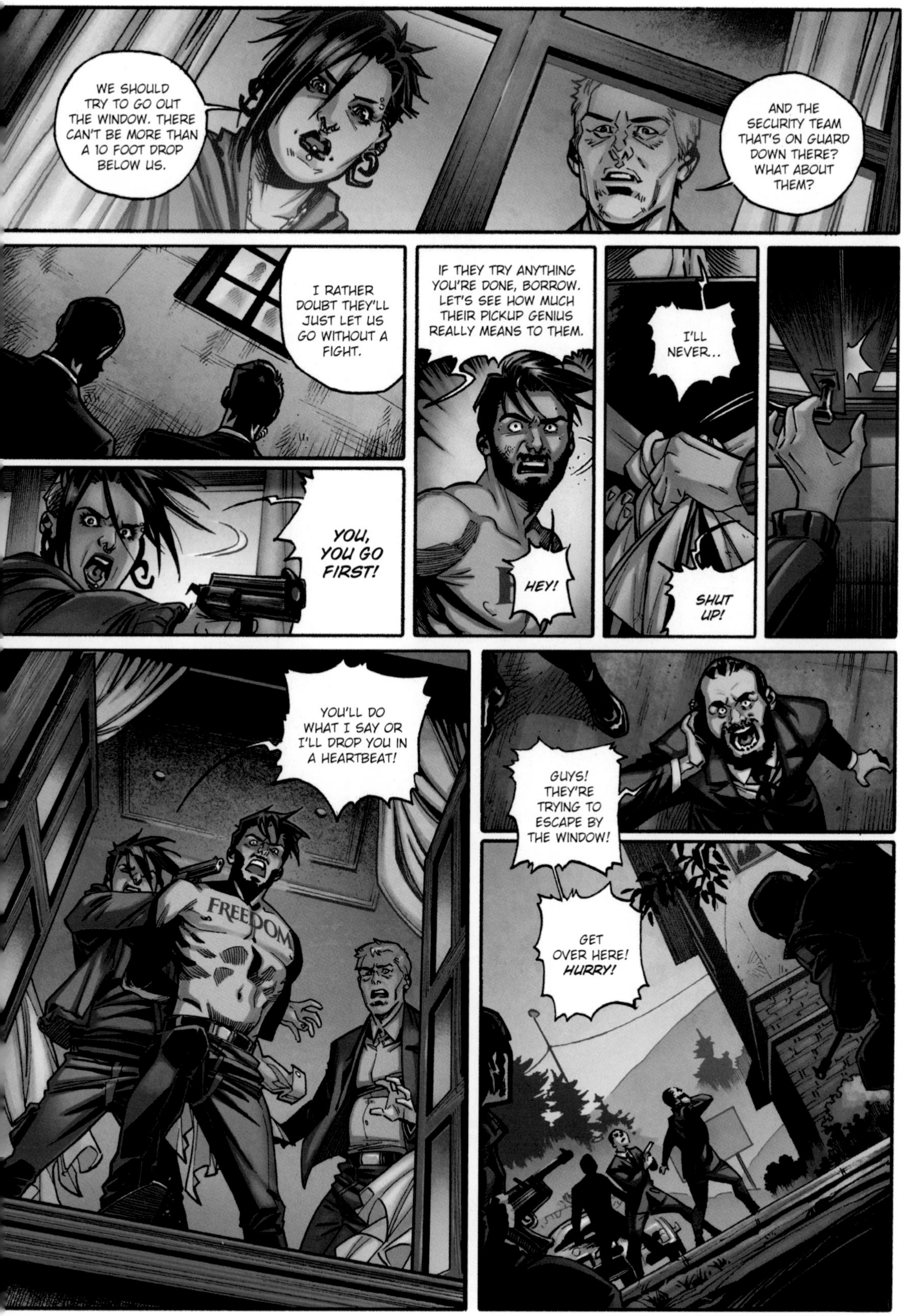
WE SHOULD TRY TO GO OUT THE WINDOW. THERE CAN'T BE MORE THAN A 10 FOOT DROP BELOW US.
AND THE SECURITY TEAM THAT'S ON GUARD DOWN THERE? WHAT ABOUT THEM?
I RATHER DOUBT THEY'LL JUST LET US GO WITHOUT A FIGHT.
IF THEY TRY ANYTHING YOU'RE DONE, BORROW. LET'S SEE HOW MUCH THEIR PICKUP GENIUS REALLY MEANS TO THEM.
I'LL NEVER..
YOU, YOU GO FIRST!
HEY!
SHUT UP!
YOU'LL DO WHAT I SAY OR I'LL DROP YOU IN A HEARTBEAT!
FREEDOM
GUYS! THEY'RE TRYING TO ESCAPE BY THE WINDOW!
GET OVER HERE! HURRY!

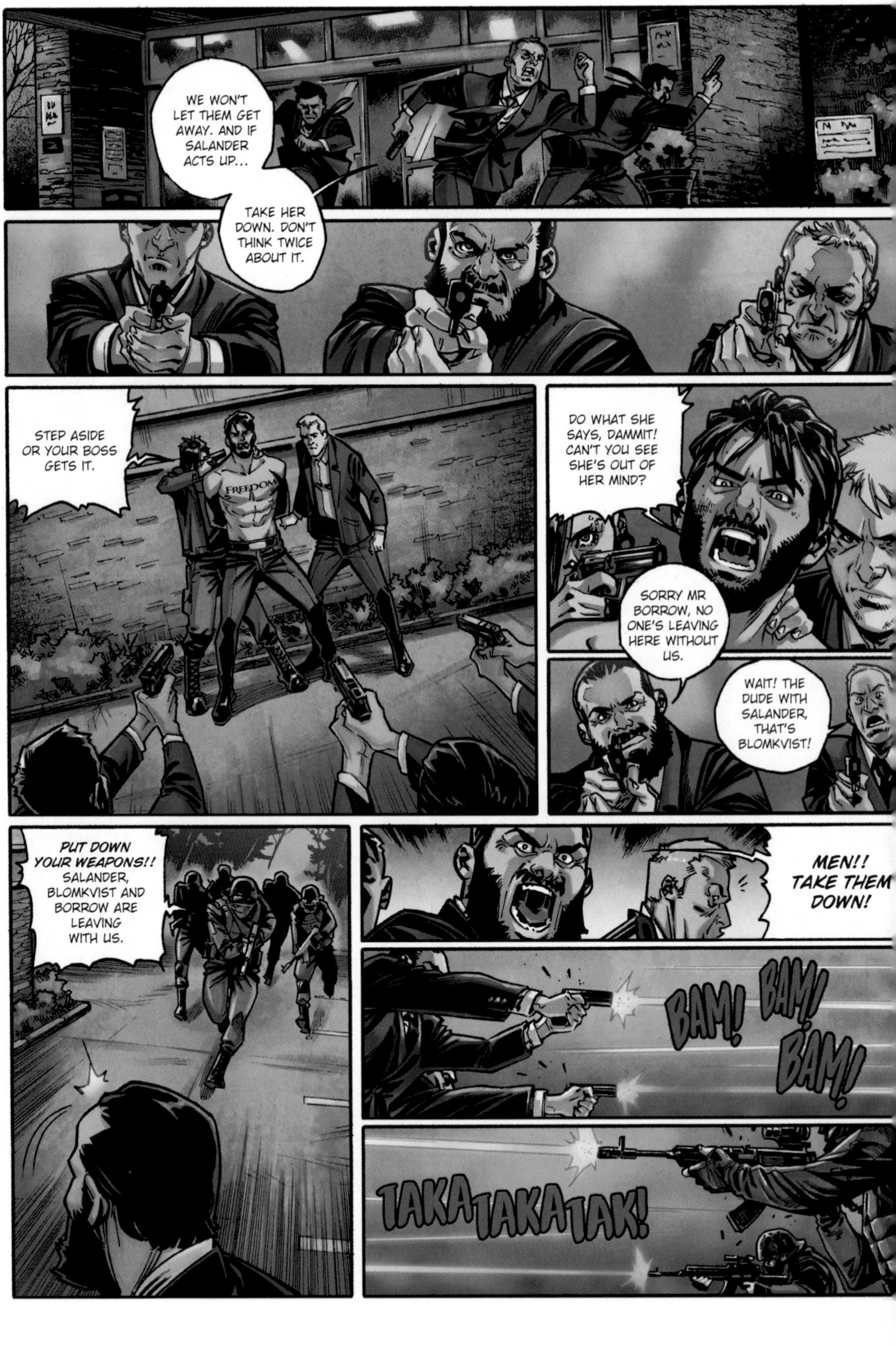
WE WON'T LET THEM GET AWAY. AND IF SALANDER ACTS UP...
TAKE HER DOWN. DON'T THINK TWICE ABOUT IT.
STEP ASIDE OR YOUR BOSS GETS IT.
FREEDOM
DO WHAT SHE SAYS, DAMMIT! CAN'T YOU SEE SHE'S OUT OF HER MIND?
SORRY MR BORROW, NO ONE'S LEAVING HERE WITHOUT US.
WAIT! THE DUDE WITH SALANDER, THAT'S BLOMKVIST!
PUT DOWN YOUR WEAPONS!! SALANDER, BLOMKVIST AND BORROW ARE LEAVING WITH US.
MEN!! TAKE THEM DOWN!
BAM! BAM! BAM!
TAKATAKATAK!

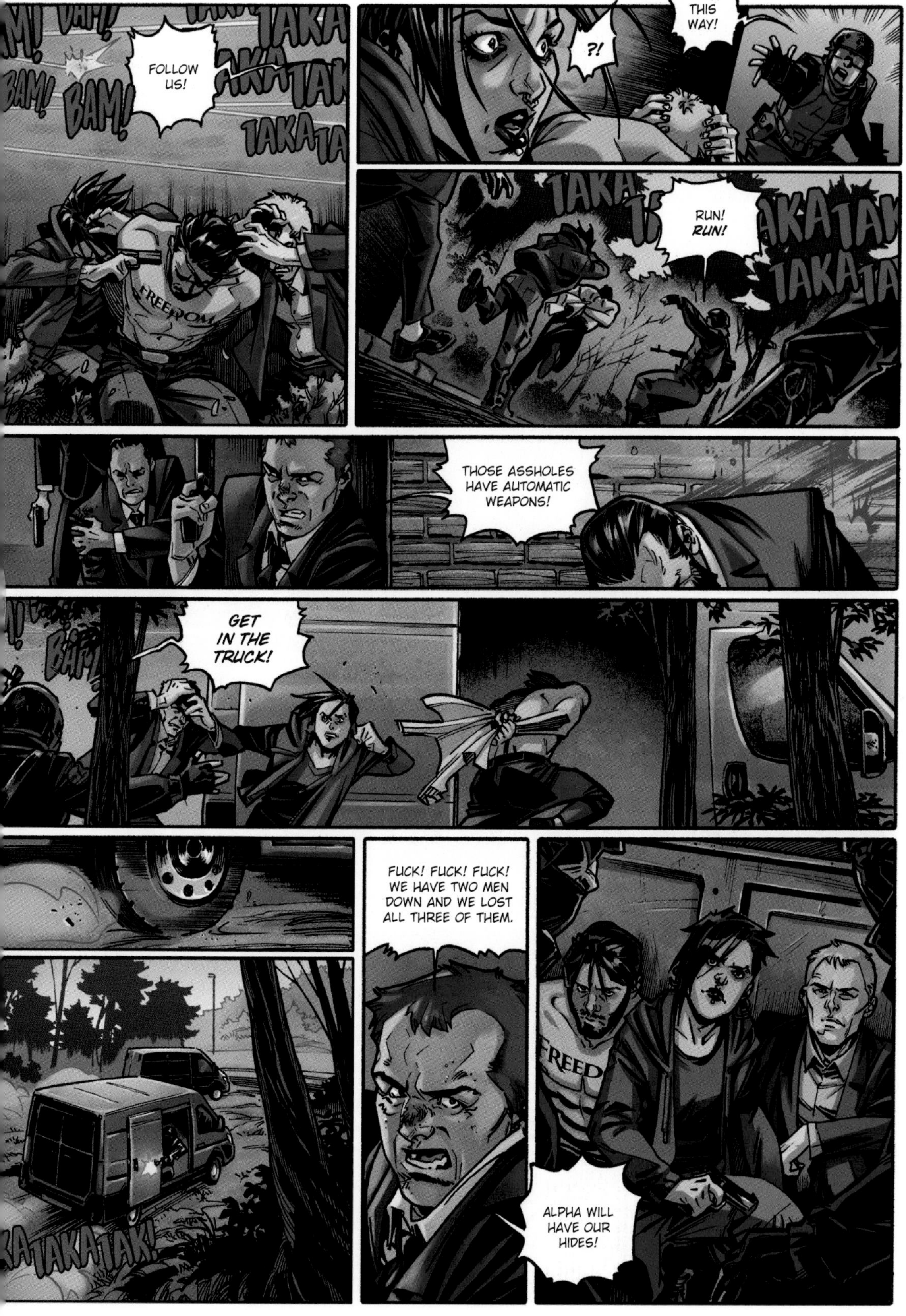
BAM! BAM!
BAM! BAM!
TAKA TAKA TAKA TAKA
FOLLOW US!
?!
THIS WAY!
TAKA TAKA TAKA TAKA
RUN! RUN!
THOSE ASSHOLES HAVE AUTOMATIC WEAPONS!
BAM!
GET IN THE TRUCK!
TAKATAKATAK!
FUCK! FUCK! FUCK! WE HAVE TWO MEN DOWN AND WE LOST ALL THREE OF THEM.
ALPHA WILL HAVE OUR HIDES!

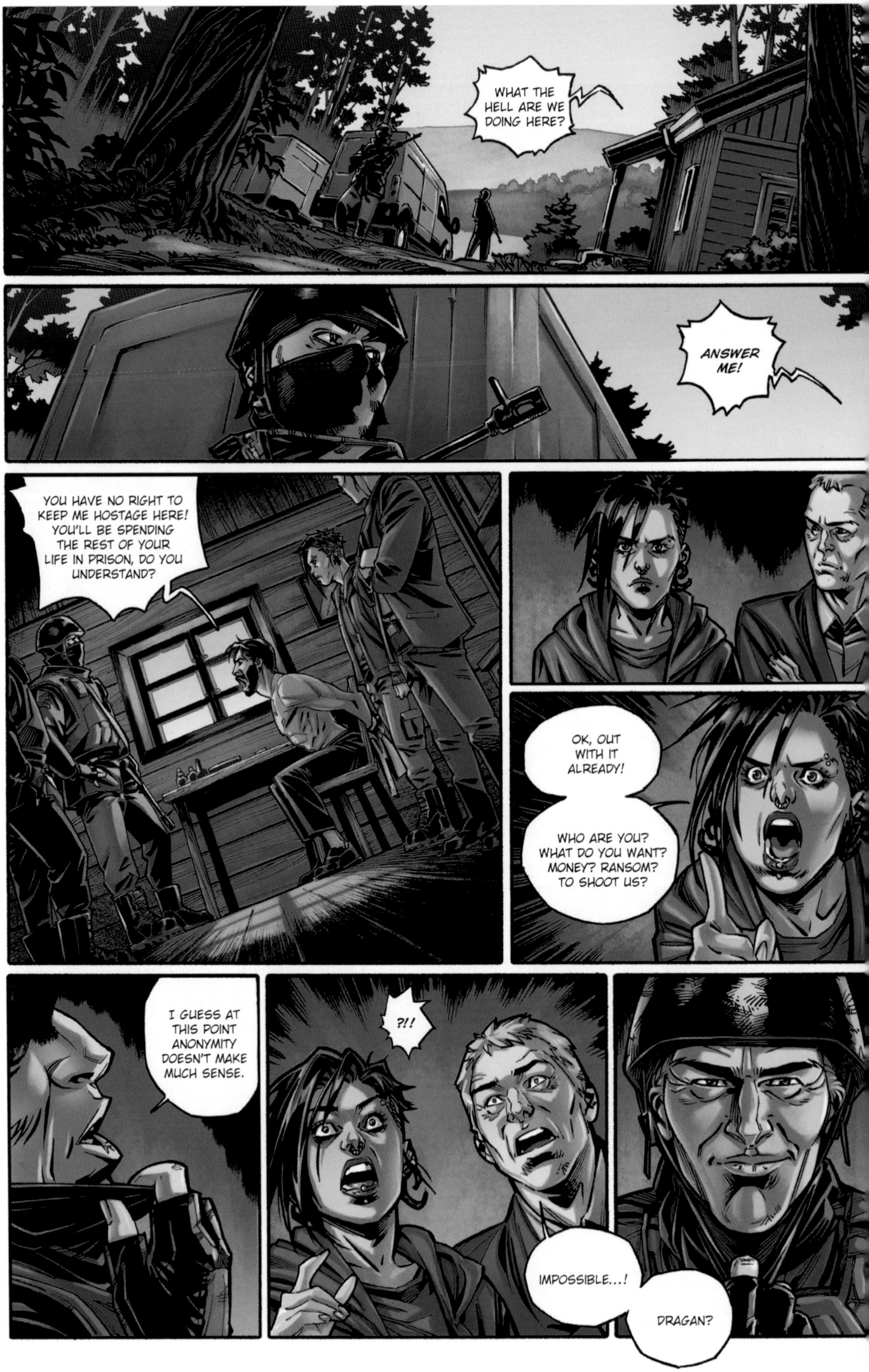
WHAT THE HELL ARE WE DOING HERE?
ANSWER ME!
YOU HAVE NO RIGHT TO KEEP ME HOSTAGE HERE! YOU'LL BE SPENDING THE REST OF YOUR LIFE IN PRISON, DO YOU UNDERSTAND?
OK, OUT WITH IT ALREADY!
WHO ARE YOU? WHAT DO YOU WANT? MONEY? RANSOM? TO SHOOT US?
I GUESS AT THIS POINT ANONYMITY DOESN'T MAKE MUCH SENSE.
?!!
IMPOSSIBLE...!
DRAGAN?

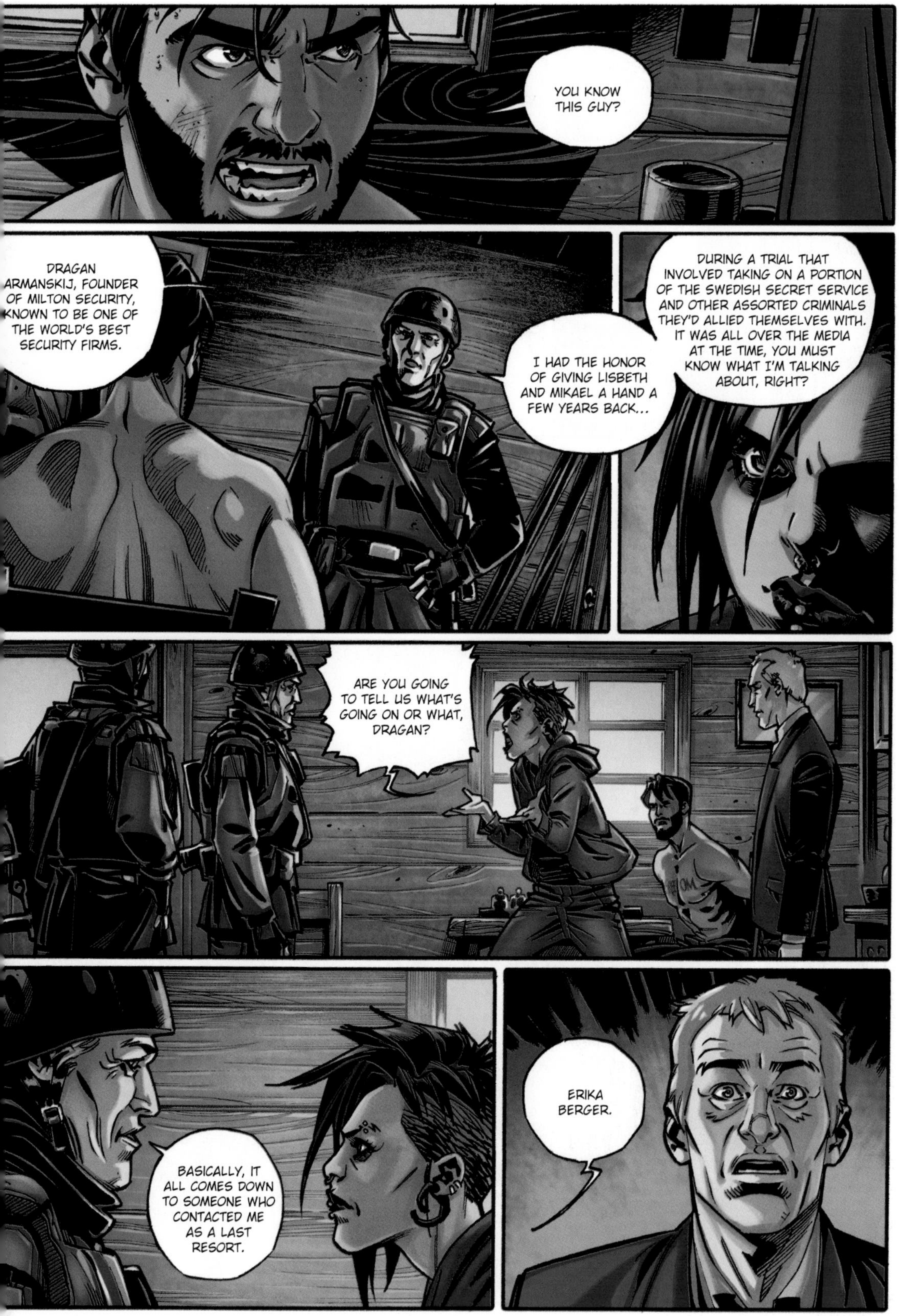
YOU KNOW THIS GUY?
DRAGAN ARMANSKIJ, FOUNDER OF MILTON SECURITY, KNOWN TO BE ONE OF THE WORLD'S BEST SECURITY FIRMS.
I HAD THE HONOR OF GIVING LISBETH AND MIKAEL A HAND A FEW YEARS BACK...
DURING A TRIAL THAT INVOLVED TAKING ON A PORTION OF THE SWEDISH SECRET SERVICE AND OTHER ASSORTED CRIMINALS THEY'D ALLIED THEMSELVES WITH. IT WAS ALL OVER THE MEDIA AT THE TIME, YOU MUST KNOW WHAT I'M TALKING ABOUT, RIGHT?
ARE YOU GOING TO TELL US WHAT'S GOING ON OR WHAT, DRAGAN?
BASICALLY, IT ALL COMES DOWN TO SOMEONE WHO CONTACTED ME AS A LAST RESORT.
ERIKA BERGER.

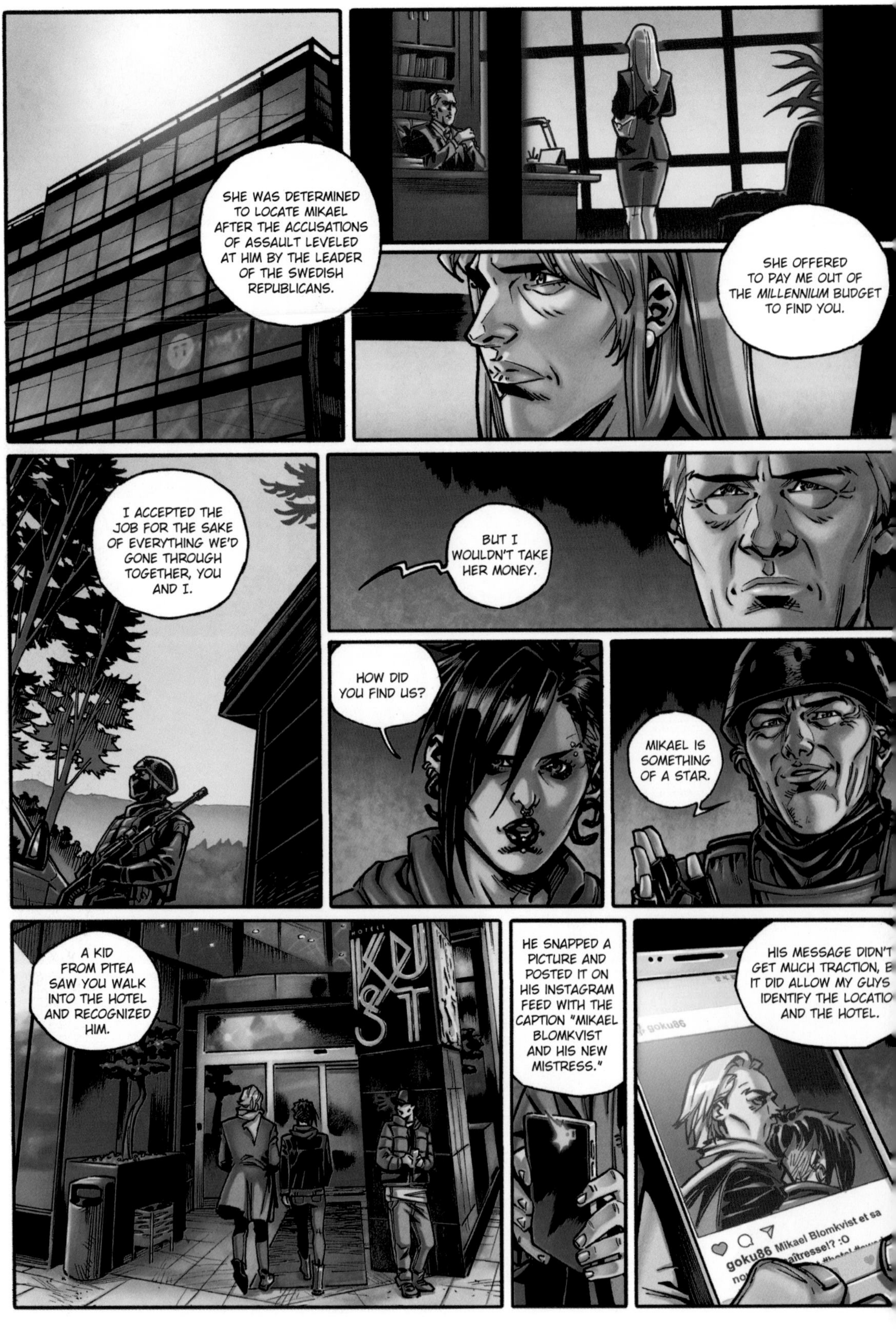
SHE WAS DETERMINED TO LOCATE MIKAEL AFTER THE ACCUSATIONS OF ASSAULT LEVELED AT HIM BY THE LEADER OF THE SWEDISH REPUBLICANS.
SHE OFFERED TO PAY ME OUT OF THE *MILLENNIUM* BUDGET TO FIND YOU.
I ACCEPTED THE JOB FOR THE SAKE OF EVERYTHING WE'D GONE THROUGH TOGETHER, YOU AND I.
BUT I WOULDN'T TAKE HER MONEY.
HOW DID YOU FIND US?
MIKAEL IS SOMETHING OF A STAR.
A KID FROM PITEA SAW YOU WALK INTO THE HOTEL AND RECOGNIZED HIM.
HE SNAPPED A PICTURE AND POSTED IT ON HIS INSTAGRAM FEED WITH THE CAPTION "MIKAEL BLOMKVIST AND HIS NEW MISTRESS."
HIS MESSAGE DIDN'T GET MUCH TRACTION, B
IT DID ALLOW MY GUYS
IDENTIFY THE LOCATIO
AND THE HOTEL.
goku86
goku86 Mikael Blomkvist et sa

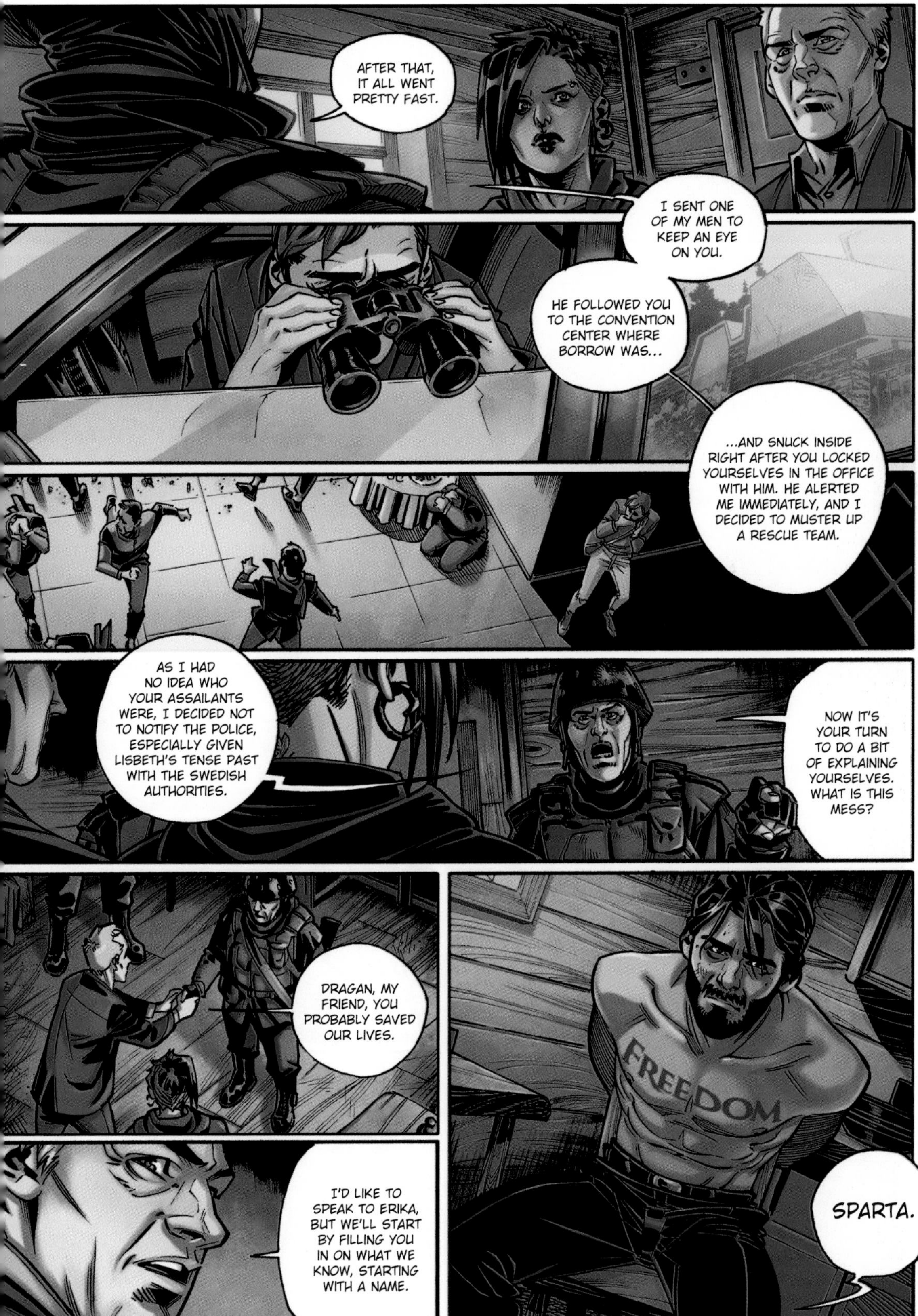
AFTER THAT, IT ALL WENT PRETTY FAST.
I SENT ONE OF MY MEN TO KEEP AN EYE ON YOU.
HE FOLLOWED YOU TO THE CONVENTION CENTER WHERE BORROW WAS...
...AND SNUCK INSIDE RIGHT AFTER YOU LOCKED YOURSELVES IN THE OFFICE WITH HIM. HE ALERTED ME IMMEDIATELY, AND I DECIDED TO MUSTER UP A RESCUE TEAM.
AS I HAD NO IDEA WHO YOUR ASSAILANTS WERE, I DECIDED NOT TO NOTIFY THE POLICE, ESPECIALLY GIVEN LISBETH'S TENSE PAST WITH THE SWEDISH AUTHORITIES.
NOW IT'S YOUR TURN TO DO A BIT OF EXPLAINING YOURSELVES. WHAT IS THIS MESS?
DRAGAN, MY FRIEND, YOU PROBABLY SAVED OUR LIVES.
FREEDOM
I'D LIKE TO SPEAK TO ERIKA, BUT WE'LL START BY FILLING YOU IN ON WHAT WE KNOW, STARTING WITH A NAME.
SPARTA.

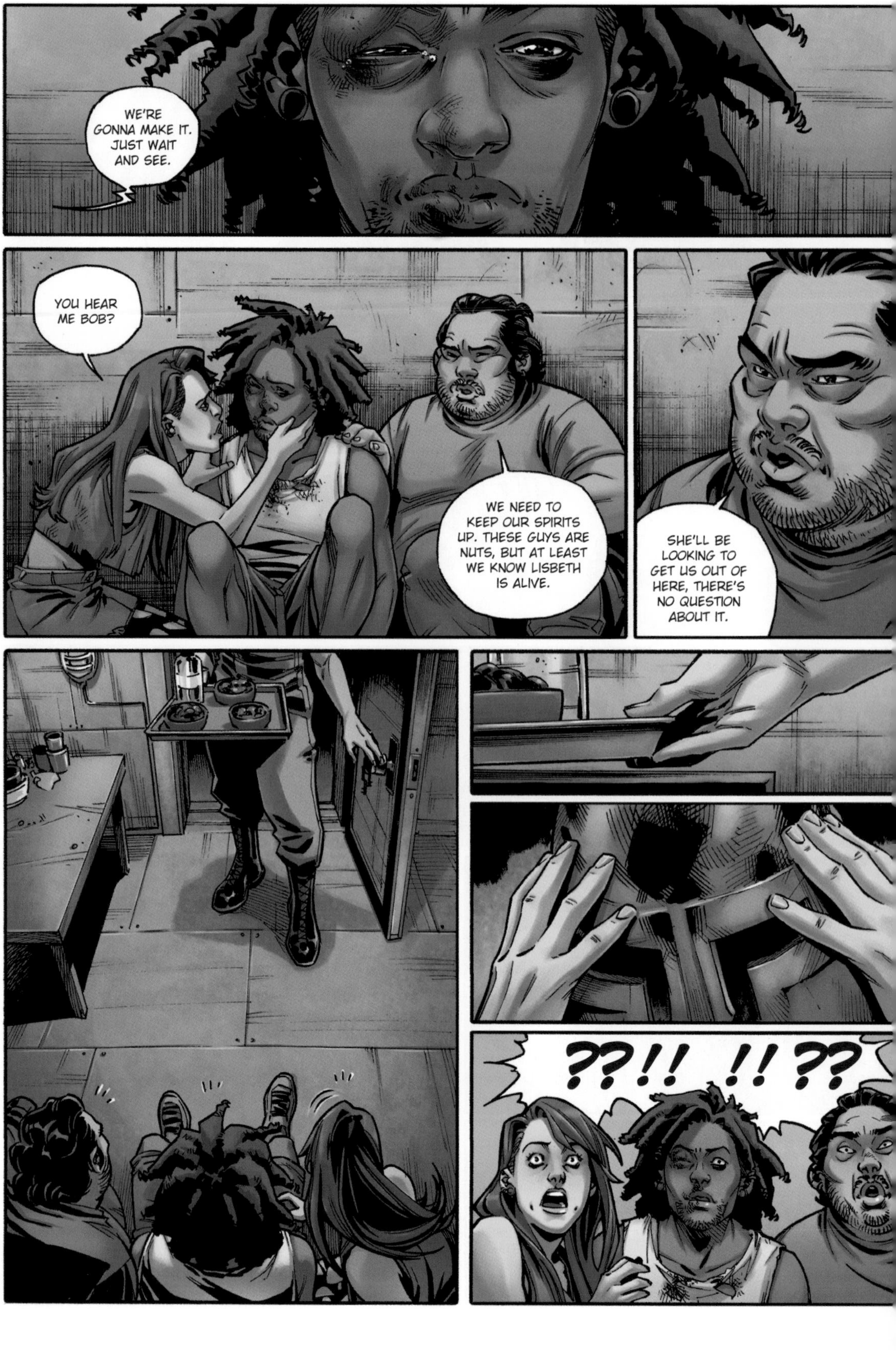
WE'RE GONNA MAKE IT. JUST WAIT AND SEE.
YOU HEAR ME BOB?
WE NEED TO KEEP OUR SPIRITS UP. THESE GUYS ARE NUTS, BUT AT LEAST WE KNOW LISBETH IS ALIVE.
SHE'LL BE LOOKING TO GET US OUT OF HERE, THERE'S NO QUESTION ABOUT IT.
??!! !!??

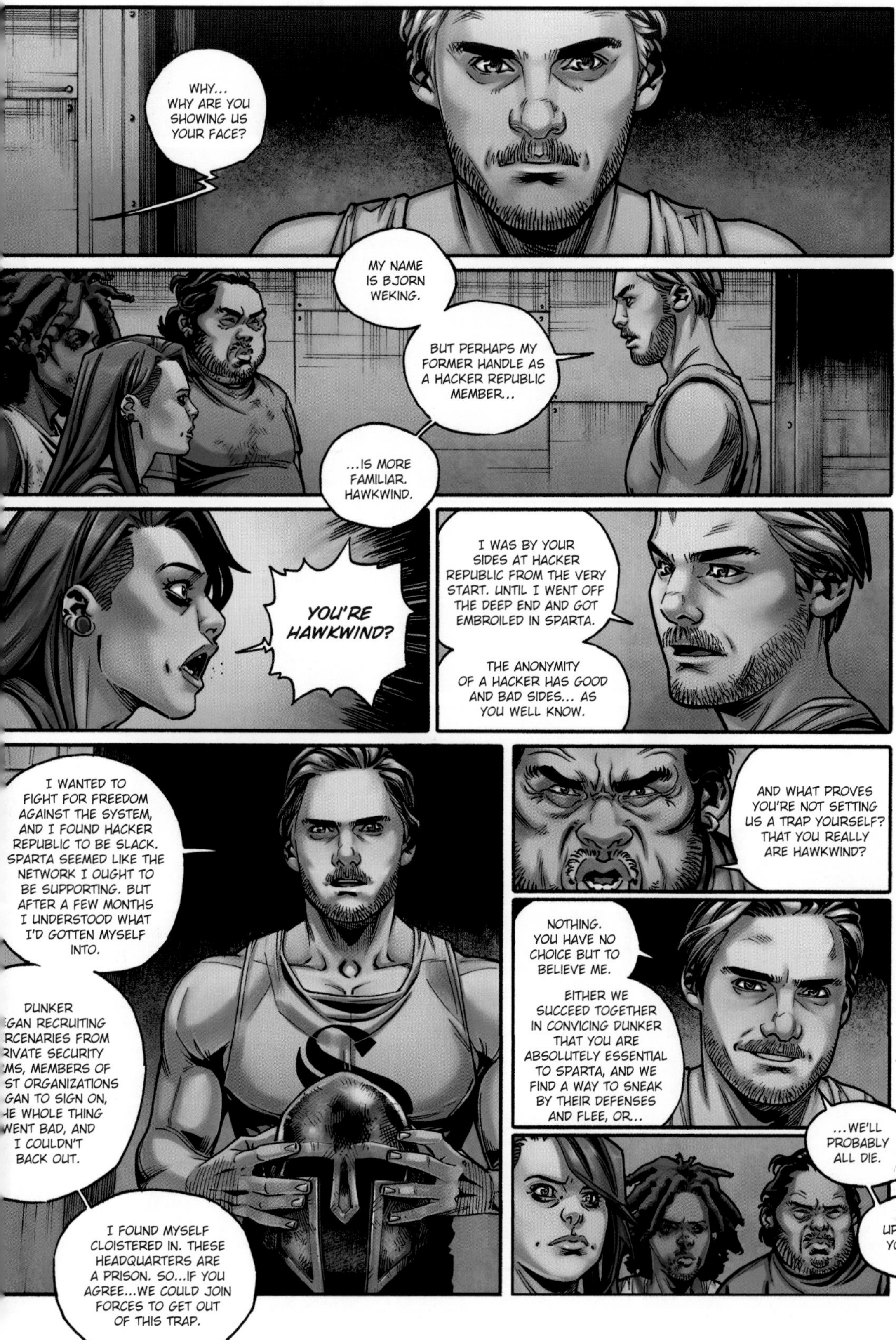

WHY... WHY ARE YOU SHOWING US YOUR FACE?
MY NAME IS BJORN WEKING.
BUT PERHAPS MY FORMER HANDLE AS A HACKER REPUBLIC MEMBER...
...IS MORE FAMILIAR. HAWKWIND.
YOU'RE HAWKWIND?
I WAS BY YOUR SIDES AT HACKER REPUBLIC FROM THE VERY START. UNTIL I WENT OFF THE DEEP END AND GOT EMBROILED IN SPARTA.
THE ANONYMITY OF A HACKER HAS GOOD AND BAD SIDES... AS YOU WELL KNOW.
I WANTED TO FIGHT FOR FREEDOM AGAINST THE SYSTEM, AND I FOUND HACKER REPUBLIC TO BE SLACK. SPARTA SEEMED LIKE THE NETWORK I OUGHT TO BE SUPPORTING. BUT AFTER A FEW MONTHS I UNDERSTOOD WHAT I'D GOTTEN MYSELF INTO.
DUNKER EGAN RECRUITING RCENARIES FROM RIVATE SECURITY MS, MEMBERS OF ST ORGANIZATIONS GAN TO SIGN ON, HE WHOLE THING WENT BAD, AND I COULDN'T BACK OUT.
I FOUND MYSELF CLOISTERED IN. THESE HEADQUARTERS ARE A PRISON. SO...IF YOU AGREE...WE COULD JOIN FORCES TO GET OUT OF THIS TRAP.
AND WHAT PROVES YOU'RE NOT SETTING US A TRAP YOURSELF? THAT YOU REALLY ARE HAWKWIND?
NOTHING. YOU HAVE NO CHOICE BUT TO BELIEVE ME.
EITHER WE SUCCEED TOGETHER IN CONVICING DUNKER THAT YOU ARE ABSOLUTELY ESSENTIAL TO SPARTA, AND WE FIND A WAY TO SNEAK BY THEIR DEFENSES AND FLEE, OR...
...WE'LL PROBABLY ALL DIE.
UP TO YOU.

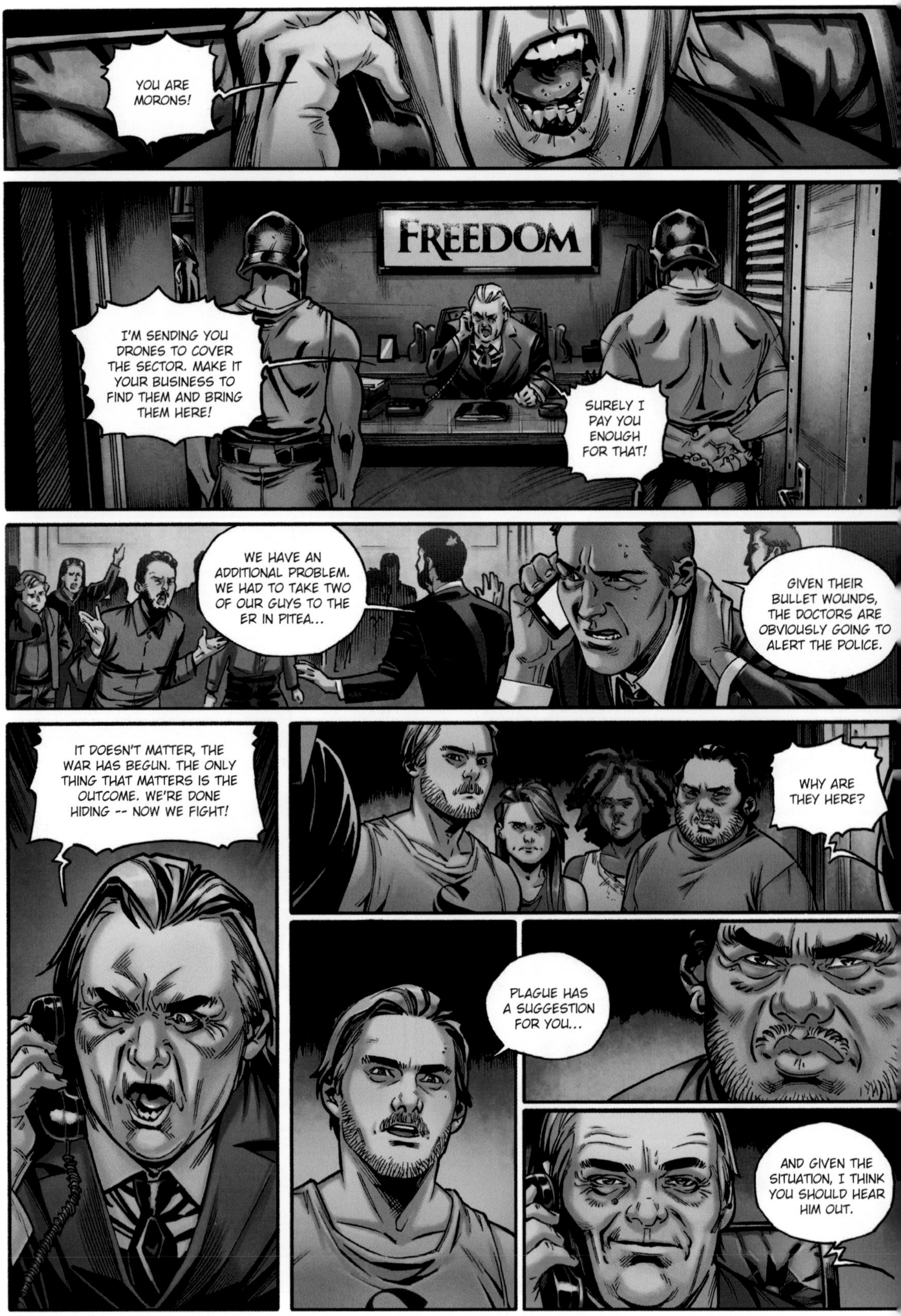
YOU ARE MORONS!
FREEDOM
I'M SENDING YOU DRONES TO COVER THE SECTOR. MAKE IT YOUR BUSINESS TO FIND THEM AND BRING THEM HERE!
SURELY I PAY YOU ENOUGH FOR THAT!
WE HAVE AN ADDITIONAL PROBLEM. WE HAD TO TAKE TWO OF OUR GUYS TO THE ER IN PITEA...
GIVEN THEIR BULLET WOUNDS, THE DOCTORS ARE OBVIOUSLY GOING TO ALERT THE POLICE.
IT DOESN'T MATTER, THE WAR HAS BEGUN. THE ONLY THING THAT MATTERS IS THE OUTCOME. WE'RE DONE HIDING -- NOW WE FIGHT!
WHY ARE THEY HERE?
PLAGUE HAS A SUGGESTION FOR YOU...
AND GIVEN THE SITUATION, I THINK YOU SHOULD HEAR HIM OUT.

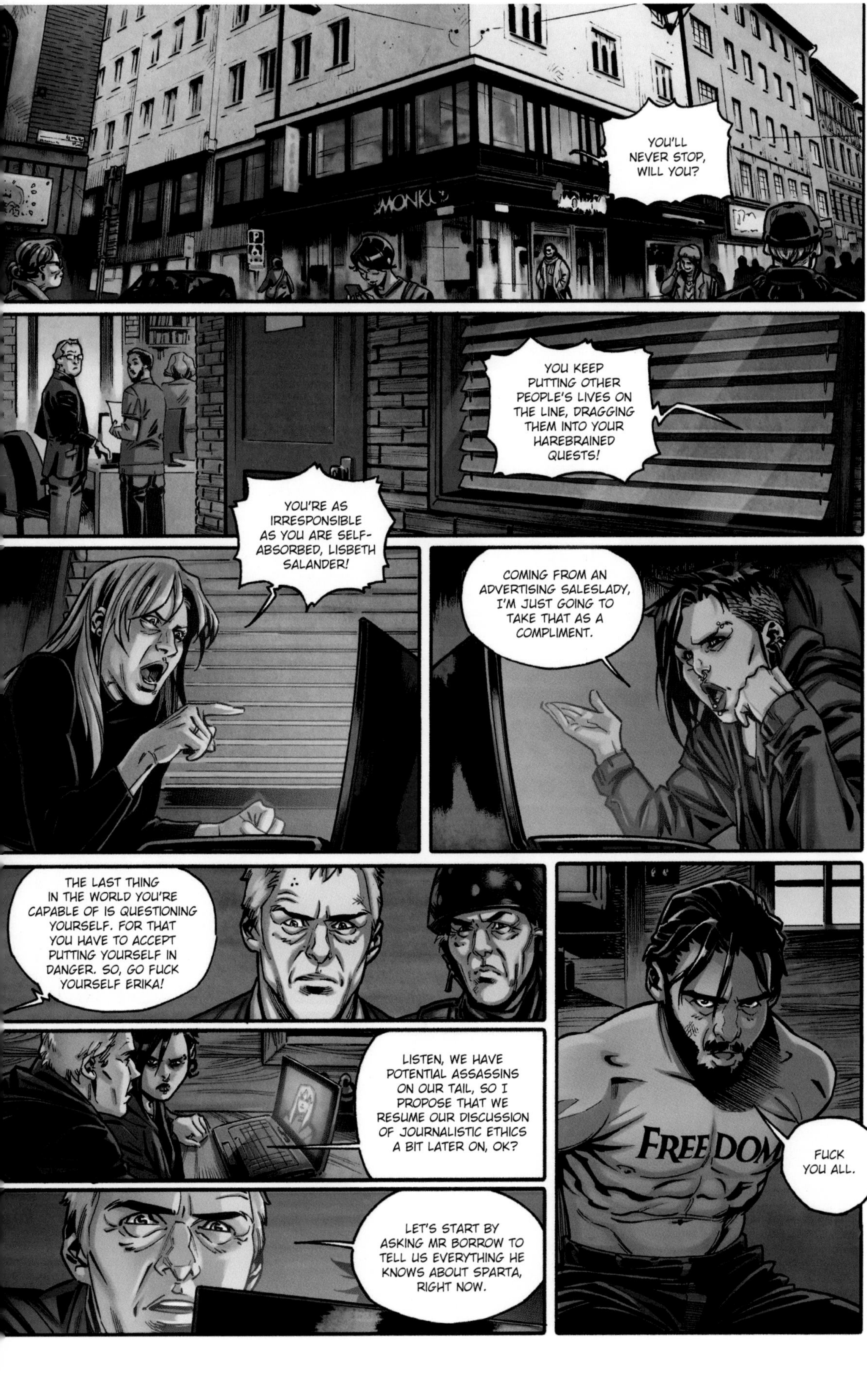
YOU'LL NEVER STOP, WILL YOU?
YOU KEEP PUTTING OTHER PEOPLE'S LIVES ON THE LINE, DRAGGING THEM INTO YOUR HAREBRAINED QUESTS!
YOU'RE AS IRRESPONSIBLE AS YOU ARE SELF-ABSORBED, LISBETH SALANDER!
COMING FROM AN ADVERTISING SALESLADY, I'M JUST GOING TO TAKE THAT AS A COMPLIMENT.
THE LAST THING IN THE WORLD YOU'RE CAPABLE OF IS QUESTIONING YOURSELF. FOR THAT YOU HAVE TO ACCEPT PUTTING YOURSELF IN DANGER. SO, GO FUCK YOURSELF ERIKA!
LISTEN, WE HAVE POTENTIAL ASSASSINS ON OUR TAIL, SO I PROPOSE THAT WE RESUME OUR DISCUSSION OF JOURNALISTIC ETHICS A BIT LATER ON, OK?
LET'S START BY ASKING MR BORROW TO TELL US EVERYTHING HE KNOWS ABOUT SPARTA, RIGHT NOW.
FREEDOM
FUCK YOU ALL.

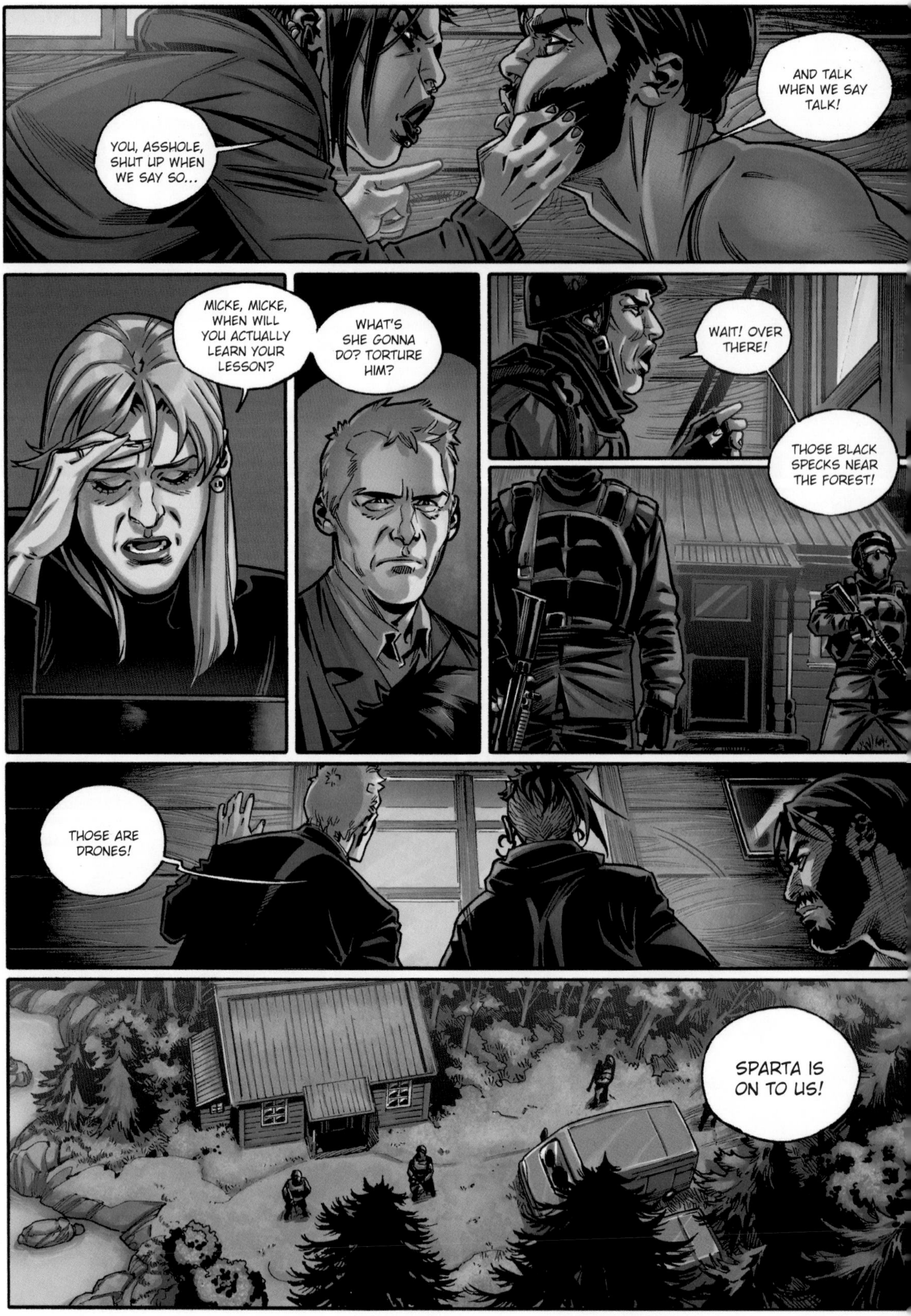
YOU, ASSHOLE, SHUT UP WHEN WE SAY SO...
AND TALK WHEN WE SAY TALK!
MICKE, MICKE, WHEN WILL YOU ACTUALLY LEARN YOUR LESSON?
WHAT'S SHE GONNA DO? TORTURE HIM?
WAIT! OVER THERE!
THOSE BLACK SPECKS NEAR THE FOREST!
THOSE ARE DRONES!
SPARTA IS ON TO US!

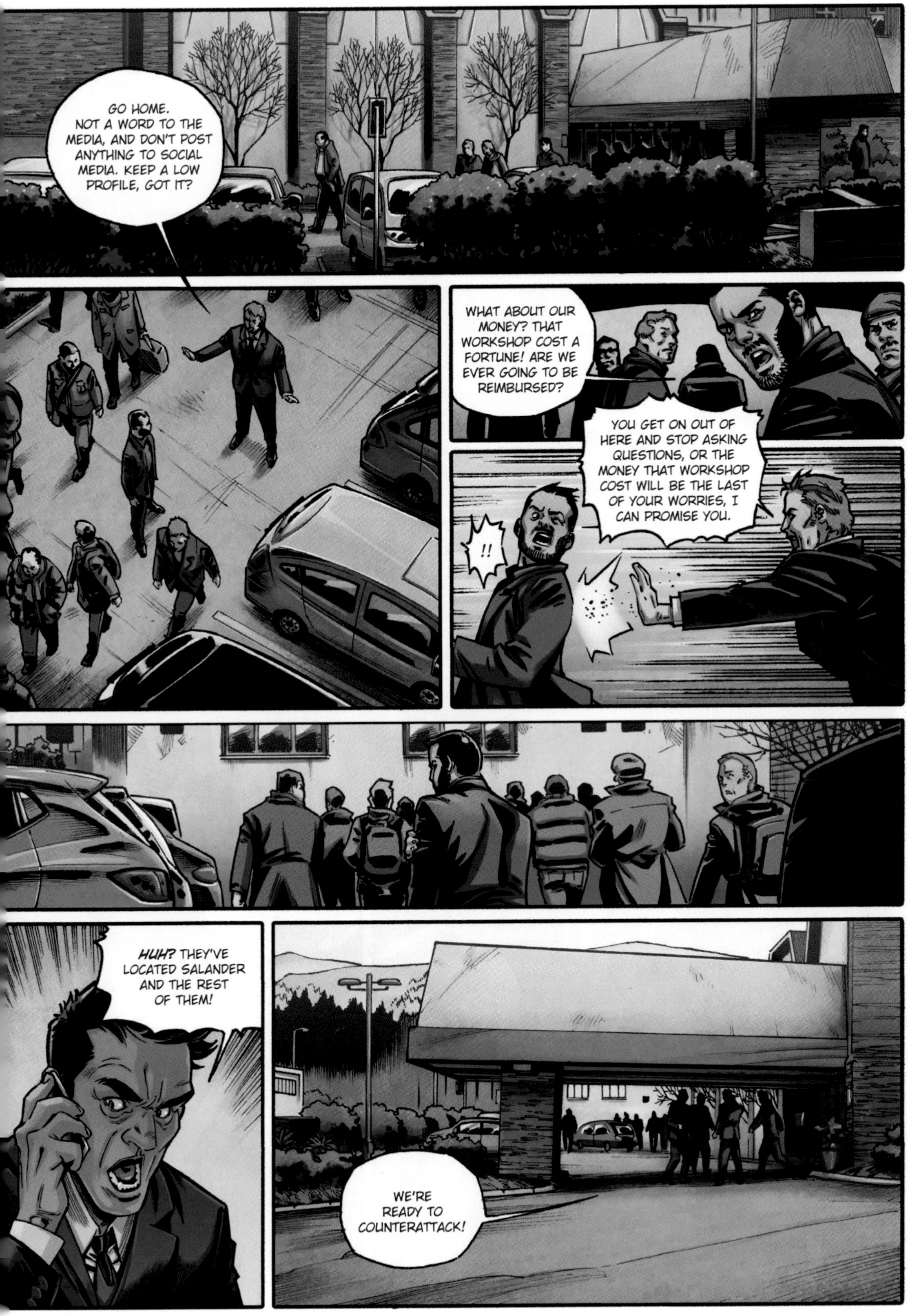
GO HOME. NOT A WORD TO THE MEDIA, AND DON'T POST ANYTHING TO SOCIAL MEDIA. KEEP A LOW PROFILE, GOT IT?
WHAT ABOUT OUR MONEY? THAT WORKSHOP COST A FORTUNE! ARE WE EVER GOING TO BE REIMBURSED?
YOU GET ON OUT OF HERE AND STOP ASKING QUESTIONS, OR THE MONEY THAT WORKSHOP COST WILL BE THE LAST OF YOUR WORRIES, I CAN PROMISE YOU.
!!
HUH? THEY'VE LOCATED SALANDER AND THE REST OF THEM!
WE'RE READY TO COUNTERATTACK!

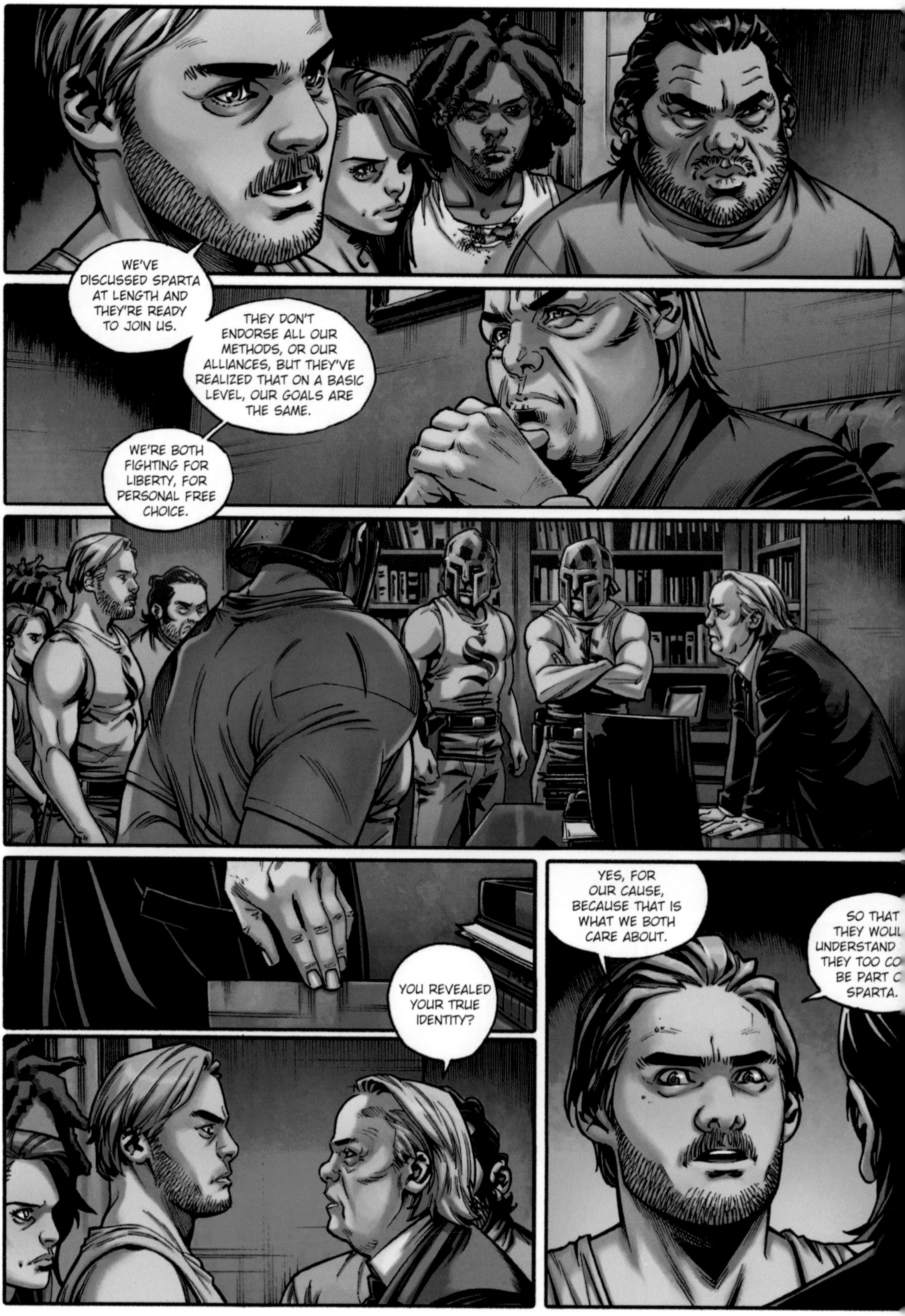
WE'VE DISCUSSED SPARTA AT LENGTH AND THEY'RE READY TO JOIN US.
THEY DON'T ENDORSE ALL OUR METHODS, OR OUR ALLIANCES, BUT THEY'VE REALIZED THAT ON A BASIC LEVEL, OUR GOALS ARE THE SAME.
WE'RE BOTH FIGHTING FOR LIBERTY, FOR PERSONAL FREE CHOICE.
YOU REVEALED YOUR TRUE IDENTITY?
YES, FOR OUR CAUSE, BECAUSE THAT IS WHAT WE BOTH CARE ABOUT.
SO THAT THEY WOUL UNDERSTAND THEY TOO CO BE PART O SPARTA.

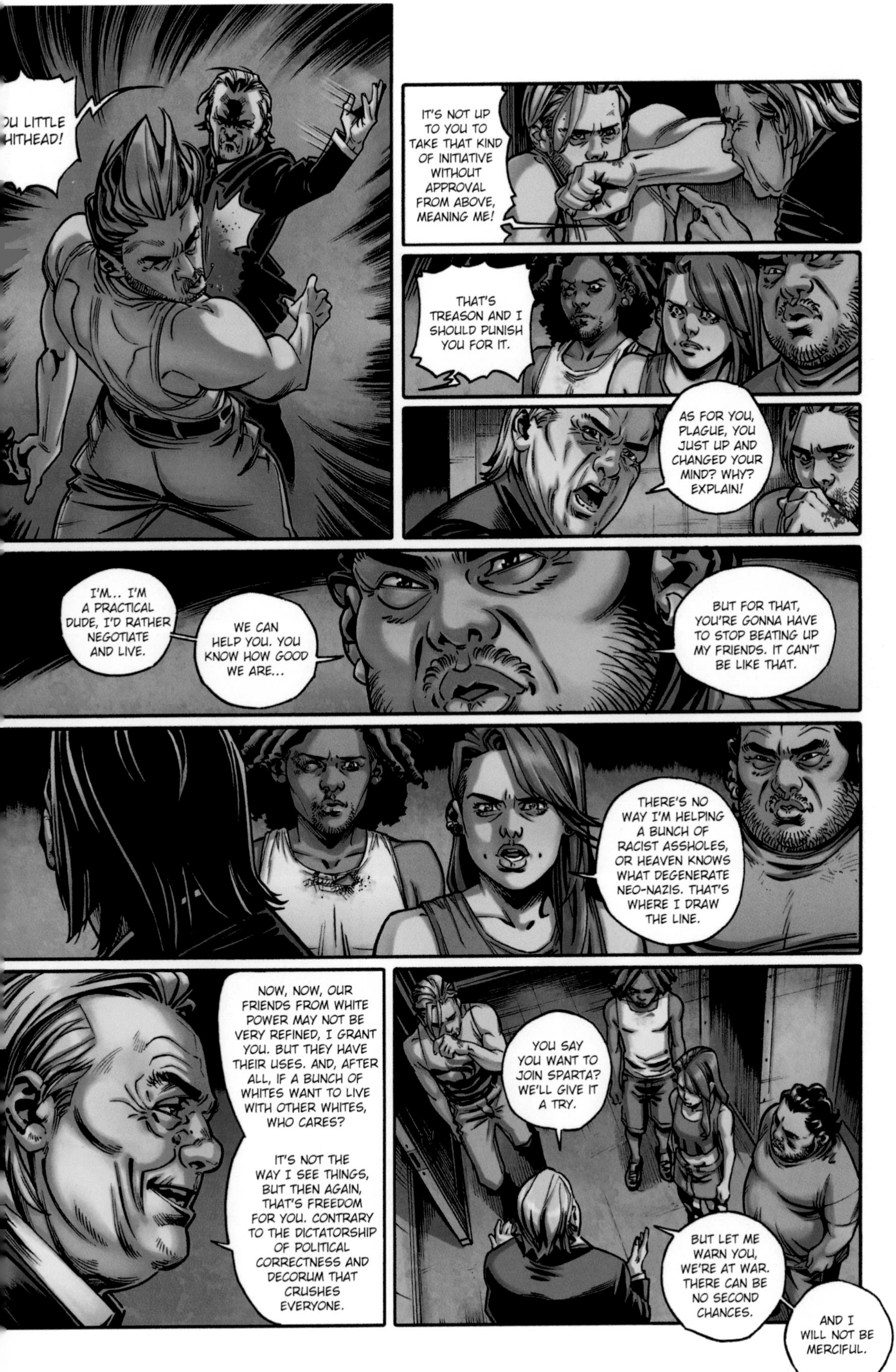
OU LITTLE
HITHEAD!
IT'S NOT UP TO YOU TO TAKE THAT KIND OF INITIATIVE WITHOUT APPROVAL FROM ABOVE, MEANING ME!
THAT'S TREASON AND I SHOULD PUNISH YOU FOR IT.
AS FOR YOU, PLAGUE, YOU JUST UP AND CHANGED YOUR MIND? WHY? EXPLAIN!
I'M... I'M A PRACTICAL DUDE, I'D RATHER NEGOTIATE AND LIVE.
WE CAN HELP YOU. YOU KNOW HOW GOOD WE ARE...
BUT FOR THAT, YOU'RE GONNA HAVE TO STOP BEATING UP MY FRIENDS. IT CAN'T BE LIKE THAT.
THERE'S NO WAY I'M HELPING A BUNCH OF RACIST ASSHOLES, OR HEAVEN KNOWS WHAT DEGENERATE NEO-NAZIS. THAT'S WHERE I DRAW THE LINE.
NOW, NOW, OUR FRIENDS FROM WHITE POWER MAY NOT BE VERY REFINED, I GRANT YOU. BUT THEY HAVE THEIR USES. AND, AFTER ALL, IF A BUNCH OF WHITES WANT TO LIVE WITH OTHER WHITES, WHO CARES?
IT'S NOT THE WAY I SEE THINGS, BUT THEN AGAIN, THAT'S FREEDOM FOR YOU. CONTRARY TO THE DICTATORSHIP OF POLITICAL CORRECTNESS AND DECORUM THAT CRUSHES EVERYONE.
YOU SAY YOU WANT TO JOIN SPARTA? WE'LL GIVE IT A TRY.
BUT LET ME WARN YOU, WE'RE AT WAR. THERE CAN BE NO SECOND CHANCES.
AND I WILL NOT BE MERCIFUL.

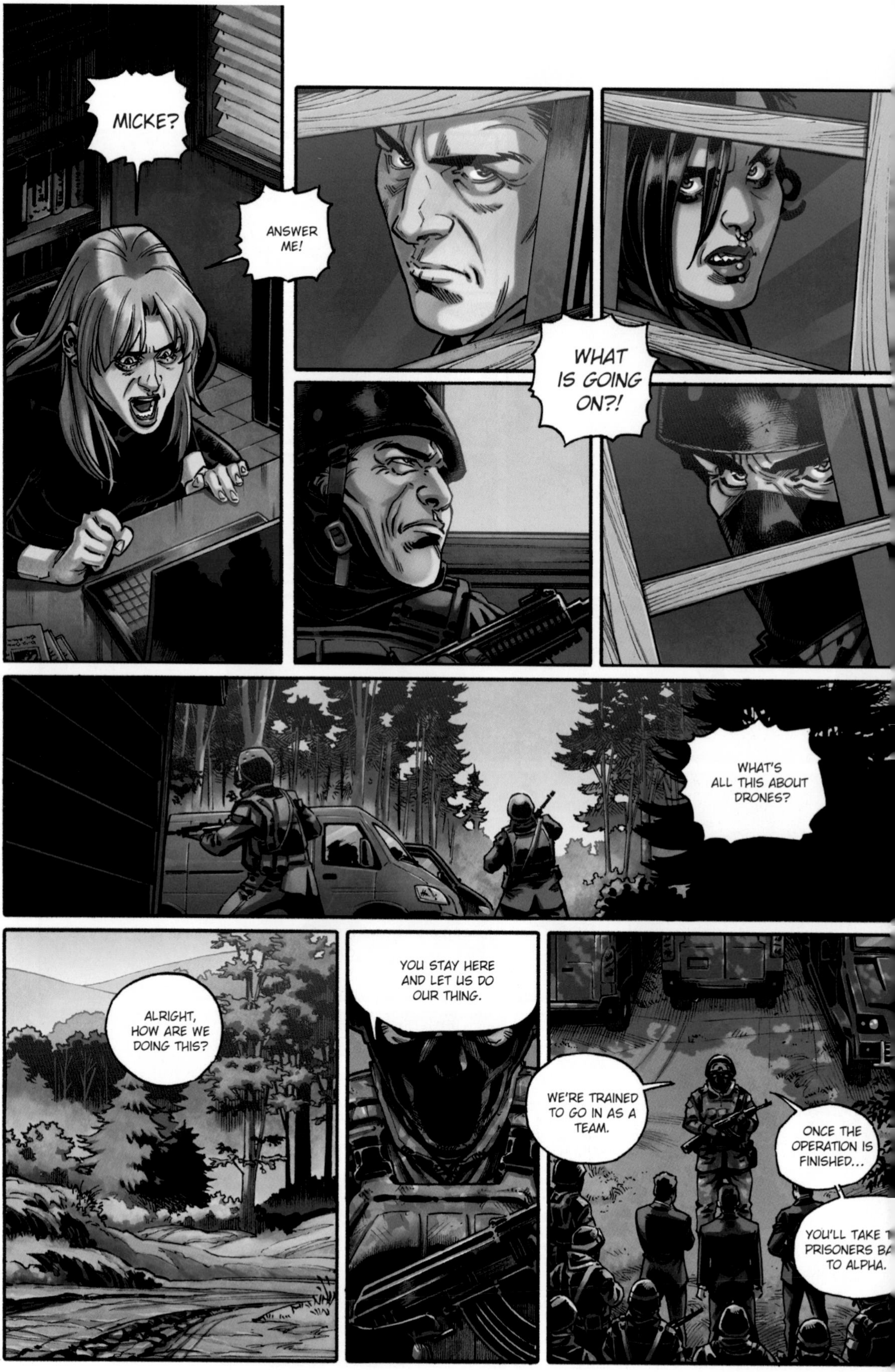
MICKE?
ANSWER ME!
WHAT IS GOING ON?!
WHAT'S ALL THIS ABOUT DRONES?
ALRIGHT, HOW ARE WE DOING THIS?
YOU STAY HERE AND LET US DO OUR THING.
WE'RE TRAINED TO GO IN AS A TEAM.
ONCE THE OPERATION IS FINISHED...
YOU'LL TAKE T
PRISONERS BA
TO ALPHA.

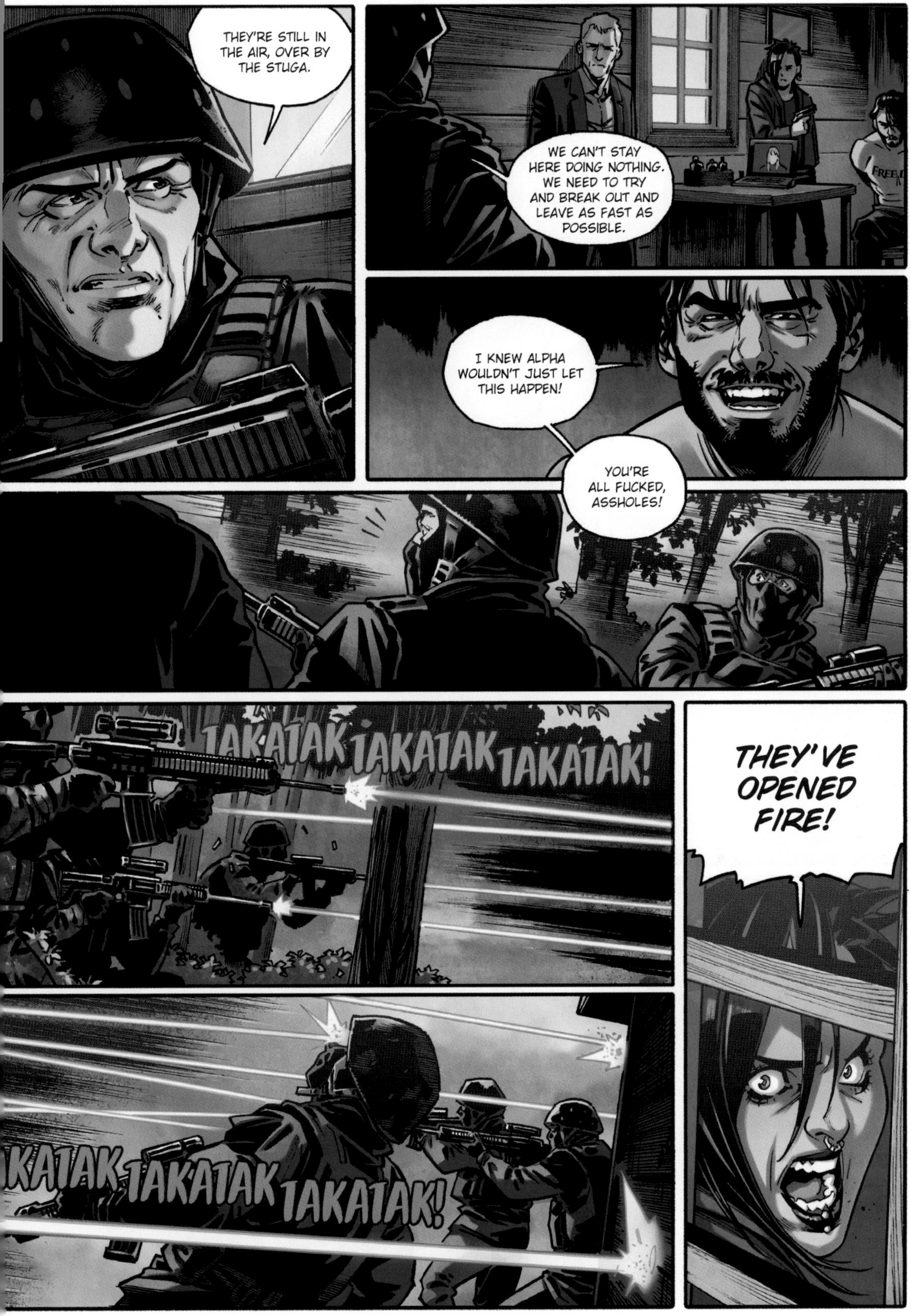
THEY'RE STILL IN THE AIR, OVER BY THE STUGA.
WE CAN'T STAY HERE DOING NOTHING. WE NEED TO TRY AND BREAK OUT AND LEAVE AS FAST AS POSSIBLE.
I KNEW ALPHA WOULDN'T JUST LET THIS HAPPEN!
YOU'RE ALL FUCKED, ASSHOLES!
TAKATAK TAKATAK TAKATAK!
THEY'VE OPENED FIRE!
TAKATAK TAKATAK TAKATAK!

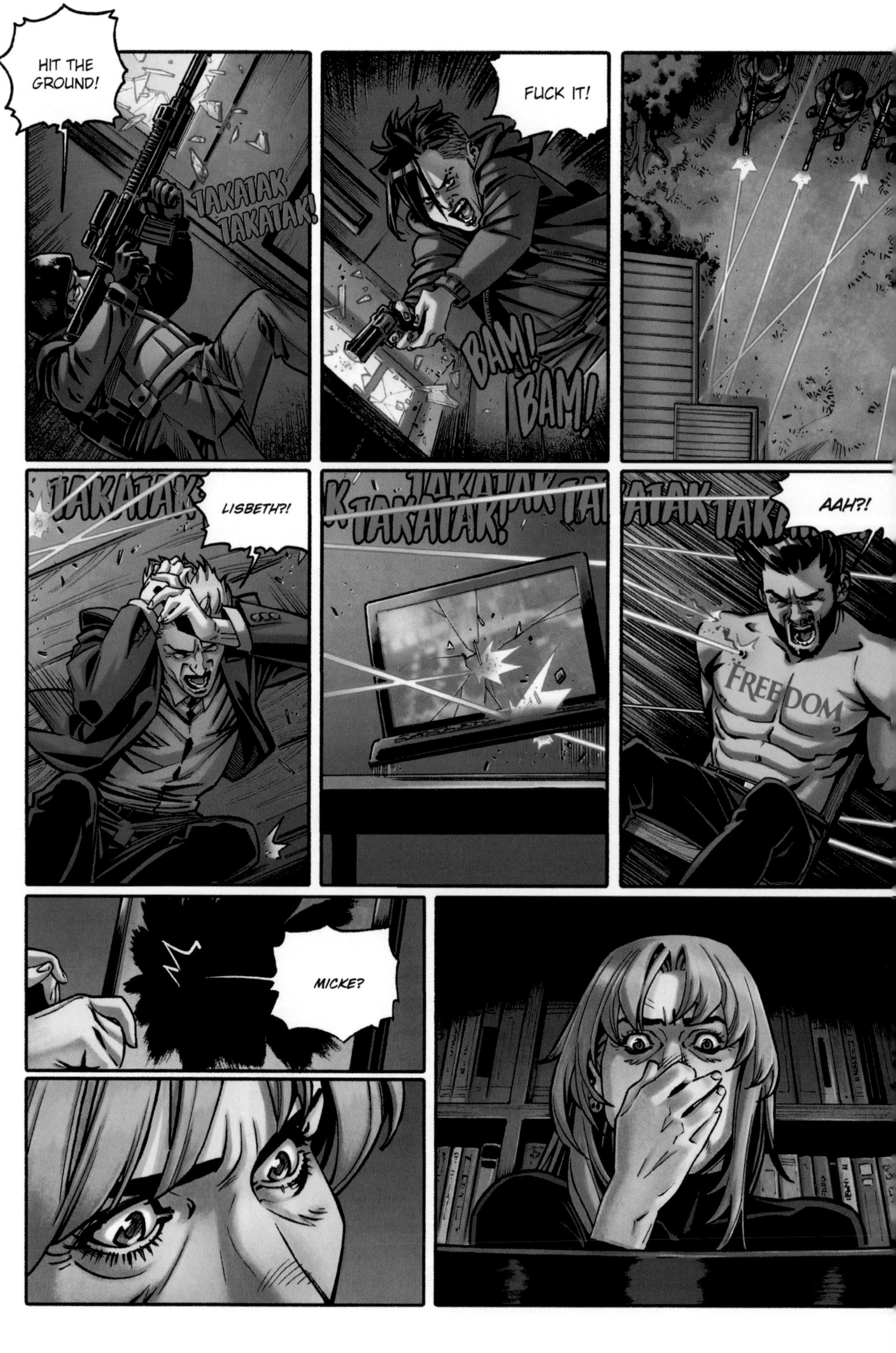
HIT THE GROUND!
TAKATAK TAKATAK!
FUCK IT!
BAM! BAM!
TAKATAK
LISBETH?!
TAKATAK!
TAKATAK
AAH?!
FREEDOM
MICKE?

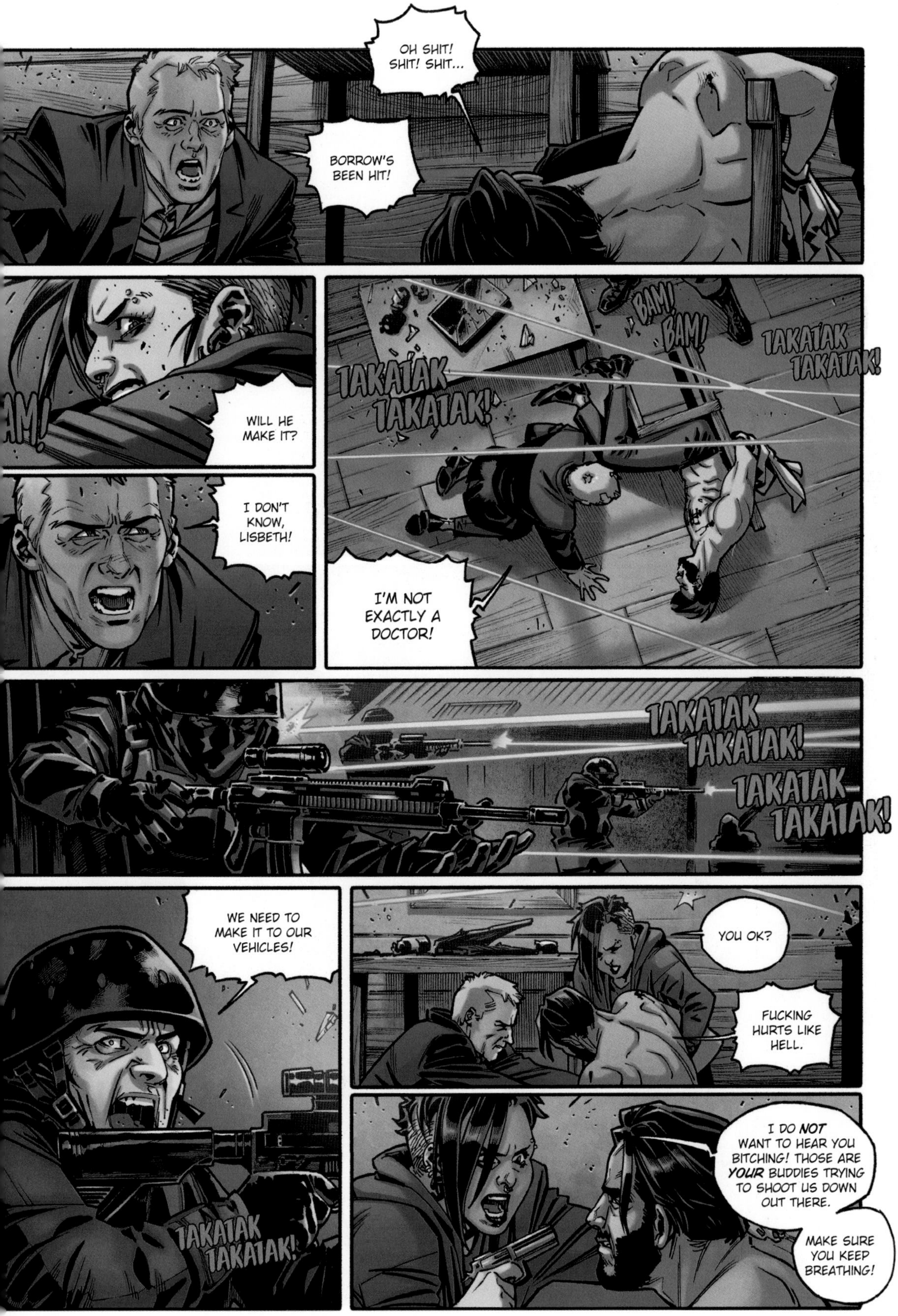
OH SHIT! SHIT! SHIT...
BORROW'S BEEN HIT!
AM!
WILL HE MAKE IT?
I DON'T KNOW, LISBETH!
BAM! BAM!
TAKATAK TAKATAK!
TAKATAK TAKATAK!
I'M NOT EXACTLY A DOCTOR!
TAKATAK TAKATAK!
TAKATAK TAKATAK!
WE NEED TO MAKE IT TO OUR VEHICLES!
TAKATAK TAKATAK!
YOU OK?
FUCKING HURTS LIKE HELL.
I DO **NOT** WANT TO HEAR YOU BITCHING! THOSE ARE ***YOUR*** BUDDIES TRYING TO SHOOT US DOWN OUT THERE.
MAKE SURE YOU KEEP BREATHING!

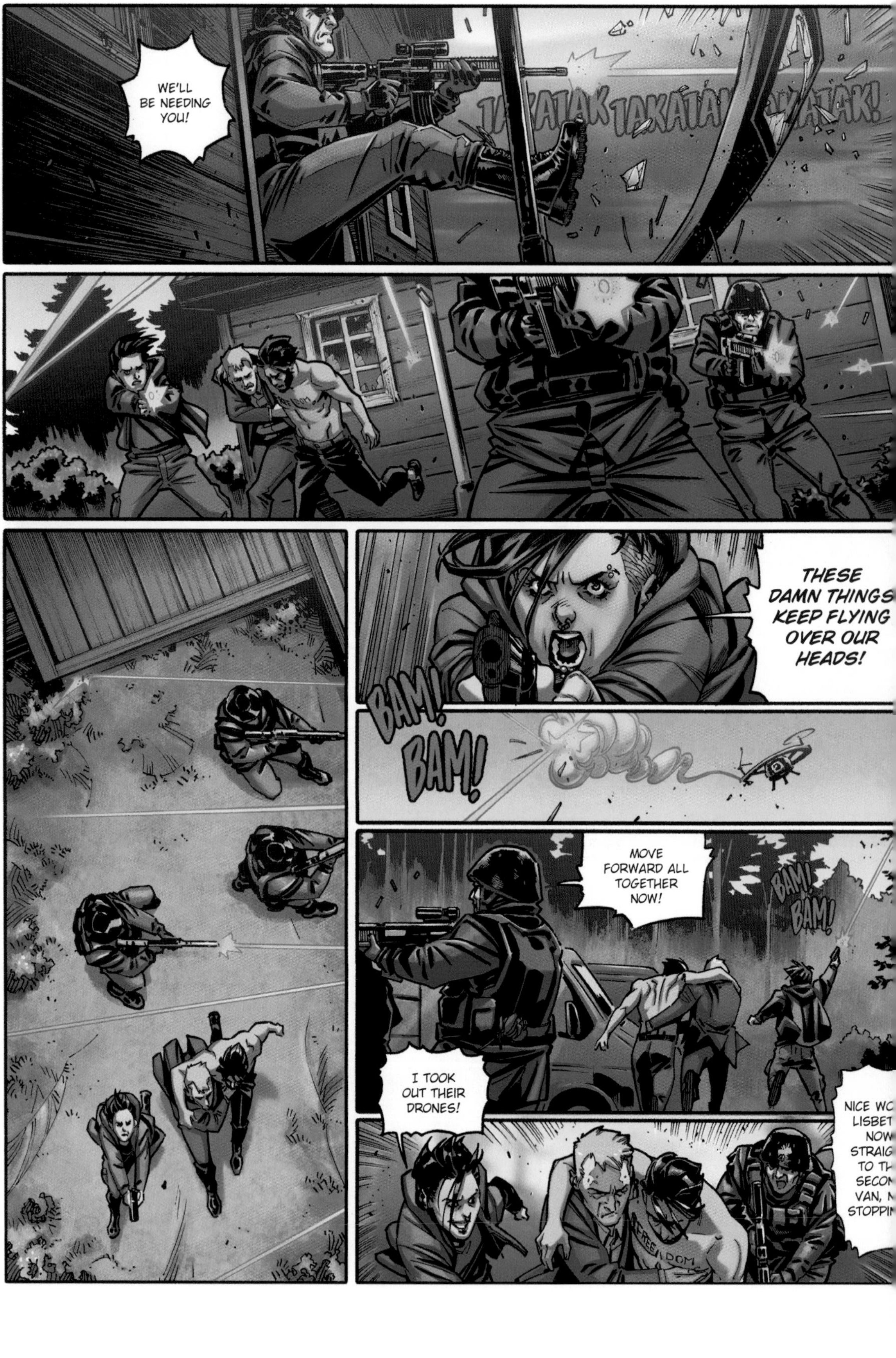
WE'LL BE NEEDING YOU!
TAKATAK TAKATAK
THESE DAMN THINGS KEEP FLYING OVER OUR HEADS!
BAM! BAM!
MOVE FORWARD ALL TOGETHER NOW!
BAM! BAM!
I TOOK OUT THEIR DRONES!
NICE WO LISBET NOW STRAIG TO TH SECON VAN, N STOPPIN

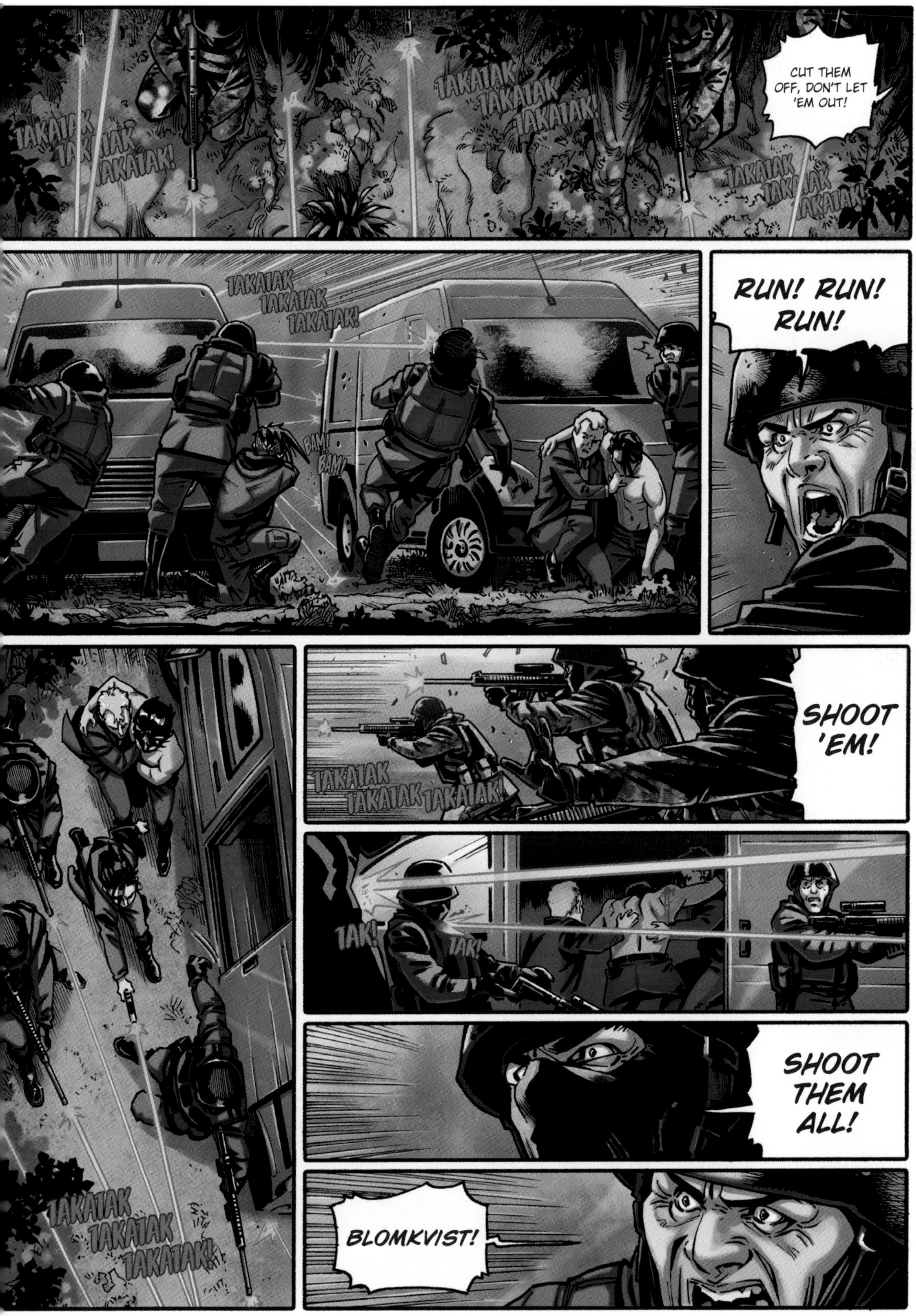
TAKATAK TAKATAK TAKATAK!
TAKATAK TAKATAK TAKATAK!
CUT THEM OFF, DON'T LET 'EM OUT!
TAKATAK TAKATAK TAKATAK!
TAKATAK TAKATAK TAKATAK!
BAM! BAM!
RUN! RUN! RUN!
TAKATAK TAKATAK TAKATAK!
SHOOT 'EM!
TAKATAK TAKATAK TAKATAK!
TAK! TAK!
SHOOT THEM ALL!
BLOMKVIST!

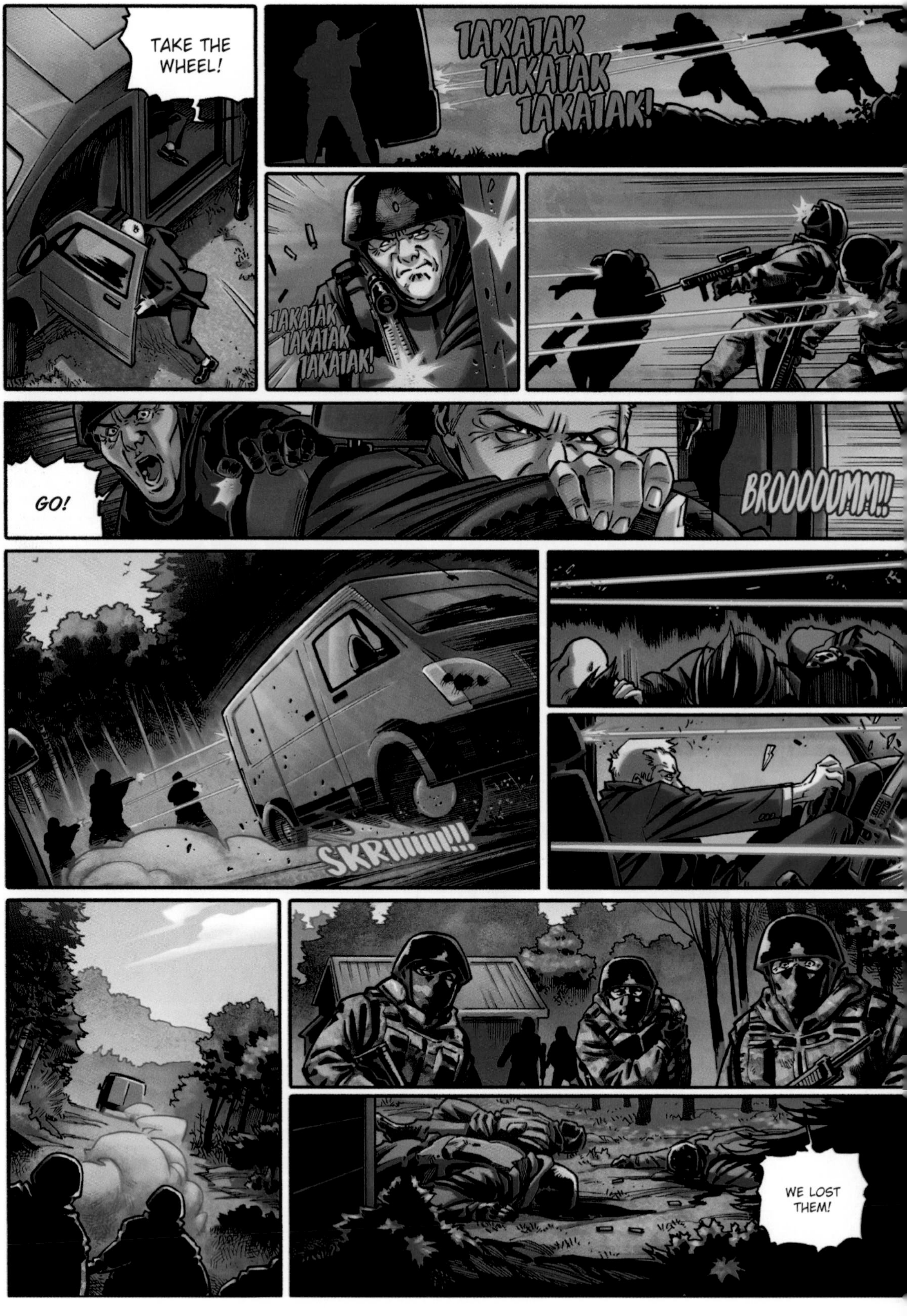
TAKE THE WHEEL!
TAKATAK TAKATAK TAKATAK!
TAKATAK TAKATAK TAKATAK!
GO!
BROOOOUMM!!
SKRIIIIIII!!!
WE LOST THEM!

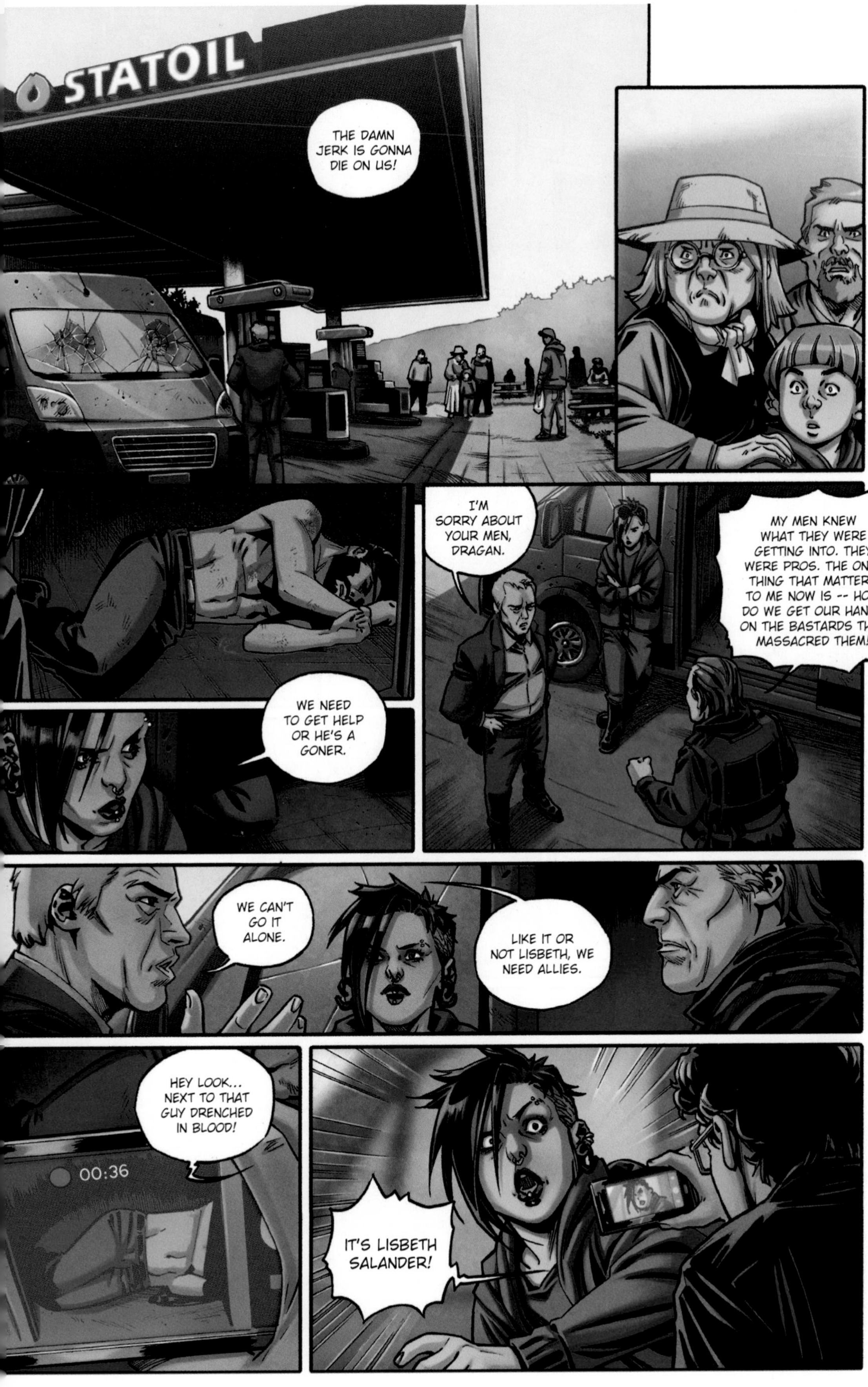
STATOIL
THE DAMN JERK IS GONNA DIE ON US!
WE NEED TO GET HELP OR HE'S A GONER.
I'M SORRY ABOUT YOUR MEN, DRAGAN.
MY MEN KNEW WHAT THEY WERE GETTING INTO. THEY WERE PROS. THE ONLY THING THAT MATTERS TO ME NOW IS -- HOW DO WE GET OUR HANDS ON THE BASTARDS THAT MASSACRED THEM!
WE CAN'T GO IT ALONE.
LIKE IT OR NOT LISBETH, WE NEED ALLIES.
HEY LOOK... NEXT TO THAT GUY DRENCHED IN BLOOD!
00:36
IT'S LISBETH SALANDER!

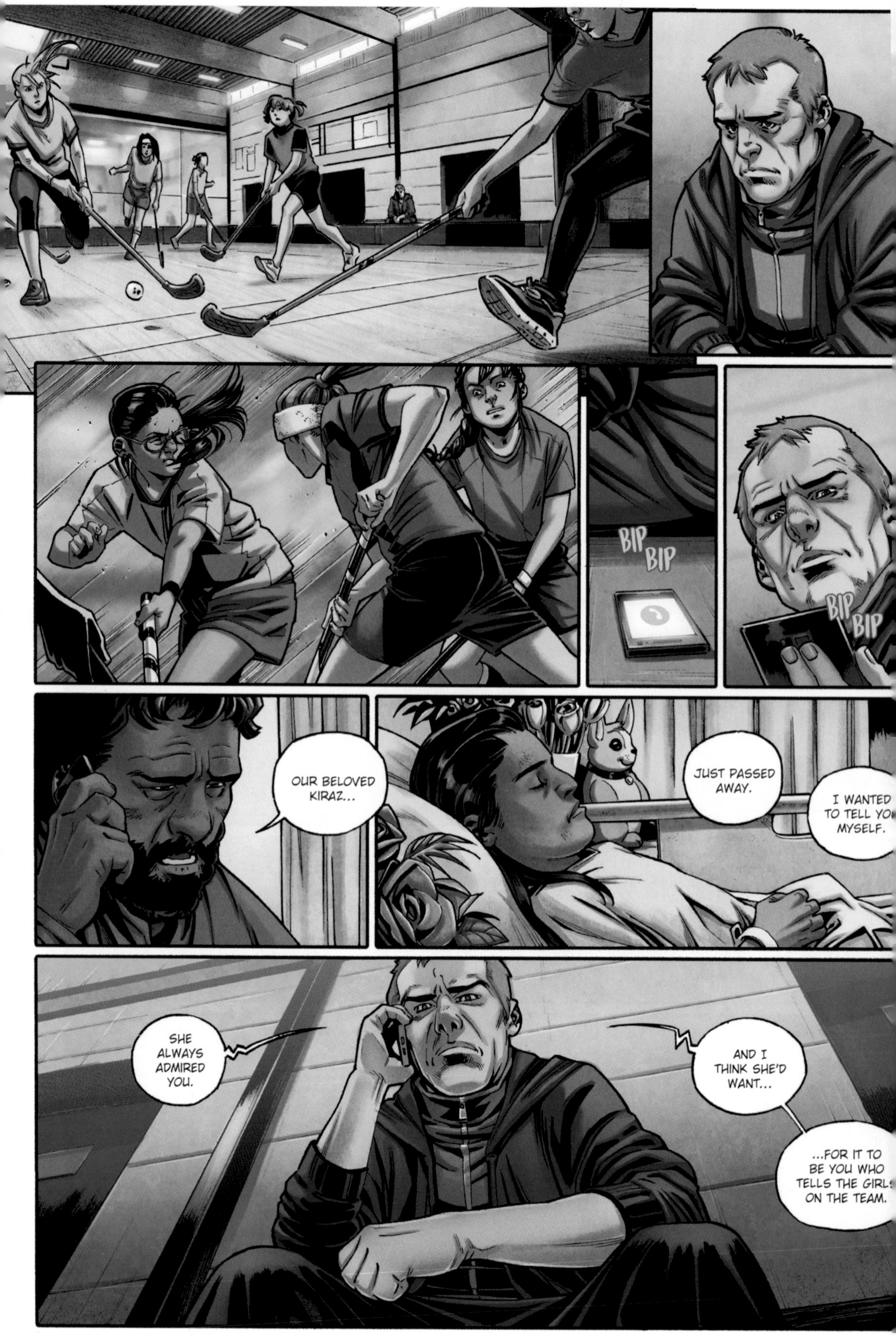
BIP BIP
BIP BIP
OUR BELOVED KIRAZ...
JUST PASSED AWAY.
I WANTED TO TELL YO MYSELF.
SHE ALWAYS ADMIRED YOU.
AND I THINK SHE'D WANT...
...FOR IT TO BE YOU WHO TELLS THE GIRLS ON THE TEAM.

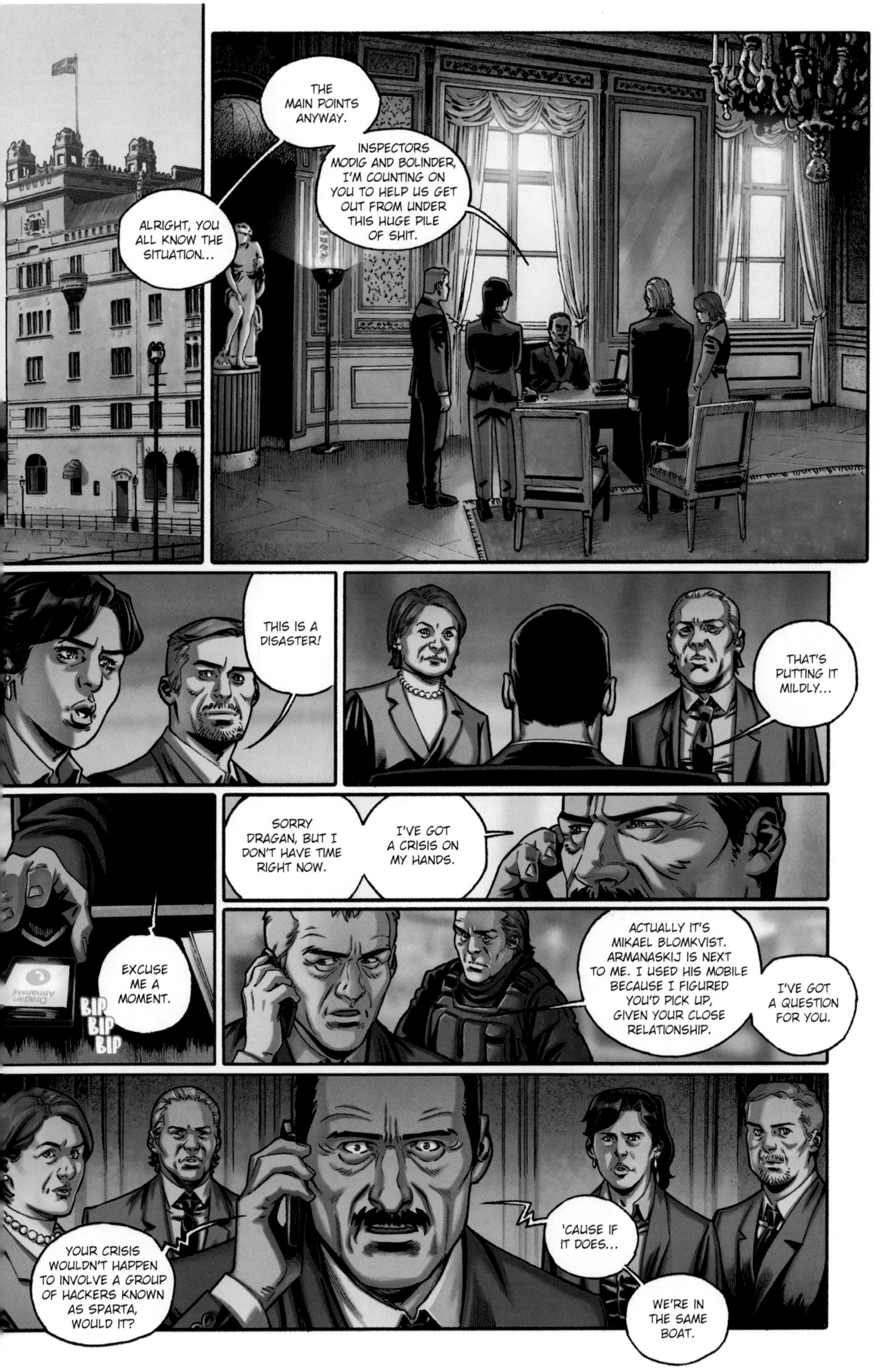
ALRIGHT, YOU ALL KNOW THE SITUATION...
THE MAIN POINTS ANYWAY.
INSPECTORS MODIG AND BOLINDER, I'M COUNTING ON YOU TO HELP US GET OUT FROM UNDER THIS HUGE PILE OF SHIT.
THIS IS A DISASTER!
THAT'S PUTTING IT MILDLY...
BIP BIP BIP
EXCUSE ME A MOMENT.
SORRY DRAGAN, BUT I DON'T HAVE TIME RIGHT NOW.
I'VE GOT A CRISIS ON MY HANDS.
ACTUALLY IT'S MIKAEL BLOMKVIST. ARMANASKIJ IS NEXT TO ME. I USED HIS MOBILE BECAUSE I FIGURED YOU'D PICK UP, GIVEN YOUR CLOSE RELATIONSHIP.
I'VE GOT A QUESTION FOR YOU.
YOUR CRISIS WOULDN'T HAPPEN TO INVOLVE A GROUP OF HACKERS KNOWN AS SPARTA, WOULD IT?
'CAUSE IF IT DOES...
WE'RE IN THE SAME BOAT.

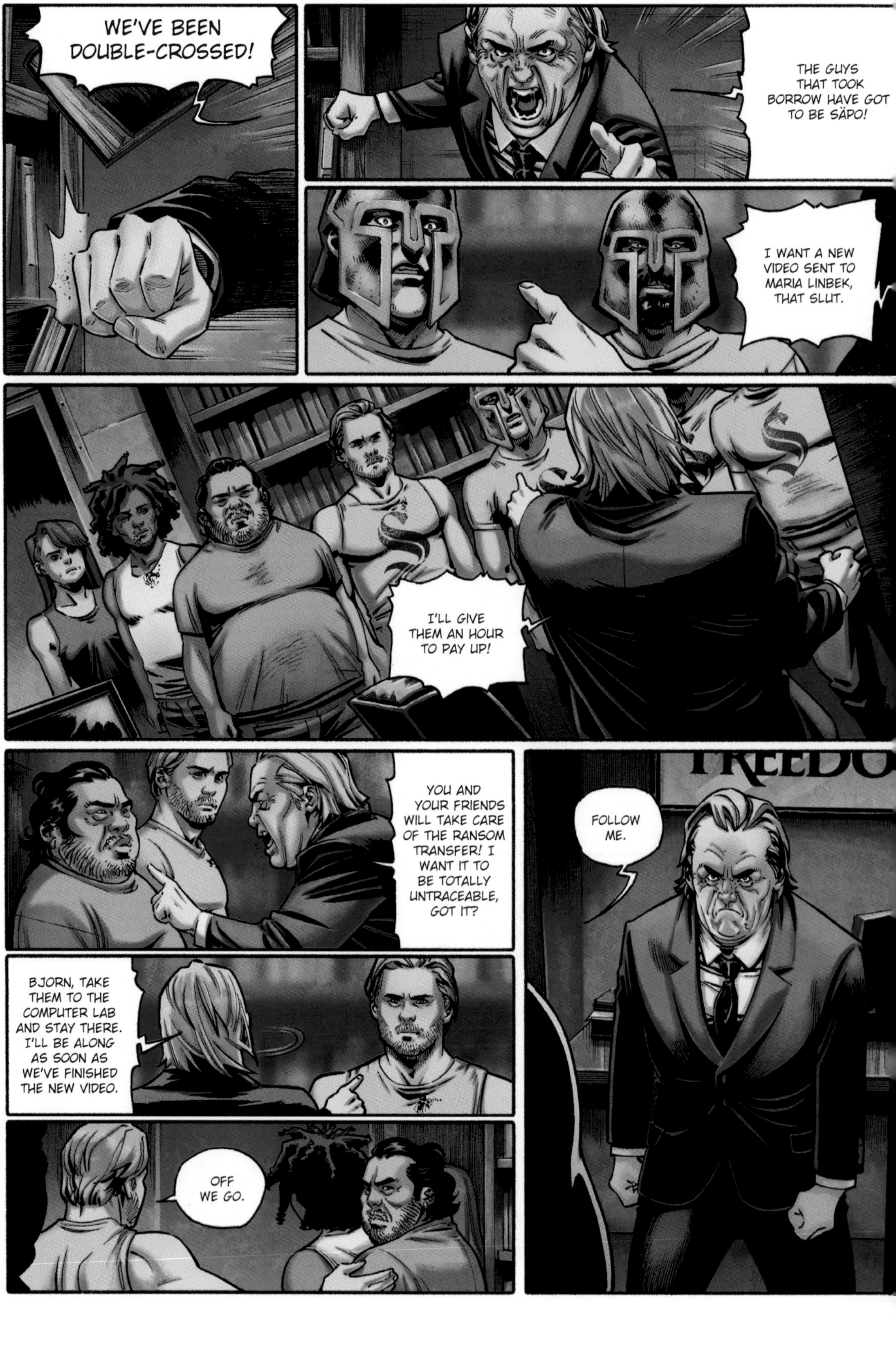
WE'VE BEEN DOUBLE-CROSSED!
THE GUYS THAT TOOK BORROW HAVE GOT TO BE SÄPO!
I WANT A NEW VIDEO SENT TO MARIA LINBEK, THAT SLUT.
I'LL GIVE THEM AN HOUR TO PAY UP!
YOU AND YOUR FRIENDS WILL TAKE CARE OF THE RANSOM TRANSFER! I WANT IT TO BE TOTALLY UNTRACEABLE, GOT IT?
BJORN, TAKE THEM TO THE COMPUTER LAB AND STAY THERE. I'LL BE ALONG AS SOON AS WE'VE FINISHED THE NEW VIDEO.
OFF WE GO.
FREEDO
FOLLOW ME.

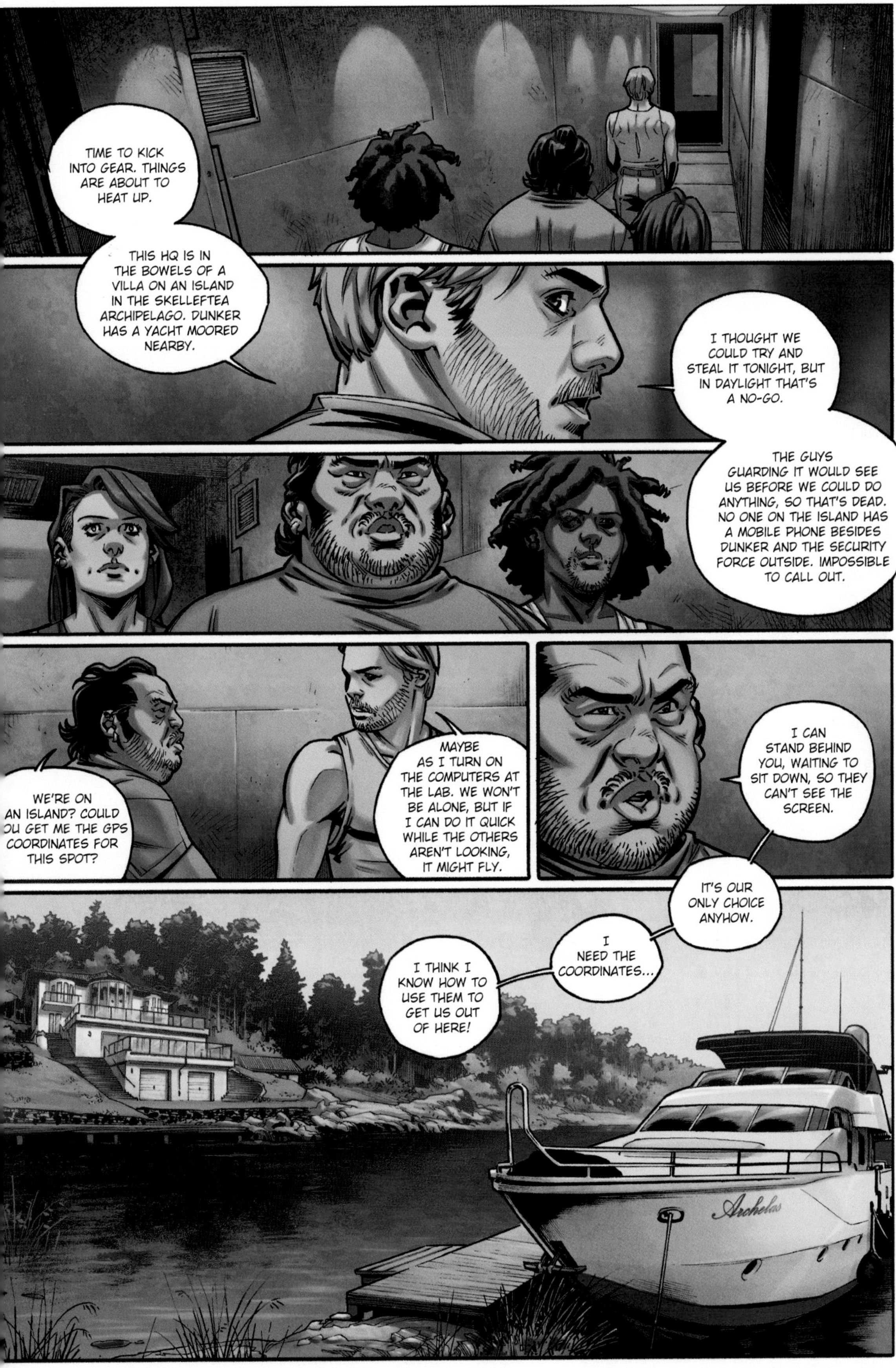
TIME TO KICK INTO GEAR. THINGS ARE ABOUT TO HEAT UP.
THIS HQ IS IN THE BOWELS OF A VILLA ON AN ISLAND IN THE SKELLEFTEA ARCHIPELAGO. DUNKER HAS A YACHT MOORED NEARBY.
I THOUGHT WE COULD TRY AND STEAL IT TONIGHT, BUT IN DAYLIGHT THAT'S A NO-GO.
THE GUYS GUARDING IT WOULD SEE US BEFORE WE COULD DO ANYTHING, SO THAT'S DEAD. NO ONE ON THE ISLAND HAS A MOBILE PHONE BESIDES DUNKER AND THE SECURITY FORCE OUTSIDE. IMPOSSIBLE TO CALL OUT.
WE'RE ON AN ISLAND? COULD OU GET ME THE GPS COORDINATES FOR THIS SPOT?
MAYBE AS I TURN ON THE COMPUTERS AT THE LAB. WE WON'T BE ALONE, BUT IF I CAN DO IT QUICK WHILE THE OTHERS AREN'T LOOKING, IT MIGHT FLY.
I CAN STAND BEHIND YOU, WAITING TO SIT DOWN, SO THEY CAN'T SEE THE SCREEN.
IT'S OUR ONLY CHOICE ANYHOW.
I NEED THE COORDINATES...
I THINK I KNOW HOW TO USE THEM TO GET US OUT OF HERE!
Archelas

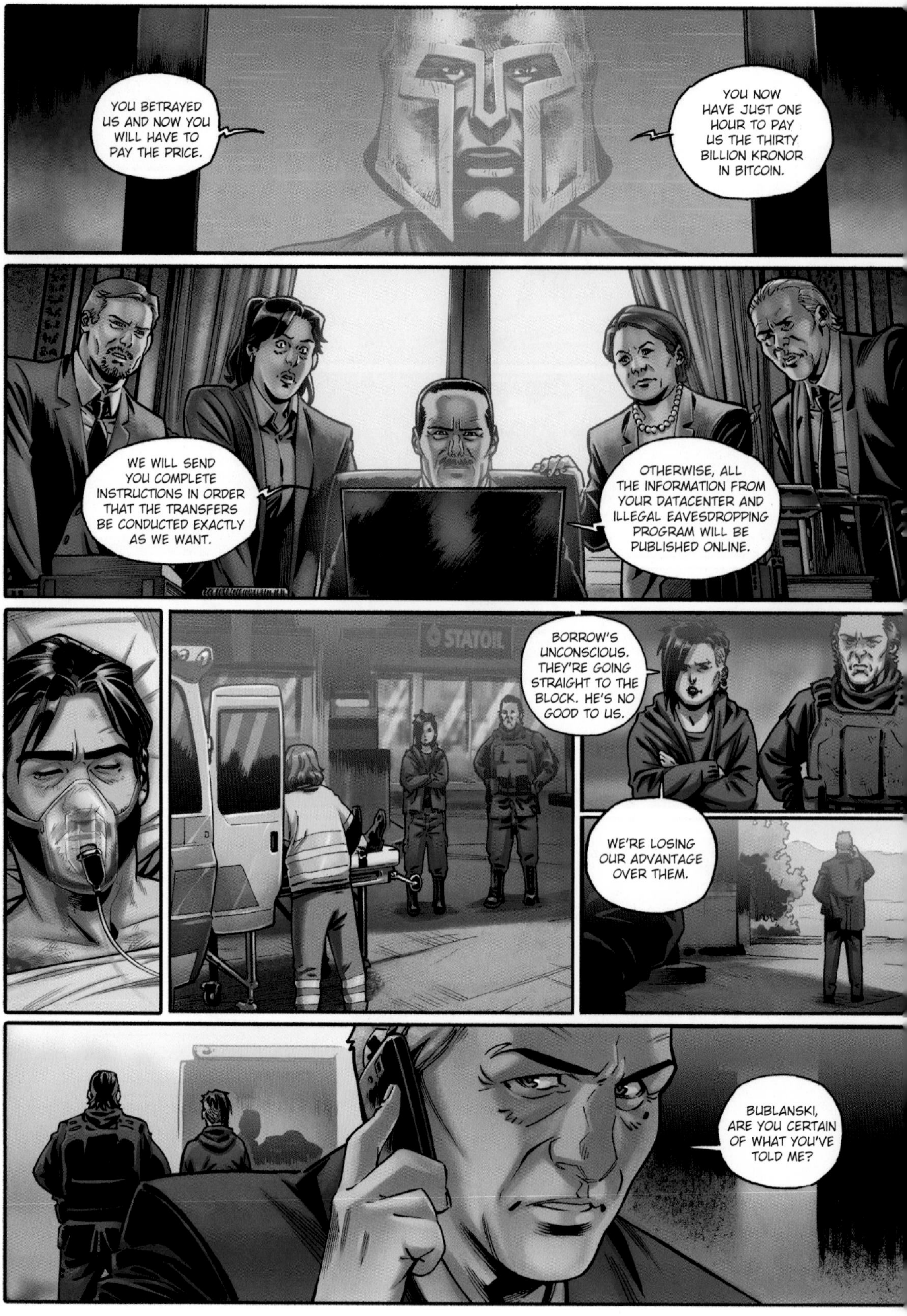
YOU BETRAYED US AND NOW YOU WILL HAVE TO PAY THE PRICE.
YOU NOW HAVE JUST ONE HOUR TO PAY US THE THIRTY BILLION KRONOR IN BITCOIN.
WE WILL SEND YOU COMPLETE INSTRUCTIONS IN ORDER THAT THE TRANSFERS BE CONDUCTED EXACTLY AS WE WANT.
OTHERWISE, ALL THE INFORMATION FROM YOUR DATACENTER AND ILLEGAL EAVESDROPPING PROGRAM WILL BE PUBLISHED ONLINE.
STATOIL
BORROW'S UNCONSCIOUS. THEY'RE GOING STRAIGHT TO THE BLOCK. HE'S NO GOOD TO US.
WE'RE LOSING OUR ADVANTAGE OVER THEM.
BUBLANSKI, ARE YOU CERTAIN OF WHAT YOU'VE TOLD ME?

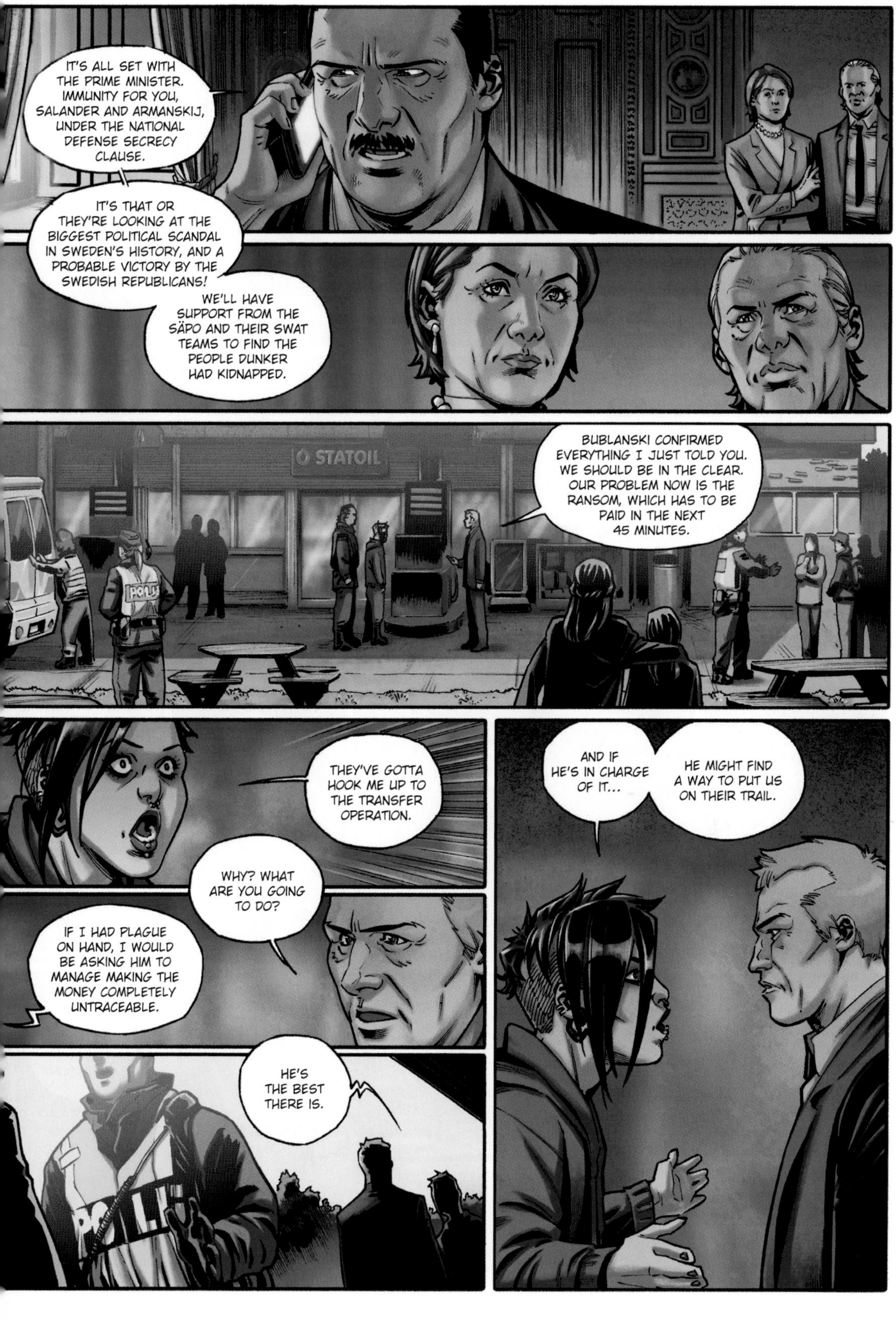
IT'S ALL SET WITH THE PRIME MINISTER. IMMUNITY FOR YOU, SALANDER AND ARMANSKIJ, UNDER THE NATIONAL DEFENSE SECRECY CLAUSE.
IT'S THAT OR THEY'RE LOOKING AT THE BIGGEST POLITICAL SCANDAL IN SWEDEN'S HISTORY, AND A PROBABLE VICTORY BY THE SWEDISH REPUBLICANS!
WE'LL HAVE SUPPORT FROM THE SÄPO AND THEIR SWAT TEAMS TO FIND THE PEOPLE DUNKER HAD KIDNAPPED.
STATOIL
BUBLANSKI CONFIRMED EVERYTHING I JUST TOLD YOU. WE SHOULD BE IN THE CLEAR. OUR PROBLEM NOW IS THE RANSOM, WHICH HAS TO BE PAID IN THE NEXT 45 MINUTES.
THEY'VE GOTTA HOOK ME UP TO THE TRANSFER OPERATION.
WHY? WHAT ARE YOU GOING TO DO?
IF I HAD PLAGUE ON HAND, I WOULD BE ASKING HIM TO MANAGE MAKING THE MONEY COMPLETELY UNTRACEABLE.
HE'S THE BEST THERE IS.
AND IF HE'S IN CHARGE OF IT...
HE MIGHT FIND A WAY TO PUT US ON THEIR TRAIL.

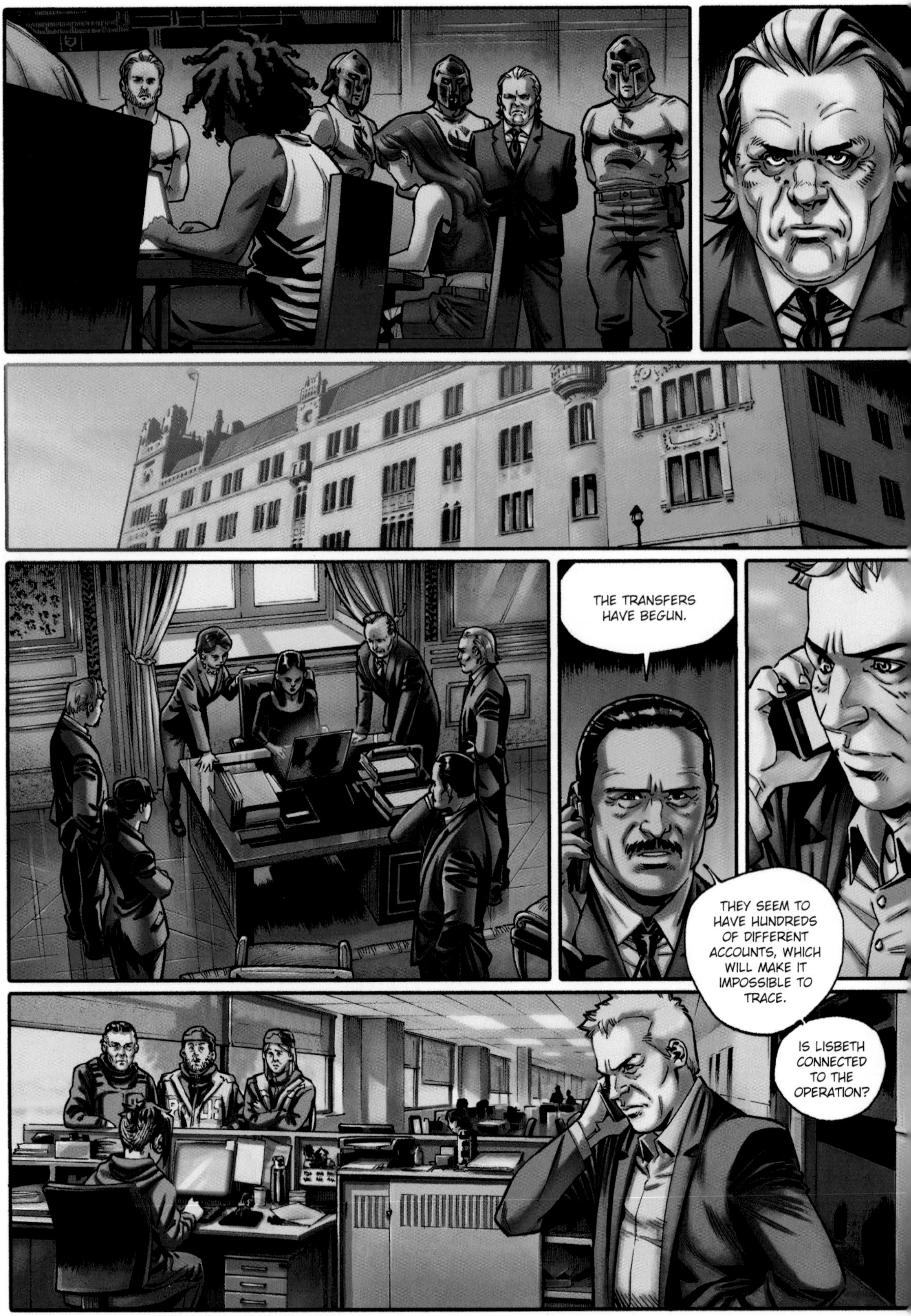
THE TRANSFERS HAVE BEGUN.
THEY SEEM TO HAVE HUNDREDS OF DIFFERENT ACCOUNTS, WHICH WILL MAKE IT IMPOSSIBLE TO TRACE.
IS LISBETH CONNECTED TO THE OPERATION?

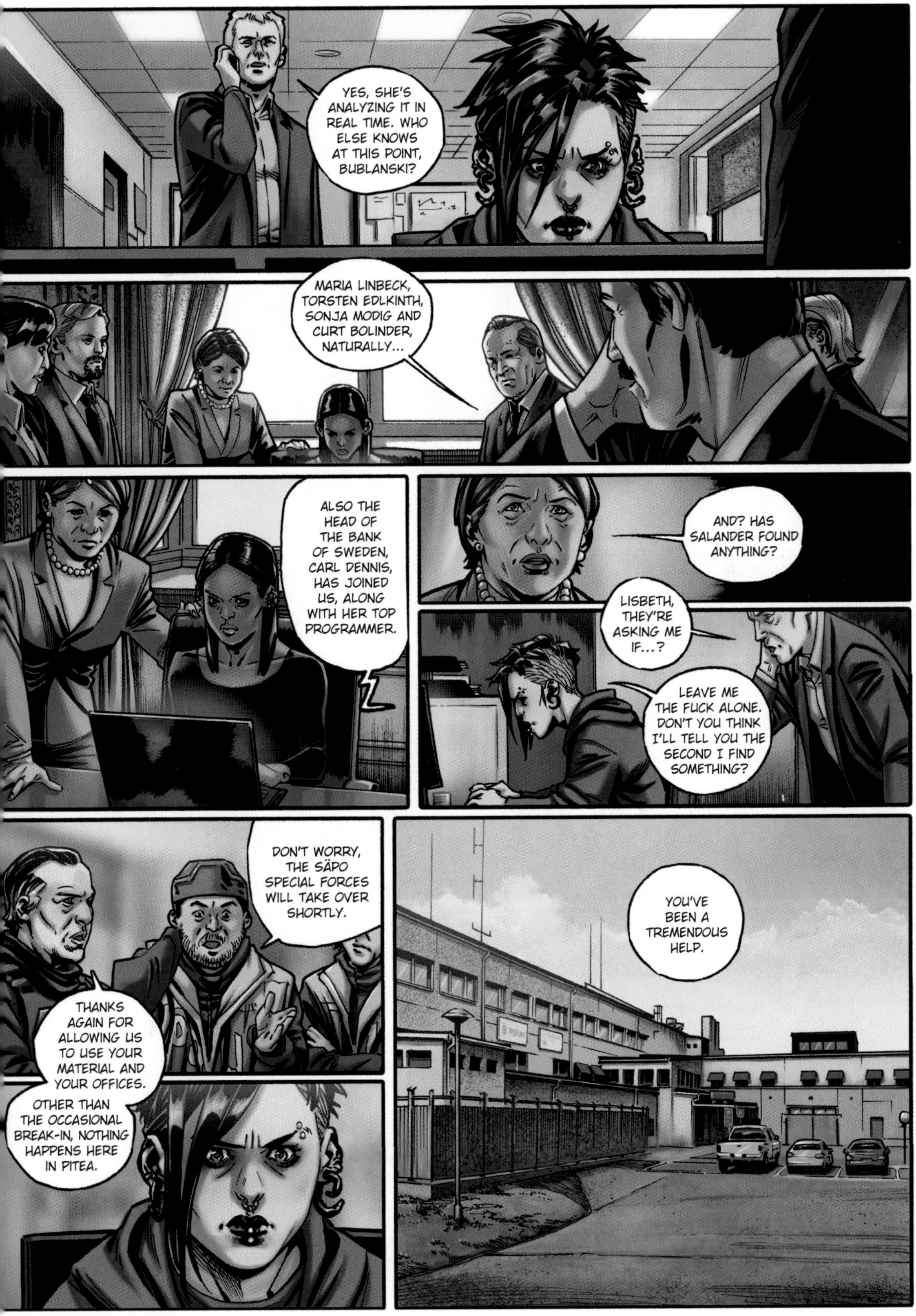
YES, SHE'S ANALYZING IT IN REAL TIME. WHO ELSE KNOWS AT THIS POINT, BUBLANSKI?
MARIA LINBECK, TORSTEN EDLKINTH, SONJA MODIG AND CURT BOLINDER, NATURALLY...
ALSO THE HEAD OF THE BANK OF SWEDEN, CARL DENNIS, HAS JOINED US, ALONG WITH HER TOP PROGRAMMER.
AND? HAS SALANDER FOUND ANYTHING?
LISBETH, THEY'RE ASKING ME IF...?
LEAVE ME THE FUCK ALONE. DON'T YOU THINK I'LL TELL YOU THE SECOND I FIND SOMETHING?
DON'T WORRY, THE SÄPO SPECIAL FORCES WILL TAKE OVER SHORTLY.
THANKS AGAIN FOR ALLOWING US TO USE YOUR MATERIAL AND YOUR OFFICES.
OTHER THAN THE OCCASIONAL BREAK-IN, NOTHING HAPPENS HERE IN PITEA.
YOU'VE BEEN A TREMENDOUS HELP.

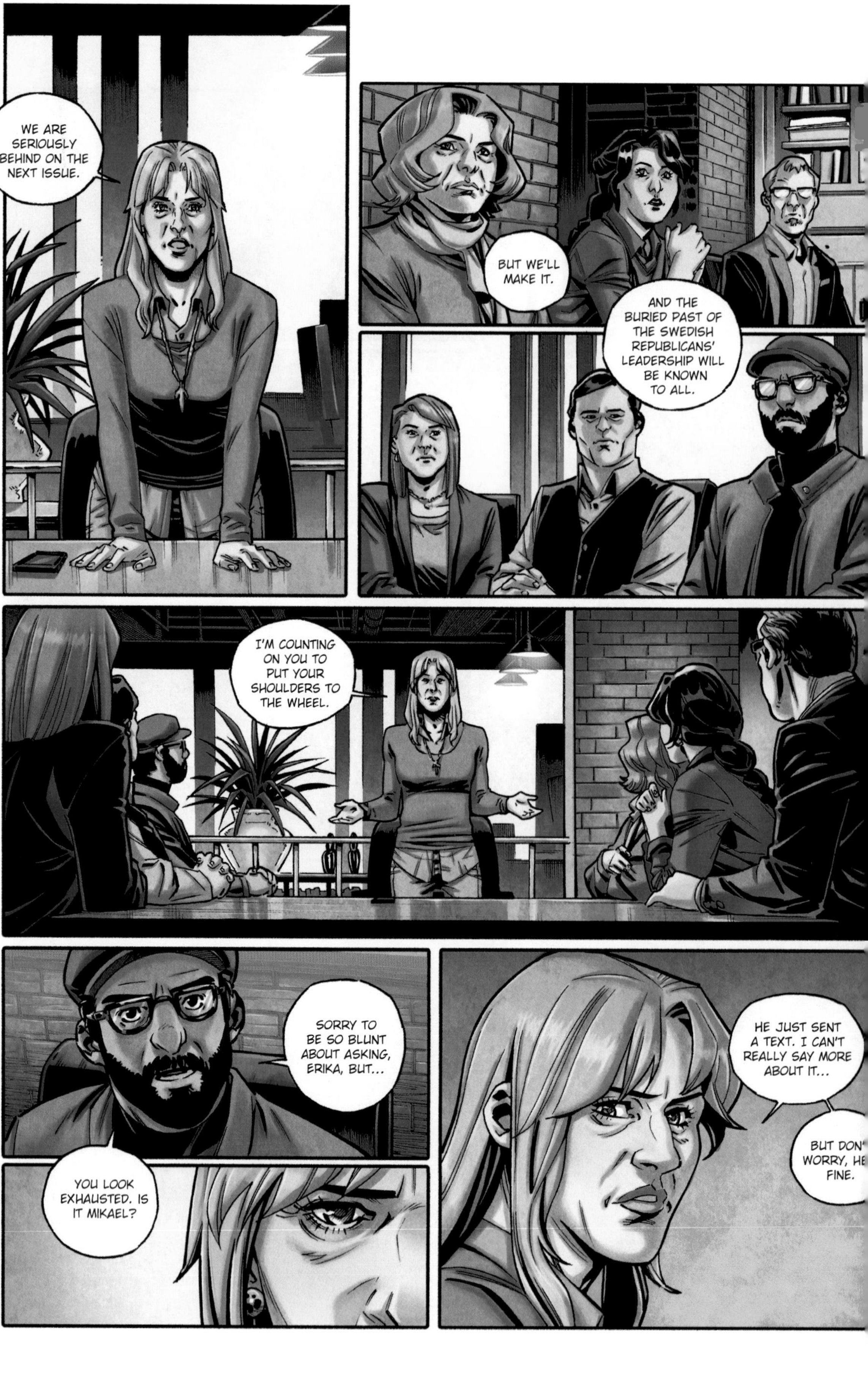

WE ARE SERIOUSLY BEHIND ON THE NEXT ISSUE.
BUT WE'LL MAKE IT.
AND THE BURIED PAST OF THE SWEDISH REPUBLICANS' LEADERSHIP WILL BE KNOWN TO ALL.
I'M COUNTING ON YOU TO PUT YOUR SHOULDERS TO THE WHEEL.
SORRY TO BE SO BLUNT ABOUT ASKING, ERIKA, BUT...
YOU LOOK EXHAUSTED. IS IT MIKAEL?
HE JUST SENT A TEXT. I CAN'T REALLY SAY MORE ABOUT IT...
BUT DON' WORRY, HE FINE.

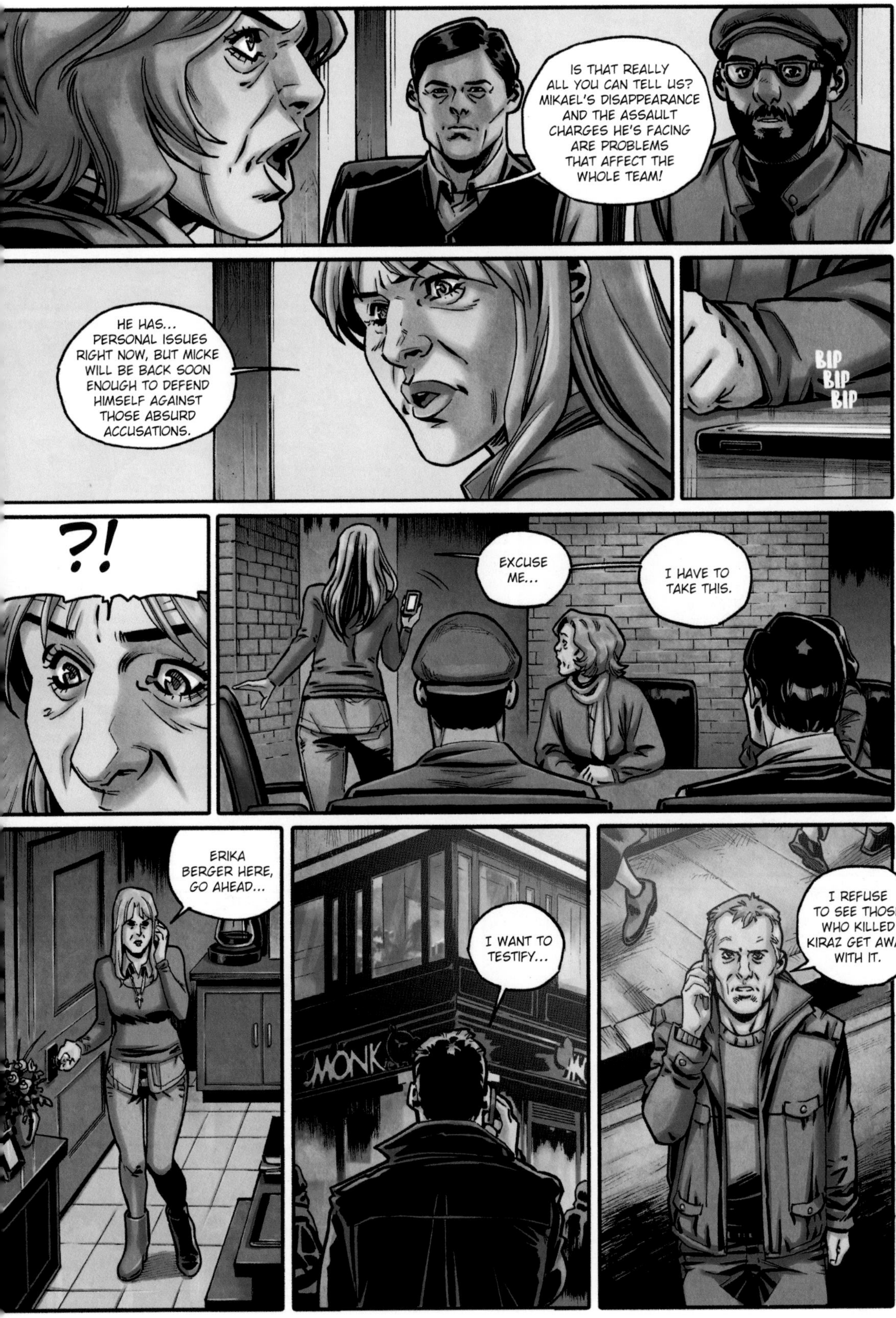
IS THAT REALLY ALL YOU CAN TELL US? MIKAEL'S DISAPPEARANCE AND THE ASSAULT CHARGES HE'S FACING ARE PROBLEMS THAT AFFECT THE WHOLE TEAM!
HE HAS... PERSONAL ISSUES RIGHT NOW, BUT MICKE WILL BE BACK SOON ENOUGH TO DEFEND HIMSELF AGAINST THOSE ABSURD ACCUSATIONS.
BIP BIP BIP
?!
EXCUSE ME...
I HAVE TO TAKE THIS.
ERIKA BERGER HERE, GO AHEAD...
I WANT TO TESTIFY...
MONK
I REFUSE TO SEE THOSE WHO KILLED KIRAZ GET AWAY WITH IT.

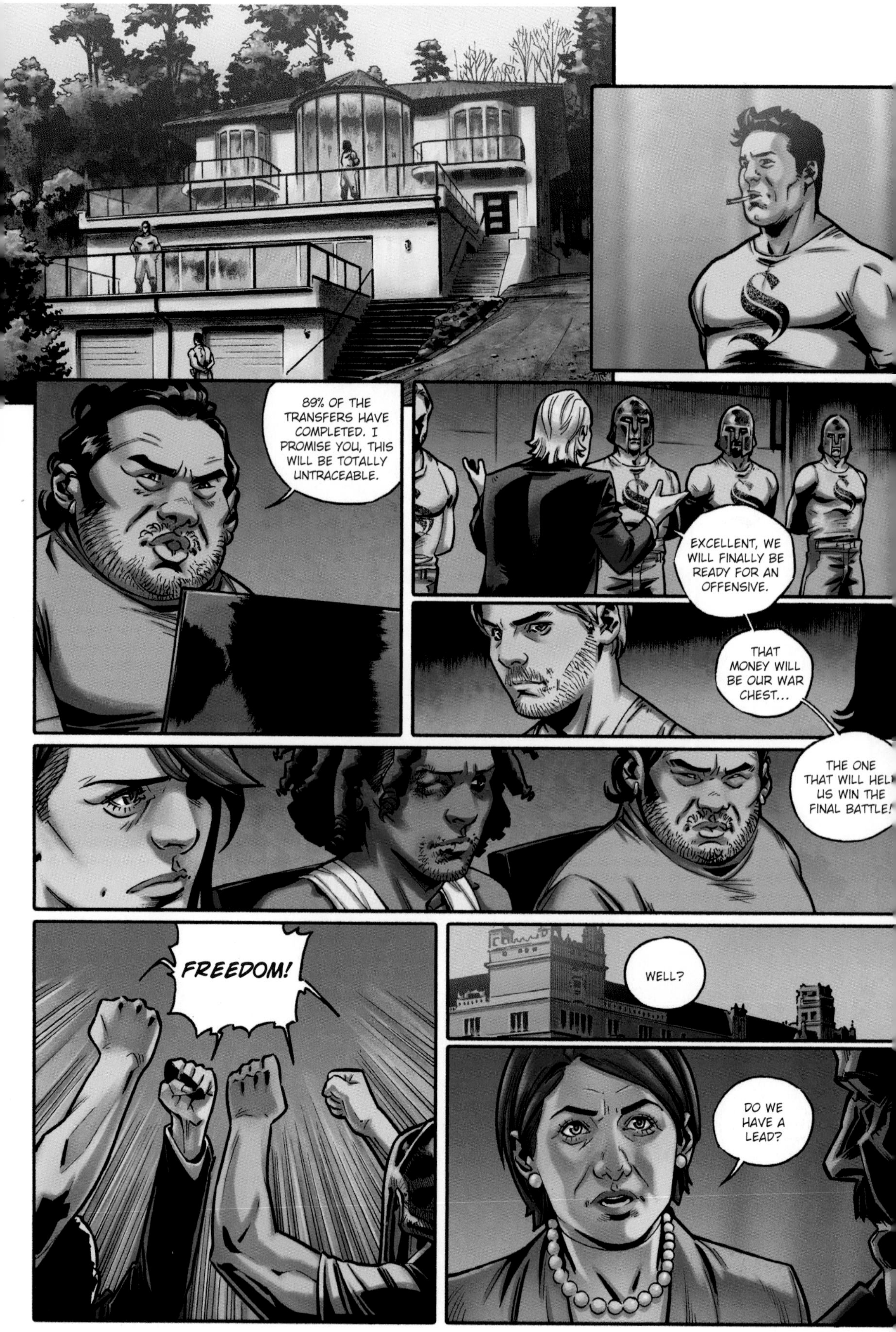
89% OF THE TRANSFERS HAVE COMPLETED. I PROMISE YOU, THIS WILL BE TOTALLY UNTRACEABLE.
EXCELLENT, WE WILL FINALLY BE READY FOR AN OFFENSIVE.
THAT MONEY WILL BE OUR WAR CHEST...
THE ONE THAT WILL HEL US WIN THE FINAL BATTLE!
FREEDOM!
WELL?
DO WE HAVE A LEAD?

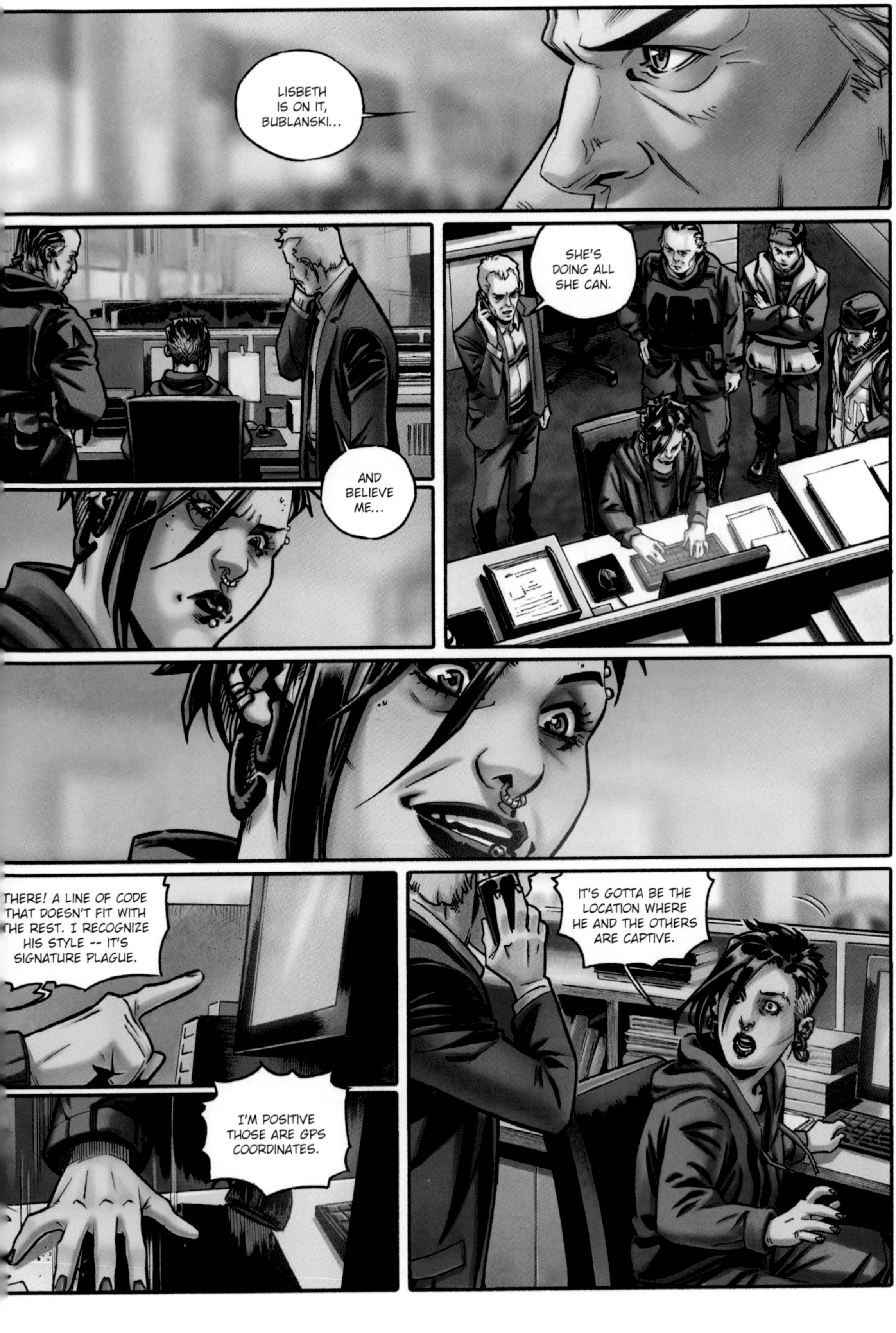
LISBETH IS ON IT, BUBLANSKI...
SHE'S DOING ALL SHE CAN.
AND BELIEVE ME...
THERE! A LINE OF CODE THAT DOESN'T FIT WITH THE REST. I RECOGNIZE HIS STYLE -- IT'S SIGNATURE PLAGUE.
I'M POSITIVE THOSE ARE GPS COORDINATES.
IT'S GOTTA BE THE LOCATION WHERE HE AND THE OTHERS ARE CAPTIVE.

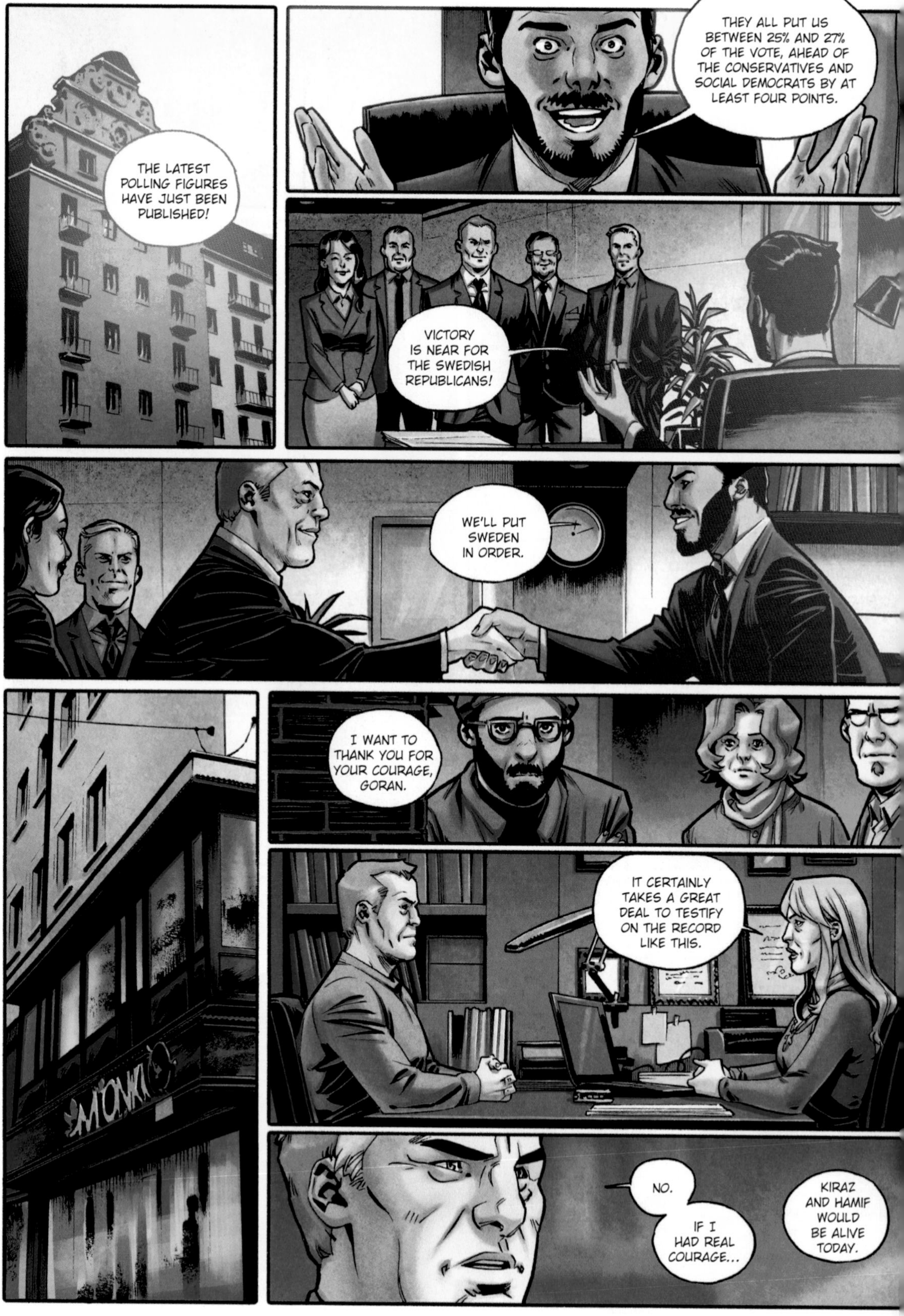
THE LATEST POLLING FIGURES HAVE JUST BEEN PUBLISHED!
THEY ALL PUT US BETWEEN 25% AND 27% OF THE VOTE, AHEAD OF THE CONSERVATIVES AND SOCIAL DEMOCRATS BY AT LEAST FOUR POINTS.
VICTORY IS NEAR FOR THE SWEDISH REPUBLICANS!
WE'LL PUT SWEDEN IN ORDER.
MONKI
I WANT TO THANK YOU FOR YOUR COURAGE, GORAN.
IT CERTAINLY TAKES A GREAT DEAL TO TESTIFY ON THE RECORD LIKE THIS.
NO.
IF I HAD REAL COURAGE...
KIRAZ AND HAMIF WOULD BE ALIVE TODAY.

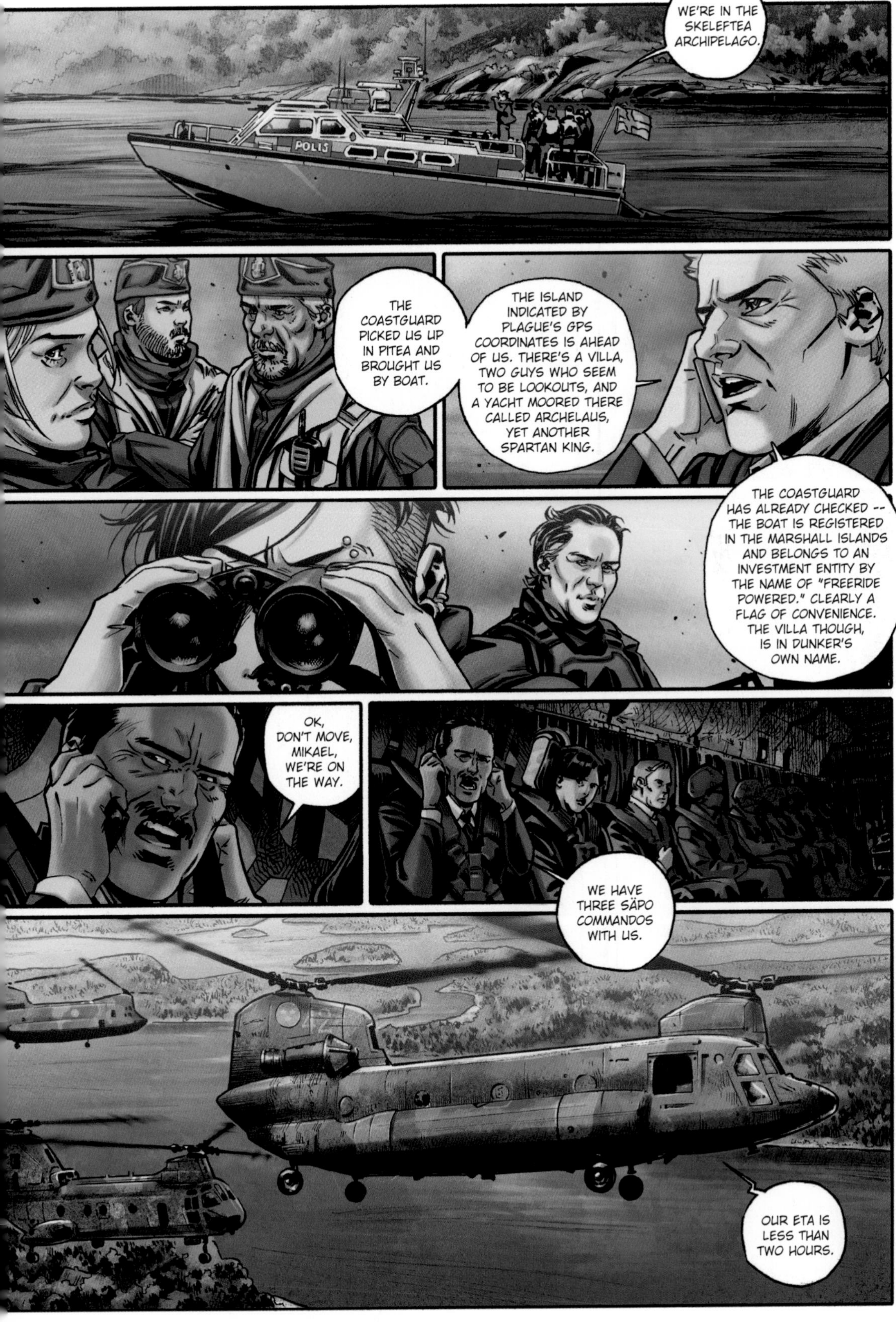
WE'RE IN THE SKELEFTEA ARCHIPELAGO.
THE COASTGUARD PICKED US UP IN PITEA AND BROUGHT US BY BOAT.
THE ISLAND INDICATED BY PLAGUE'S GPS COORDINATES IS AHEAD OF US. THERE'S A VILLA, TWO GUYS WHO SEEM TO BE LOOKOUTS, AND A YACHT MOORED THERE CALLED ARCHELAUS, YET ANOTHER SPARTAN KING.
THE COASTGUARD HAS ALREADY CHECKED -- THE BOAT IS REGISTERED IN THE MARSHALL ISLANDS AND BELONGS TO AN INVESTMENT ENTITY BY THE NAME OF "FREERIDE POWERED." CLEARLY A FLAG OF CONVENIENCE. THE VILLA THOUGH, IS IN DUNKER'S OWN NAME.
OK, DON'T MOVE, MIKAEL, WE'RE ON THE WAY.
WE HAVE THREE SÄPO COMMANDOS WITH US.
OUR ETA IS LESS THAN TWO HOURS.
POLIS

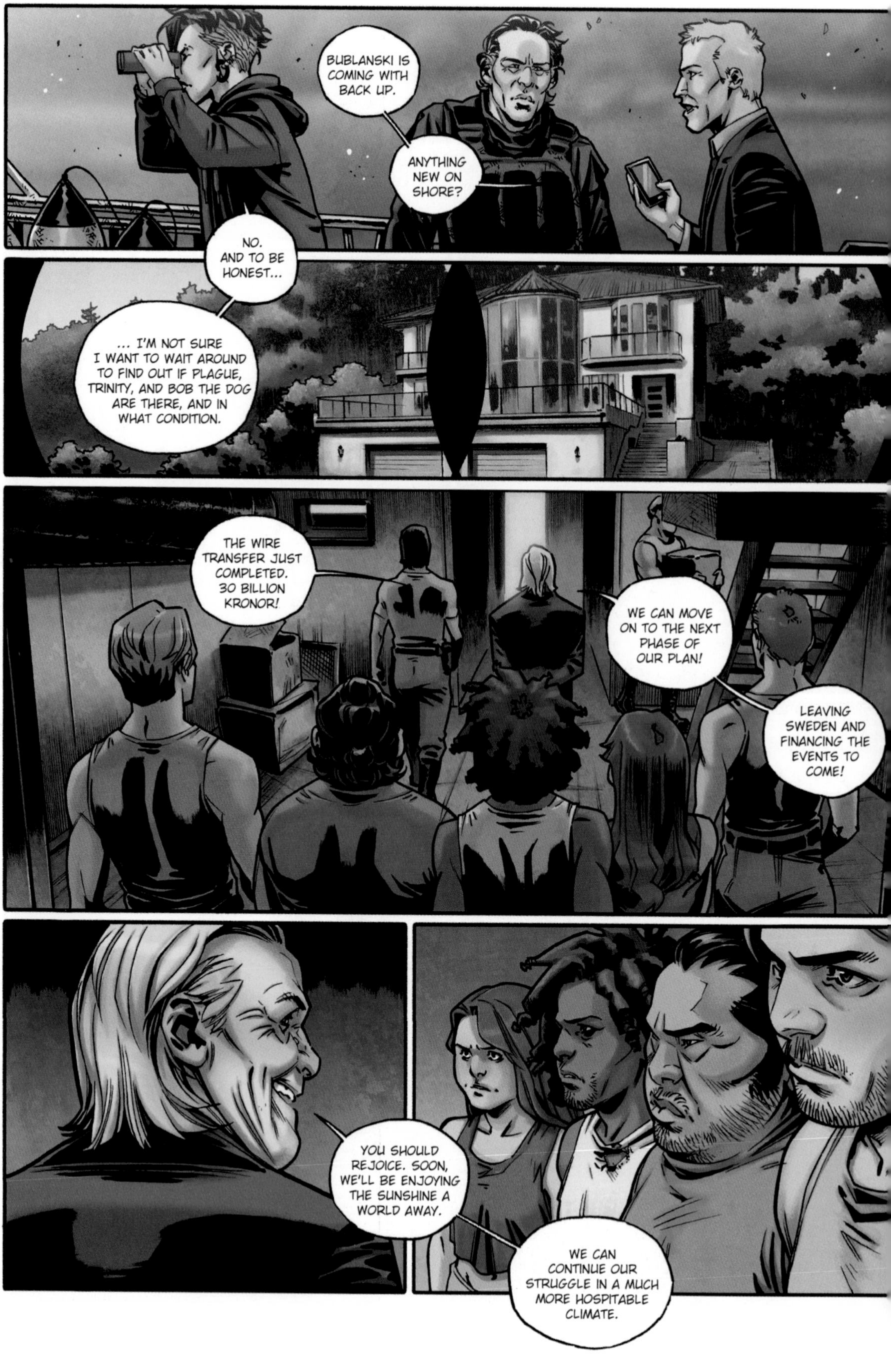
BUBLANSKI IS COMING WITH BACK UP.
ANYTHING NEW ON SHORE?
NO. AND TO BE HONEST...
... I'M NOT SURE I WANT TO WAIT AROUND TO FIND OUT IF PLAGUE, TRINITY, AND BOB THE DOG ARE THERE, AND IN WHAT CONDITION.
THE WIRE TRANSFER JUST COMPLETED. 30 BILLION KRONOR!
WE CAN MOVE ON TO THE NEXT PHASE OF OUR PLAN!
LEAVING SWEDEN AND FINANCING THE EVENTS TO COME!
YOU SHOULD REJOICE. SOON, WE'LL BE ENJOYING THE SUNSHINE A WORLD AWAY.
WE CAN CONTINUE OUR STRUGGLE IN A MUCH MORE HOSPITABLE CLIMATE.

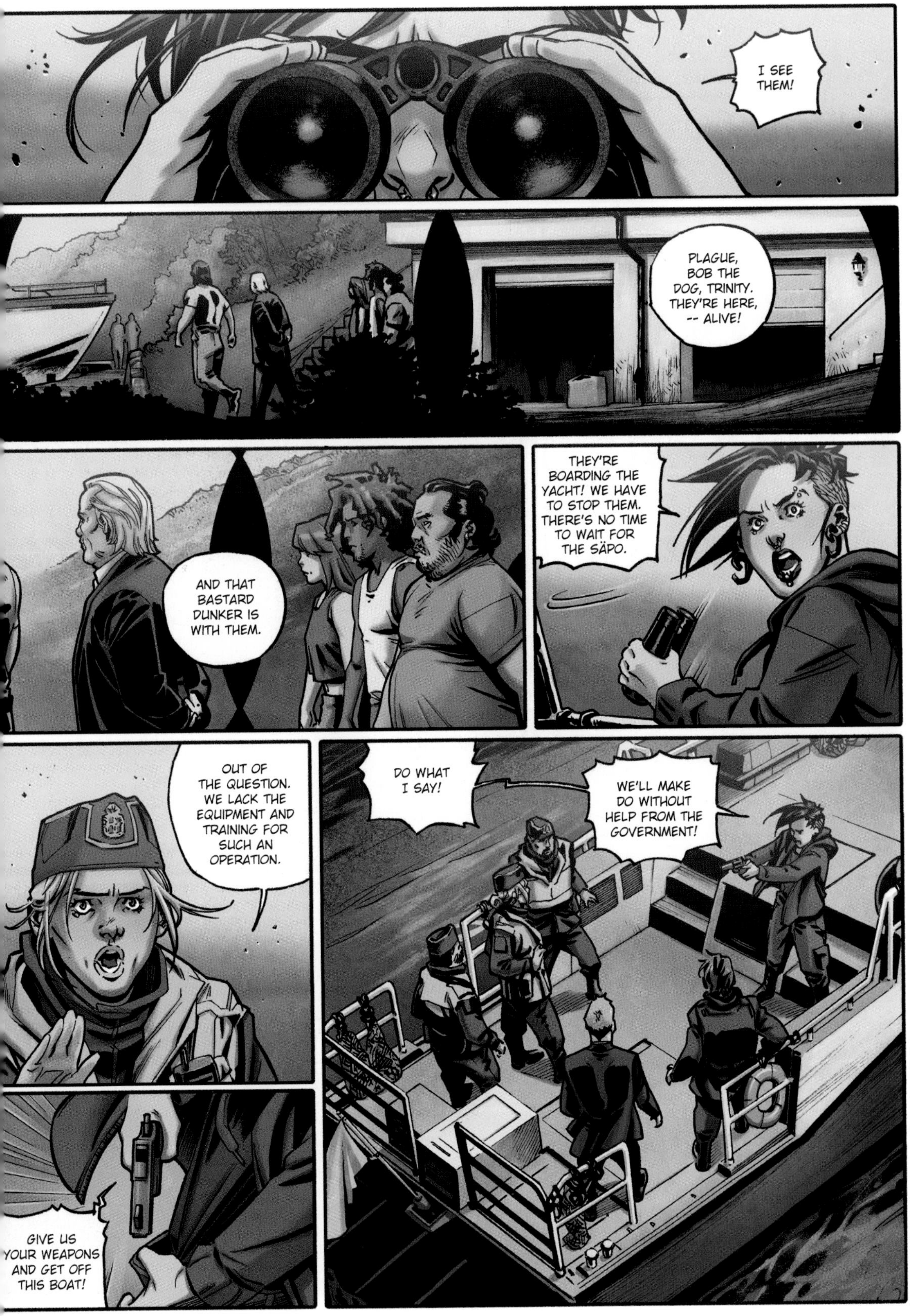
I SEE THEM!
PLAGUE, BOB THE DOG, TRINITY. THEY'RE HERE, -- ALIVE!
AND THAT BASTARD DUNKER IS WITH THEM.
THEY'RE BOARDING THE YACHT! WE HAVE TO STOP THEM. THERE'S NO TIME TO WAIT FOR THE SÄPO.
OUT OF THE QUESTION. WE LACK THE EQUIPMENT AND TRAINING FOR SUCH AN OPERATION.
GIVE US YOUR WEAPONS AND GET OFF THIS BOAT!
DO WHAT I SAY!
WE'LL MAKE DO WITHOUT HELP FROM THE GOVERNMENT!

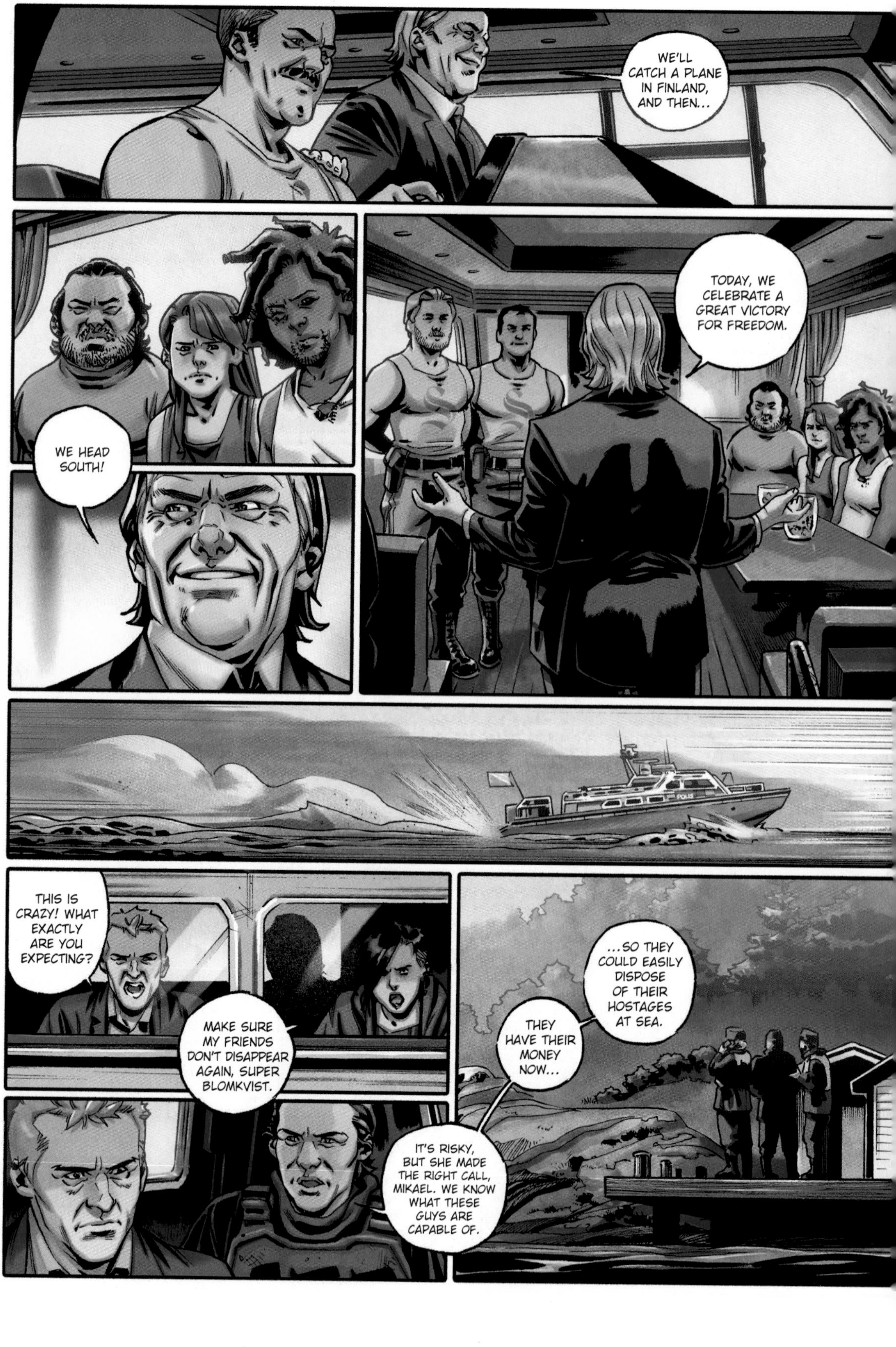
WE'LL CATCH A PLANE IN FINLAND, AND THEN...
WE HEAD SOUTH!
TODAY, WE CELEBRATE A GREAT VICTORY FOR FREEDOM.
POLIS
THIS IS CRAZY! WHAT EXACTLY ARE YOU EXPECTING?
MAKE SURE MY FRIENDS DON'T DISAPPEAR AGAIN, SUPER BLOMKVIST.
IT'S RISKY, BUT SHE MADE THE RIGHT CALL, MIKAEL. WE KNOW WHAT THESE GUYS ARE CAPABLE OF.
THEY HAVE THEIR MONEY NOW...
...SO THEY COULD EASILY DISPOSE OF THEIR HOSTAGES AT SEA.

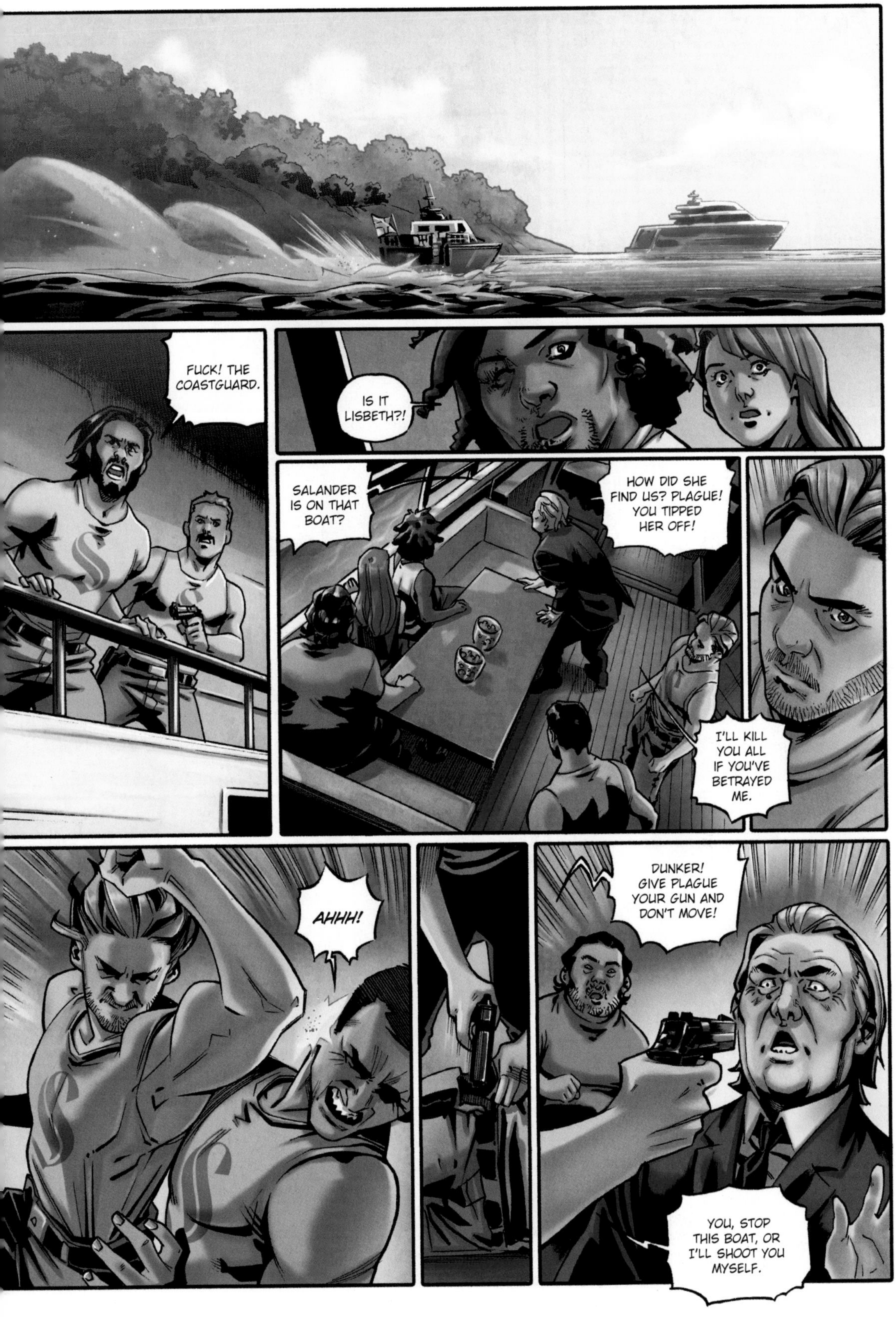
FUCK! THE COASTGUARD.
IS IT LISBETH?!
SALANDER IS ON THAT BOAT?
HOW DID SHE FIND US? PLAGUE! YOU TIPPED HER OFF!
I'LL KILL YOU ALL IF YOU'VE BETRAYED ME.
AHHH!
DUNKER! GIVE PLAGUE YOUR GUN AND DON'T MOVE!
YOU, STOP THIS BOAT, OR I'LL SHOOT YOU MYSELF.

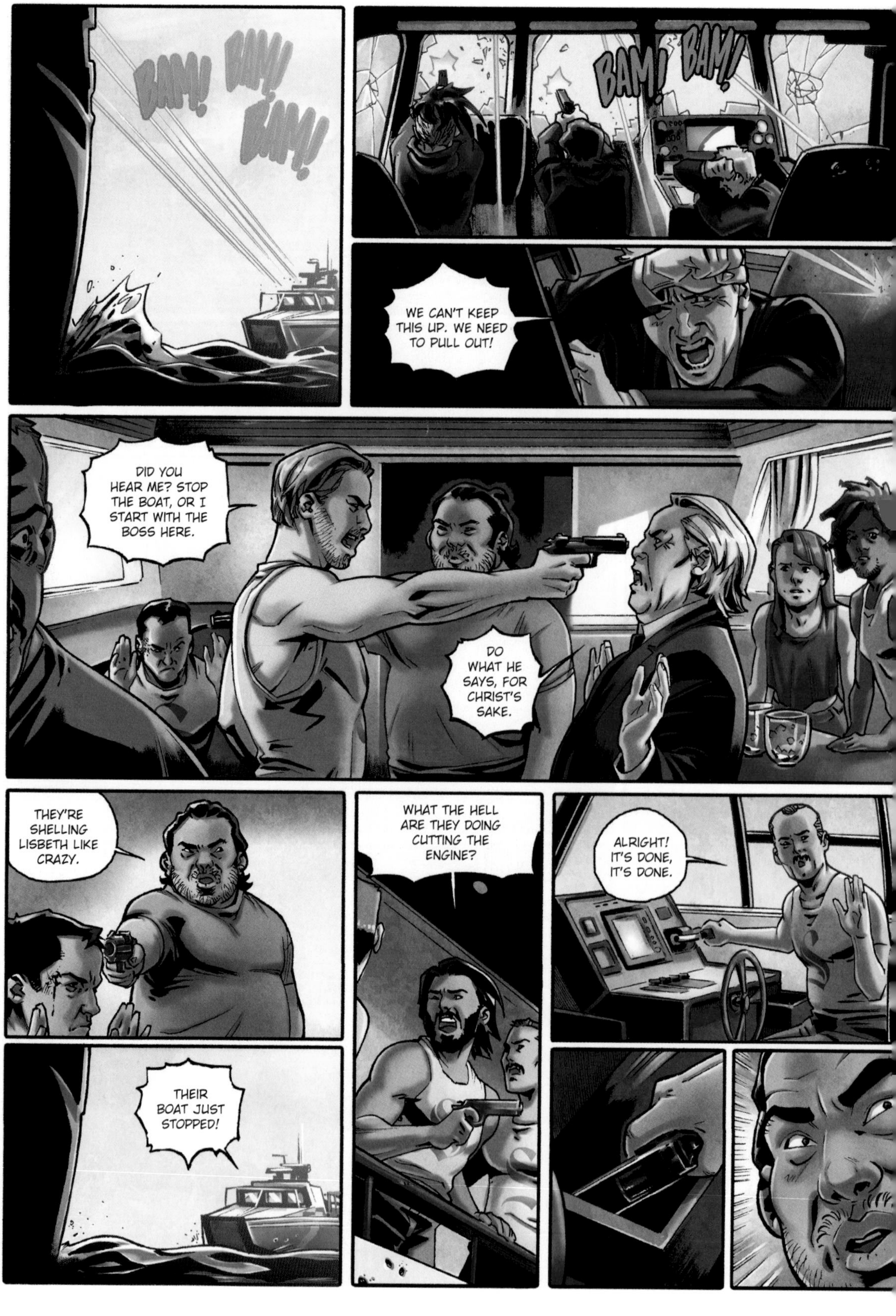
BAM! BAM! BAM!
BAM! BAM!
WE CAN'T KEEP THIS UP. WE NEED TO PULL OUT!
DID YOU HEAR ME? STOP THE BOAT, OR I START WITH THE BOSS HERE.
DO WHAT HE SAYS, FOR CHRIST'S SAKE.
THEY'RE SHELLING LISBETH LIKE CRAZY.
WHAT THE HELL ARE THEY DOING CUTTING THE ENGINE?
ALRIGHT! IT'S DONE, IT'S DONE.
THEIR BOAT JUST STOPPED!

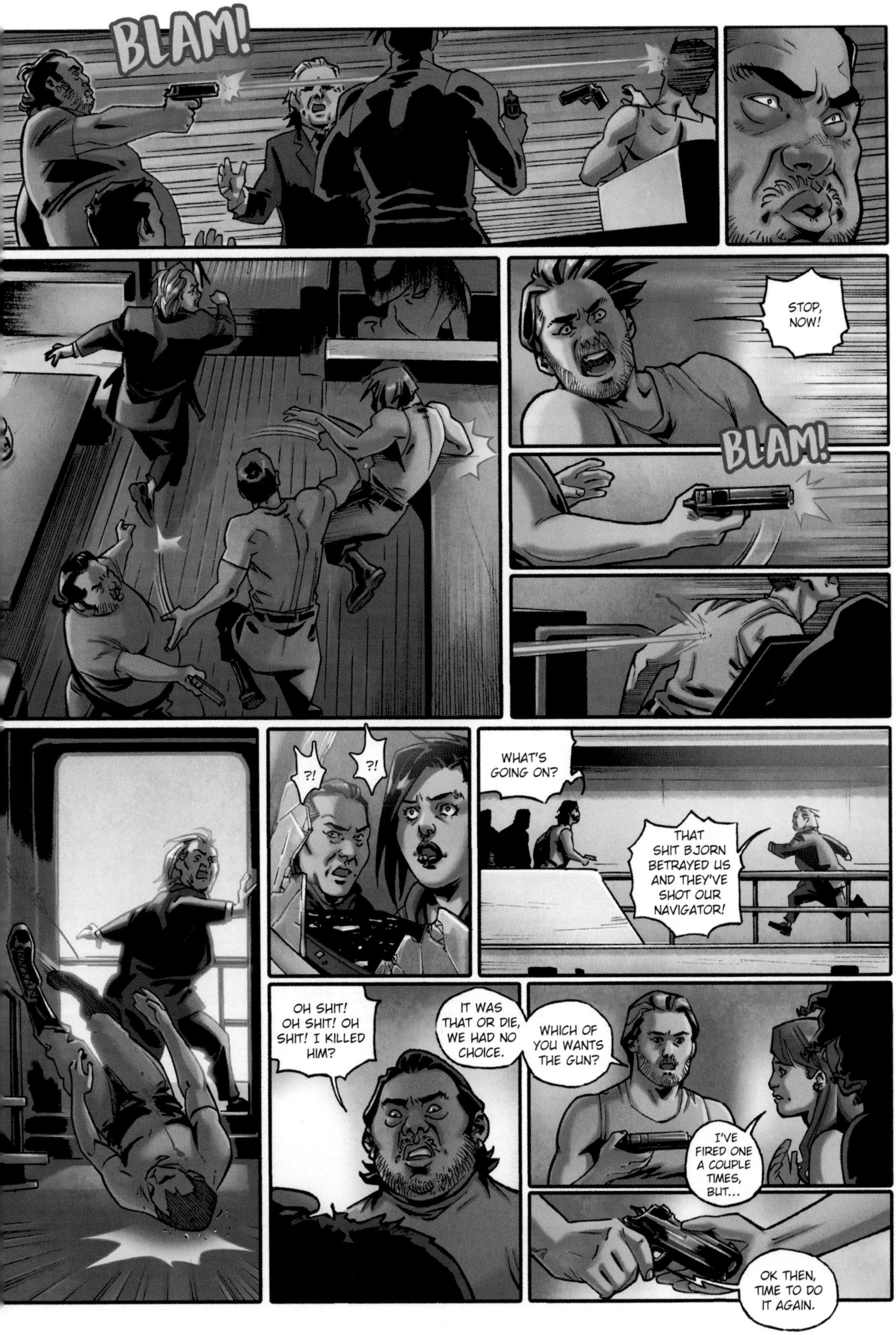
BLAM!
STOP, NOW!
BLAM!
?!
?!
WHAT'S GOING ON?
THAT SHIT BJORN BETRAYED US AND THEY'VE SHOT OUR NAVIGATOR!
OH SHIT! OH SHIT! OH SHIT! I KILLED HIM?
IT WAS THAT OR DIE, WE HAD NO CHOICE.
WHICH OF YOU WANTS THE GUN?
I'VE FIRED ONE A COUPLE TIMES, BUT...
OK THEN, TIME TO DO IT AGAIN.

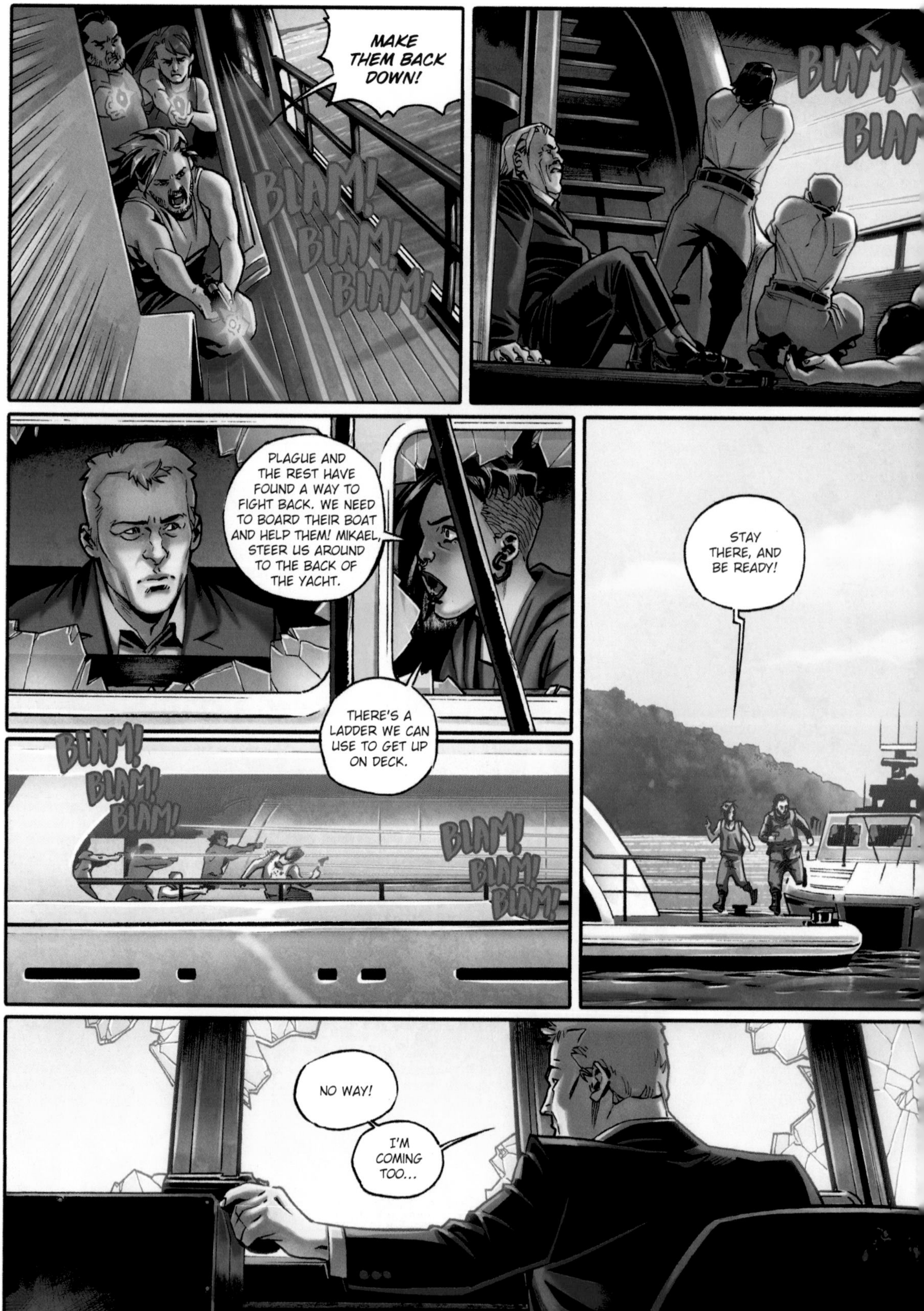
MAKE THEM BACK DOWN!
BLAM! BLAM! BLAM!
BLAM! BLAM!
PLAGUE AND THE REST HAVE FOUND A WAY TO FIGHT BACK. WE NEED TO BOARD THEIR BOAT AND HELP THEM! MIKAEL, STEER US AROUND TO THE BACK OF THE YACHT.
THERE'S A LADDER WE CAN USE TO GET UP ON DECK.
BLAM! BLAM! BLAM!
BLAM! BLAM! BLAM!
STAY THERE, AND BE READY!
NO WAY!
I'M COMING TOO...

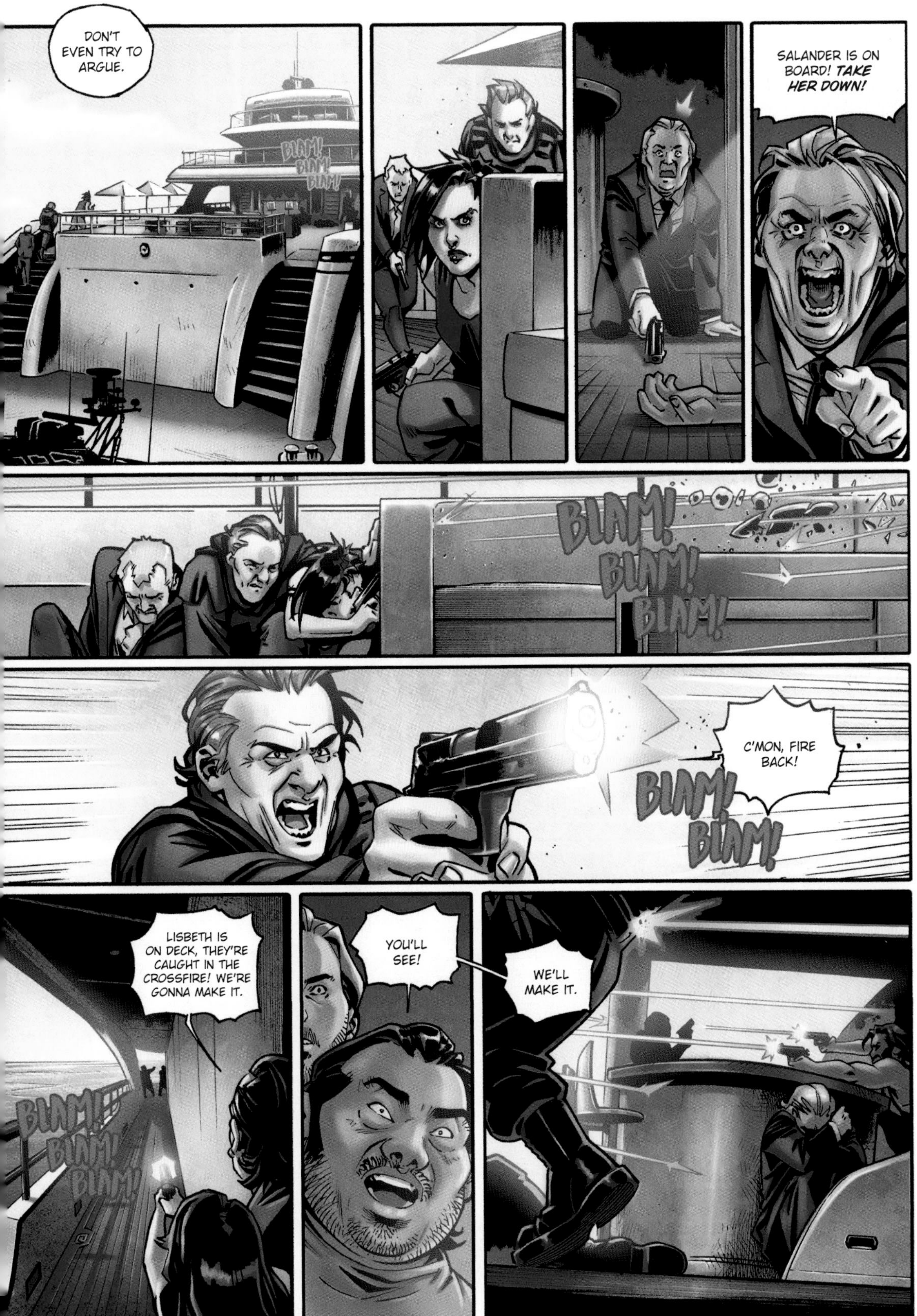
DON'T EVEN TRY TO ARGUE.
BLAM! BLAM! BLAM!
SALANDER IS ON BOARD! TAKE HER DOWN!
BLAM! BLAM! BLAM!
C'MON, FIRE BACK!
BLAM! BLAM!
LISBETH IS ON DECK, THEY'RE CAUGHT IN THE CROSSFIRE! WE'RE GONNA MAKE IT.
BLAM! BLAM! BLAM!
YOU'LL SEE!
WE'LL MAKE IT.

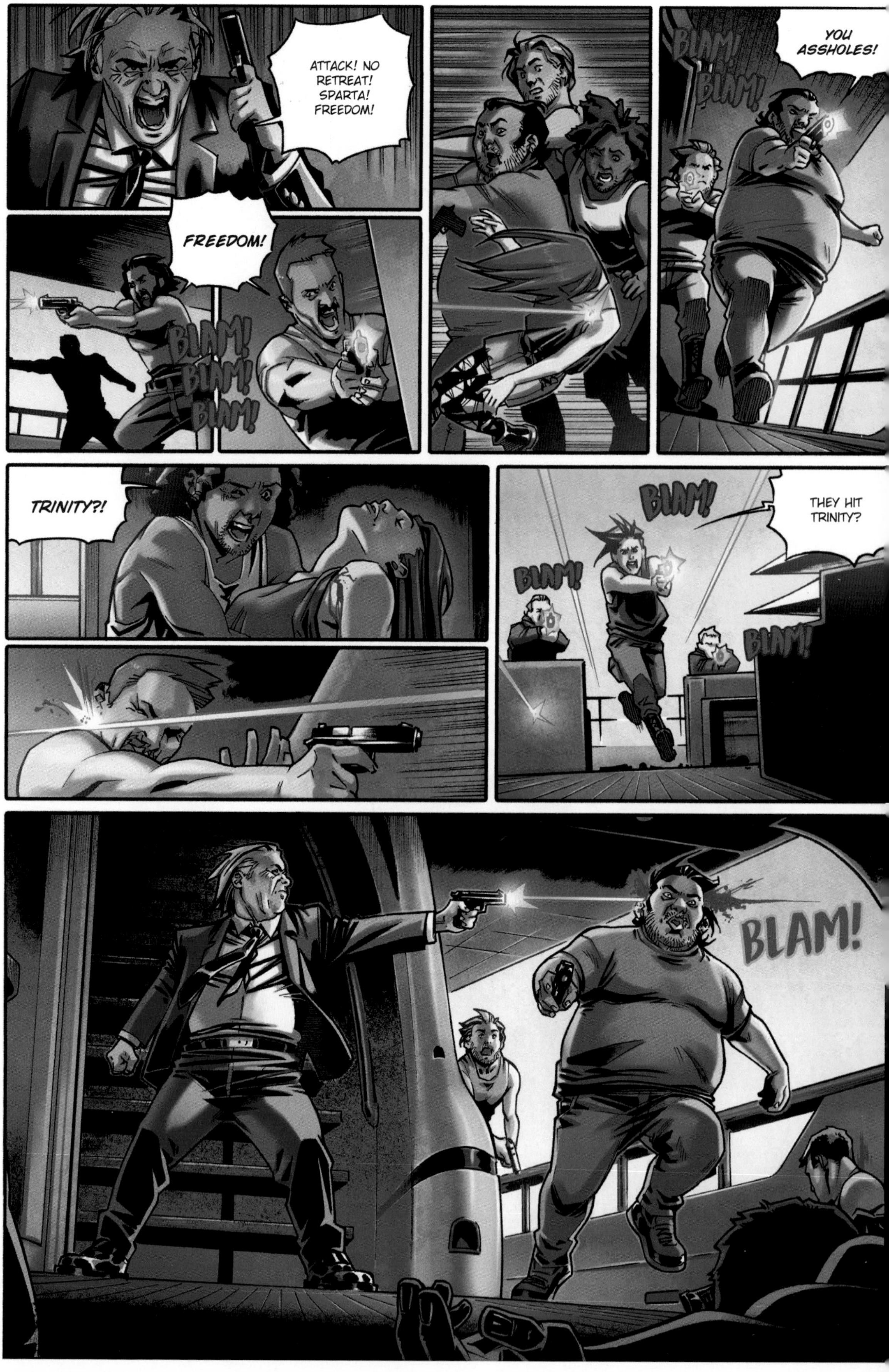
ATTACK! NO RETREAT! SPARTA! FREEDOM!
BLAM! BLAM!
YOU ASSHOLES!
FREEDOM!
BLAM! BLAM! BLAM!
TRINITY?!
BLAM!
THEY HIT TRINITY?
BLAM!
BLAM!
BLAM!

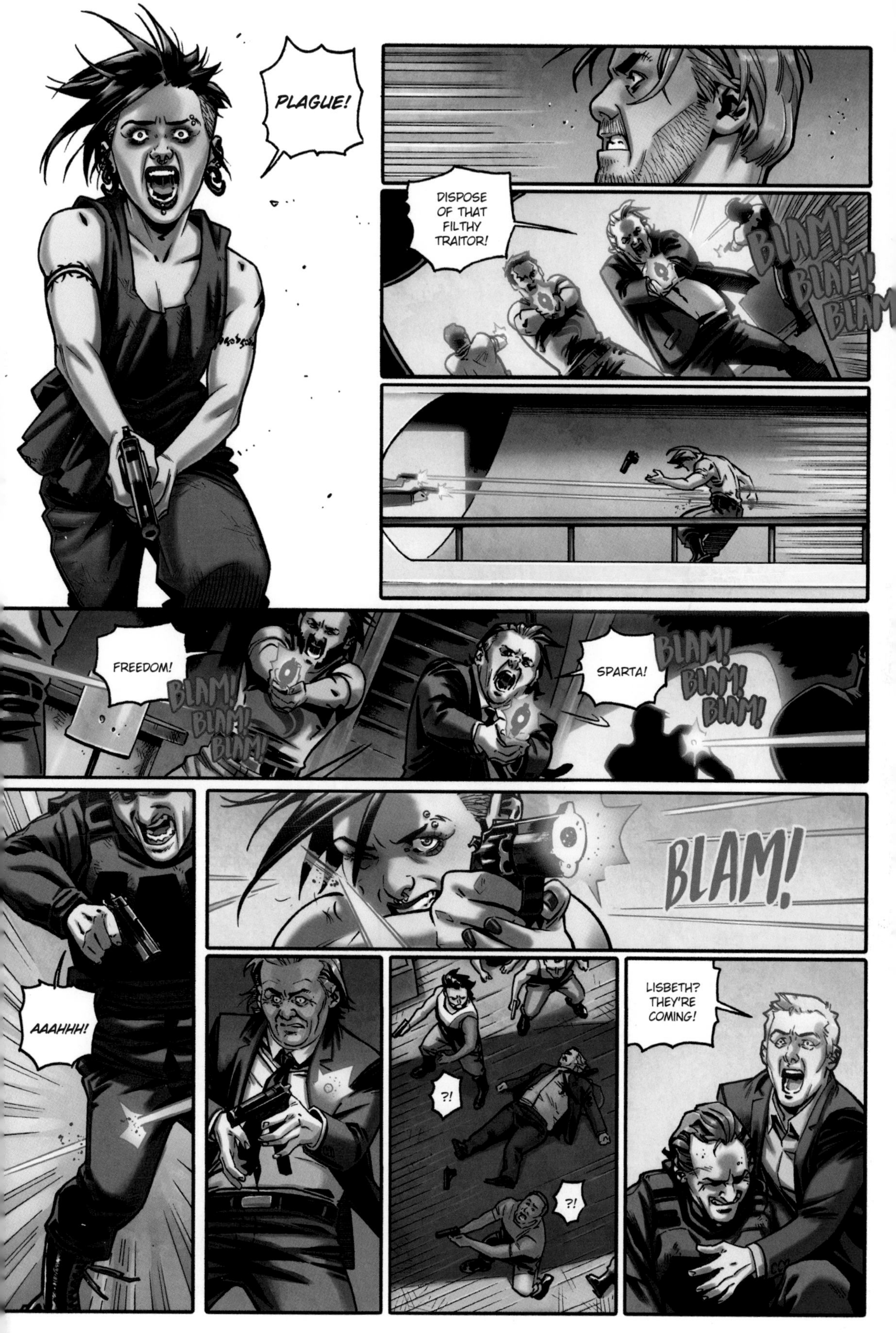
PLAGUE!
DISPOSE OF THAT FILTHY TRAITOR!
BLAM! BLAM! BLAM
FREEDOM!
BLAM! BLAM! BLAM!
SPARTA!
BLAM! BLAM! BLAM!
BLAM!
AAAHHH!
?!
?!
LISBETH? THEY'RE COMING!

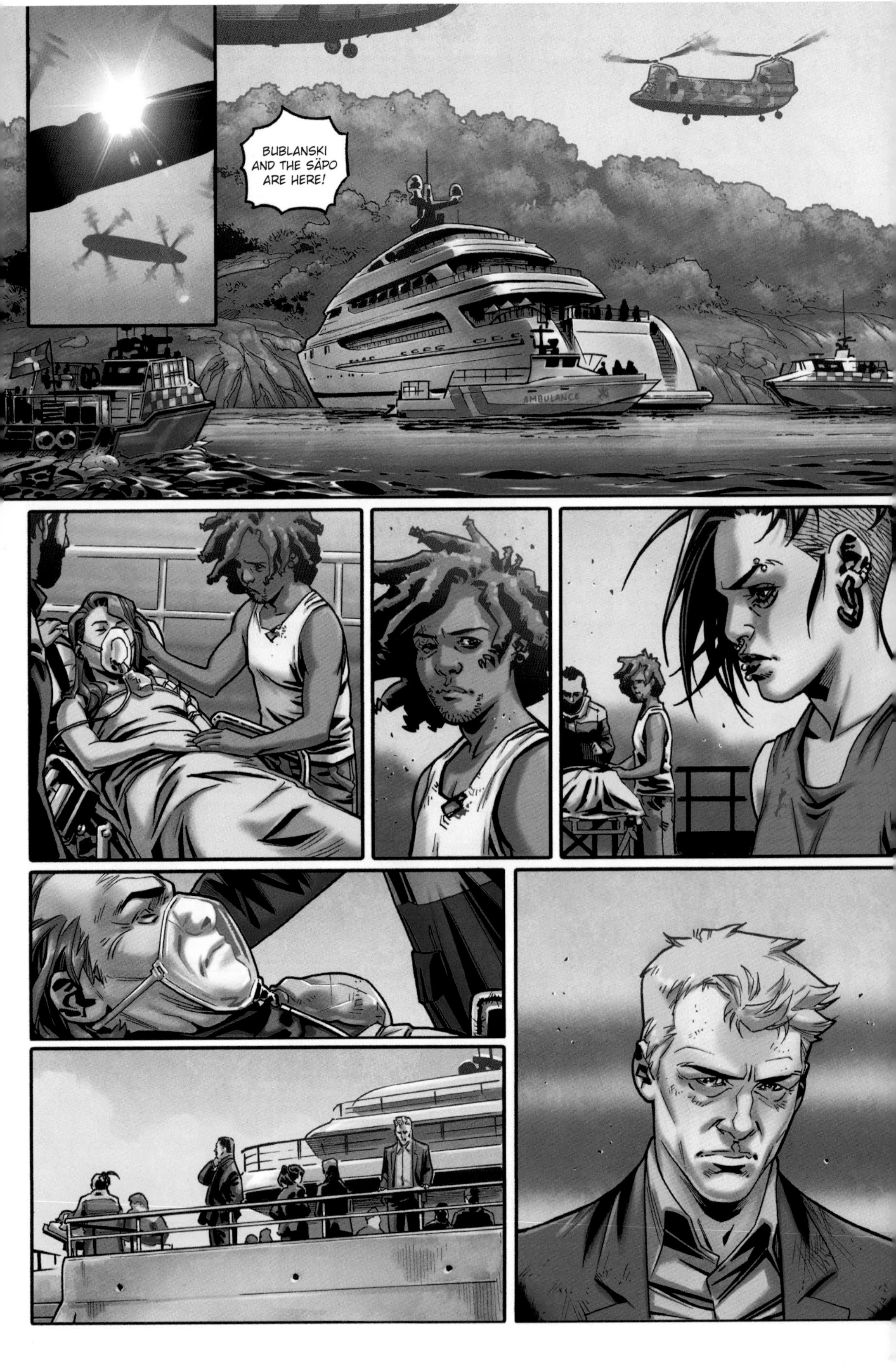
BUBLANSKI AND THE SÄPO ARE HERE!
AMBULANCE

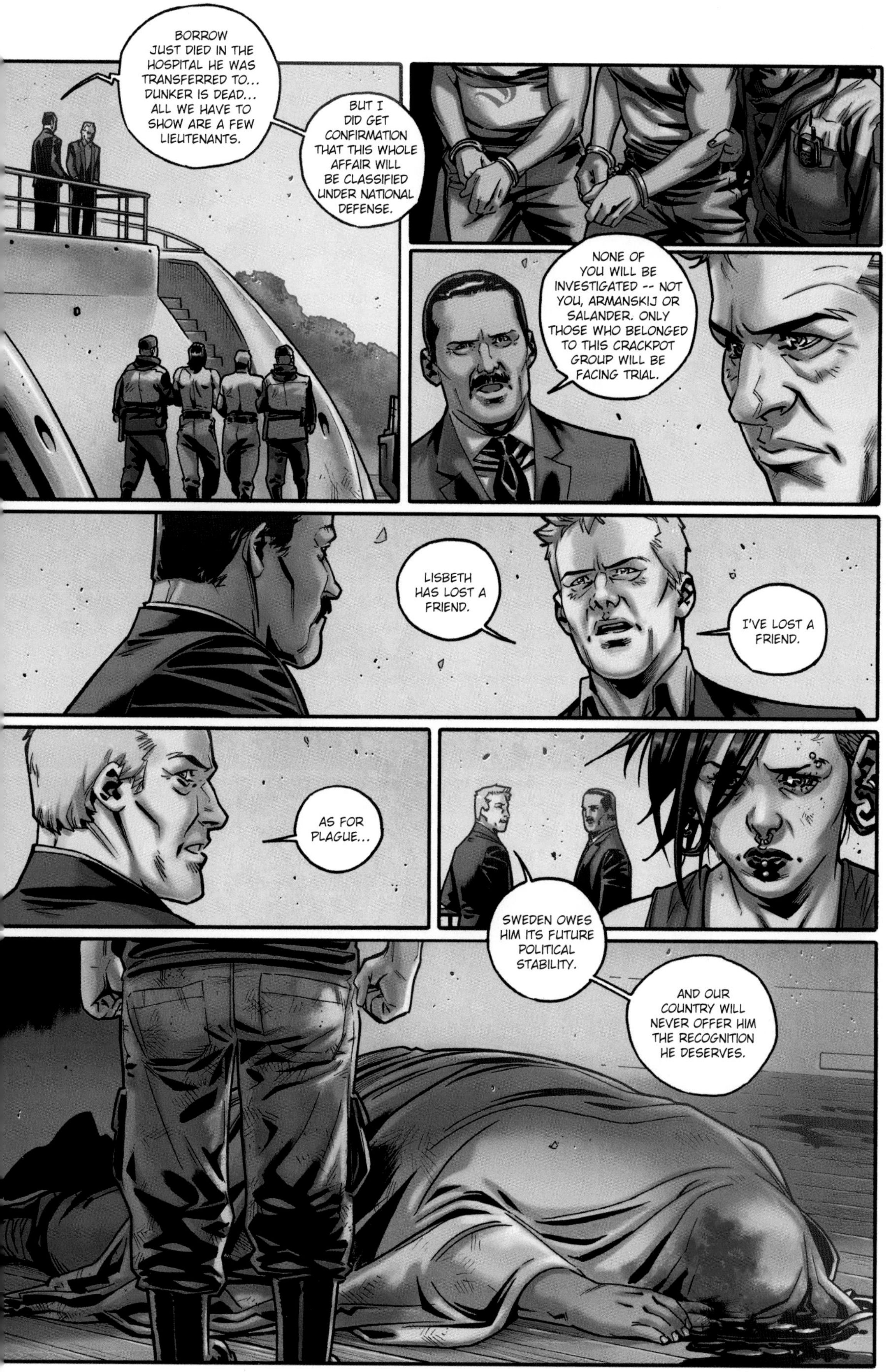
BORROW JUST DIED IN THE HOSPITAL HE WAS TRANSFERRED TO... DUNKER IS DEAD... ALL WE HAVE TO SHOW ARE A FEW LIEUTENANTS.
BUT I DID GET CONFIRMATION THAT THIS WHOLE AFFAIR WILL BE CLASSIFIED UNDER NATIONAL DEFENSE.
NONE OF YOU WILL BE INVESTIGATED -- NOT YOU, ARMANSKIJ OR SALANDER. ONLY THOSE WHO BELONGED TO THIS CRACKPOT GROUP WILL BE FACING TRIAL.
LISBETH HAS LOST A FRIEND.
I'VE LOST A FRIEND.
AS FOR PLAGUE...
SWEDEN OWES HIM ITS FUTURE POLITICAL STABILITY.
AND OUR COUNTRY WILL NEVER OFFER HIM THE RECOGNITION HE DESERVES.

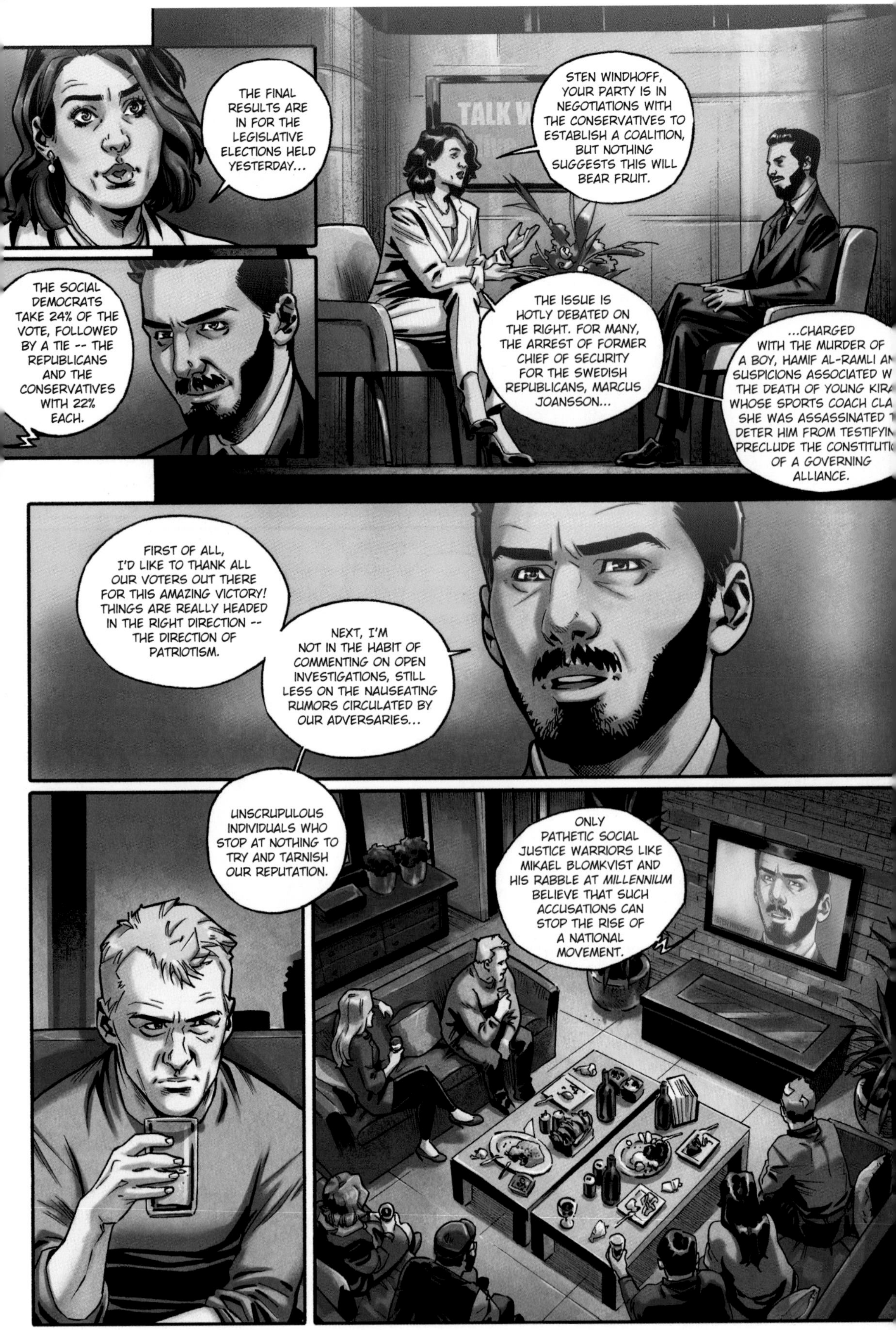
THE FINAL RESULTS ARE IN FOR THE LEGISLATIVE ELECTIONS HELD YESTERDAY...
THE SOCIAL DEMOCRATS TAKE 24% OF THE VOTE, FOLLOWED BY A TIE -- THE REPUBLICANS AND THE CONSERVATIVES WITH 22% EACH.
TALK
STEN WINDHOFF, YOUR PARTY IS IN NEGOTIATIONS WITH THE CONSERVATIVES TO ESTABLISH A COALITION, BUT NOTHING SUGGESTS THIS WILL BEAR FRUIT.
THE ISSUE IS HOTLY DEBATED ON THE RIGHT. FOR MANY, THE ARREST OF FORMER CHIEF OF SECURITY FOR THE SWEDISH REPUBLICANS, MARCUS JOANSSON...
...CHARGED WITH THE MURDER OF A BOY, HAMIF AL-RAMLI AN SUSPICIONS ASSOCIATED W THE DEATH OF YOUNG KIRA WHOSE SPORTS COACH CLA SHE WAS ASSASSINATED T DETER HIM FROM TESTIFYIN PRECLUDE THE CONSTITUTIO OF A GOVERNING ALLIANCE.
FIRST OF ALL, I'D LIKE TO THANK ALL OUR VOTERS OUT THERE FOR THIS AMAZING VICTORY! THINGS ARE REALLY HEADED IN THE RIGHT DIRECTION -- THE DIRECTION OF PATRIOTISM.
NEXT, I'M NOT IN THE HABIT OF COMMENTING ON OPEN INVESTIGATIONS, STILL LESS ON THE NAUSEATING RUMORS CIRCULATED BY OUR ADVERSARIES...
UNSCRUPULOUS INDIVIDUALS WHO STOP AT NOTHING TO TRY AND TARNISH OUR REPUTATION.
ONLY PATHETIC SOCIAL JUSTICE WARRIORS LIKE MIKAEL BLOMKVIST AND HIS RABBLE AT *MILLENNIUM* BELIEVE THAT SUCH ACCUSATIONS CAN STOP THE RISE OF A NATIONAL MOVEMENT.
STEN WINDHOFF

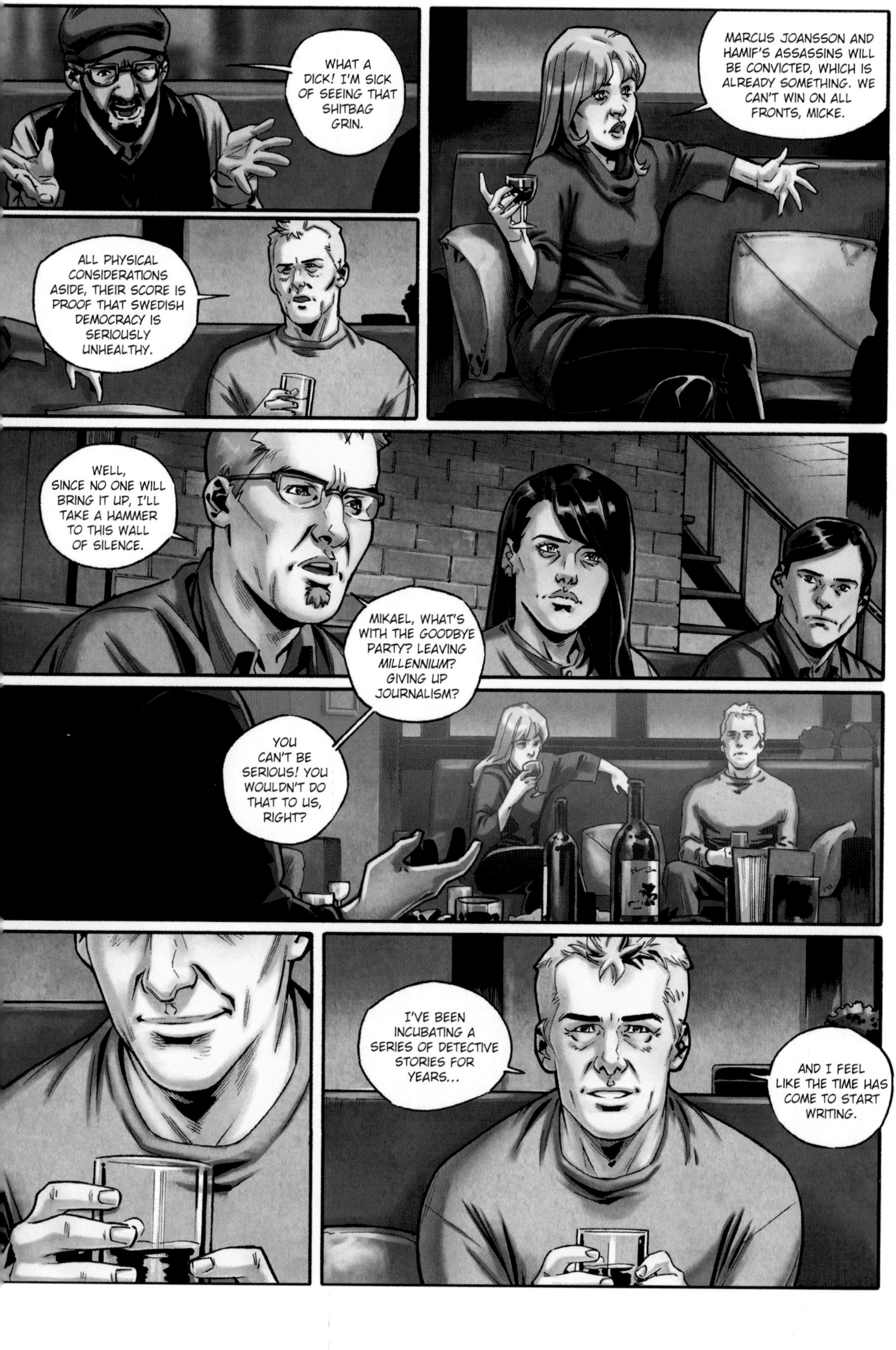
WHAT A DICK! I'M SICK OF SEEING THAT SHITBAG GRIN.
ALL PHYSICAL CONSIDERATIONS ASIDE, THEIR SCORE IS PROOF THAT SWEDISH DEMOCRACY IS SERIOUSLY UNHEALTHY.
MARCUS JOANSSON AND HAMIF'S ASSASSINS WILL BE CONVICTED, WHICH IS ALREADY SOMETHING. WE CAN'T WIN ON ALL FRONTS, MICKE.
WELL, SINCE NO ONE WILL BRING IT UP, I'LL TAKE A HAMMER TO THIS WALL OF SILENCE.
MIKAEL, WHAT'S WITH THE GOODBYE PARTY? LEAVING MILLENNIUM? GIVING UP JOURNALISM?
YOU CAN'T BE SERIOUS! YOU WOULDN'T DO THAT TO US, RIGHT?
I'VE BEEN INCUBATING A SERIES OF DETECTIVE STORIES FOR YEARS...
AND I FEEL LIKE THE TIME HAS COME TO START WRITING.

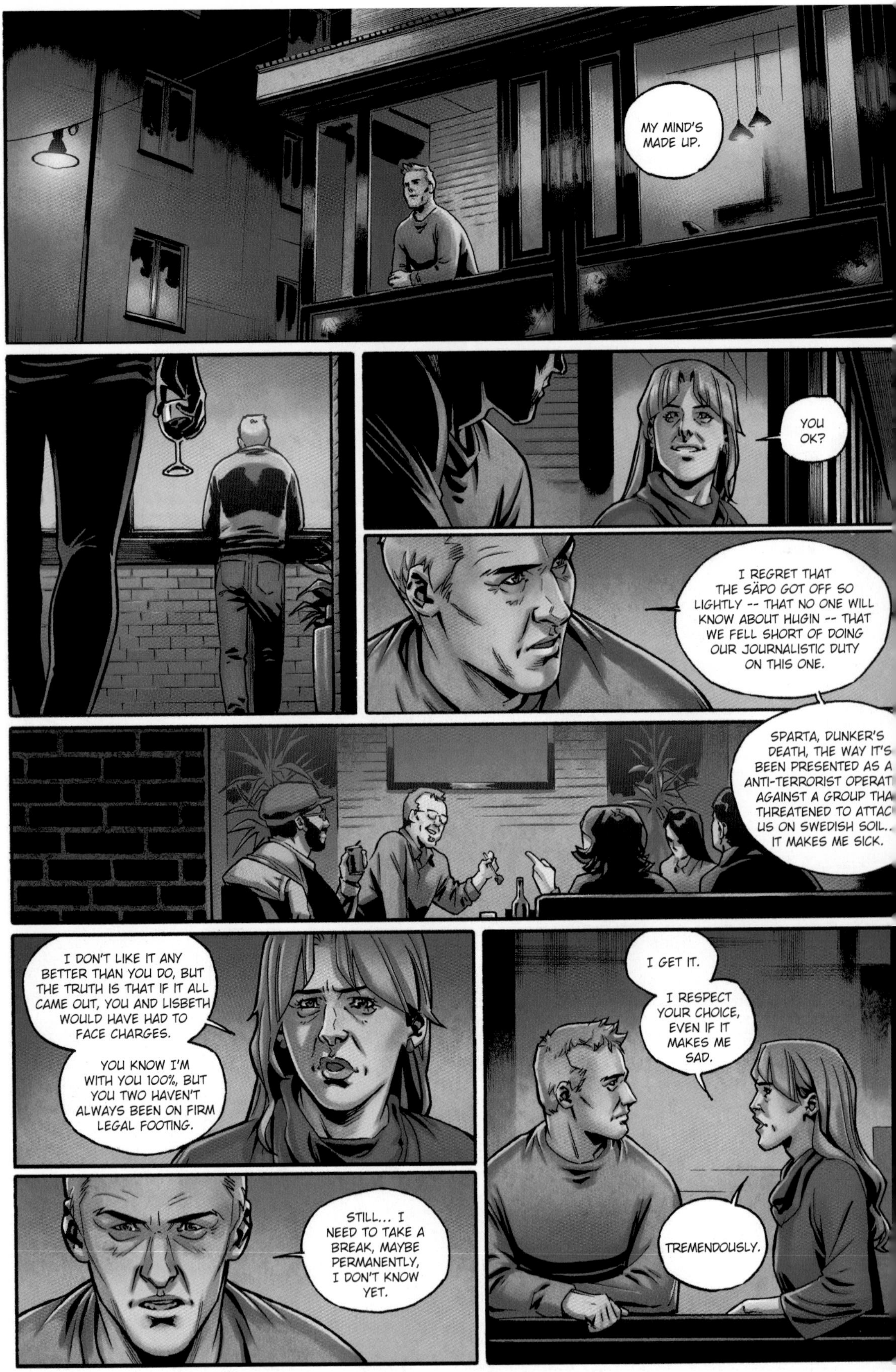
MY MIND'S MADE UP.
YOU OK?
I REGRET THAT THE SÄPO GOT OFF SO LIGHTLY -- THAT NO ONE WILL KNOW ABOUT HUGIN -- THAT WE FELL SHORT OF DOING OUR JOURNALISTIC DUTY ON THIS ONE.
SPARTA, DUNKER'S DEATH, THE WAY IT'S BEEN PRESENTED AS A ANTI-TERRORIST OPERAT AGAINST A GROUP THA THREATENED TO ATTAC US ON SWEDISH SOIL... IT MAKES ME SICK.
I DON'T LIKE IT ANY BETTER THAN YOU DO, BUT THE TRUTH IS THAT IF IT ALL CAME OUT, YOU AND LISBETH WOULD HAVE HAD TO FACE CHARGES.
YOU KNOW I'M WITH YOU 100%, BUT YOU TWO HAVEN'T ALWAYS BEEN ON FIRM LEGAL FOOTING.
STILL... I NEED TO TAKE A BREAK, MAYBE PERMANENTLY, I DON'T KNOW YET.
I GET IT.
I RESPECT YOUR CHOICE, EVEN IF IT MAKES ME SAD.
TREMENDOUSLY.

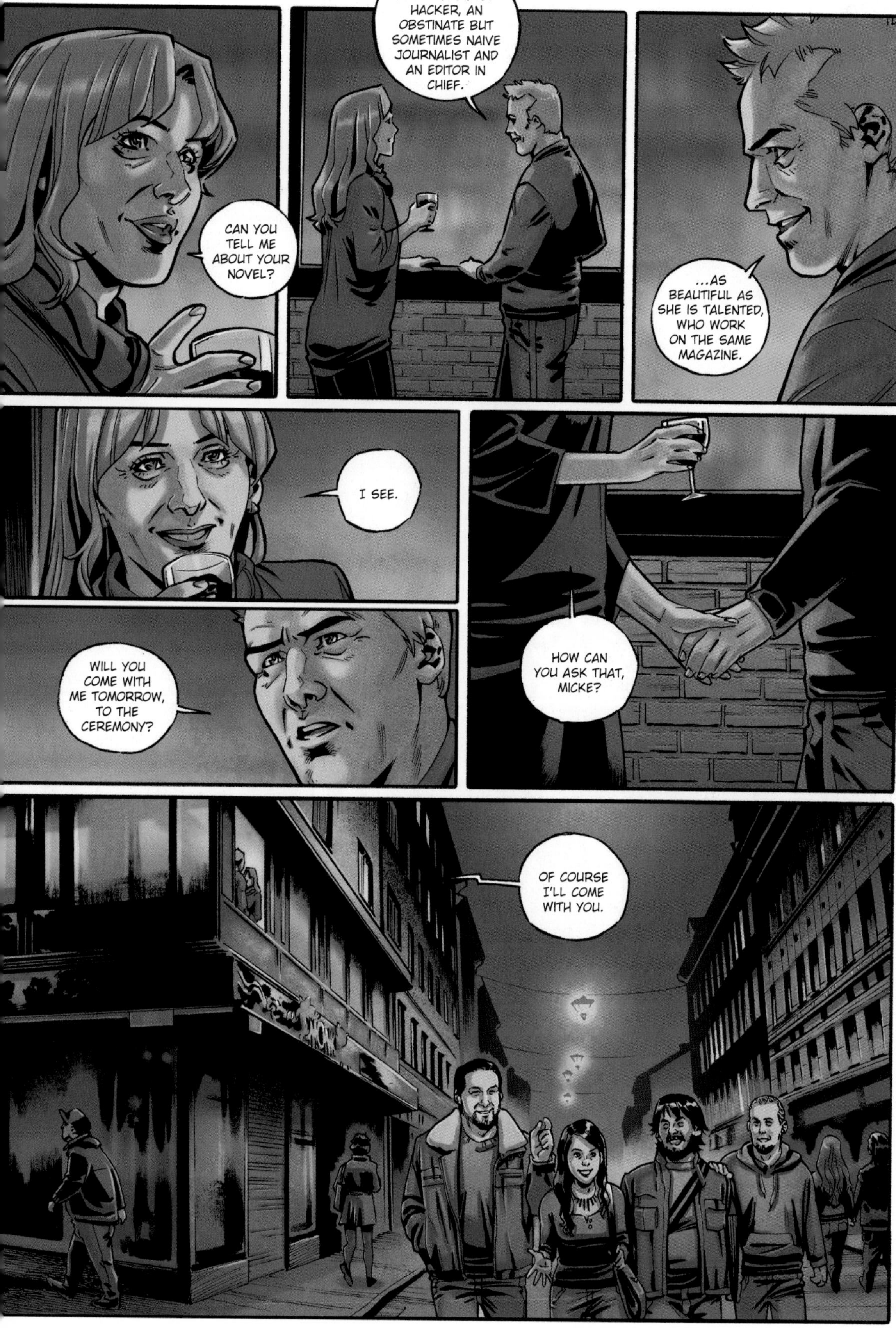
CAN YOU TELL ME ABOUT YOUR NOVEL?
IT'LL BE ABOUT A GIFTED HACKER, AN OBSTINATE BUT SOMETIMES NAIVE JOURNALIST AND AN EDITOR IN CHIEF...
...AS BEAUTIFUL AS SHE IS TALENTED, WHO WORK ON THE SAME MAGAZINE.
I SEE.
WILL YOU COME WITH ME TOMORROW, TO THE CEREMONY?
HOW CAN YOU ASK THAT, MICKE?
OF COURSE I'LL COME WITH YOU.

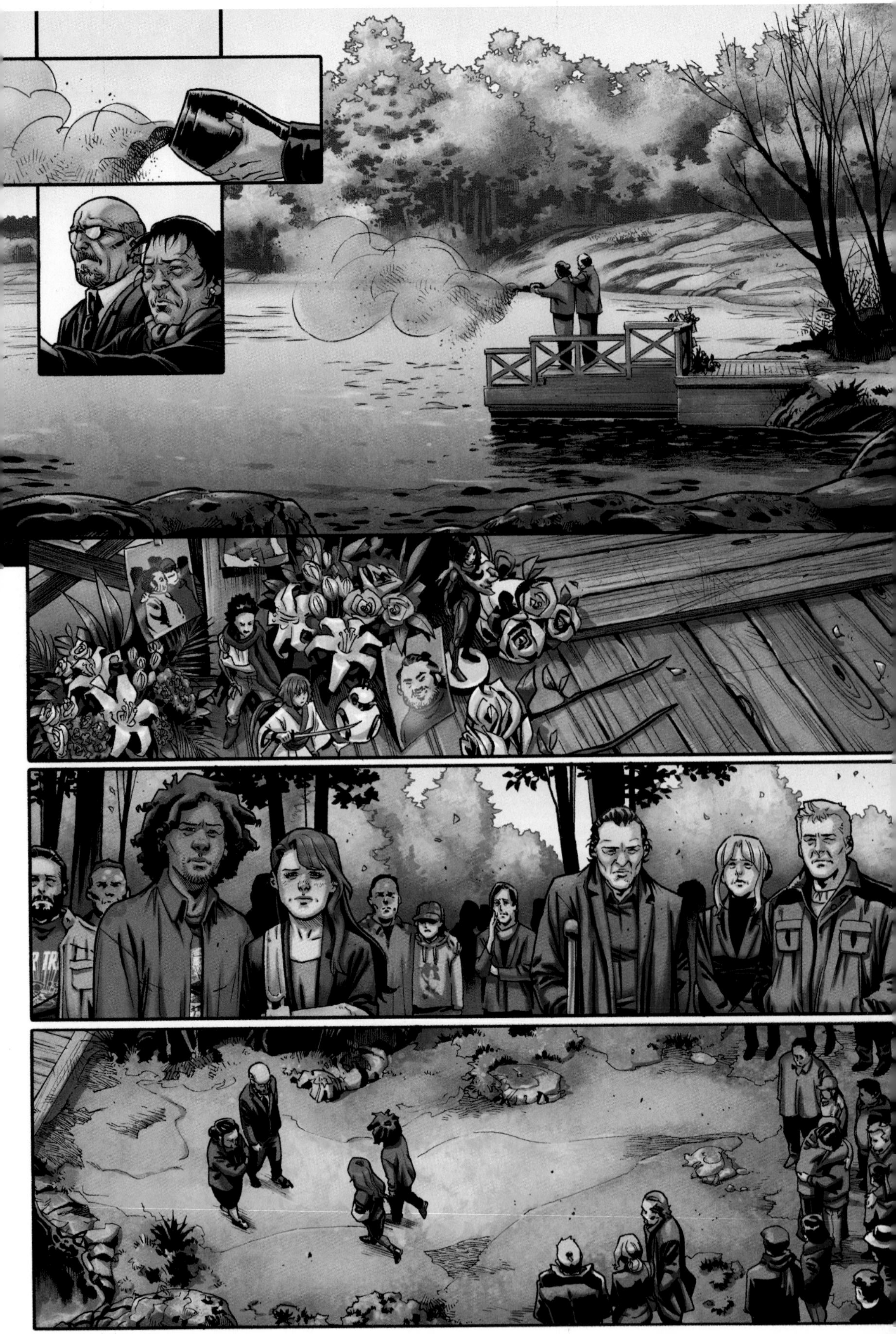

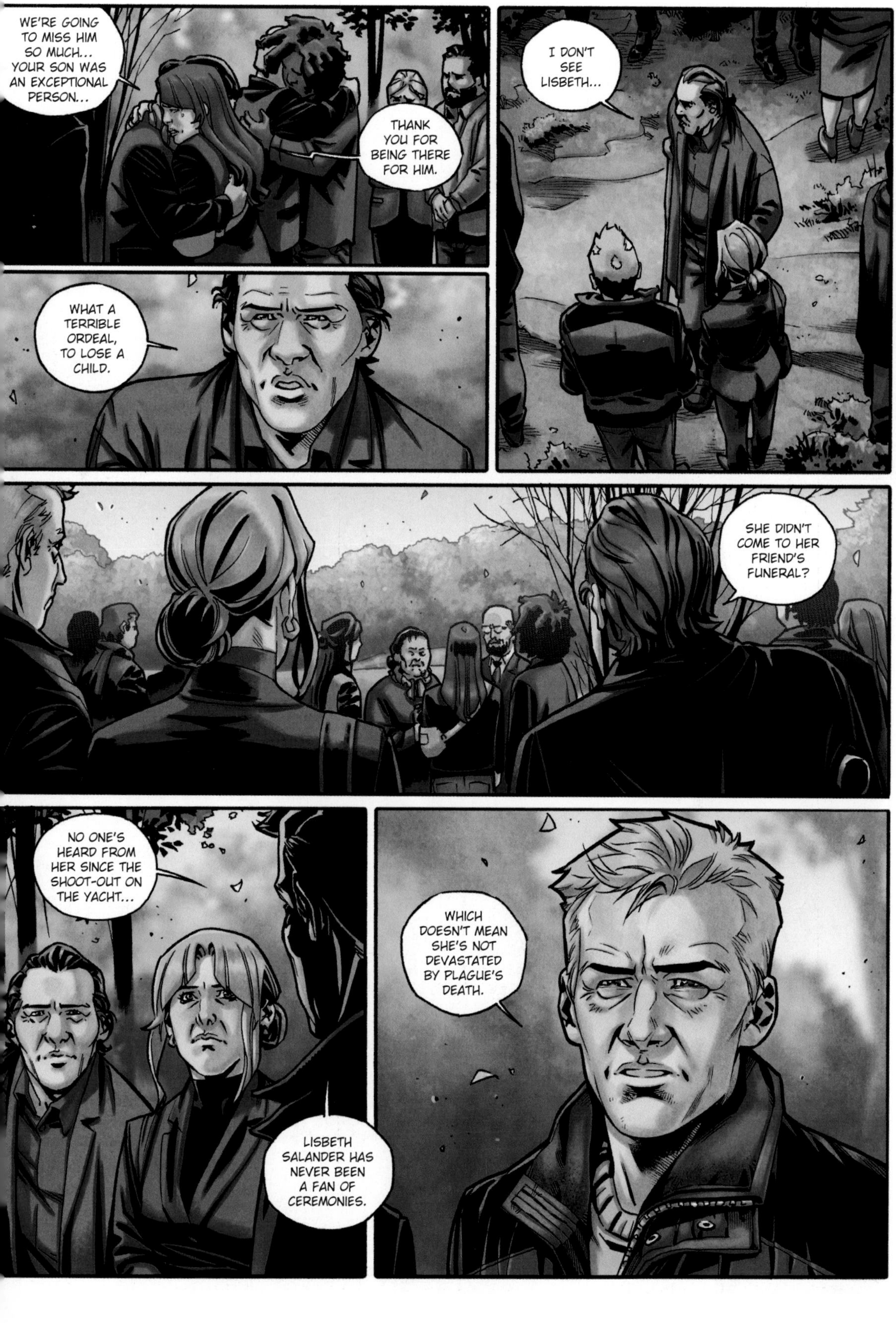
WE'RE GOING TO MISS HIM SO MUCH... YOUR SON WAS AN EXCEPTIONAL PERSON...
THANK YOU FOR BEING THERE FOR HIM.
I DON'T SEE LISBETH...
WHAT A TERRIBLE ORDEAL, TO LOSE A CHILD.
SHE DIDN'T COME TO HER FRIEND'S FUNERAL?
NO ONE'S HEARD FROM HER SINCE THE SHOOT-OUT ON THE YACHT...
LISBETH SALANDER HAS NEVER BEEN A FAN OF CEREMONIES.
WHICH DOESN'T MEAN SHE'S NOT DEVASTATED BY PLAGUE'S DEATH.

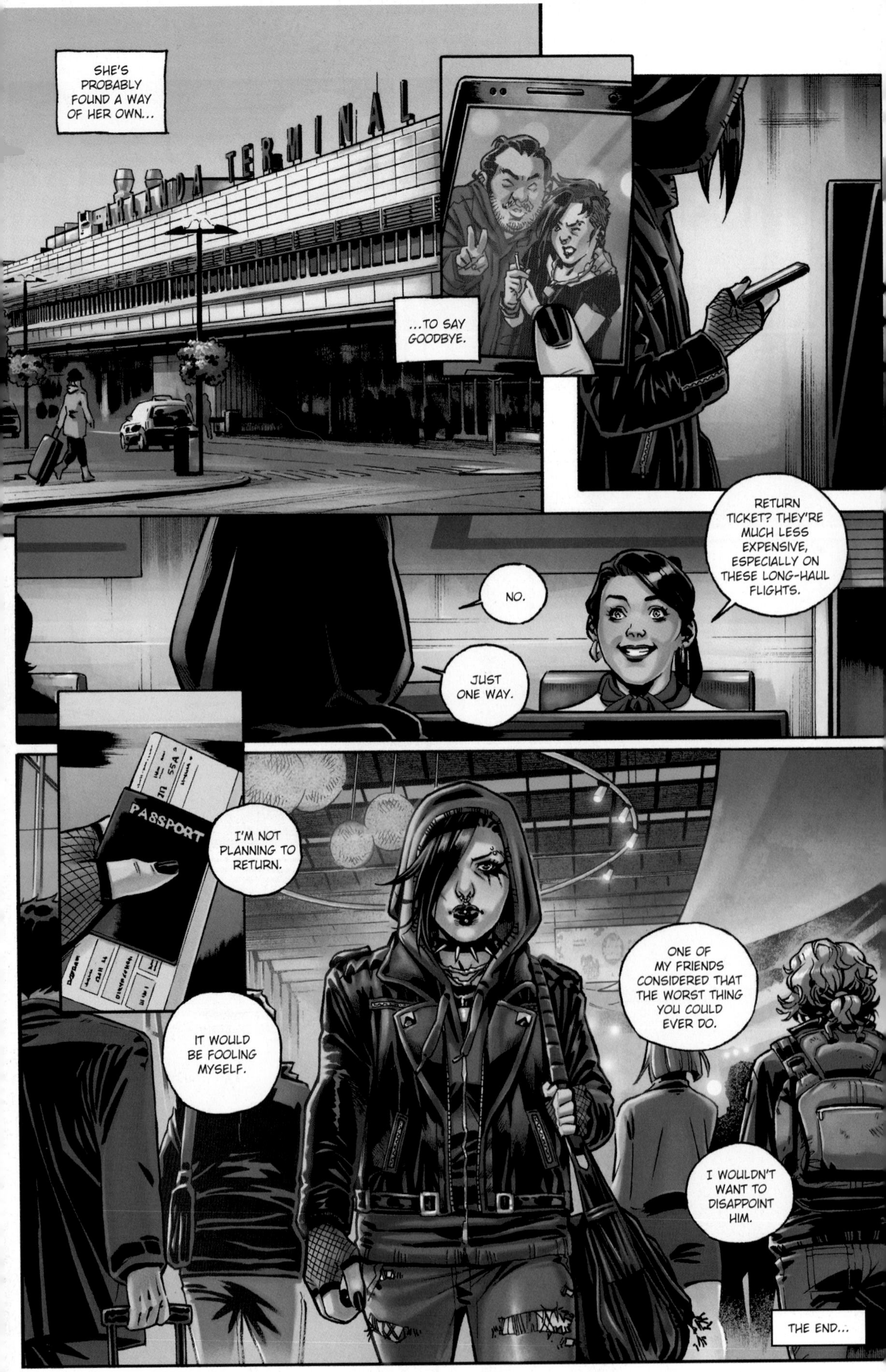
SHE'S PROBABLY FOUND A WAY OF HER OWN...
ARLANDA TERMINAL
...TO SAY GOODBYE.
RETURN TICKET? THEY'RE MUCH LESS EXPENSIVE, ESPECIALLY ON THESE LONG-HAUL FLIGHTS.
NO.
JUST ONE WAY.
PASSPORT
I'M NOT PLANNING TO RETURN.
IT WOULD BE FOOLING MYSELF.
ONE OF MY FRIENDS CONSIDERED THAT THE WORST THING YOU COULD EVER DO.
I WOULDN'T WANT TO DISAPPOINT HIM.
THE END...

THE GIRL WHO DANCED WITH DEATH

COVERS GALLERY

#1 COVER A by Claudia Ianniciello

#2 COVER A by Claudia Ianniciello

#2 COVER B by Bélen Ortega

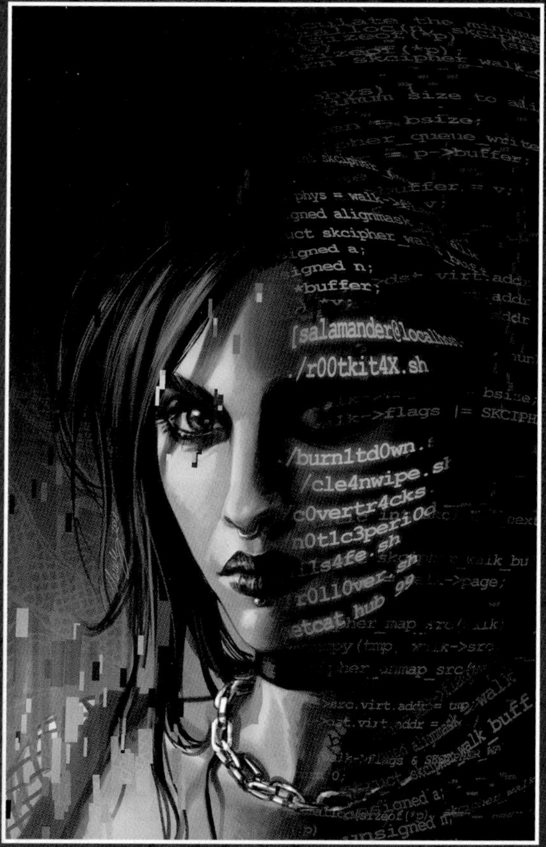
bsize;
phys = walk-
igned alignmask
uct skcipher
igned a;
igned n;
*buffer;
[salamander@localh
./r00tkit4X.sh
flags |= SKCIPH
/burn1td0wn.
/cle4nwipe.s
c0vertr4cks
n0t1c3peri0d
ls4fe.sh
->page;
etcat.hub 99
src.virt.addr
walk buff
signed a;
unsigned n;

#3 COVER A by **Claudia Ianniciello**

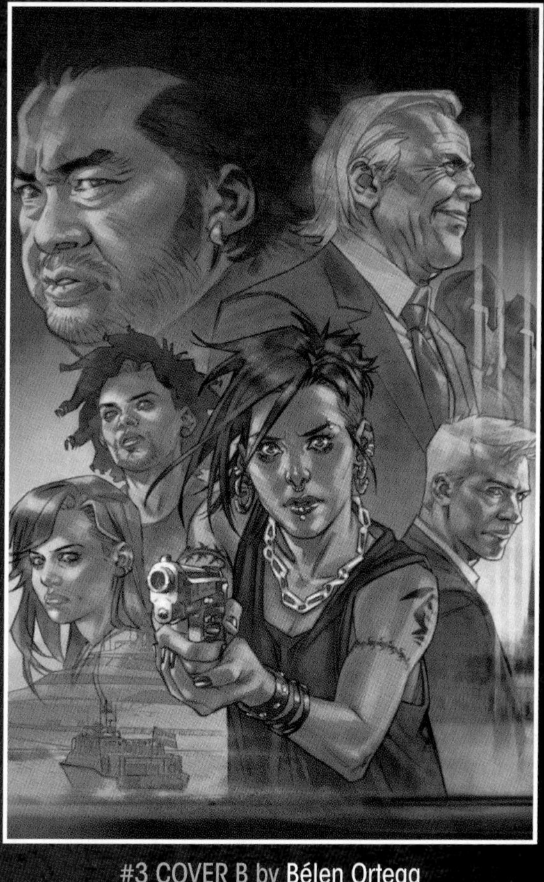

#3 COVER B by **Bélen Ortega**

HARD CASE CRIME

HARD CASE CRIME COLLECTIONS!

"STEEPED IN THE GRIT AND GRISTLE OF THE GENRE AND NOT AFRAID TO WALLOW IN IT!"
BIG COMIC PAGE
HARD CASE CRIME
CHRISTA FAUST
GARY PHILLIPS
Peepland
ANDREA CAMERINI

$19.99 OUT NOW!

ISBN: 9781785851193

WRITERS:
CHRISTA FAUST
GARY PHILLIPS

ARTIST:
ANDREA CAMERINI

"HARD CASE MAY BE THE BEST NEW AMERICAN PUBLISHER TO APPEAR IN THE LAST DECADE."
- NEAL POLLACK IN THE STRANGER
HARD CASE CRIME
NORMANDY GOLD
MEGAN ABBOTT
ALISON GAYLIN
STEVE SCOTT
LOVERN KINDZIERSKI

$19.99 OUT NOW!

ISBN: 9781785858642

WRITERS:
MEGAN ABBOTT, ALISON GAYLIN

ARTISTS:
STEVE SCOTT, RODNEY RAMOS, LOVERN KINDZIERSKI

TITAN COMICS

For information on how to subscribe to our Hard Case Crime titles, or to purchase them digitally, visit:

WWW.TITAN-COMICS.COM

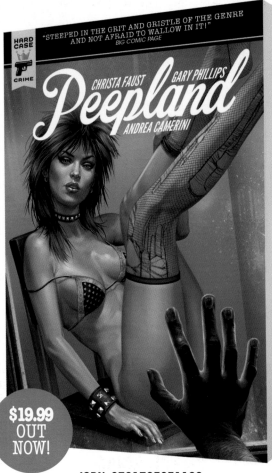

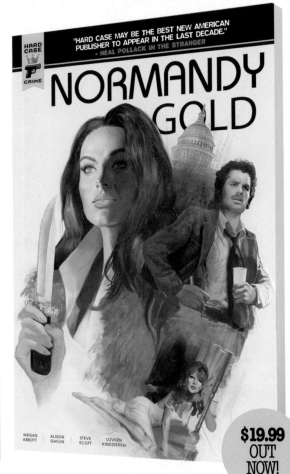

MILLENNIUM
THE GIRL WHO DANCED WITH DEATH

CREATOR BIOS

SYLVAIN RUNBERG

Sylvain Runberg is a French writer who divides his time between Stockholm, Provence, and Paris. He has a diploma in Plastic Arts and an MA in Political History. His first book was launched in 2004 and since then Runberg has had more than 70 books published by some of the largest French publishers (Glénat, Le Lombard, Dupuis, Dargaud, Casterman, Soleil, Futuropolis etc,...) and is now translated into 18 languages, having sold in total over a million copies worldwide.

Sylvain is best known for his comics adaptation of Stieg Larsson's *Millennium* trilogy. The adaptation has been acclaimed by both French and European media and readers and is already published in 13 other countries.

Runberg is currently working on several new comics and TV projects that will be published in years to come.

BÉLEN ORTEGA

Belen Ortega was trained in Fine Arts at the University of Granada and soon her passion for Japanese manga took her towards fantasy illustration and the creation of comics, completing her studies at the Human Academy in Osaka (Japan). Her most recent works include *Pájaro Indiano* (Norma Editorial), a fable located on the Costa Brava at the end of the 19th century, as well as *Artbook* (Ominiky Ediciones), a compilation book of her illustrations to date.